AF394455

From Chocolate to Cider

FROM CHOCOLATE TO CIDER

A Virtual Train Journey of Family Railway History Over 150 Years From the West Midlands to the West Country

PAUL STANFORD

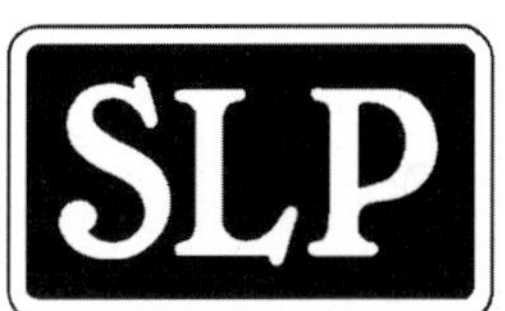

Acknowledgements

I am indebted to David Stanford who started our family railway history in 1875 and his son John, always known as Jack, who started with the GWR in 1894. My gratitude extends to my grandfather, Harry Stanford, who aside from his part in keeping the railway at Bournville serving the chocolate factory needs, also fostered and supported the railway interest in his son John and myself.

To my father John, a railwayman from 1960 until his untimely passing in 1994. His research, railway knowledge and photographs on this route feature prominently. Plus his sister Elizabeth James (nee Stanford), for recording and establishing our family history and unearthing facts about our railway past.

Friends Richard Giles, Trevor and Jill Riddle, Robbie Aston, and the late George Jenks for their photographs. Mr Don Townsley former general manager of the Hunslet Engine Company for his recollections and contribution of superb railway photographs of Cadbury locomotives. Plus Malcolm Ravensdale and Adrian Rescorla for their marvellous colour photographs of the Bournville railway system. Other photographers are credited on individual photos. Uncredited photos are by the author. Every effort has been made to identify authors of photographic work.

The Industrial Railway Society for their useful handbooks with details of locomotives at industrial sites. Cadbury UK Ltd and Mondelez international; for consenting to the use of their photos that help tell our story working on the Cadbury Bournville factory railway. With a special thank you to Sarah Foden and Jackie Jones at Cadbury Bournville and who enthusiastically supported me with access to the Cadbury Archives. To Bournville Village Trust for use of their archive and a special thank you to Daniel Callicot.

To the wider railway family for supporting father and self; with some friendships still extending now, with people who worked with us over the past 60 years.

To the team at Mortons Media, including Dan Sharp for his great support and to Steve O'Hara for his support right from the outset..

Finally, to my long-suffering wife Fiona, and our sons Olly and Toby for tolerating my hobbies and their proof-reading and critical challenge, aiding production of the book.

Published in Great Britain by Silver Link Books
an imprint of Mortons Books Ltd.
Media Centre
Morton Way
Horncastle LN9 6JR
www.mortonsbooks.co.uk

ISBN 978-1-911704-44-7

Typeset by Hinoki Design and Typesetting

The book is dedicated to my grandfather, Harry Stanford, and my auntie, Elizabeth James (nee Stanford). Both were active in meticulously recording and researching the family history aside from both working at Cadbury Bournville.

They also helped nurture my railway interest from a young age in the early 1970s. Plus grandfather was the recipient of official photographs from Cadbury Limited of their railway locomotives when he retired in 1973 and this was the initial spark for my railway interest as a small boy, so thank you.

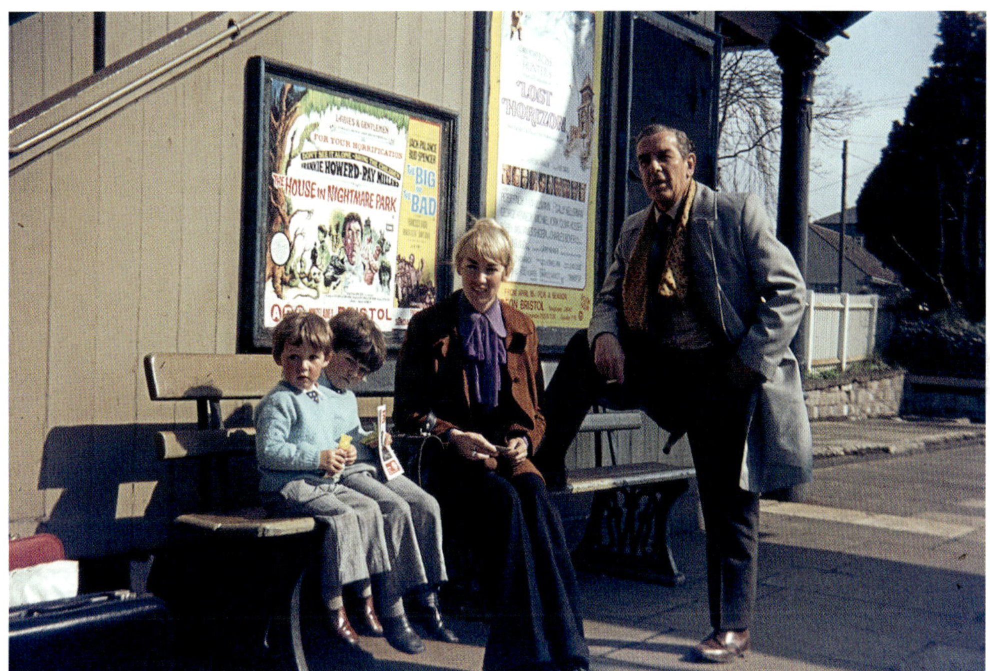

Yatton station. Elizabeth and Harry Stanford at Yatton Station in April 1973, about to catch the train home to Birmingham with the author and his brother Mark. Note the cinema poster behind them; playing at the Odeon Cinema is a Frankie Howerd film. The actor lived locally to Yatton, in Cross, near Axbridge. *Photo by John Stanford*

Contents

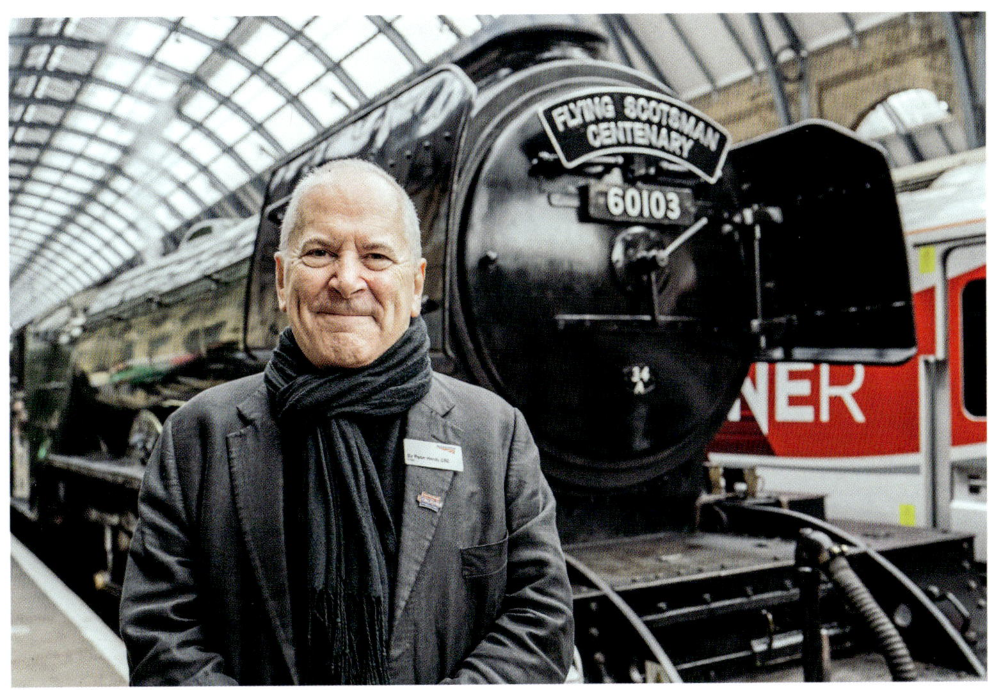

Foreword

I am delighted to have been asked to contribute this foreword. As we celebrate the 200th anniversary of the birth of the passenger railway in 2025, we remember the overwhelmingly positive contribution it has made to culture, the economy, society, and the arts, in the UK and all over the world.

But this book also inspires us to remember that the railway is more than trains and rails and engineering. It is a collection of dedicated people who believe passionately in the inherent goodness of what they do, and the social and economic value that they create.

This railway family is one which I have been privileged to represent during my time as chairman of Network Rail. During my career I have met many railway people, in every different role imaginable, and I have never failed to be impressed by their hard work, determination, and their ability to deliver on behalf of the customers that they ultimately serve.

One thing I have often been struck by, is how many people across the industry are part of a much longer lineage of railway people. In many cases their parents, grandparents, and even great grandparents also worked on or for the railway in some capacity. The fact that so many young people look at the example set by their parents and want to follow in their footsteps is a testament to the railway being more than a simple job. It inspires people to be part of something bigger.

The author is one of these people. He is a fifth-generation railway worker, with his great-great-grandfather starting on the railway at Kidderminster in 1875. It is very plausible that he would have met someone who was present at the inaugural journey of the Stockton and Darlington Railway in 1825 and who could have told him directly about the fanfare and the excitement of that moment. As we begin to deliver a new model for the railway, that historical connection should serve to remind us that we must build on the great achievements of the past to successfully deliver the future.

I end this foreword by commending the author's decision to donate all author proceeds to Headshunt, the charity that he started in 2022. This organisation does wonderful work in support of the mental health of railway workers, and to date over 5000 individuals have benefited from this service. I commend Paul for this.

Peter, Lord Hendy of Richmond Hill

STANFORD FAMILY RAILWAY TREE

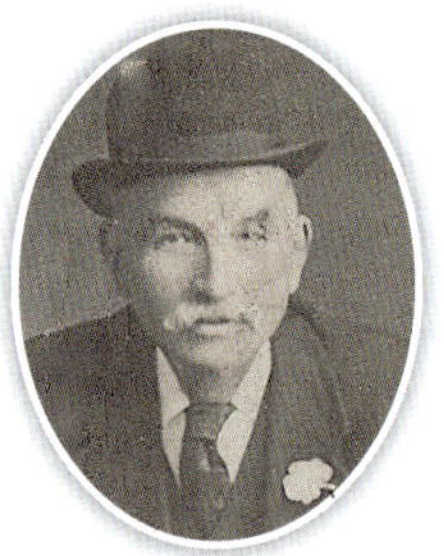

David Stanford b. 1852 d. 1925
Railway locations worked:
Kidderminster, and Dudley

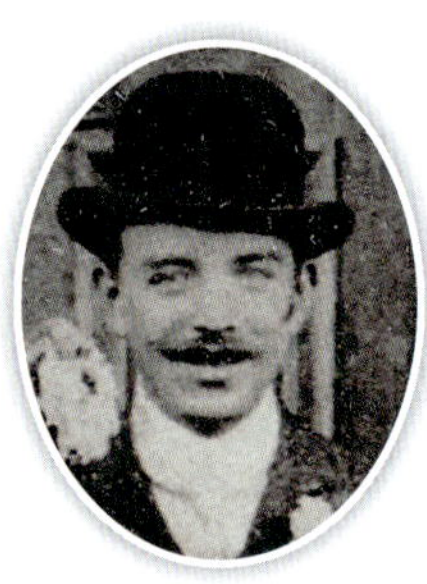

John 'Jack' Stanford b. 1880 d. 1952
Railway locations worked:
Kidderminster, Dudley and Bournville

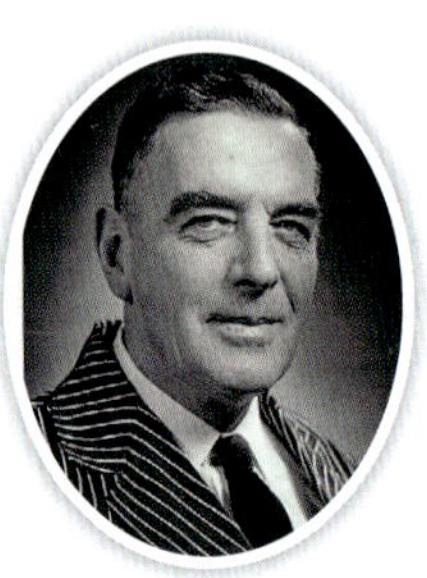

Harry Stanford b. 1911 d. 1987
Railway location worked:
Bournville

John Stanford b. 1942 d. 1994
Married 16-9-66
Railway locations worked
Bromsgrove, Wolverhampton Low Level
Birmingham (Snow Hill & Stanier House)
Bristol Temple Meads, Swindon, and Yatton

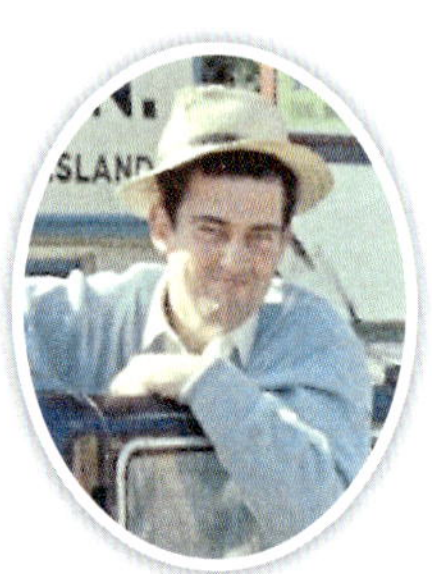

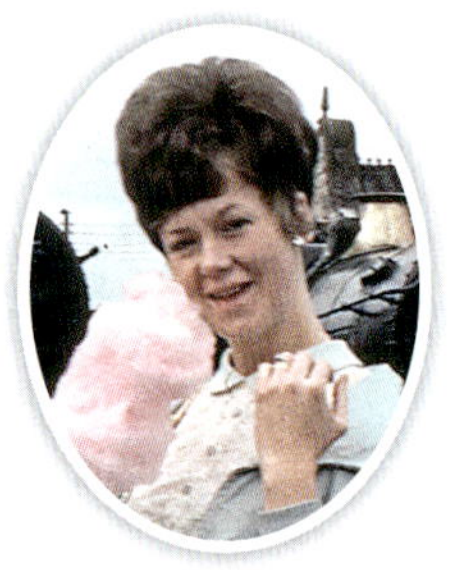

Wendy Richmond b. 1944 d. 2011
Railway locations worked
Birmingham New Street

Paul Stanford b. 1967-
Railway locations worked
Bristol Temple Meads (Twice)
Swindon (four occasions over 30 years)
Cardiff & Hereford
London Euston & Kings Cross

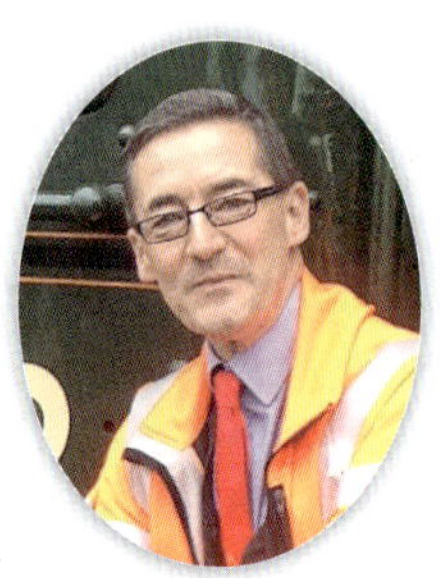

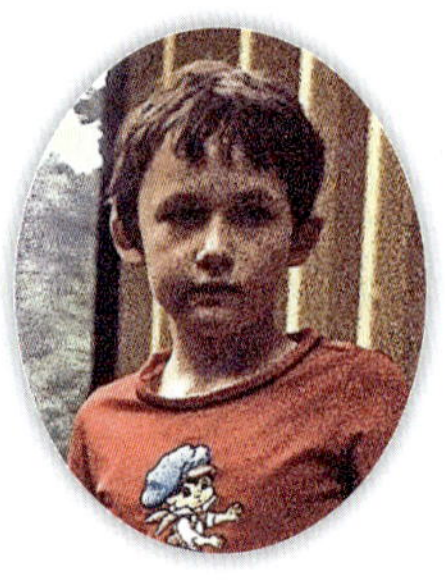

Mark Stanford b. 1970-
Railway locations worked
Weston Super Mare
Bristol Temple Meads

Introduction

The railway industry is a fascinating place; so, it was that six members of my family and I worked in and around the railway over the course of 150 years; garnering 186 years of railway service between us.

The book deals with the rail route from the West Midlands to the West Country; linking Birmingham with Bristol and on into Devon and Cornwall. This route features prominently in our family railway history.

The images presented here seek to match the family's involvement or interest with rail in each geographic area, but the goal is not to record every career step or feature on the route from the West Midlands to Penzance in detail. Instead, a selection of largely historic photos on the rail route is presented. In many cases, such as the railway around the Bournville factory or the wider Western Region where we worked, the pictures reflect our first-hand railway experience or railway interests.

The Cadbury Bournville Railway features heavily, as our history was inextricably linked with that railway's operation for circa 50 years. Most photographs in the book are from a 'lost age' but some more recent photos are included to highlight a point or to tell the story. The book is laid out in an arc, starting at Kidderminster, heading to the Black Country, then to Birmingham, Worcester, Gloucester, Bristol and into the West, to best capture our story chronologically – albeit with the odd deviation!

Inevitably, the book reflects the changes in the UK railway system, from the latter part of the 19th century when railways were being built, to the Great War and Second World War, when they were absolutely key to the war effort, through to the 1950s and beyond, where rail use declined as the spread of road usage occurred. This was of course followed by the Shaping of Britain's Railways Report in 1963 and the cuts that followed.

Happily, from the 1990s onwards there had been a reversal of the railways' fortunes with increased passenger patronage, even in spite of a huge dip linked to the COVID crisis. There was an increase in trains during the latter part of my career, with new or reopened stations on the line of route starting from the tail end of dad's career from 1989 onwards. The same cannot be said of freight traffic on the route however, with rail-freight in the West Country hanging by a thread presently, the Cadbury Bournville factory bereft of railway now for 50 years and freight in the West dwindling since 1975, concomitant with the M5 motorway opening up in Devon, the loss of wagon-load freight traffic and the conscious focus on freight train-load volumes. That said, rail has a very definite future, both for freight and the passenger business; highlighted by the Okehampton line reopening in 2021.

So, join me for a virtual journey back in time, highlighting the contribution of the railway and the ability to keep Britain moving, whilst delving into our family railway history.

Paul Stanford, FCIRO, April 2025

CHAPTER 1

In the Beginning – West Midlands

The heart of the UK saw early rail developments. The London to Birmingham Railway opened fully in 1838, with the Birmingham to Gloucester Railway opening in 1840, then four years later opening though to Bristol. Progressively in the 19th century other lines appeared to serve the needs of industry and the movement of people.

The author's great-great-grandfather started his railway career at Kidderminster in the GWR goods yard in 1875 as a drayman. By 1881 he was a goods porter at Kidderminster and then moved to the position of goods foreman at the same location by 1891, remaining in the area on the railway, such that he held a supervisor's position at Dudley in the early reign of King Edward after Queen Victoria's passing in 1901. His son John Stanford did the same, starting at Kidderminster in 1894 and then rising to a foreman's position at Dudley. He then made the move from a main line rail company to Cadbury Bournville, becoming a rail foreman in 1907 and with a successive promotion and he held the role until 1944 when he retired. With locomotives and rail staff at his behest for nearly 40 years he saw the continuing growth of the factory and its railway. His son (the author's grandfather) took on that role too, post-Second World War, following his father's retirement in 1944.

Of course, the Cadbury Brothers has established 'the factory in the garden' as Bournville chocolate factory became known in 1879 and two years later it was connected to the national rail network and progressively a rail system was established around the factory to supply raw materials and dispatch finished product for 90 years.

Later in time in 1960, with railways in his blood, young John Stanford worked on Birmingham area railways, starting at Bromsgrove and then Wolverhampton, Birmingham Snow Hill, and Stanier House meeting his wife-to-be, Wendy, in the BR staff canteen at Curzon Street in 1964. At the time, she worked in the personnel department for BR London Midland Region.

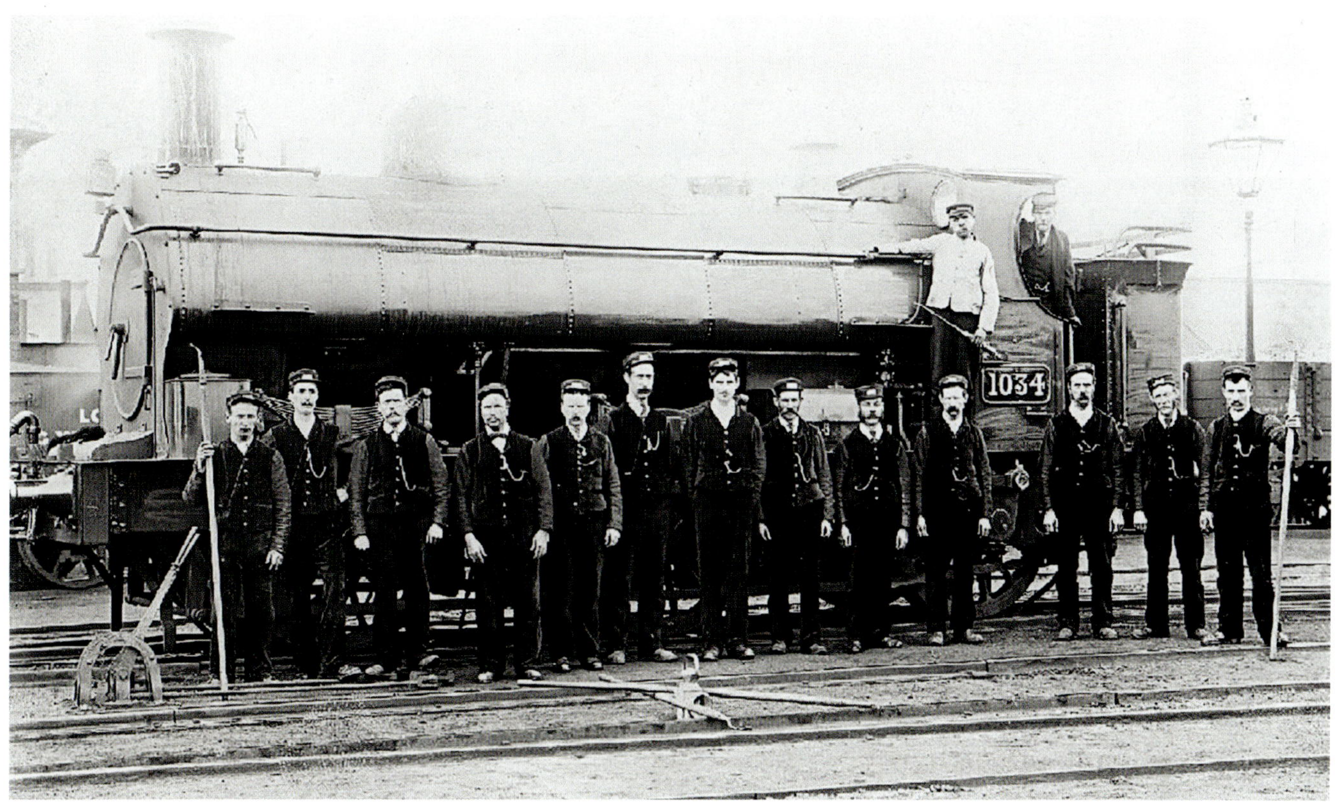

Kidderminster Goods Yard was home to David and Jack Stanford at the start of their rail careers. With a Wolverhampton-built GWR 0-6-0 saddle tank loco known to have worked in Kidderminster yard, this photo was taken pre-1900 with just such a loco and goods yard staff in typical late Victorian GWR uniforms at an unrecorded location. It is however a good indication of how David and Jack would have looked early in their rail careers. *Photo by courtesy of Local Studies (Swindon Library)*

Kidderminster Goods Yard in 1984 become home for the new terminus of the Severn Valley Railway, following the opening of the line from Bewdley. The goods shed structures survive, both built in 1878. In this view from 2024, the transhipment structure is visible where David and Jack would have worked in their initial roles as draymen. Here carpet materials were held having arrived by train, before dispatch to the carpet factories.

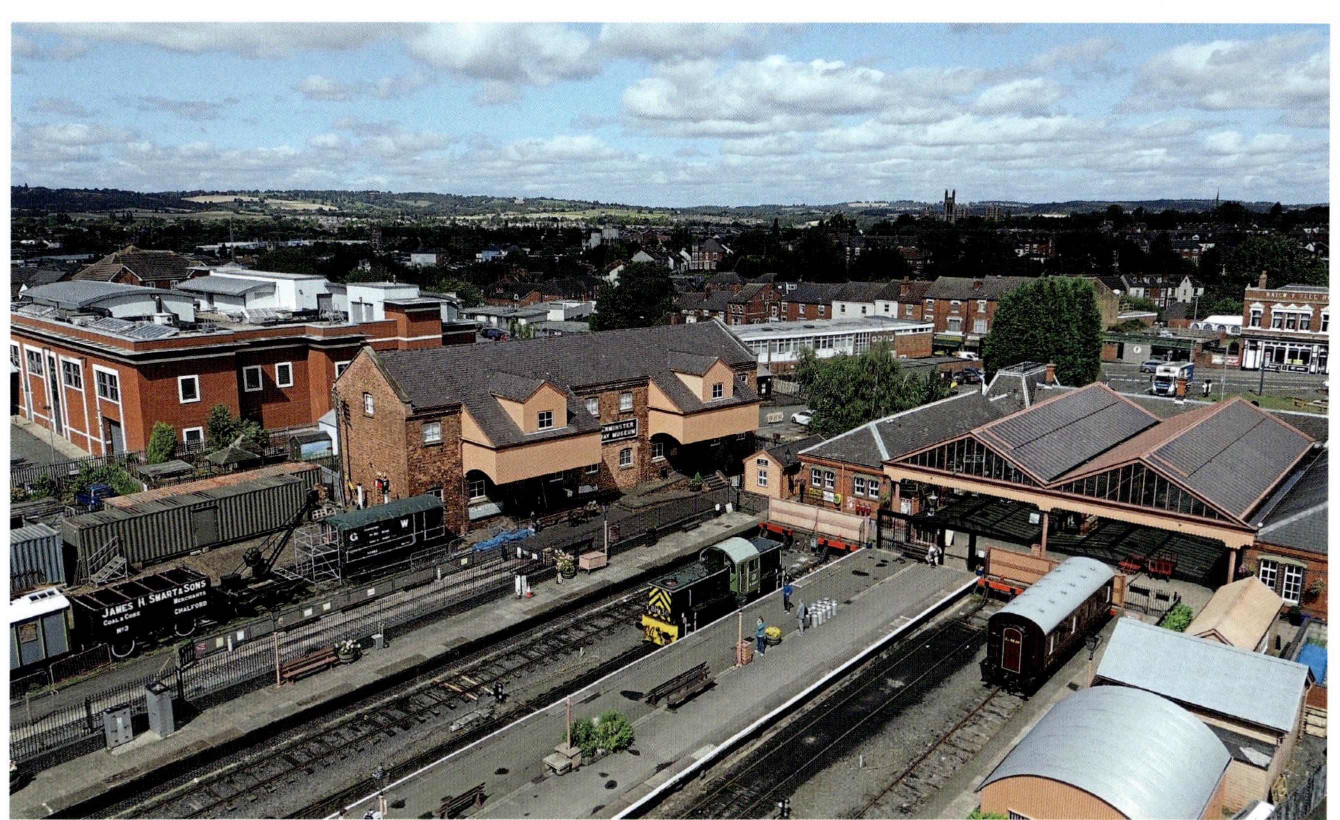

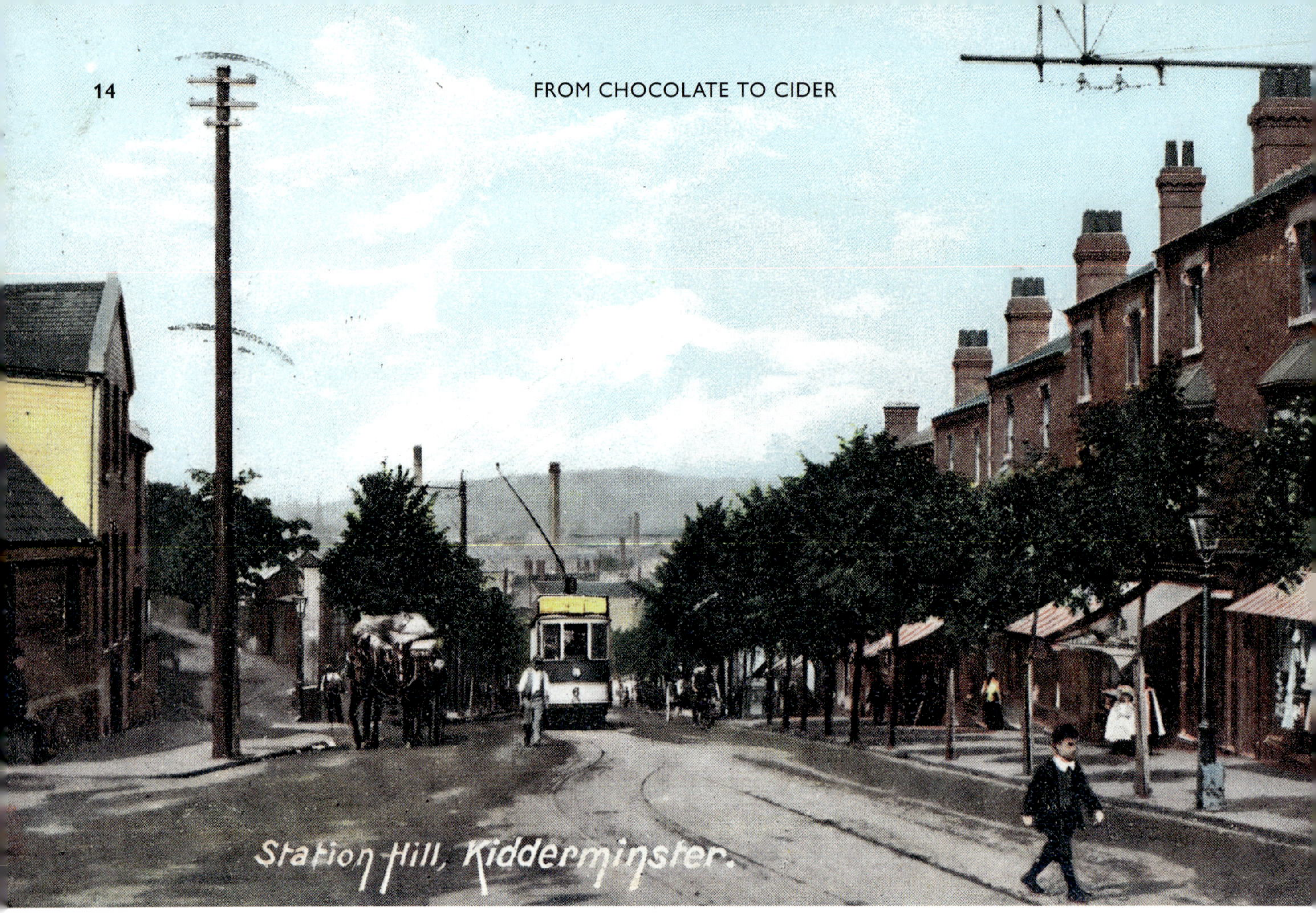

Kidderminster Station Hill in a pre-1910 scene. Jack and David Stanford would have traversed this route many times in their time at Kidderminster Goods Yard. The tram network lasted until 1929. Just out of view to the left was the goods yard.

Photo Paul Stanford Collection (a Raphael Tuck & Son postcard)

Wolverhampton Low Level was John's workplace from 1962. Here a pannier tank, 6422, sits in the bay platform. The loco gained some notoriety when stolen by two alleged criminals after a bank robbery; driving it for nearly 40 miles from Wolverhampton.

Photographer unknown – John Stanford Collection

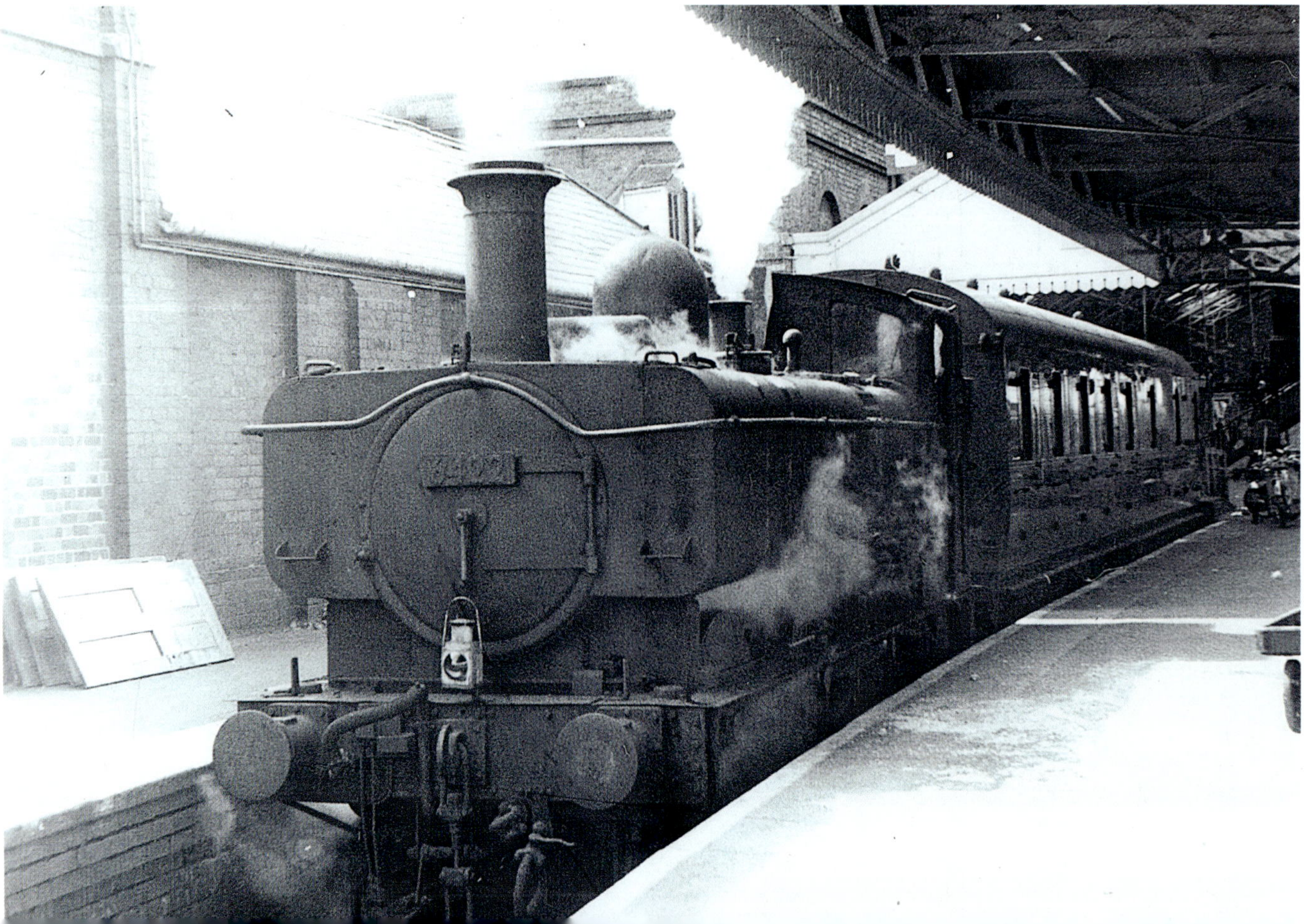

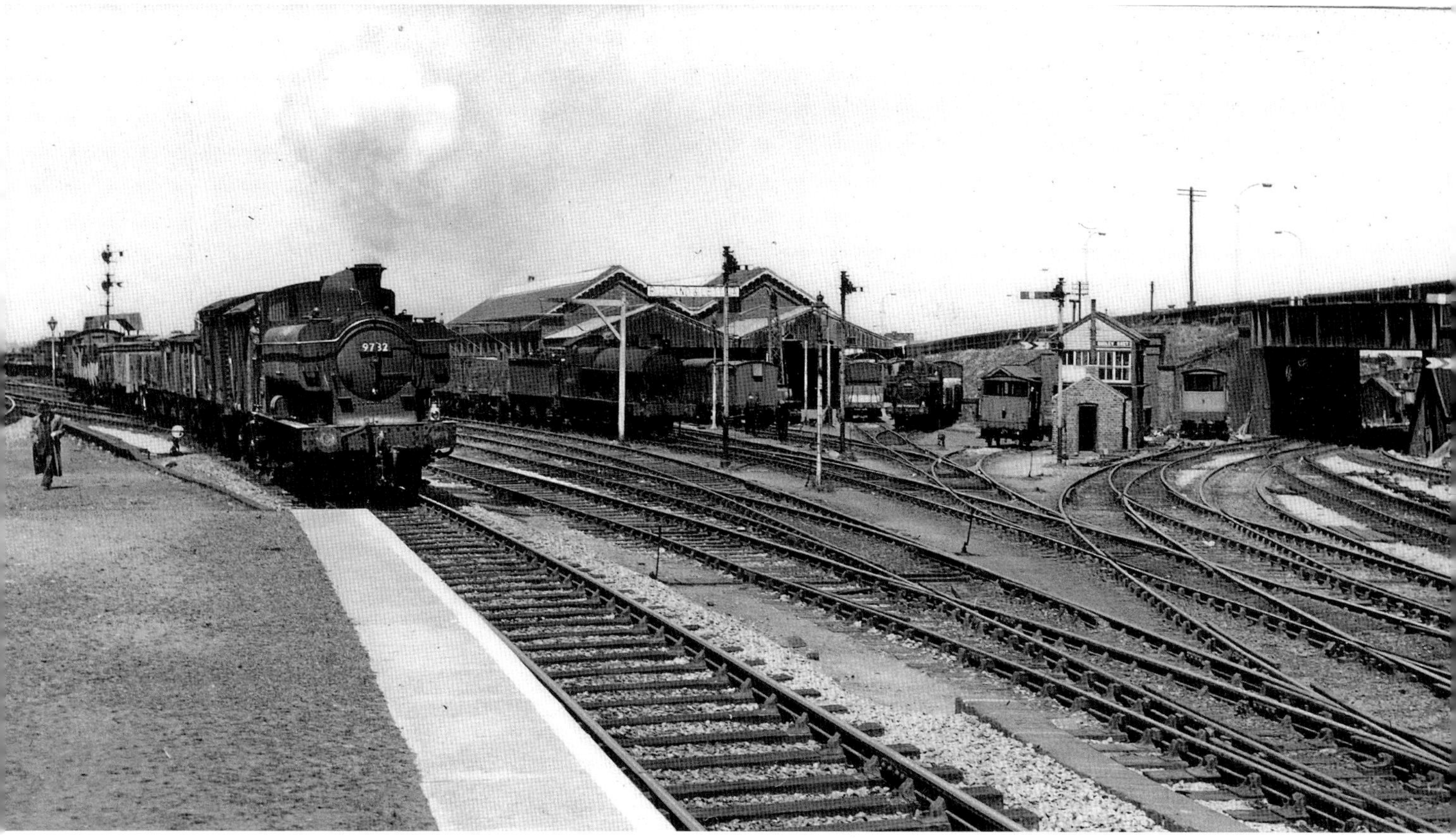

Dudley. These two excellent shots, taken in the 1950s, give a good idea of the environment where David and Jack Stanford worked from the turn of the century in the goods department as foremen. With Great Western traction in evidence and a LNWR Super D locomotive. The lower shot, featuring two GWR railcars, shows the full extent of the goods yard.

Photos by Michael Hale with special thanks to the Great Western Trust

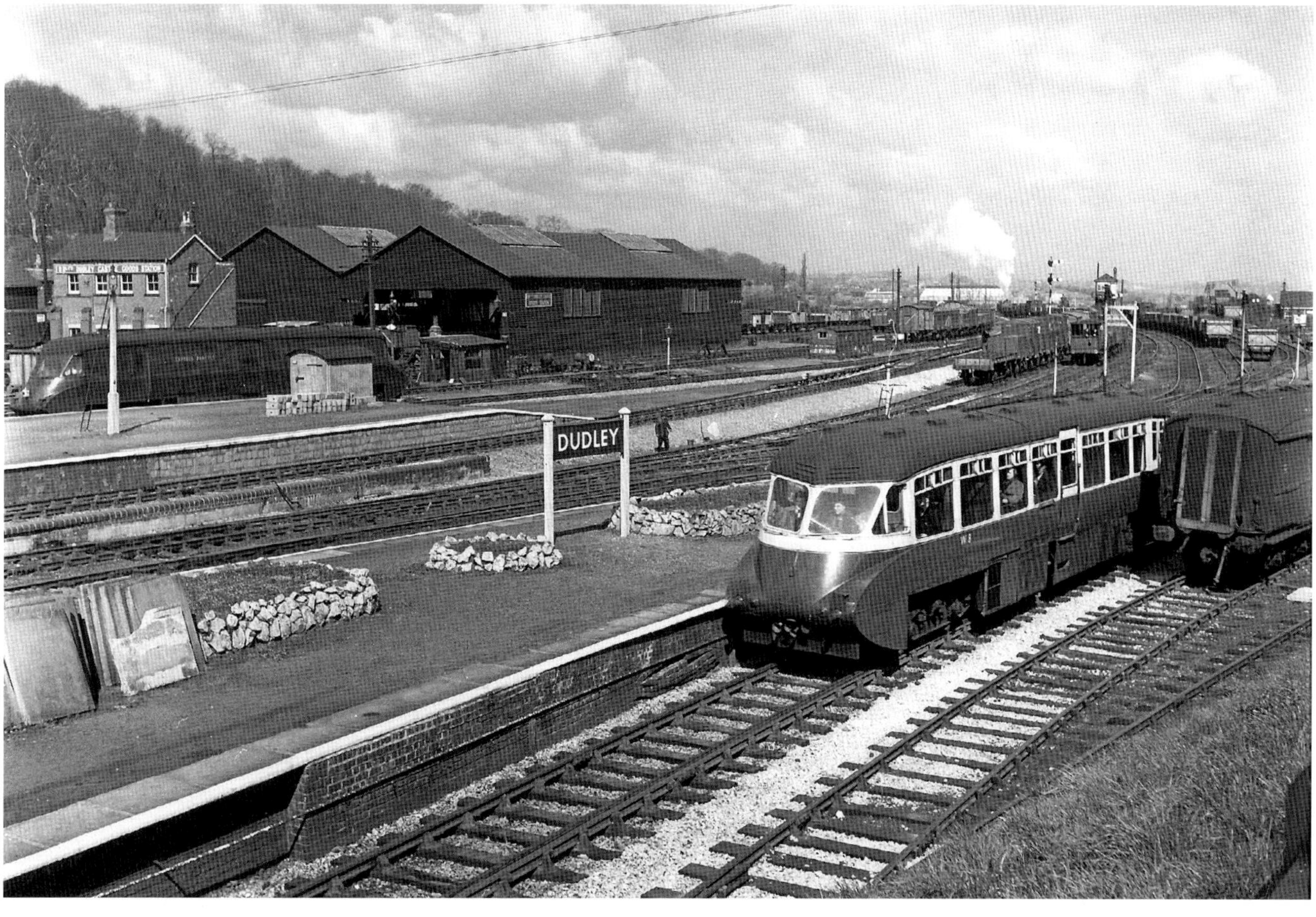

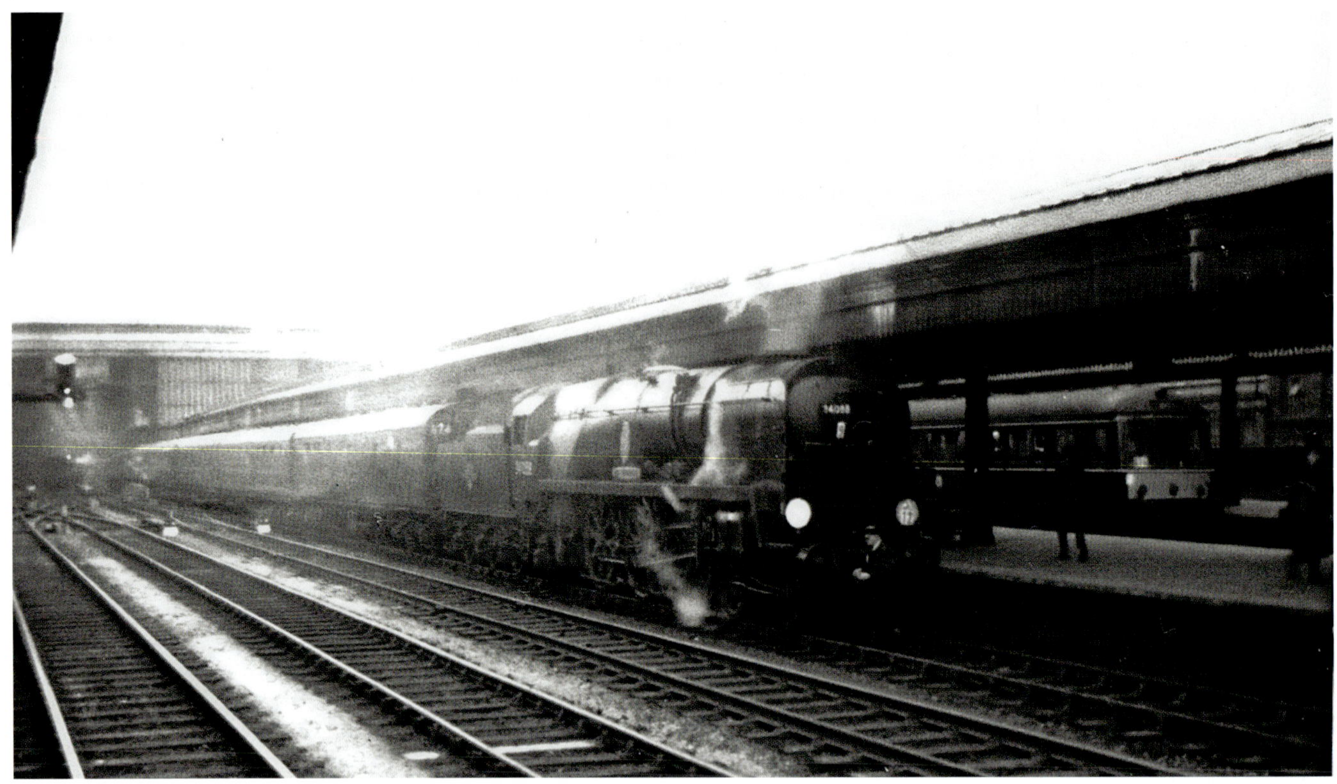

Snow Hill was John's place of work from 1963 until 1967, in the telegraph office on platform 7; experience garnered at Bromsgrove signal box meant he was good 'on the needle' – sending and receiving telegraph messages. In 1963 there was the amazing spectacle of no fewer than 17 special trains from Southampton for an FA Cup final game; each train was hauled by a Southern Railway Bullied pacific. This loco is 34088 named *213 Squadron* on train 9 of 17. Taken 27th April 1963. *Photo by John Stanford*

Birmingham Snow Hill and 7029 *Clun Castle* heads a special train to Swindon via High Wycombe on 3rd April 1965. The trip enabled enthusiasts to visit Swindon railway works and museum. *Photo by John Stanford*

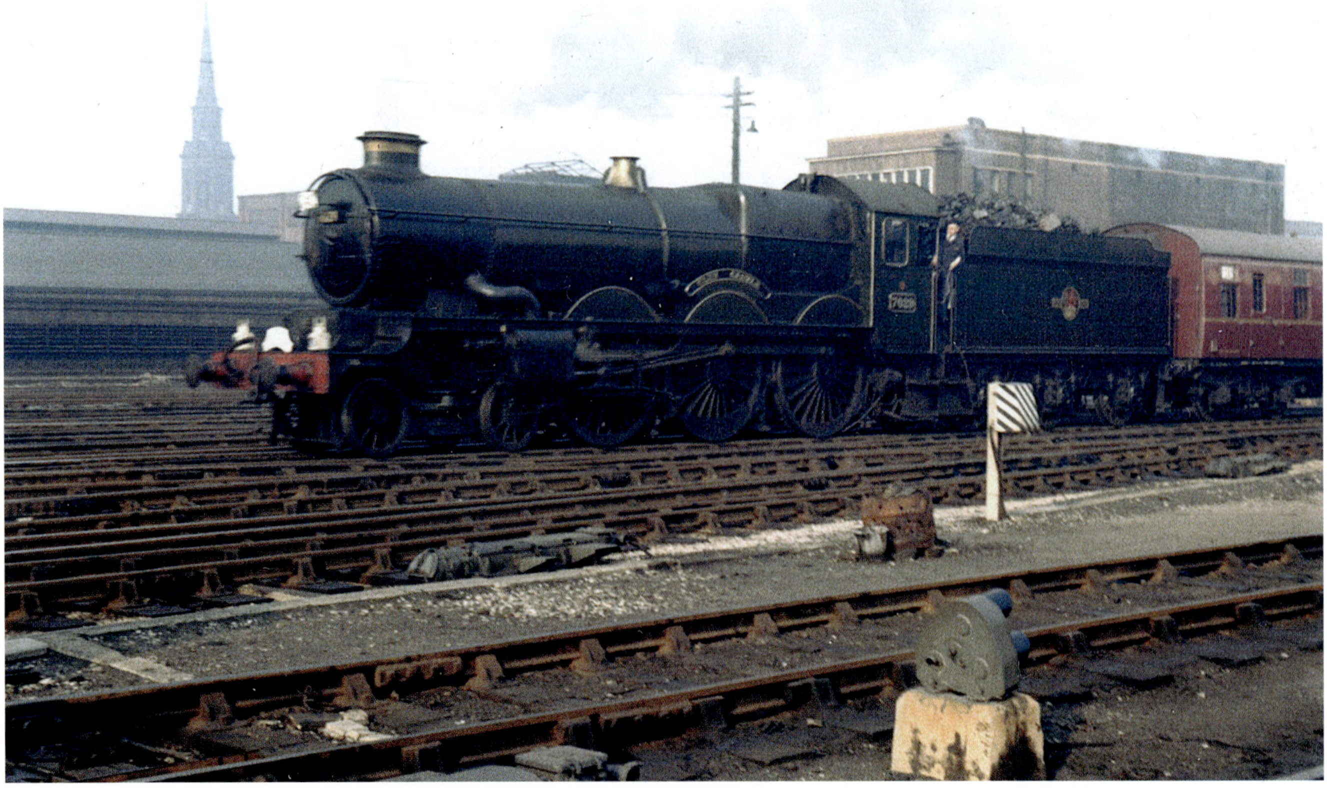

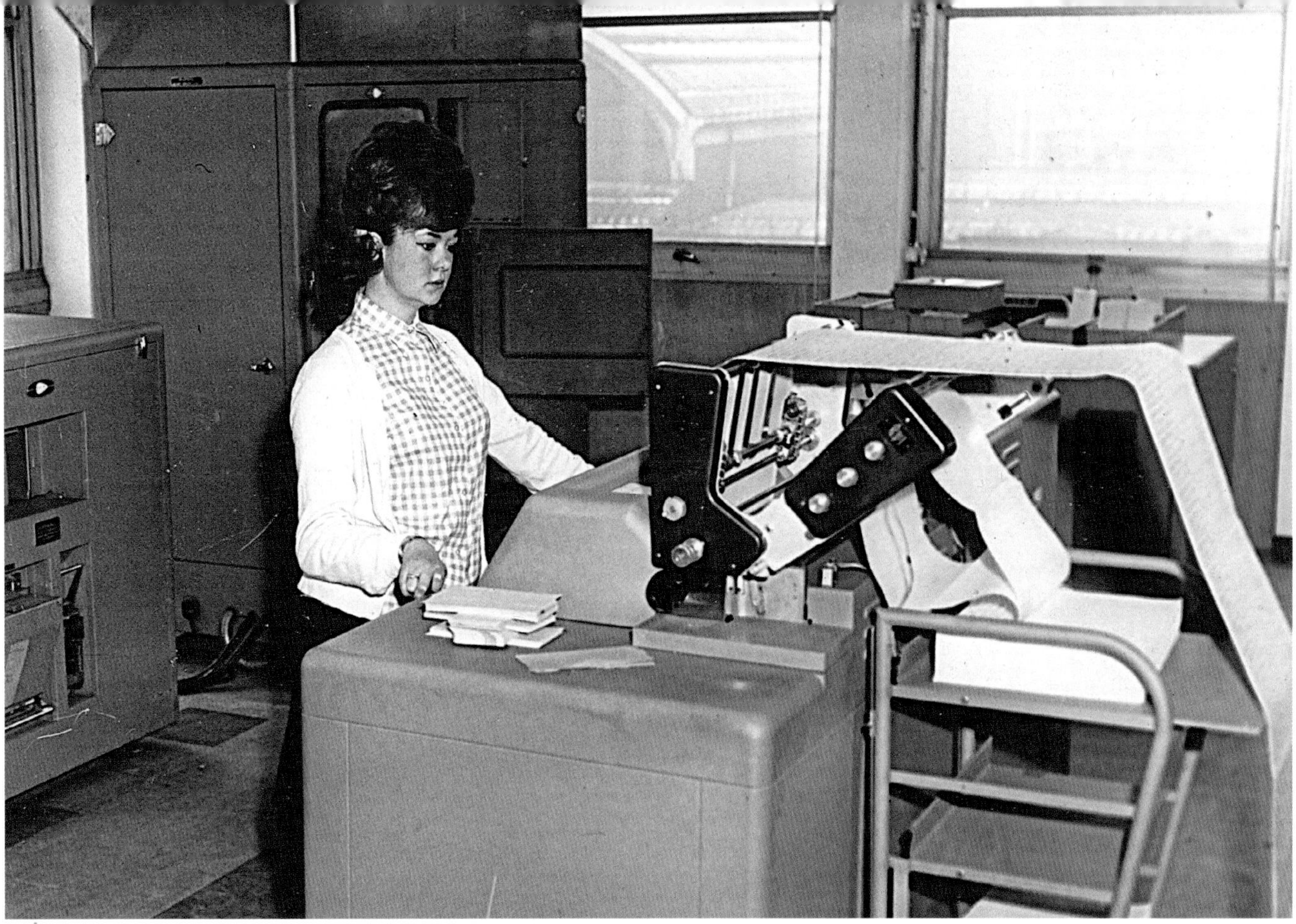

New Street. Wendy worked in the personnel function for BR London Midland Region from 1964; she would dine in the BR staff canteen at Curzon Street where she met John that year and they married two years later. Here she is captured entering data on a 'modern' computer, which these days would be accessed via a laptop device. *Photo by BR London Midland Region*

Birmingham Navigation Street 20 years earlier. The Birmingham tram system was a love of John's from an early age, open until July 1953. Just beyond here, after returning from RAF leave during the Blitz, Harry had to push a double-deck car, along with the driver and other passengers, with the overhead wires down, until operable tram wiring was found near Bristol Street. They were then all able to climb back aboard and Harry headed on down the Bristol Road to Betty and young son John who had just been born in early 1942. Further bombs were dropped on Birmingham routinely until summer 1942. *Photo John Stanford Collection (by the late R.T. Wilson)*

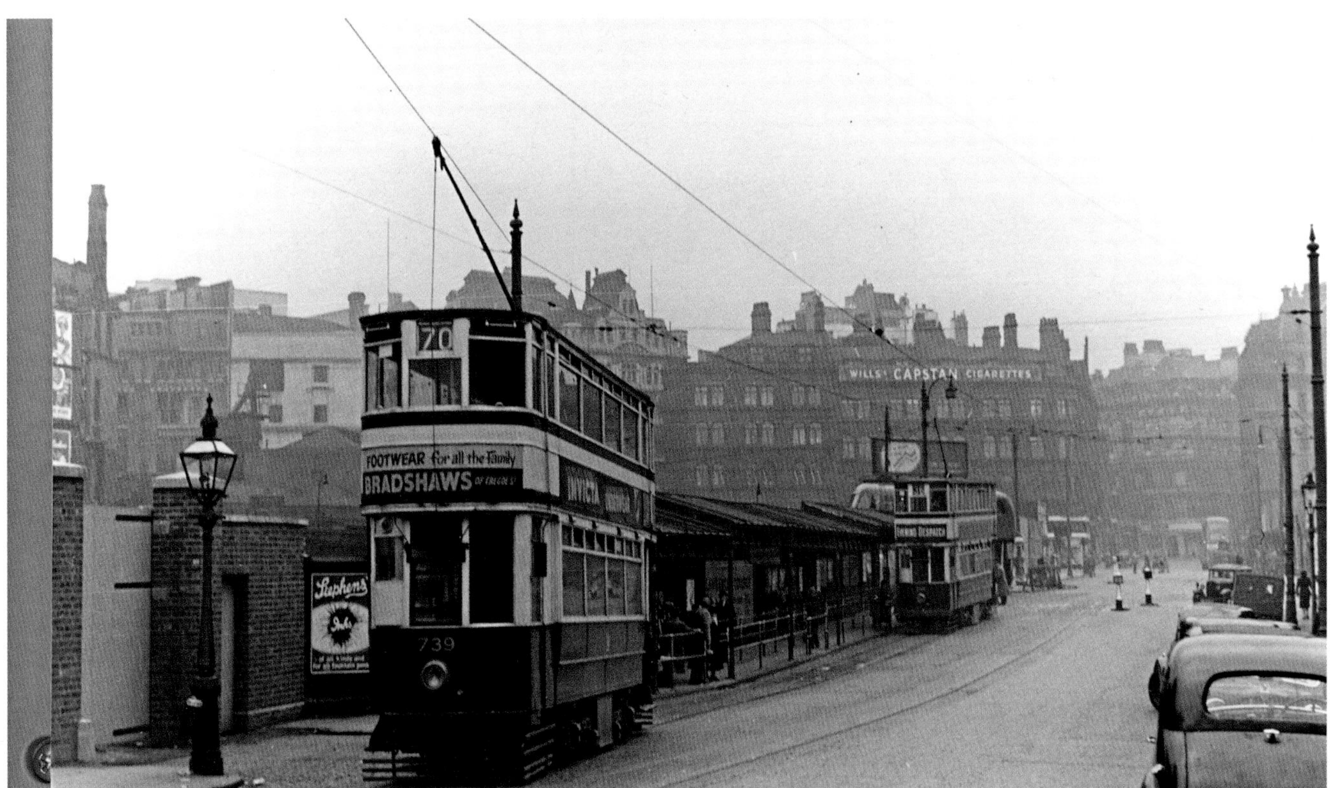

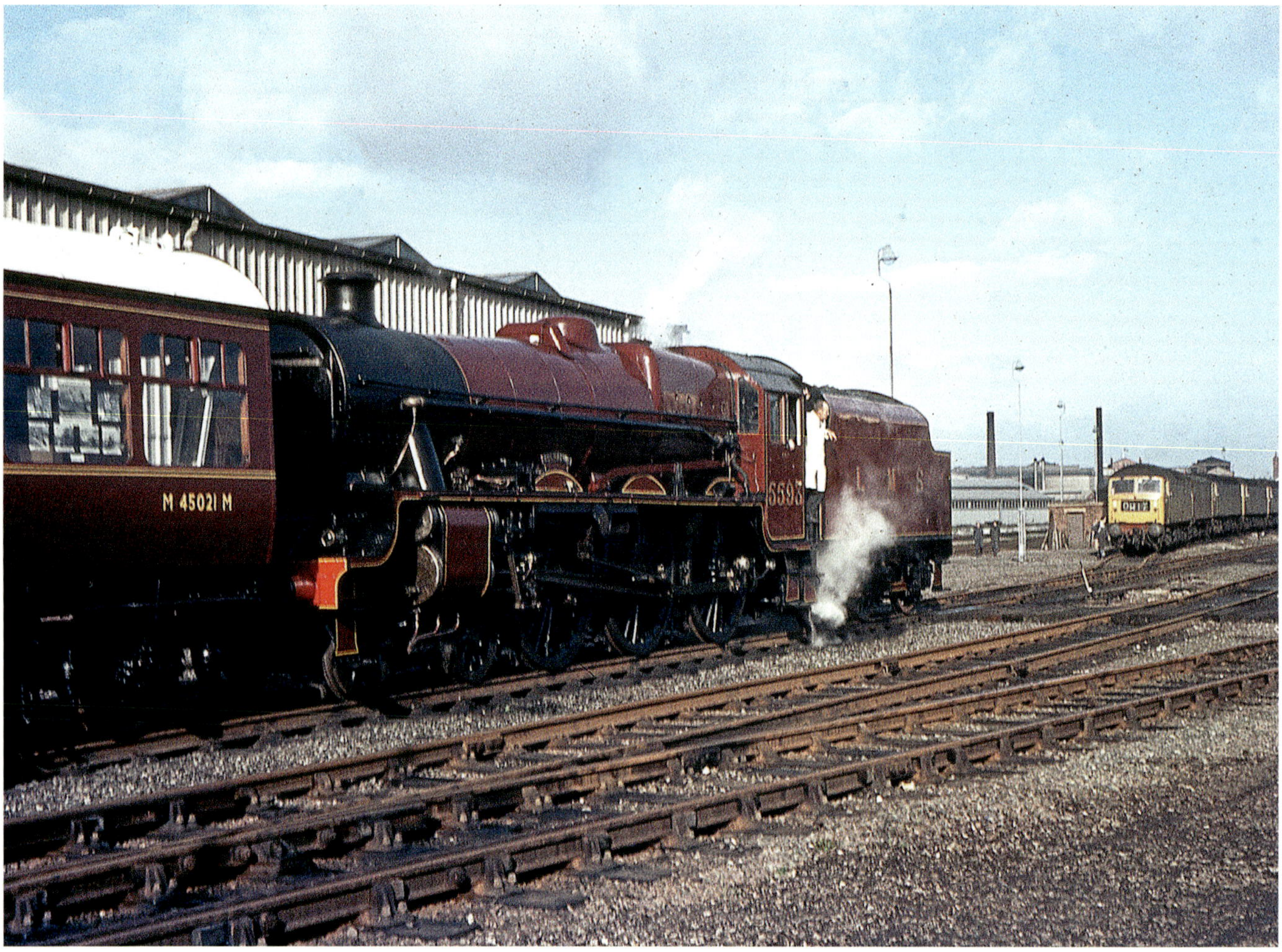

Tyseley Shed was a regular haunt for John, where he could still enjoy steam working steam; pre- and post-marriage in 1966. Here on 28th September 1968 a preserved LMS Jubilee named *Kolhapur* is seen preparing for the depot open day. Note the two-tone green class 47s in the background. The lower view the same day, shows Castle class loco 7029 *Clun Castle*, Wendy's favourite engine, operating a shuttle service in the depot confines. By 1968 the loco had been preserved. *Photos by John Stanford*

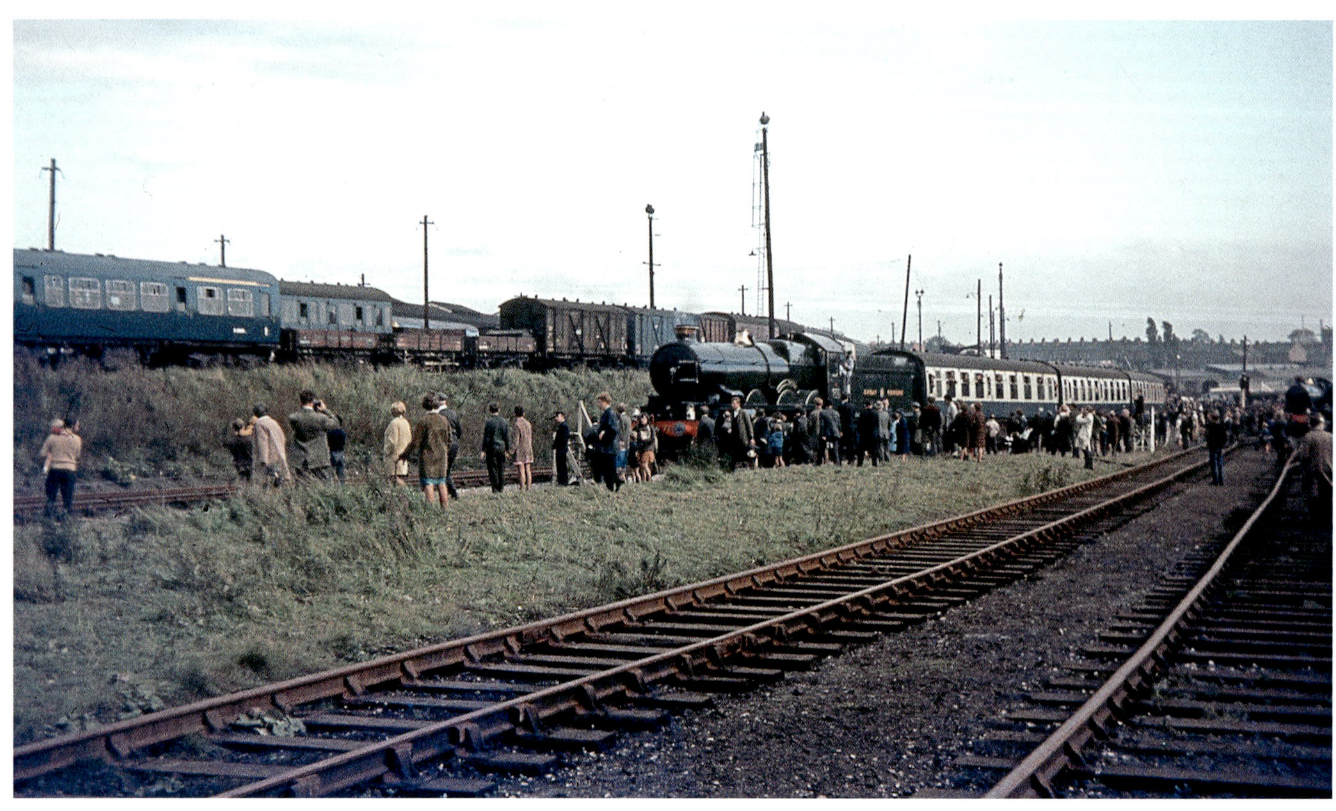

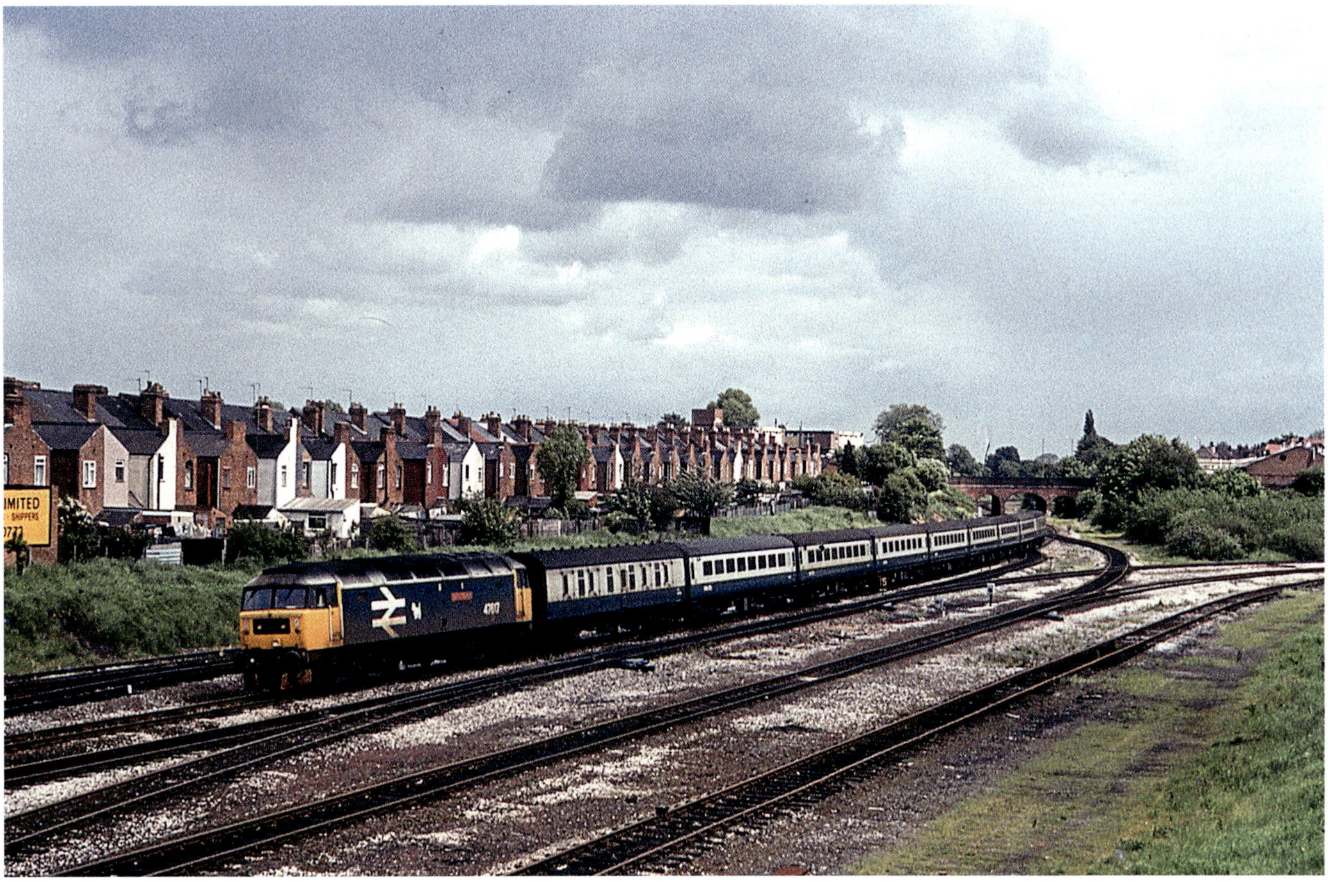

Tyseley on Sunday 8th June 1986 and the train was being conducted through Single Line Working by a pilotman. The author watched fascinated, never realising he would be doing the same eight years later as operations manager in South Wales.

Solihull in September 1966; just before John and Wendy's wedding, John came across woebegone Panier 9794 shunting new-build tractors. The loco was in service for another eight weeks, based out of Tyseley shed, in typical end of steam condition.

Photo by John Stanford

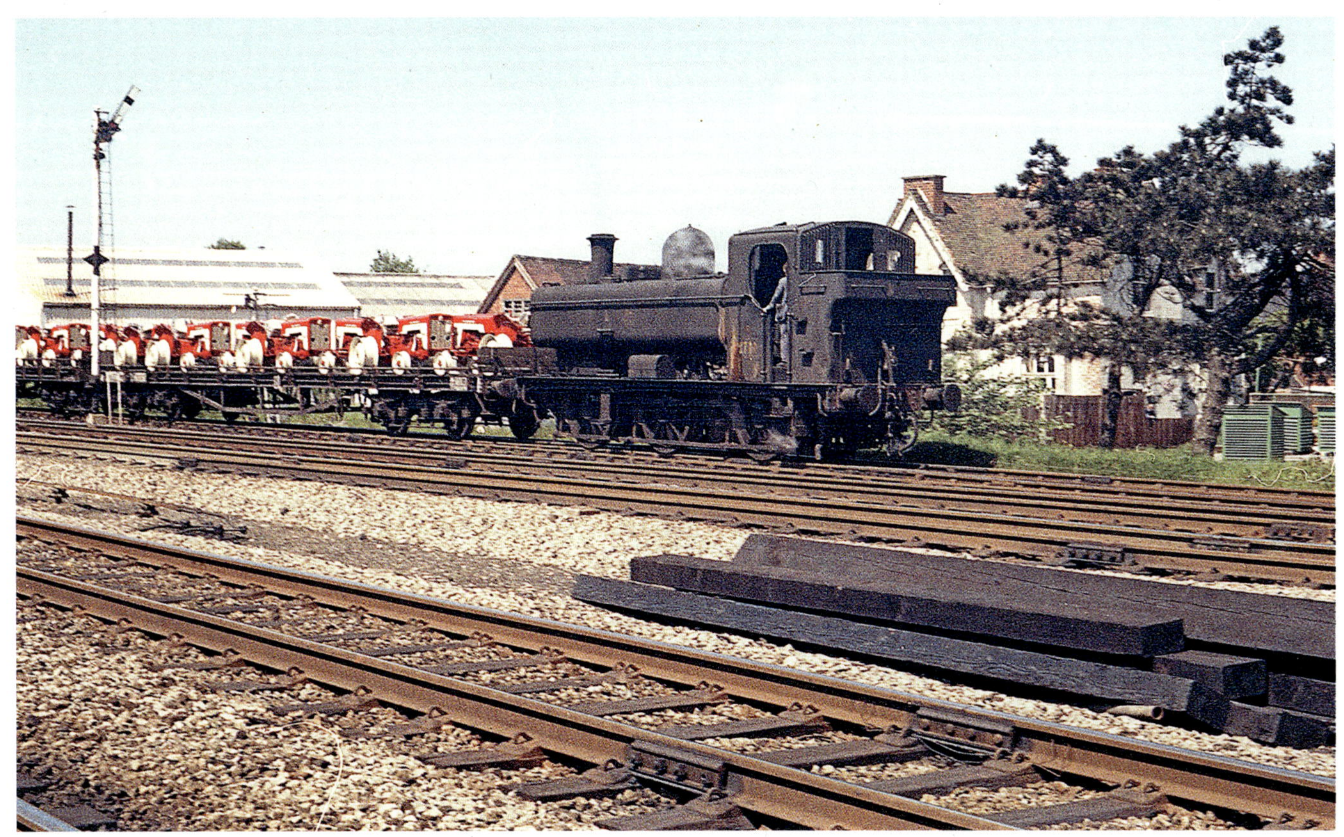

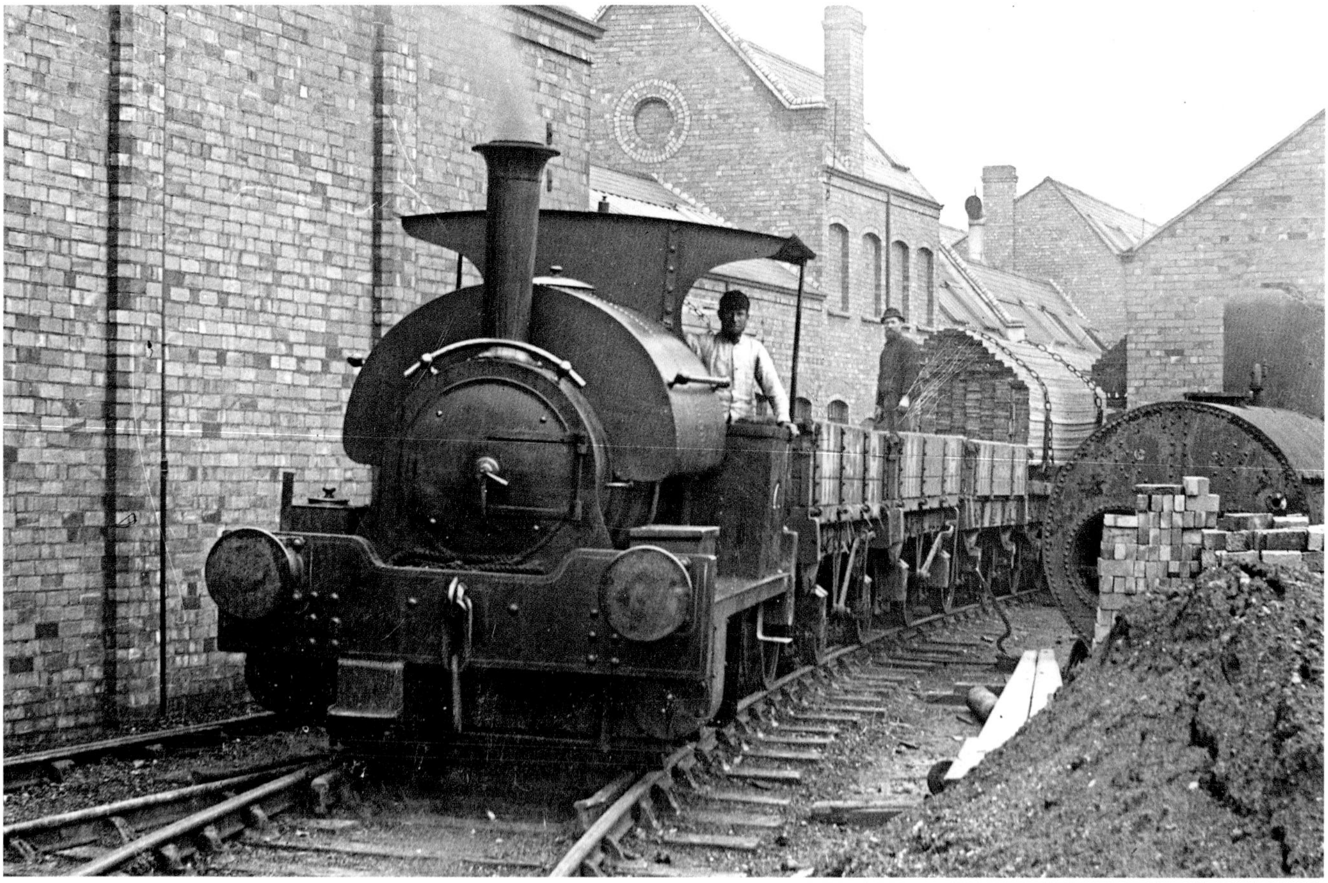

Bournville; in the heart of the first stage of the Bournville works, the first Cadbury locomotive, built by Peckett of Bristol in 1885. This locomotive remained on site until 1894 and was displaced from Bournville by the arrival of the new-build Dick Kerr-built steam locomotives, the first of which arrived in 1894. The Peckett locomotive departed to a colliery contractor in Bloxwich.

Photo Paul Stanford Collection with thanks to Cadbury Archive and Mondelez International

Bournville Dispatch Building and Cadbury Number 4 is seen at the head of a long train of chocolate-carrying vans. The photograph has obviously been 'touched up' at the processing stage, nevertheless it is a fine view taken between the First and Second World Wars; the rail wagons are carrying post-1923 colour schemes, notably the LMS railway box van.

Photo Paul Stanford Collection with thanks to Cadbury Archive and Mondelez International

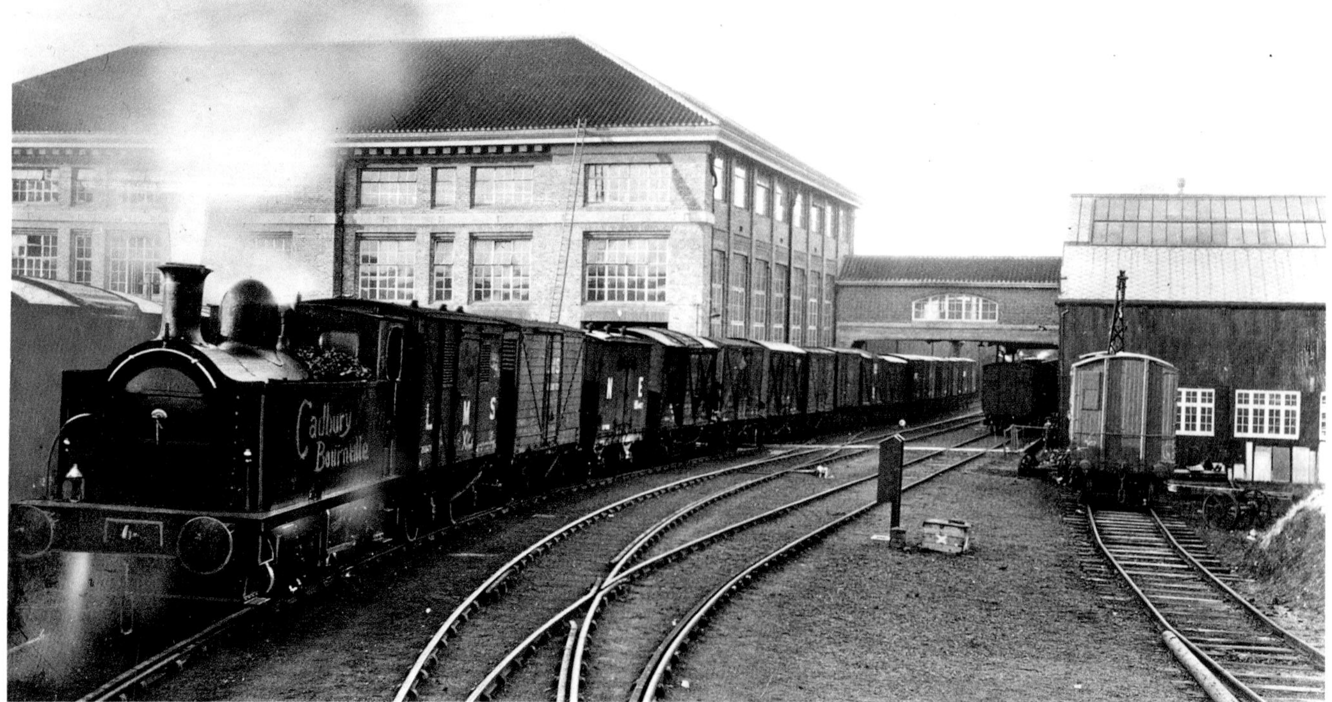

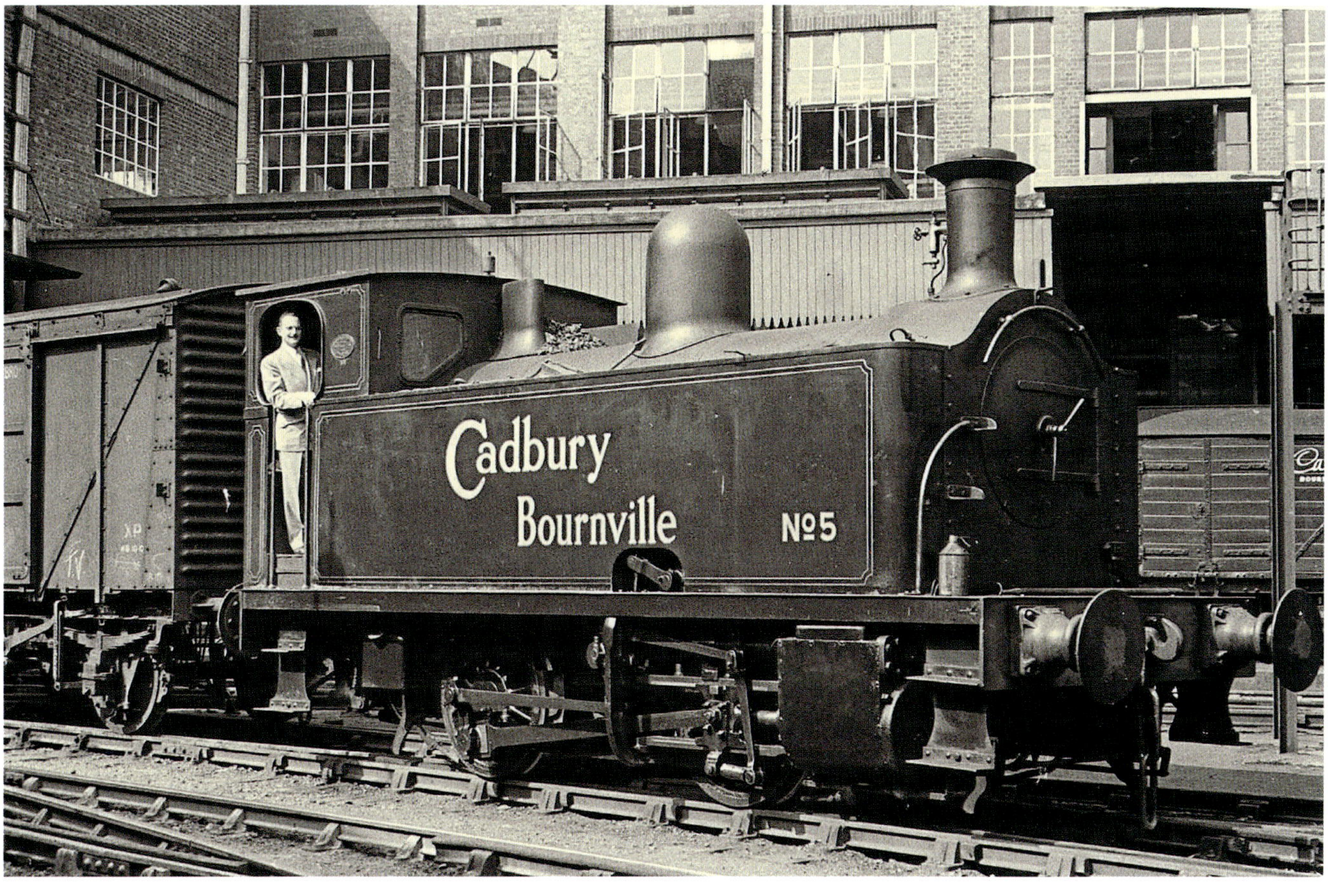

Bournville. Cadbury Number 5 is seen in the 1950s, coupled to a LMS railway box van. The locomotive carries the small Cadbury Bournville typeface, applied when it went for an overhaul in 1952 at the Hunslet Engine Co in Leeds, matching the typeface size applied to Cadbury No.9 when built in 1949. Locomotive No.5 was scrapped on site at Bournville in June 1959.

Photo Stanford Collection, with thanks to Cadbury Archive and Mondelez International

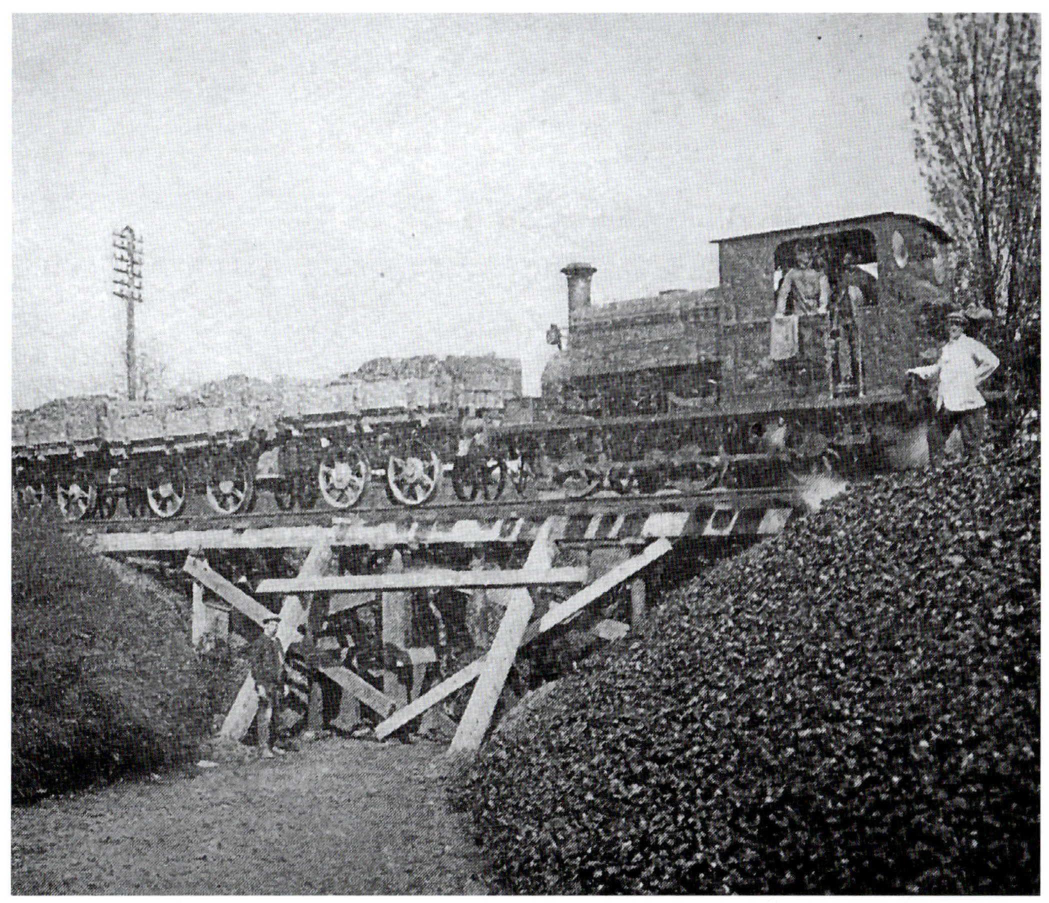

The Cadbury Railway system underwent expansion in the early 1920s and utilised a Manning Wardle 0-6-0 saddle tank locomotive named *Hollymoor* to haul trains of muck. The author's grandfather remembered the locomotive working on extending the factory railway, as a schoolboy aged 10, telling the author, as a boy, that the locomotive was painted green and was quite unlike any other Cadbury loco.

Photo courtesy of Cadbury Archives and Mondelez International

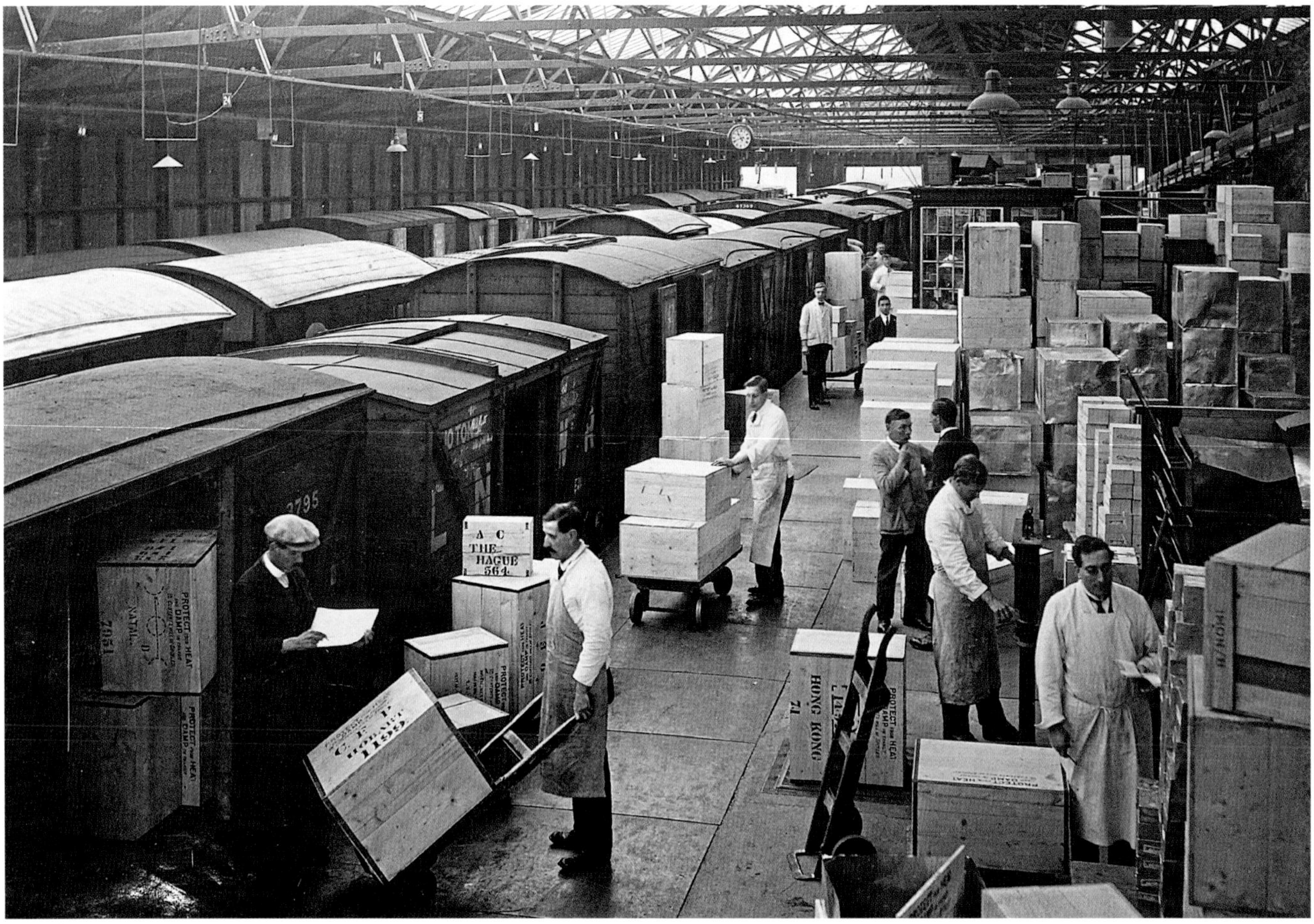

Bournville Loading Dock was akin to an important station with staff engaged in the individual loading of rail wagons for dispatch across the UK and further afield. Here in the 1920s we see just such a scene. Photo courtesy of Cadbury Archives and Mondelez International

Bournville, Despatch Building and Cadbury No.1 (AE 1977 of 1925) hauls a train up the steep gradient to the exchange sidings; either shortly before or after the Second World War; given the colour scheme of the box vans. At left is the location where the author's grandfather had a 'near miss' when he lost control of some box vans he was gravity shunting. Mercifully, he regained control of the errant wagons before they crashed into the loading deck. His only injuries were to his pride and cuts to his trousers and knees. He coached the author on shunting safety when he started training as a guard in 1987.

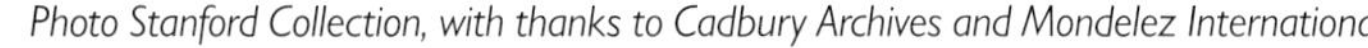

Photo Stanford Collection, with thanks to Cadbury Archives and Mondelez International

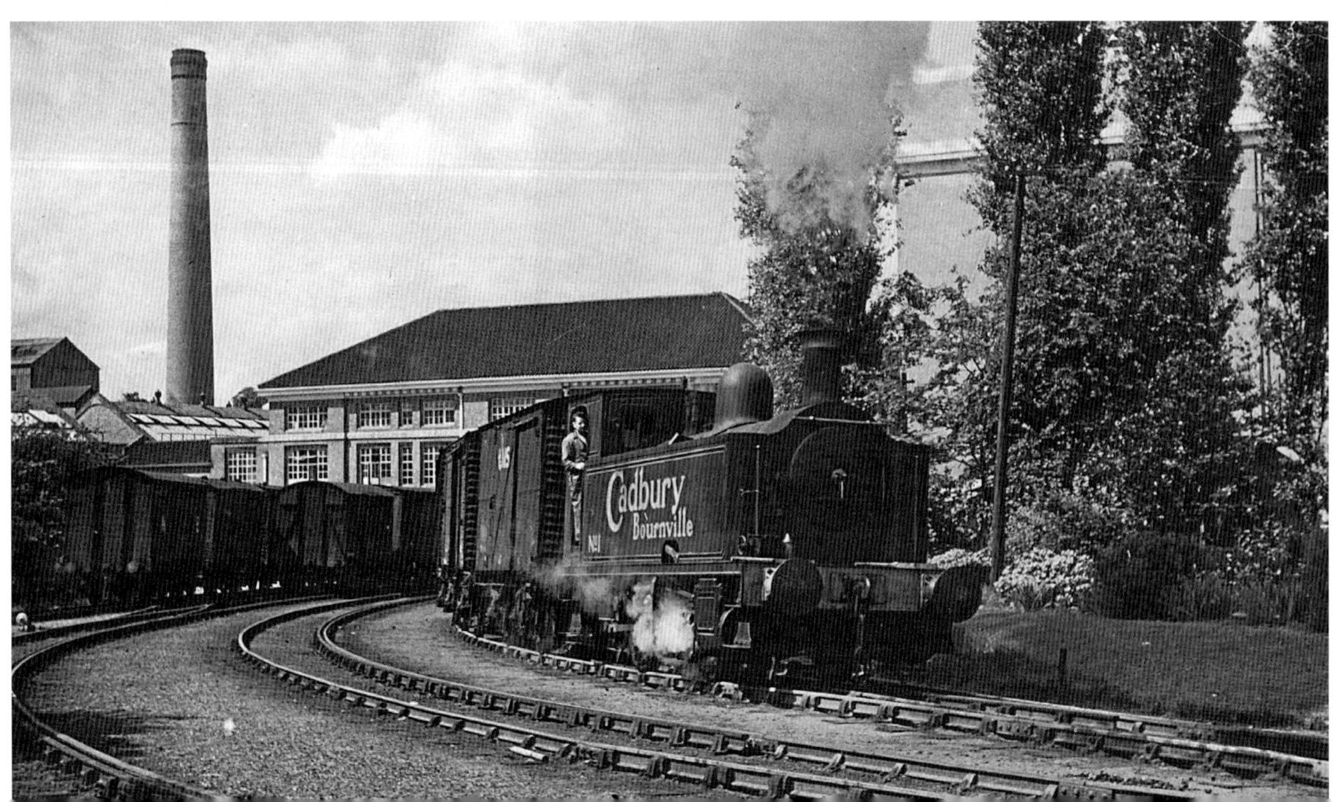

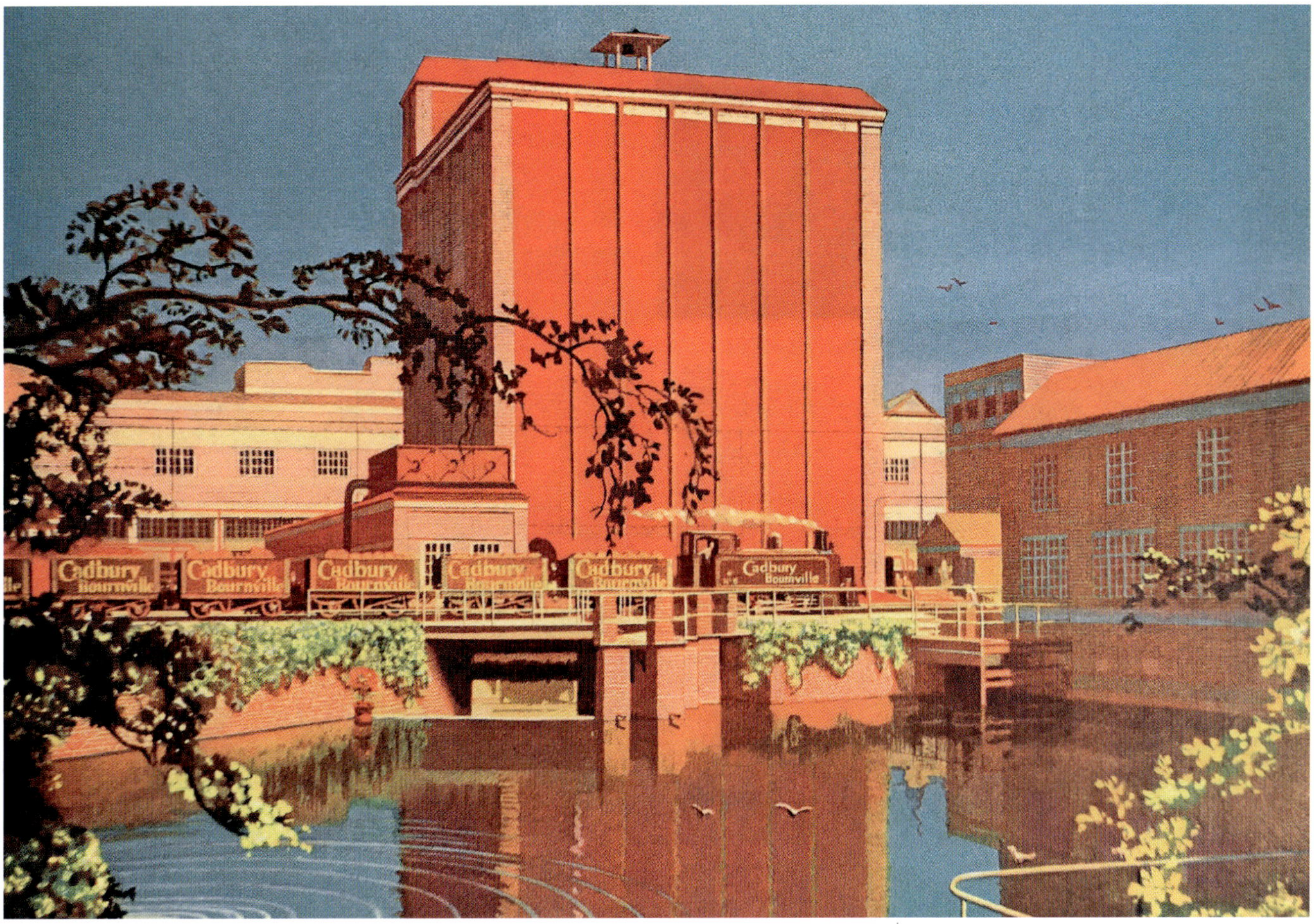

Bournville after the huge expansion of the 1920s rightly celebrated the achievement with some exceptional paintings. Superb British artist Ernest Wallcousins executed this view in the heart of the works in 1930, beautifully portraying Cadbury No.6.

Painting courtesy of Cadbury Archives and Mondelez International

Bournville Parkside in 1964; with the very first train to the Cadbury Cake Depot being pushed into the loading building. The depot was built on the site of the Midland Railway locomotive shed, closed by 1961. The site was not directly rail connected to the rest of the Cadbury Bournville system and was served by BR locomotives for depositing and collection of wagons. The author as a schoolboy recollects seeing BR blue class 25 locos in the cake depot on a number of occasions with vacuum braked box vans.

Photo Stanford Collection, with thanks to Cadbury Archive and Mondelez International

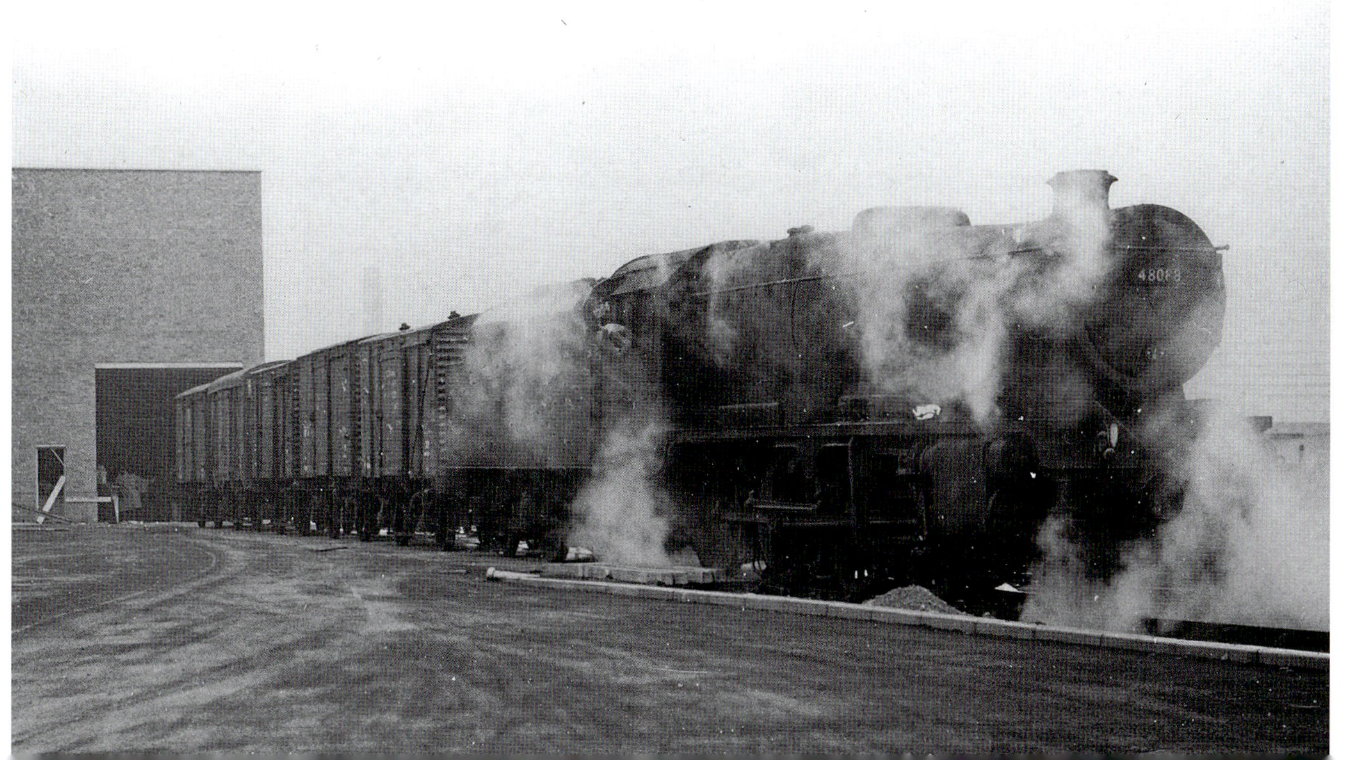

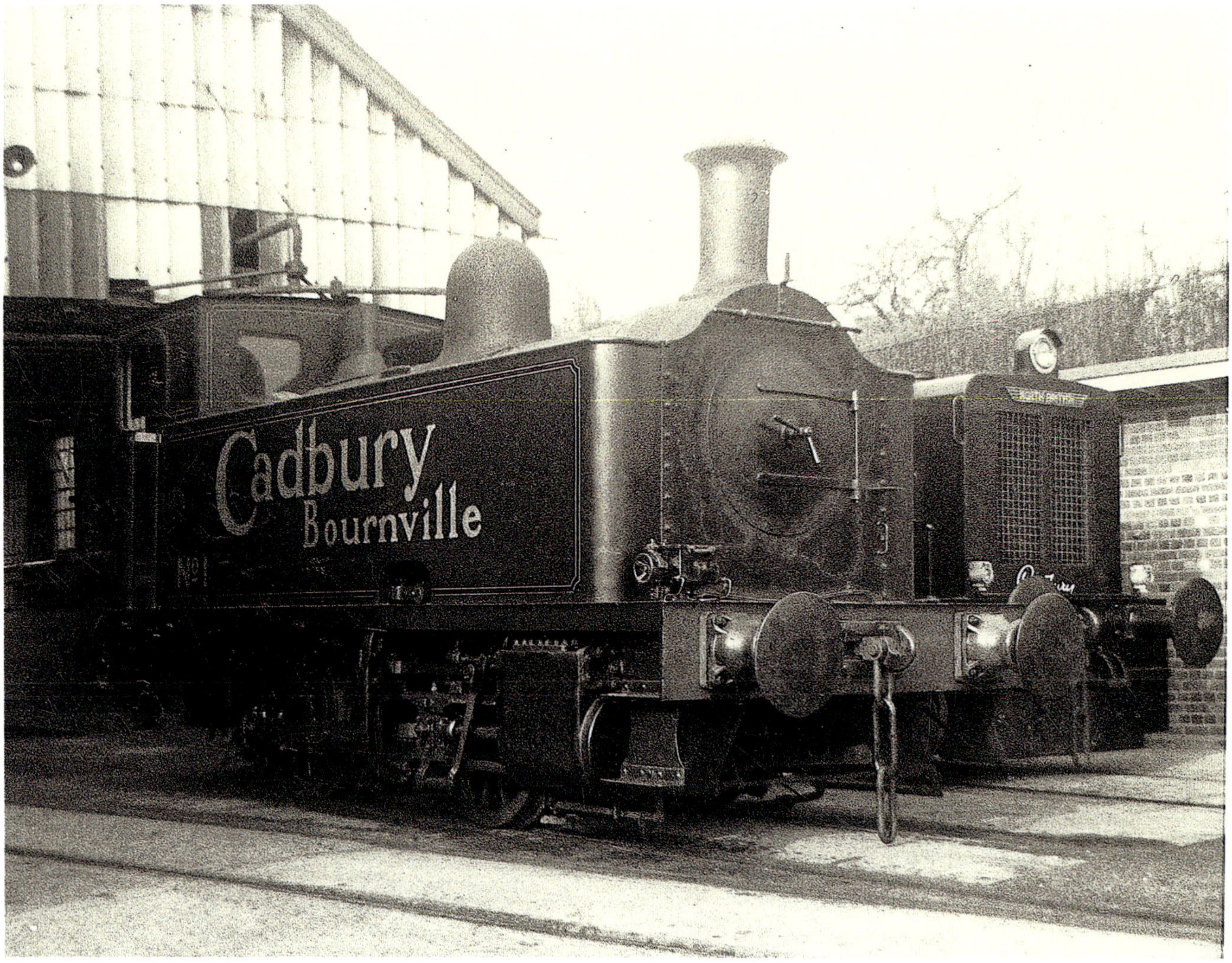

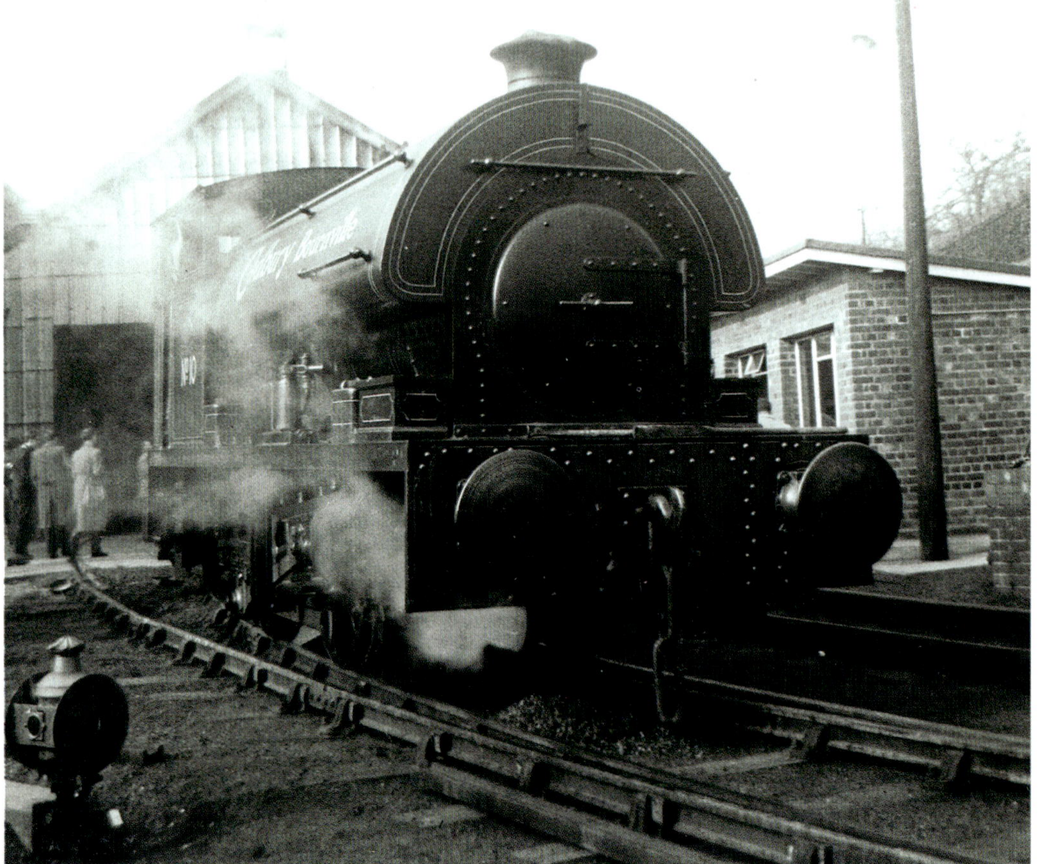

Bournville Cadbury Locomotive Shed on 4th March 1961 when the Industrial Railway Society visited. These two views were taken by family friend Trevor Riddle. In the view of Cadbury No.1, it should be noted that Jack Stanford's house is just out of sight on the right, highlighting how close he lived to his place of work from 1912 to 1944. Also pictured is the final Cadbury steam loco, No.10 built by Peckett of Bristol, who ironically built the first loco.

Photos by Trevor Riddle

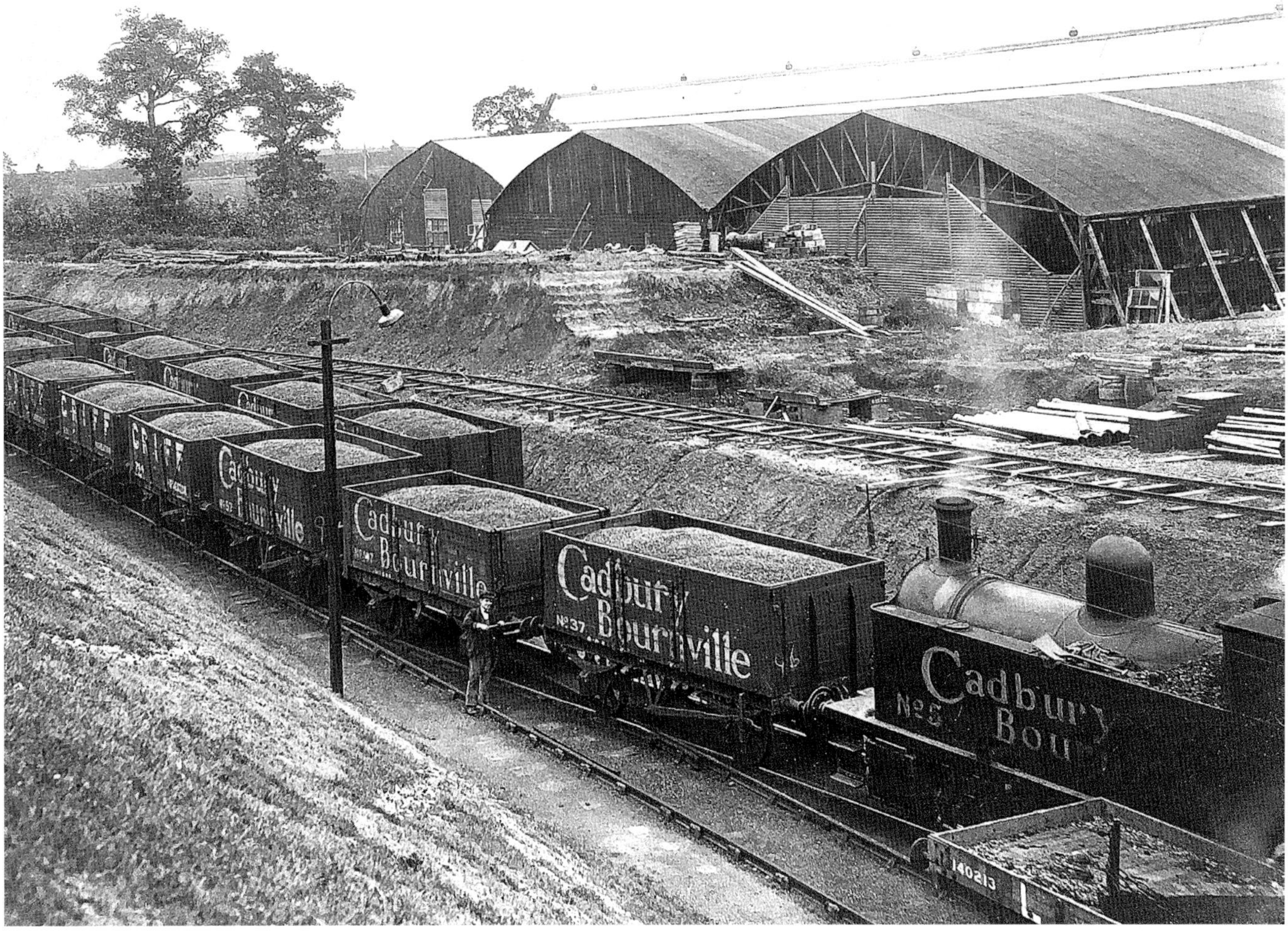

Holly Curve was situated east of the locomotive shed and in this splendid early 1920s view the locomotive shed is at right out of shot, with Cadbury number 5 stood on the line to Holly Curve and the exchange sidings. The Birmingham to Bristol line runs left to right in the background.

Photo Cadbury Archive and Mondelez International

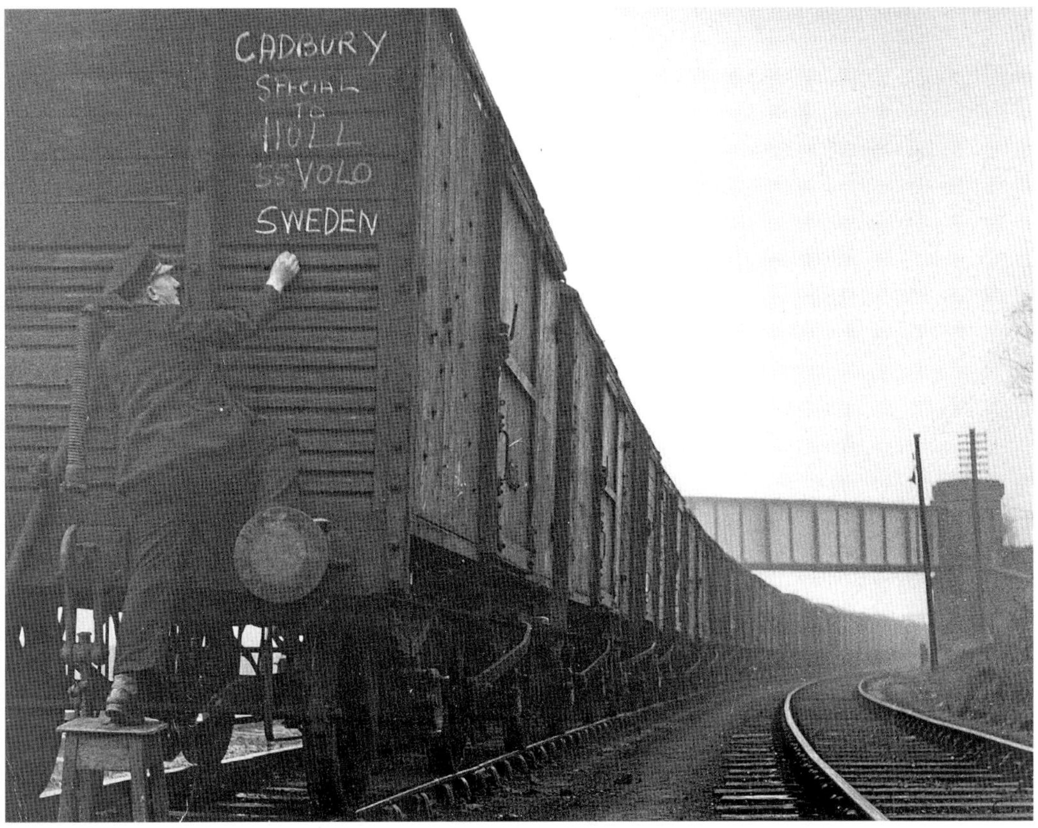

Bournville Exchange Sidings in a photo circa the start of the Second World War. This can be determined by the fact the ship, SS *Volo* as recipient of the Cadbury chocolate, was built in 1938 and sunk by a U-boat in 1941.

Photo courtesy of Cadbury Archives and Mondelez International

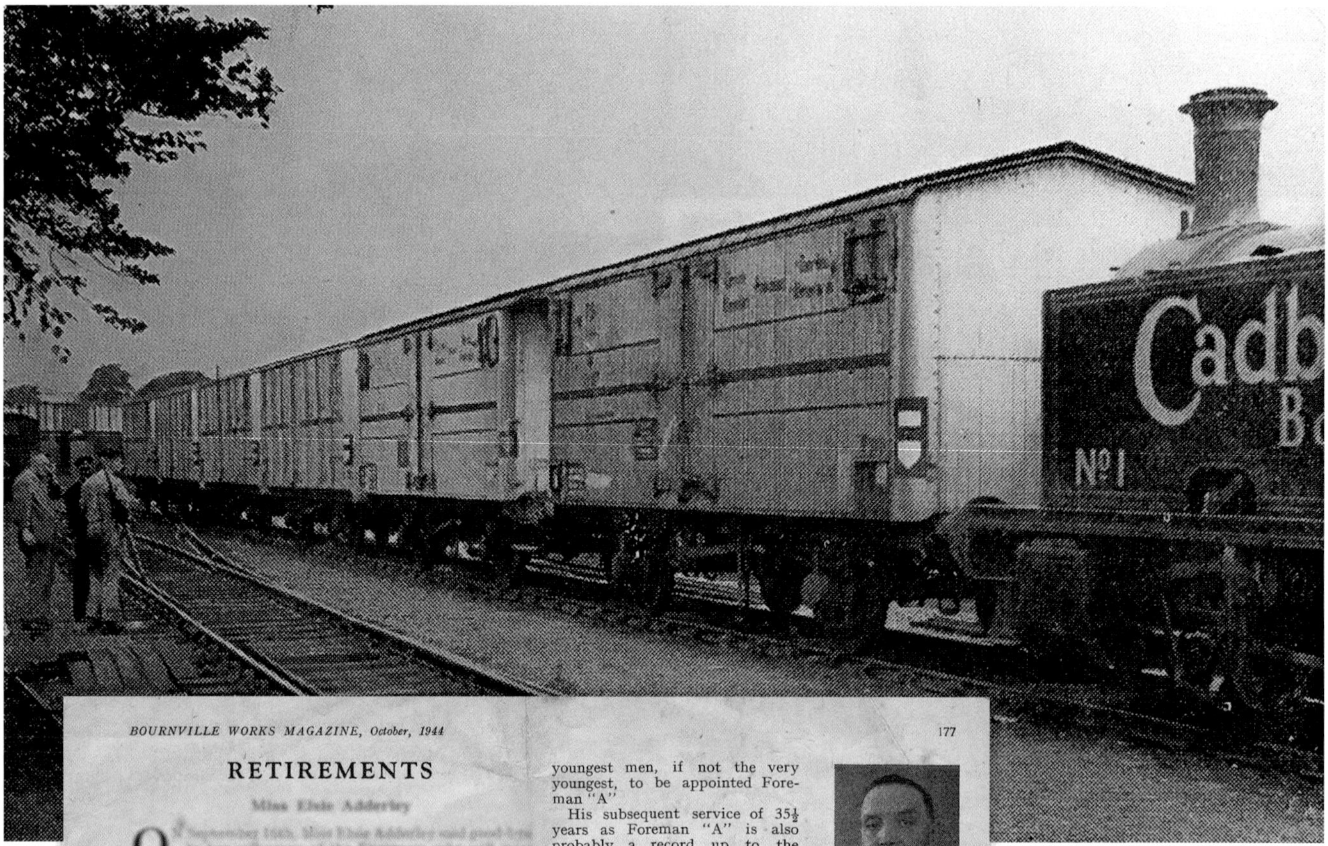

BOURNVILLE WORKS MAGAZINE, October, 1944 177

RETIREMENTS

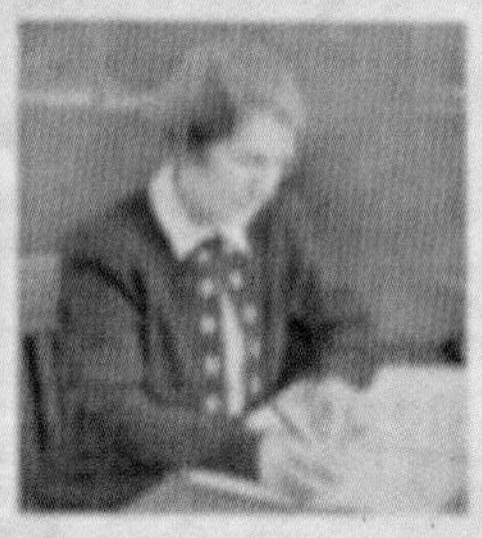

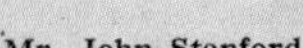

Mr. John Stanford

It is difficult to realize the break in the long association which Mr. J. Stanford had with Bournville life, both inside and outside the factory, caused by his retirement at the end of August. It has been natural for so many years to "ask Jack Stanford" when anything wanted moving, that we almost feel a Bournville institution has gone.

It is not everyone's lot to have railway engines and gangs of men at their beck and call, but, as Foreman "A" of the Unloaders' Department, that was Mr. Stanford's work. He came to Bournville in March, 1907, from a railway company's office, where he had risen to Foreman, and so he was already versed in the handling of freight. In November, 1908, he was appointed to take charge of the Unloaders, and, at the age of 28, was surely one of the youngest men, if not the very youngest, to be appointed Foreman "A"

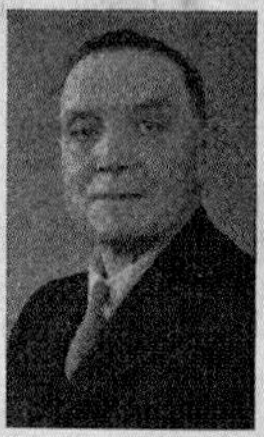

His subsequent service of 35½ years as Foreman "A" is also probably a record up to the present time.

A colleague, "W.D.," writes from the Foreman "A" Association: "His railway experience helped him to deal efficiently with the ever-increasing flow of goods in and out of the Works, and in the handling of his men he won their respect. He has always been very interested in the activities of the Association, and was for some years a member of the Committee. He is a keen and doughty opponent on the billiards and snooker tables, and we well remember he was one of those who, in earlier years, strove to get a hundred break, 'chalking' his cue with plaster from the wall! No doubt he will now be an acquisition to the Retired Foremen's team.

"He retires with the best wishes of all, and as we enjoy what we have really earned, no one will deny that he should have a happy retirement."

Mr. Stanford's name is connected with another record—or near-record — for readers will recollect that in July, 1943, we reproduced the portraits of six sons, a daughter and a son-in-law, all in uniform.

His departmental colleagues do not consider that they have said a final farewell to him, and are looking forward to meeting him again to make a presentation. They hope that retirement will enable him to make one of the crowd at Villa Park as frequently as he likes, and when happier times return, to visit Wembley at least once every Cup season.

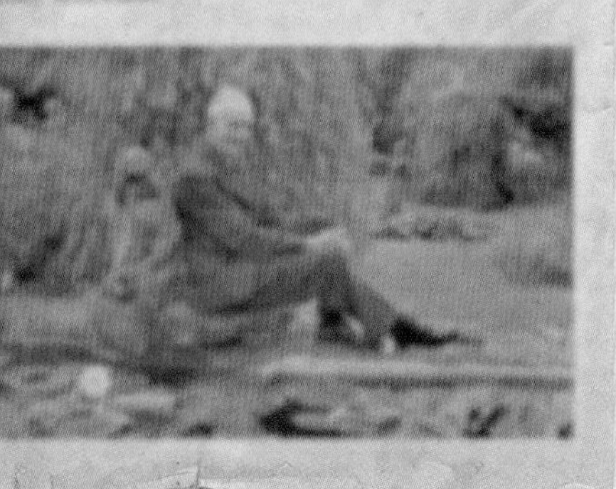

Above: Bournville Exchange Sidings in 1947; loco number 1 is in view with vans destined for the train ferry. The author's grandad told him he remembered chalking Cadbury con latte on the side of these Italian wagons at the dispatch deck. Impressively they returned with a back-load, fruit for Cadbury, coming via the Harwich train ferry.

Photo courtesy of Cadbury Archives and Mondelez International

Left: Bournville in 1944 was also significant as it was the year that Jack Stanford retired from his role looking after the railway and unloading teams at Cadbury Bournville. This touching tribute appeared in the Cadbury staff magazine

Photo courtesy of Cadbury Archives and Mondelez International

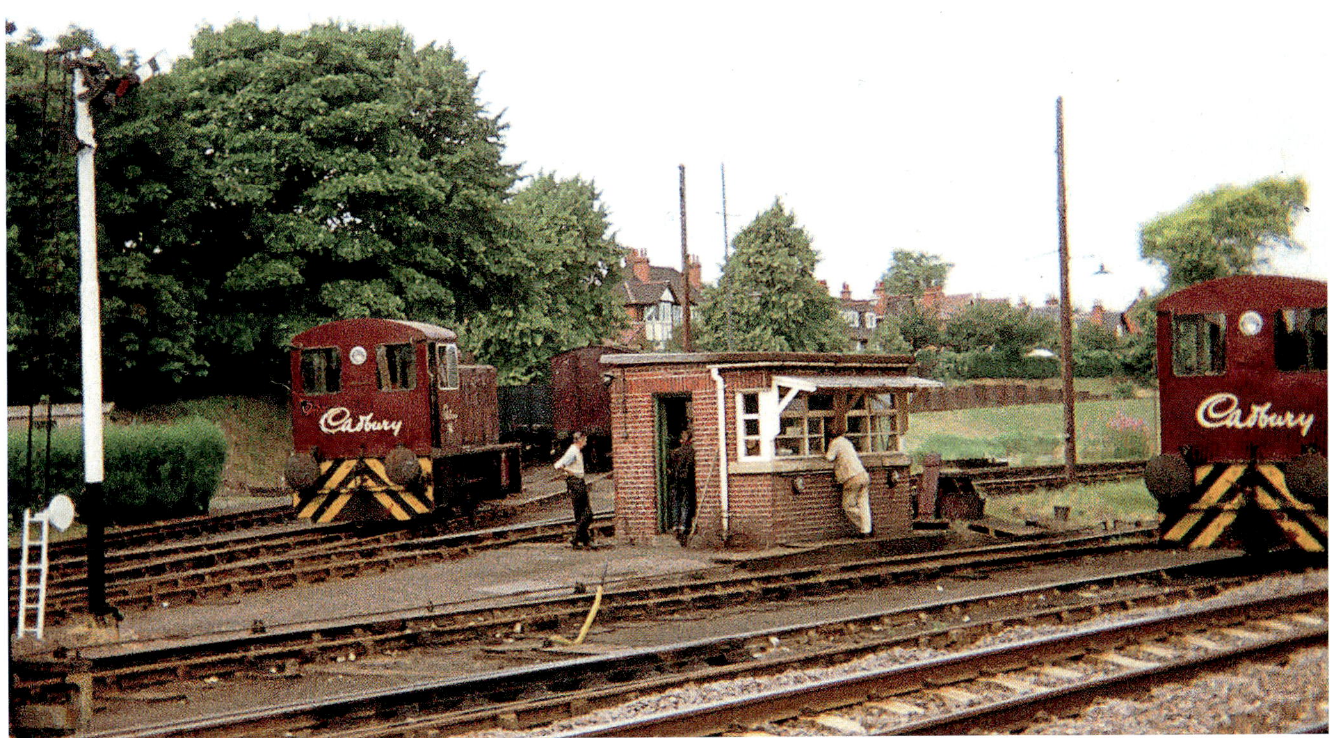

Above: Bournville Exchange Sidings in 1970, with North British Locos standing by the weighbridge building which formed the de-facto operating centre for staff. Behind loco number 15 is the end of Laburnum Road, where the author with his grandfather watched sister loco number 14 shunt box vans in February 1976. Of note from that visit, the author recollects the loco driver and shunter referring to his grandad as Mr Stanford when they greeted him some three years after his retirement.

Photo by Adrian Rescorla

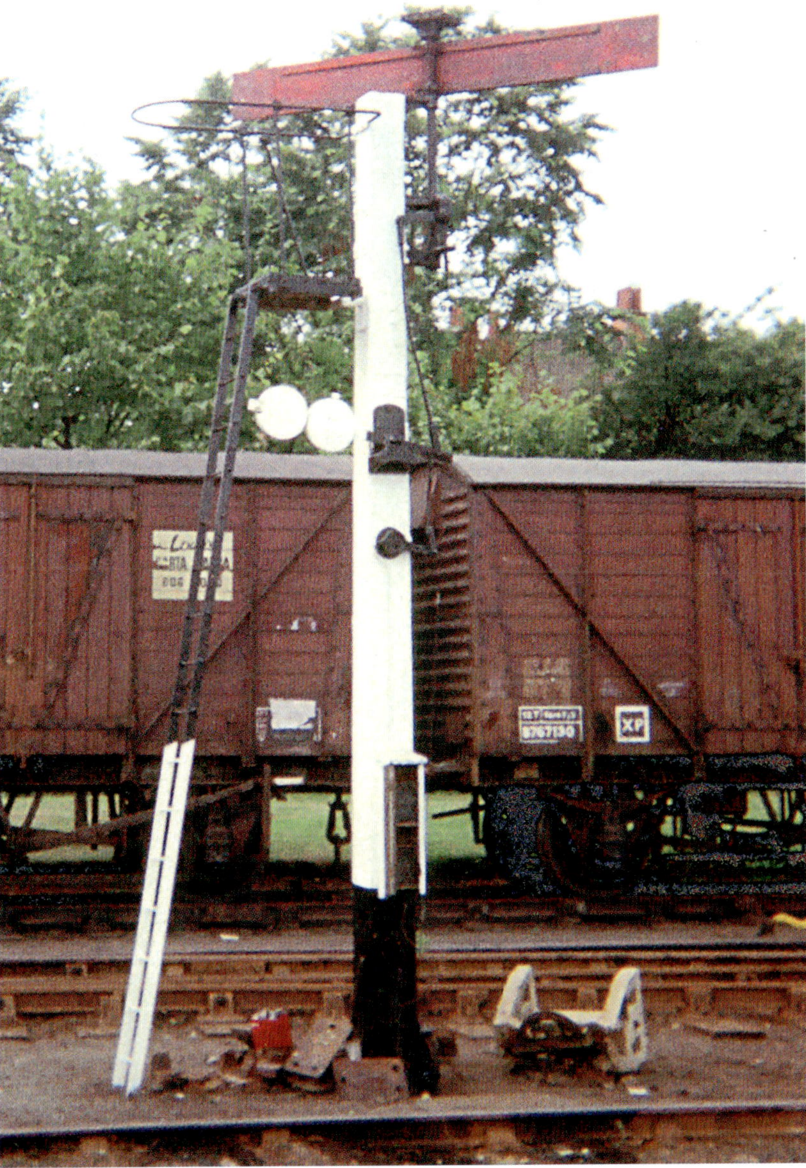

Left: Bournville Exchange Sidings and the unique crossbar signal seen in 1970. Following closure of the system, the signal was donated to the Chasewater Railway, who also have a Cadbury Bournville box van.

Photo by Adrian Rescorla

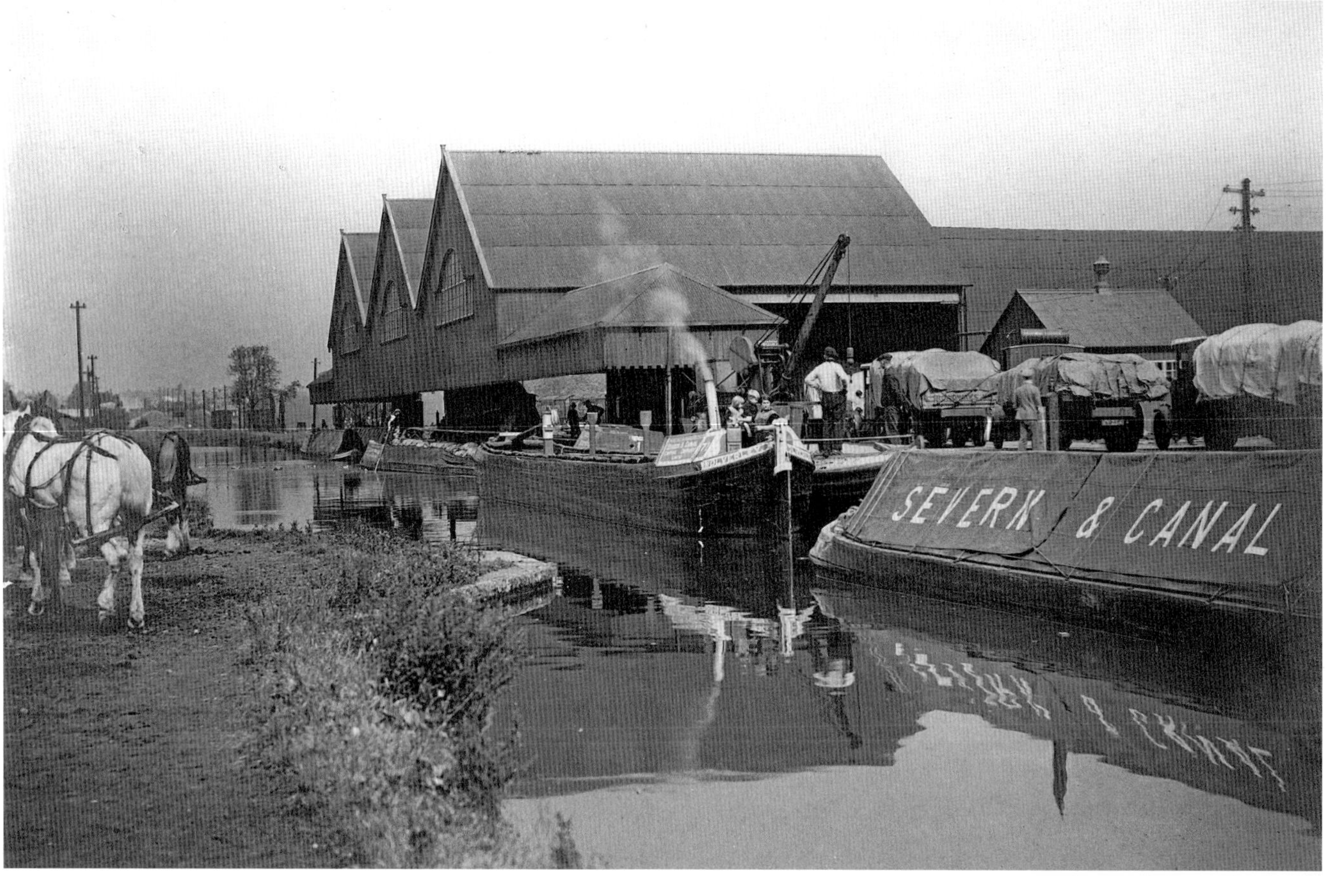

Waterside; looking towards Selly Oak. Judging by the design of the lorries this picture would appear to have been taken in the 1930s, as the Waterside Buildings, installed in 1925, look to have lost their newness. With rail stock visible in the distance the importance of the location, bringing three transport modes together as a freight hub, is evident.

Photo Stanford Collection, with thanks to Cadbury Archives and Mondelez International

Waterside with locomotive No.4 appearing to wait for the loading of wagons to be completed. Note Bournville has been painted out; suggesting the photo was taken during the Second World War. Place names were covered to make life difficult for any enemy invaders.

Photo Cadbury Archives and Mondelez International

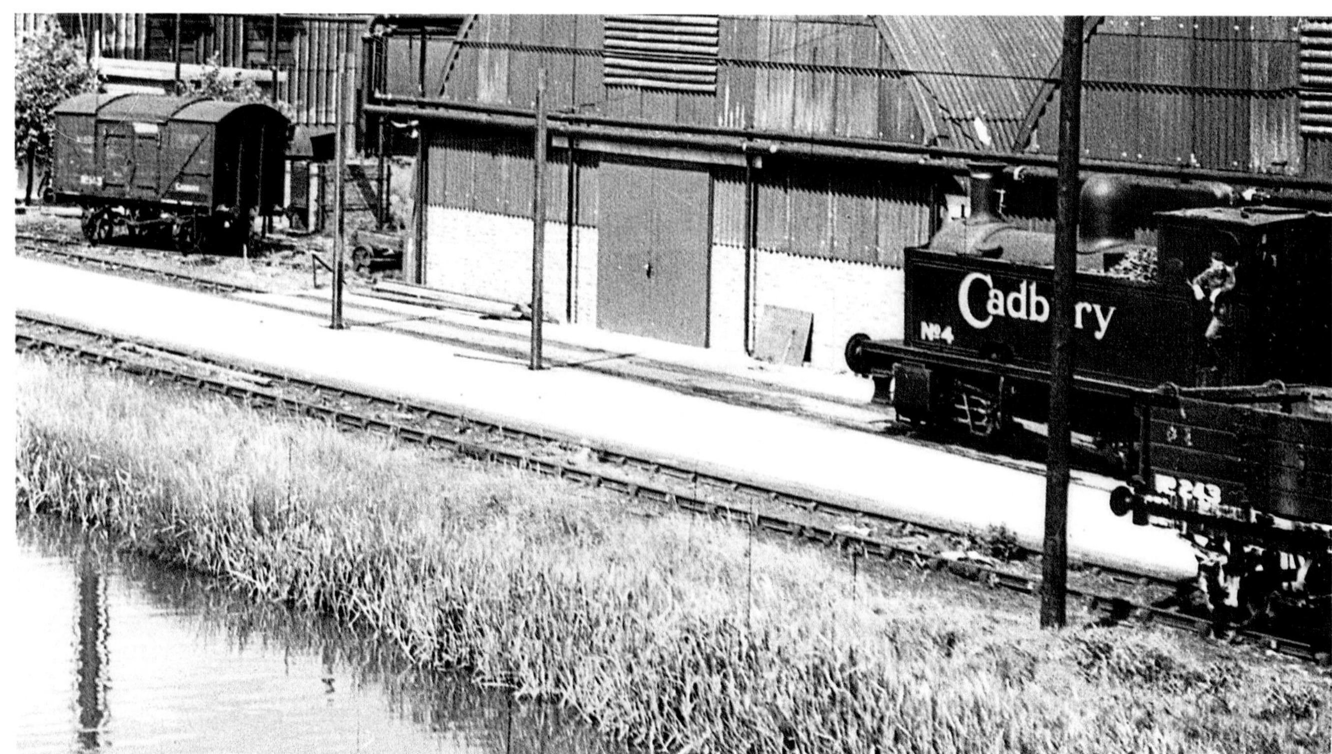

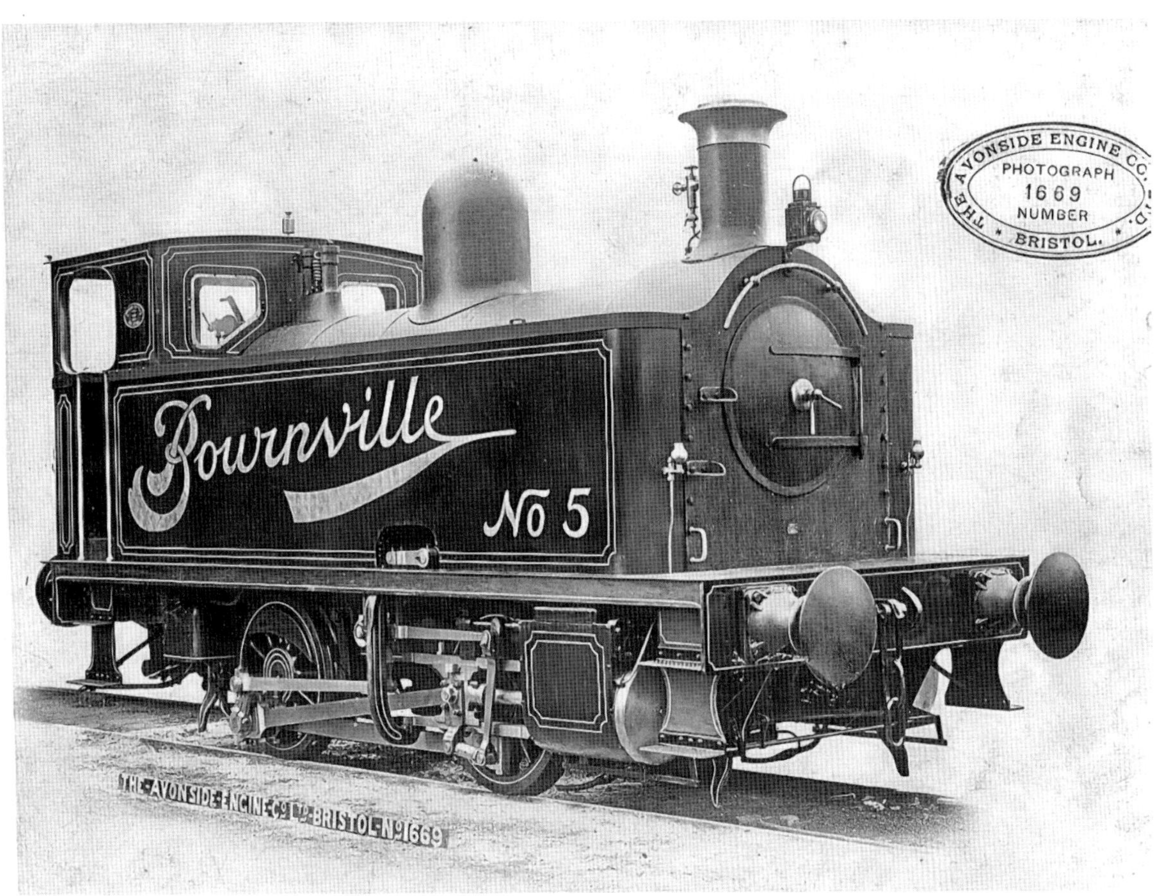

Bournville railway system around the factory had many sharp curves and steep gradients. Louis Barrow was the Chief Engineer at Cadbury Ltd during the period of railway expansion. He led the work to determine a design for a bespoke locomotive type suited to the Cadbury Railway system, which was handling increasing tonnages in the early part of the 20th century. The outcome was Cadbury Number 4, an 0-4-0 side tank locomotive built by the Avonside Engine Company in Bristol in 1911. Three further locomotives of this type were constructed, and here No.5 and No.6 are seen at Avonside. *Photos Courtesy of Don Townsley*

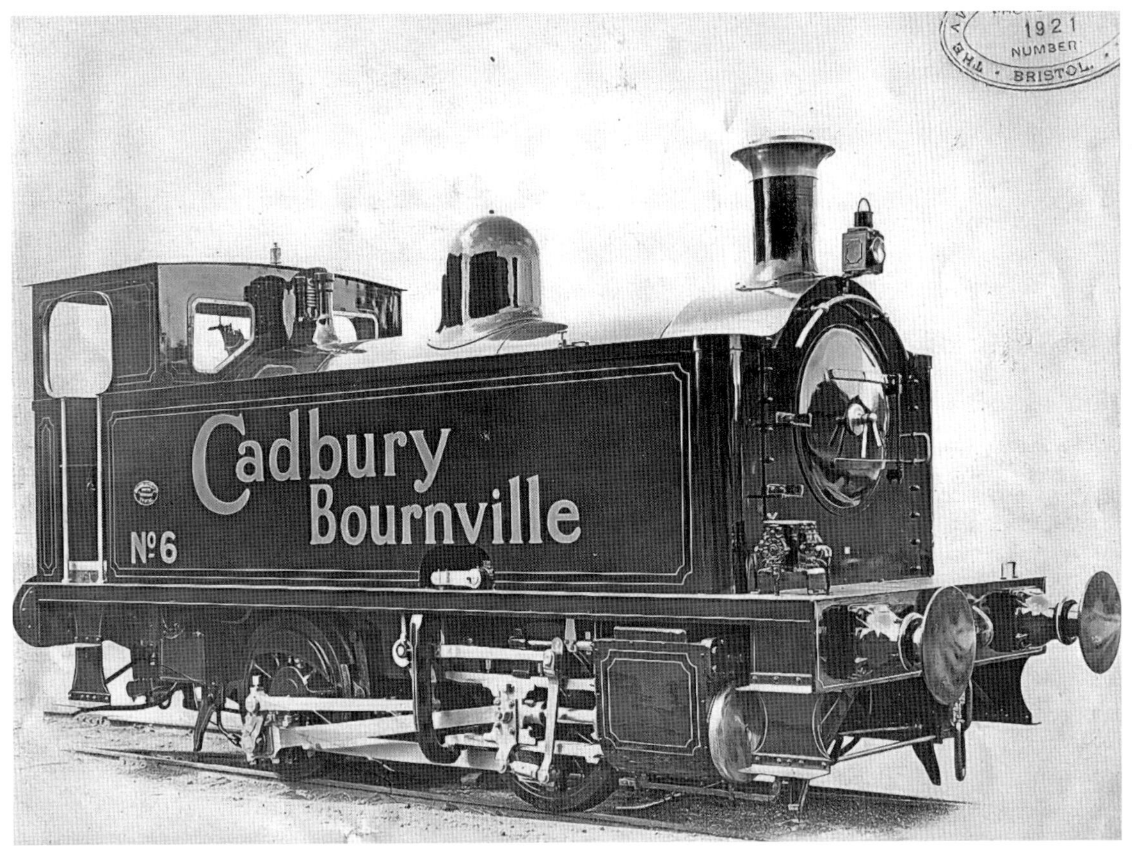

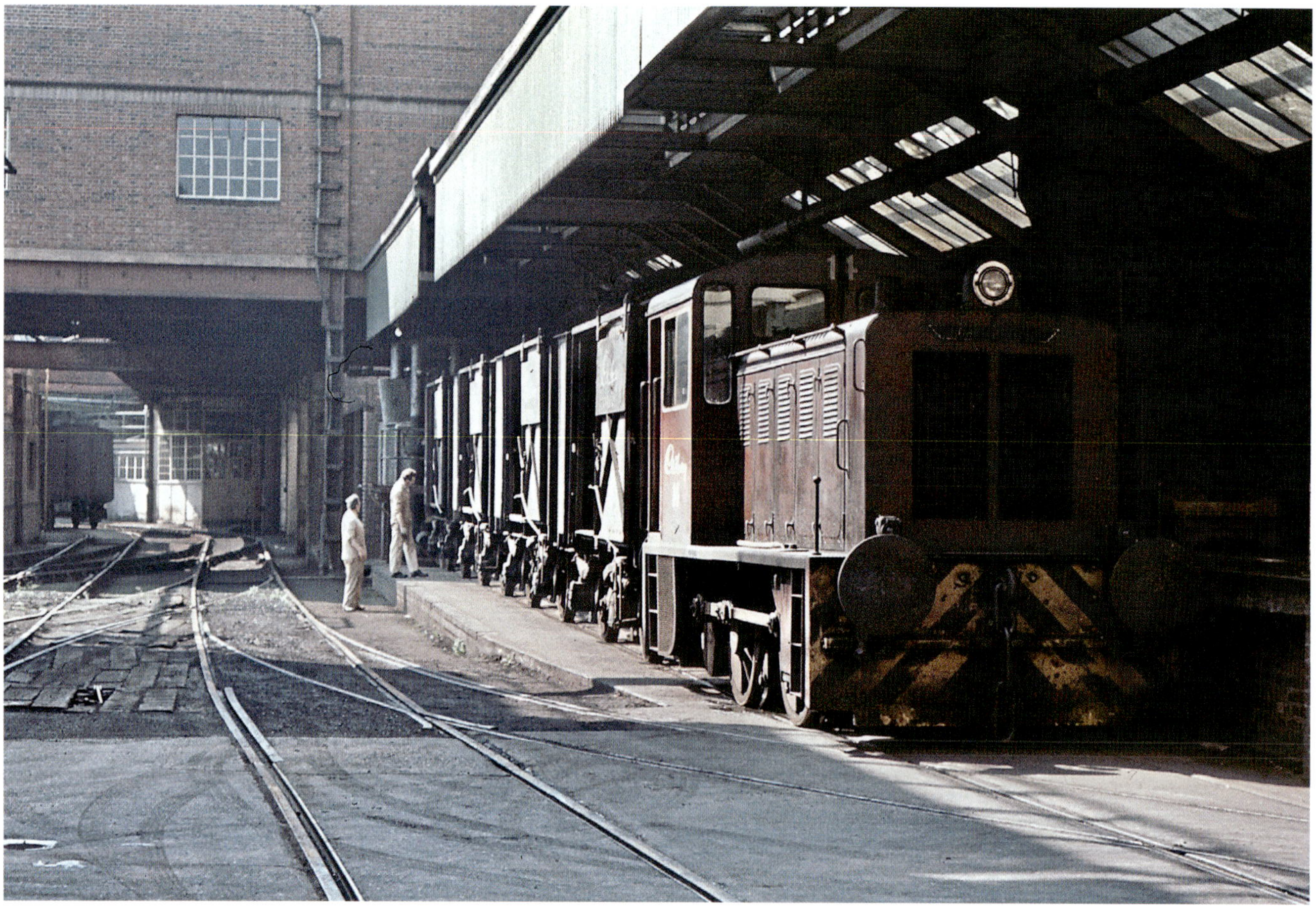

Bournville and a farewell train operated for the benefit of enthusiasts in May 1976 as the system closed to all rail traffic. These splendid pictures show how the author remembers the railway as a young boy. Indeed, loco 14 is the only one the author saw operating in February 1976. It and its sisters were built by North British in Glasgow. *Photos by Malcolm Ravensdale*

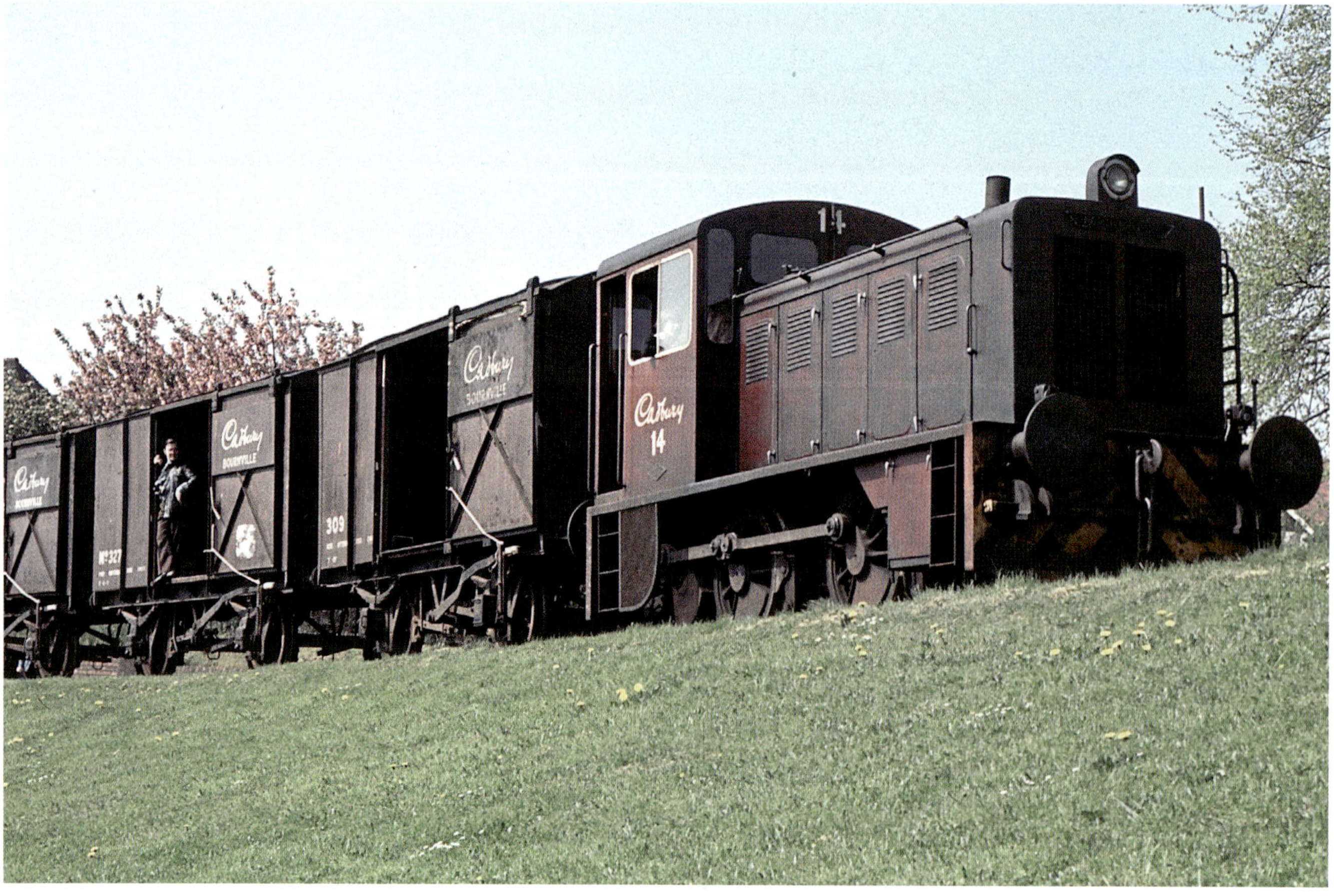

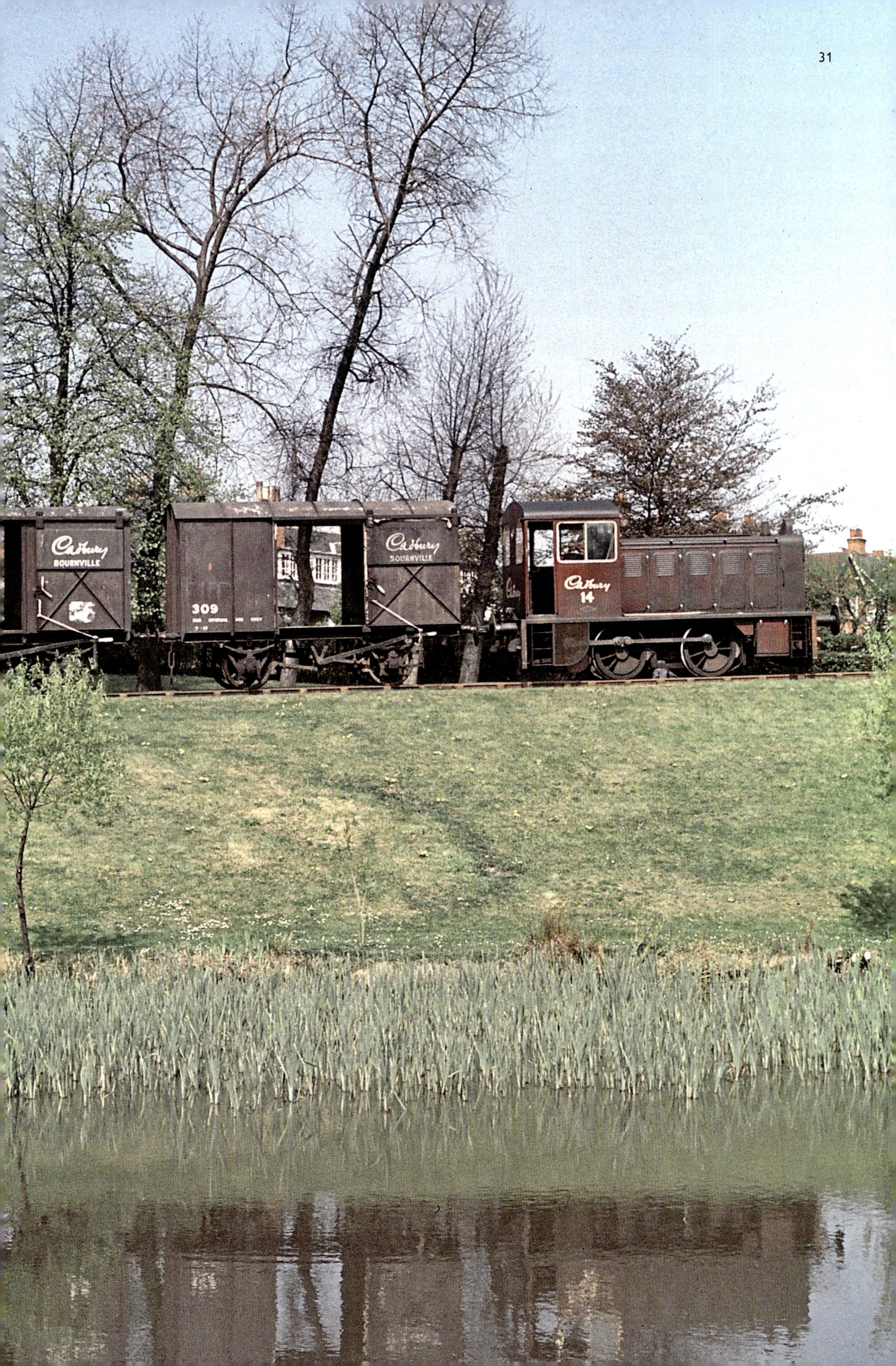
Cadbury
BOURNVILLE
309
Cadbury
BOURNVILLE
Cadbury
14

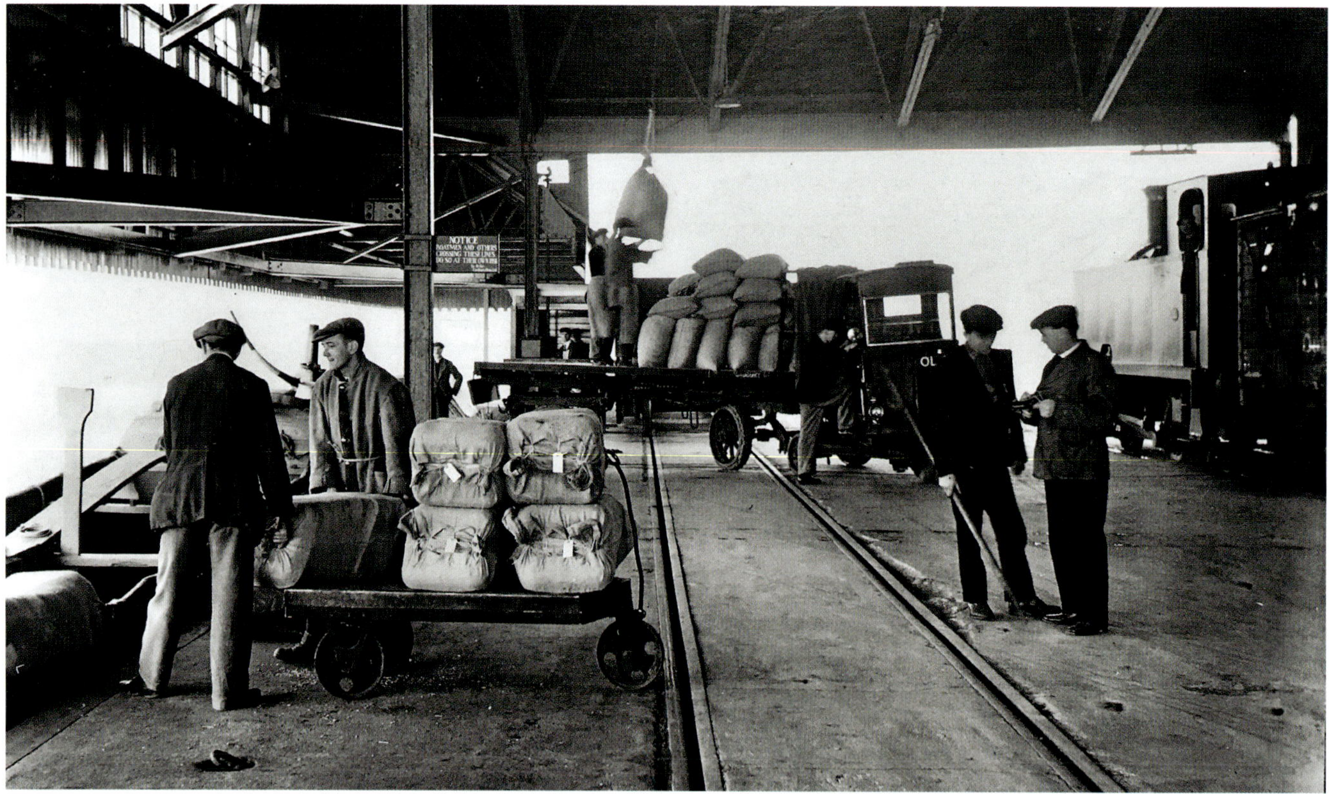

Bournville Waterside in a photo that looks posed but which nevertheless gives a great insight into what was daily activity on the quayside with barges unloading product to rail. The building still had a newness; it was opened in 1925.

Photo Cadbury Archives and Mondelez International

Bournville Waterside and Cadbury No.6 is loaded to head off for overhaul at the Hunslet Engine Co in Leeds, 1956. The original builders, the Avonside Engine Co of Bristol, had ceased trading more than 20 years earlier.

Photo Stanford Collection with thanks to Cadbury Archive and Mondelez International

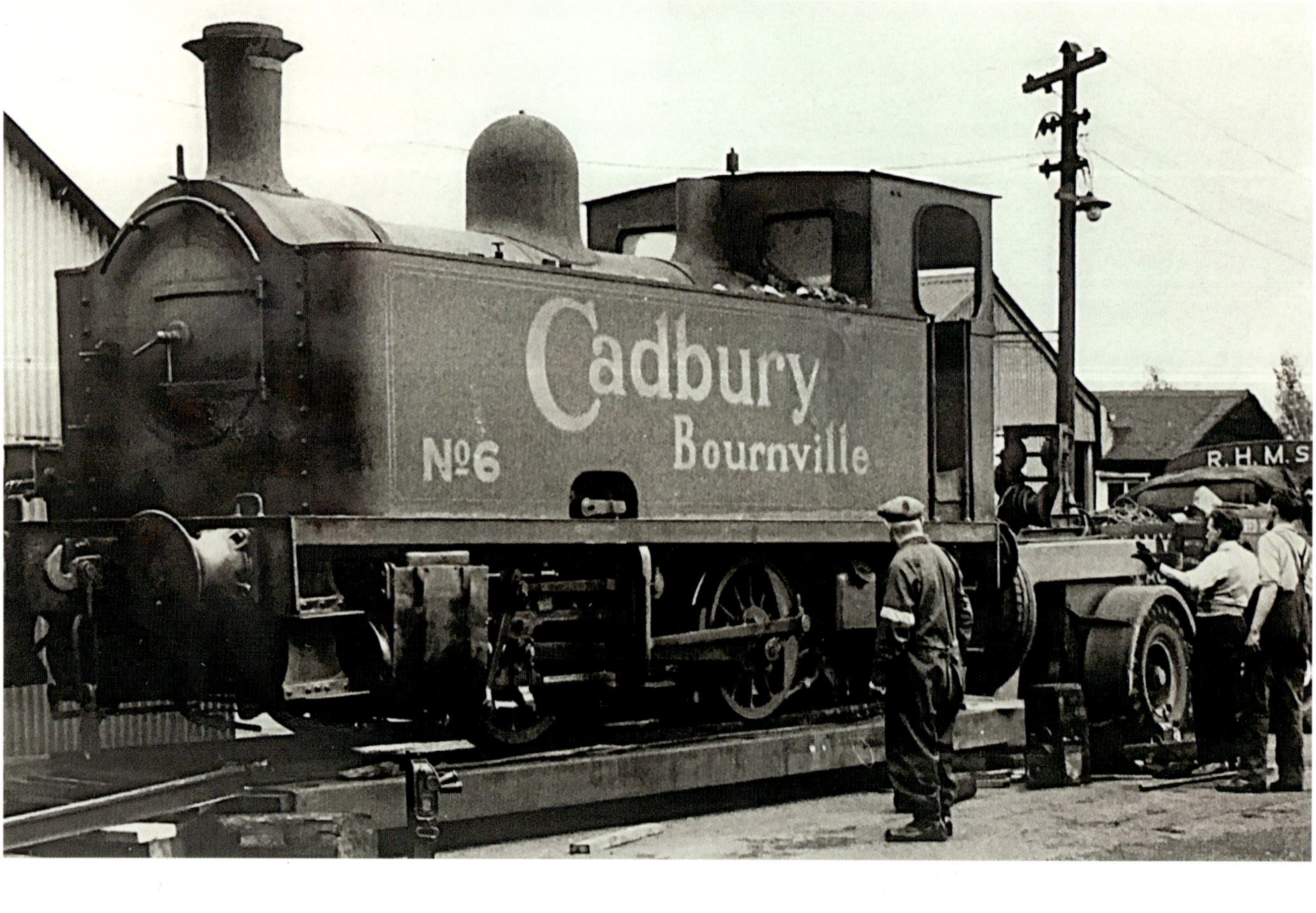

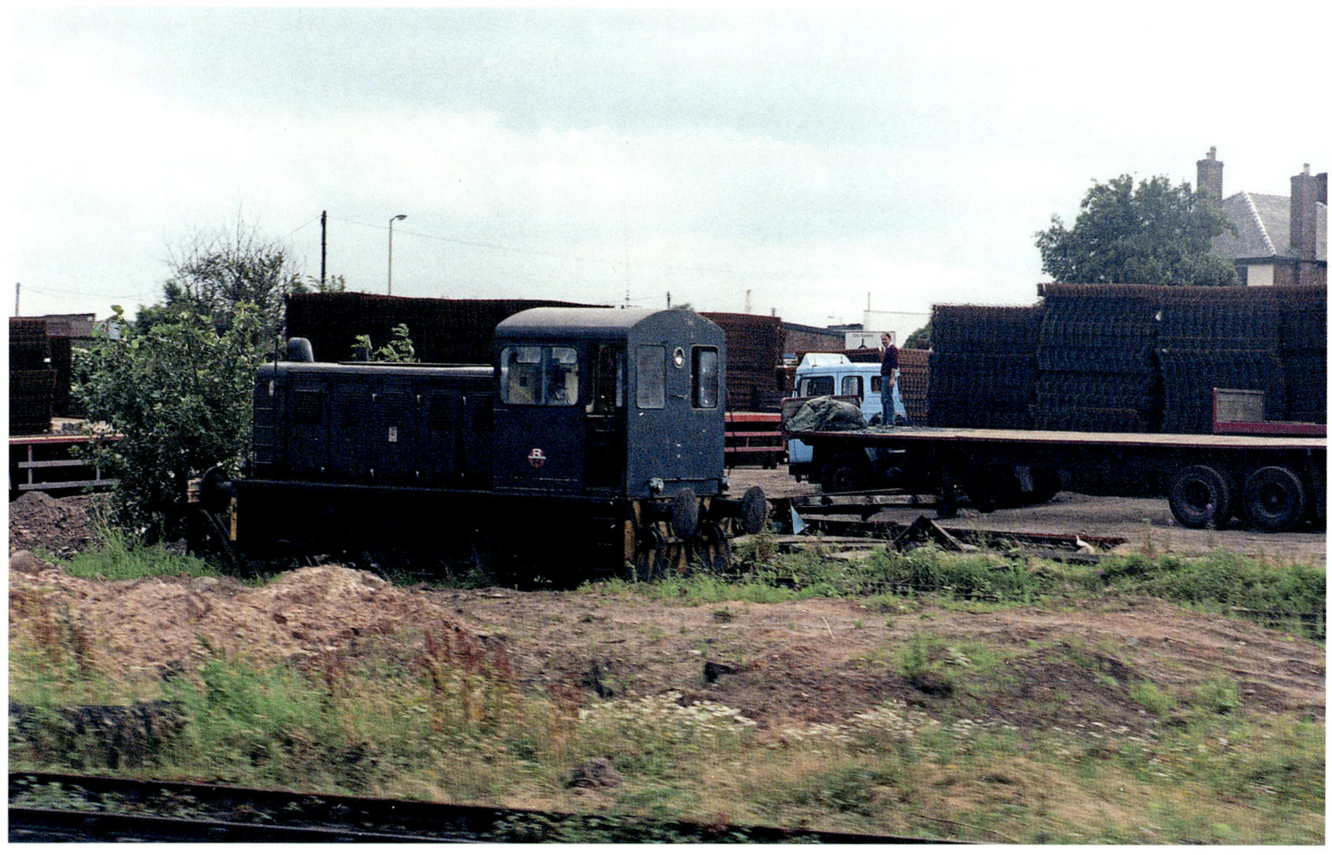

Lichfield and Rom River Steel Reinforcements became home to Cadbury No.12 after the Bournville system closed in 1976. It was used to shunt wagons of steel. From a young age the author was fascinated by the Cadbury Railway system and its history. Sadly all the Cadbury North British diesel locomotives had been scrapped by the 2000s. This was taken 31st July 1987.

Bournville Station was just south of the connection to the factory railway. This excellent late 1920s view captures the arrival of a special train from Weston-super-Mare with people to visit the factory, which is left of this shot featuring GWR coaches.

Photo by Cadbury Archive and Mondelez International

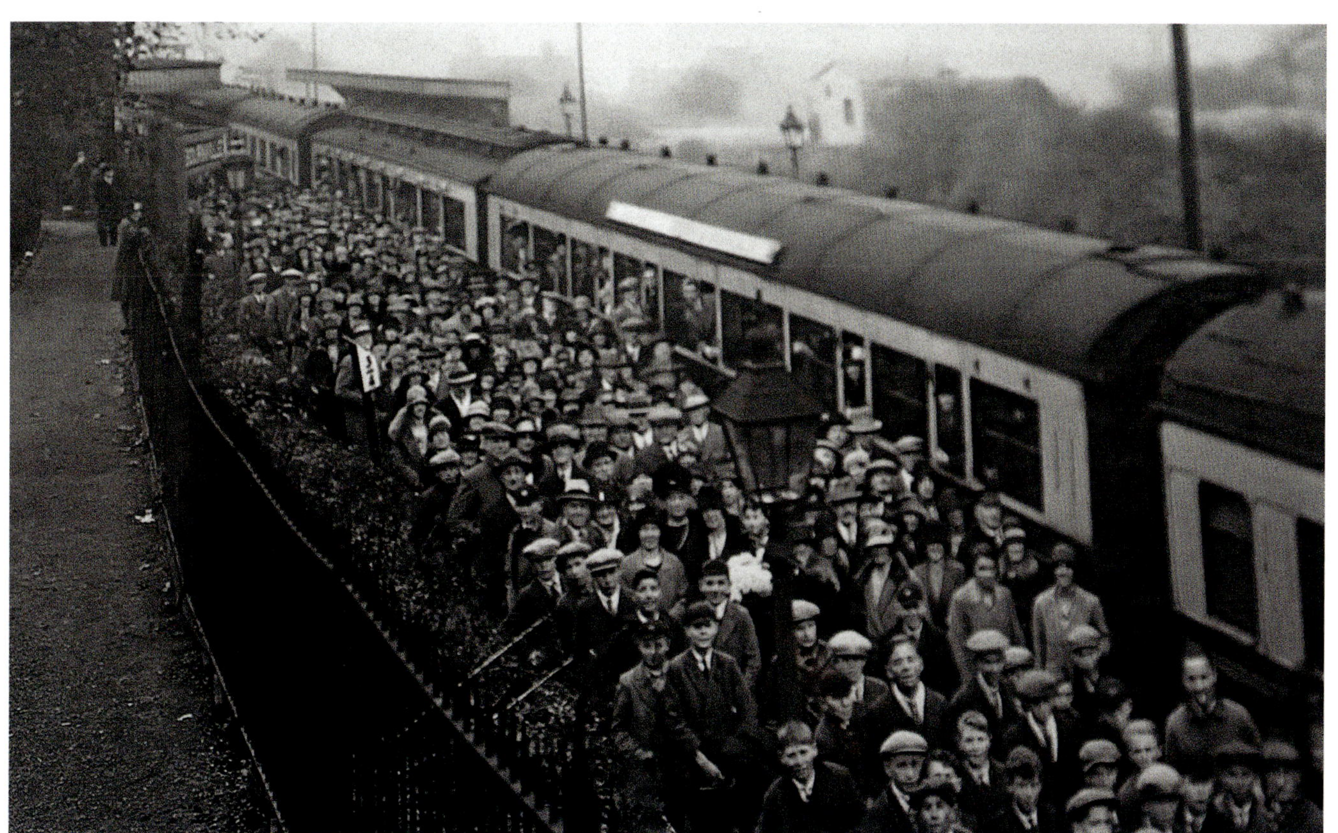

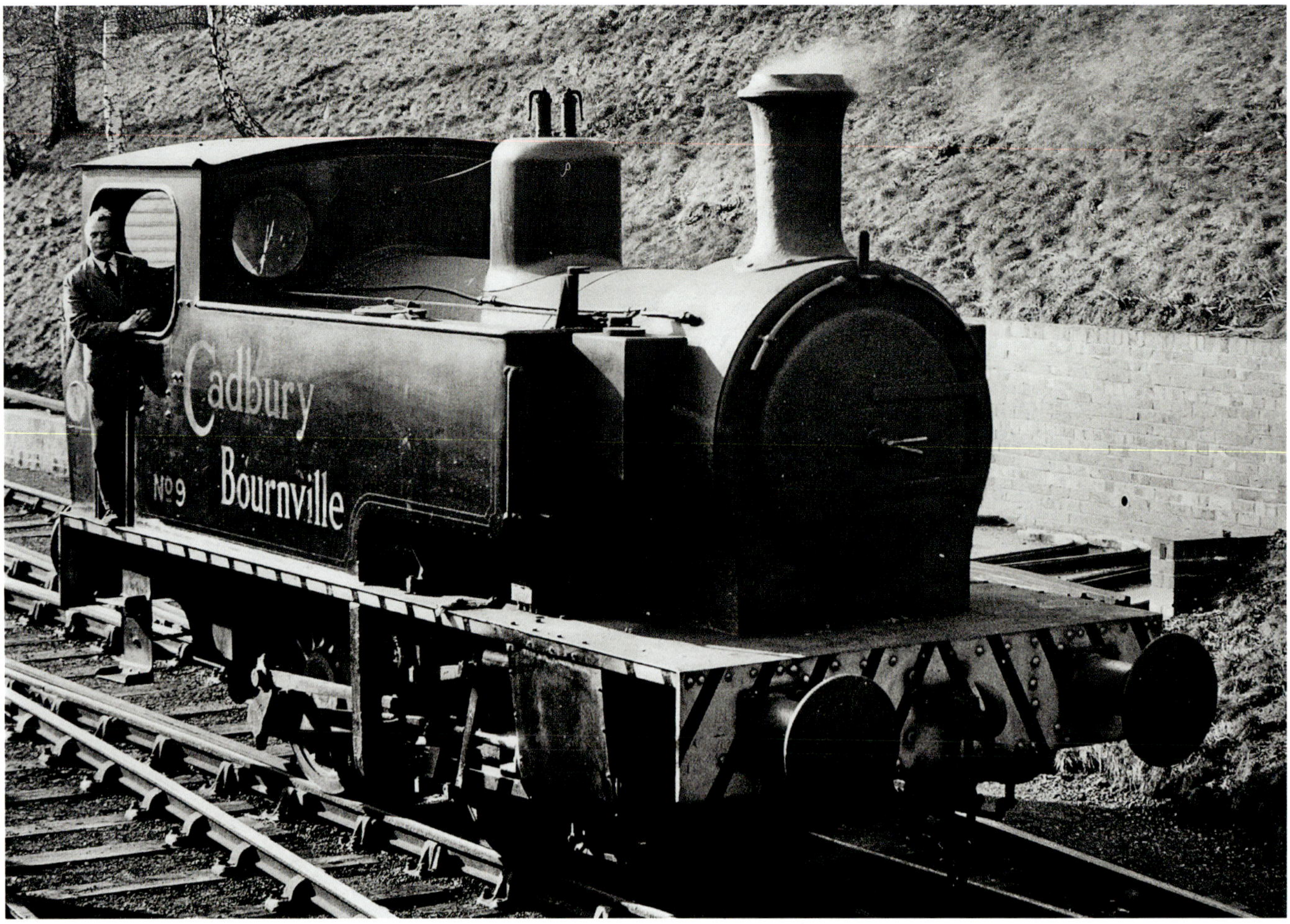

Bournville and many years after cessation of rail activities at Cadbury great affection remains for the railway system, with models of Cadbury locomotives appearing in OO and O scales. Master locomotive builder Graham Duncan Smith constructed one in Gauge 3, with a track gauge of 2½ inches. Here his model of Cadbury No.9 is seen in front of the factory in November 2023 in almost the same location as the prototype 60 years earlier, with thanks to Cadbury Archive and Mondelez International.

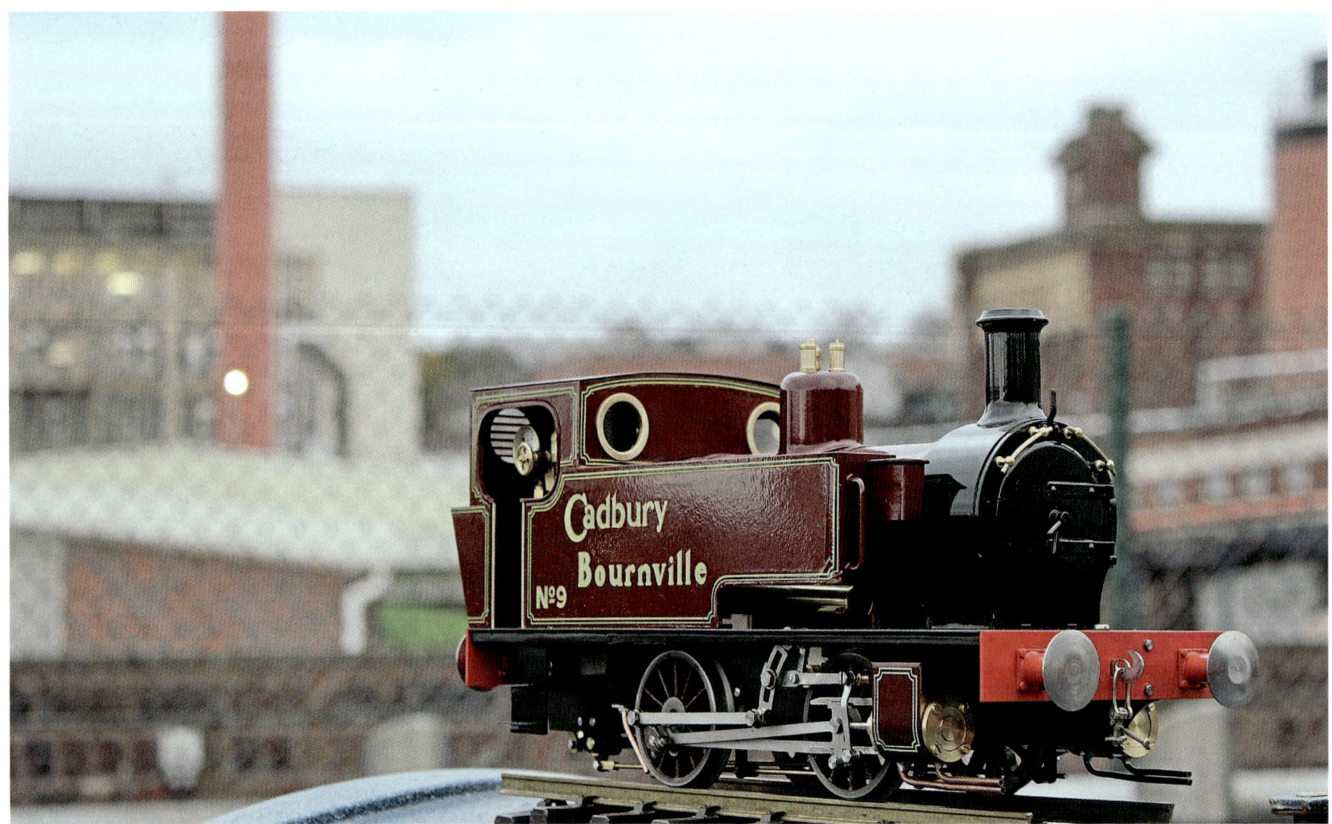

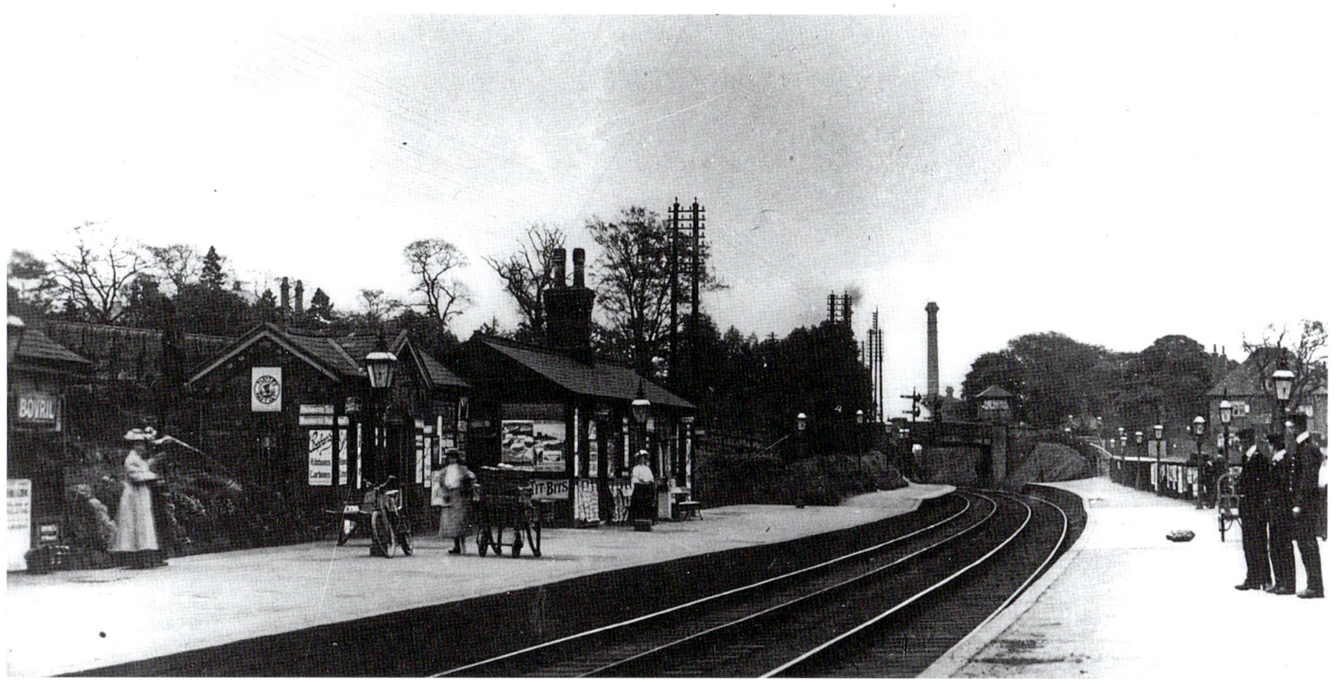

Kings Norton Station looking towards Birmingham New Street in what appears to be the early 20th century. *Photo John Stanford Collection*

Between Kings Norton and Northfield on 25th September 1961 and an 8f (4831) hurries along a mixed freight towards Cheltenham. Of note in the train formation are three loaded Cadbury box vans nearest the locomotive. Visible in the distance are large construction cranes used for the two tower blocks; which still exist today, albeit the original 1960s design features have been lost with the inevitable cladding applied. *Photo by John Stanford*

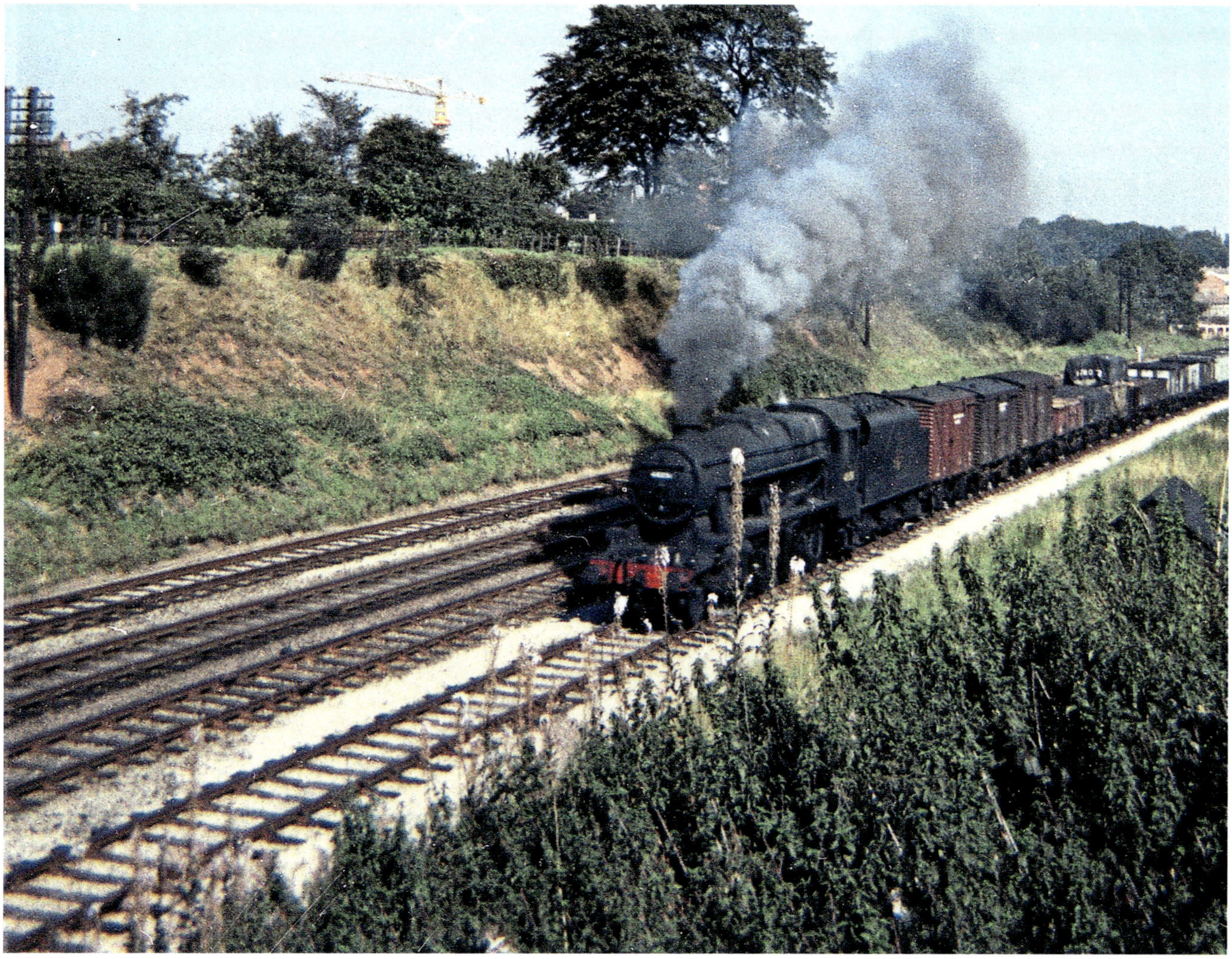

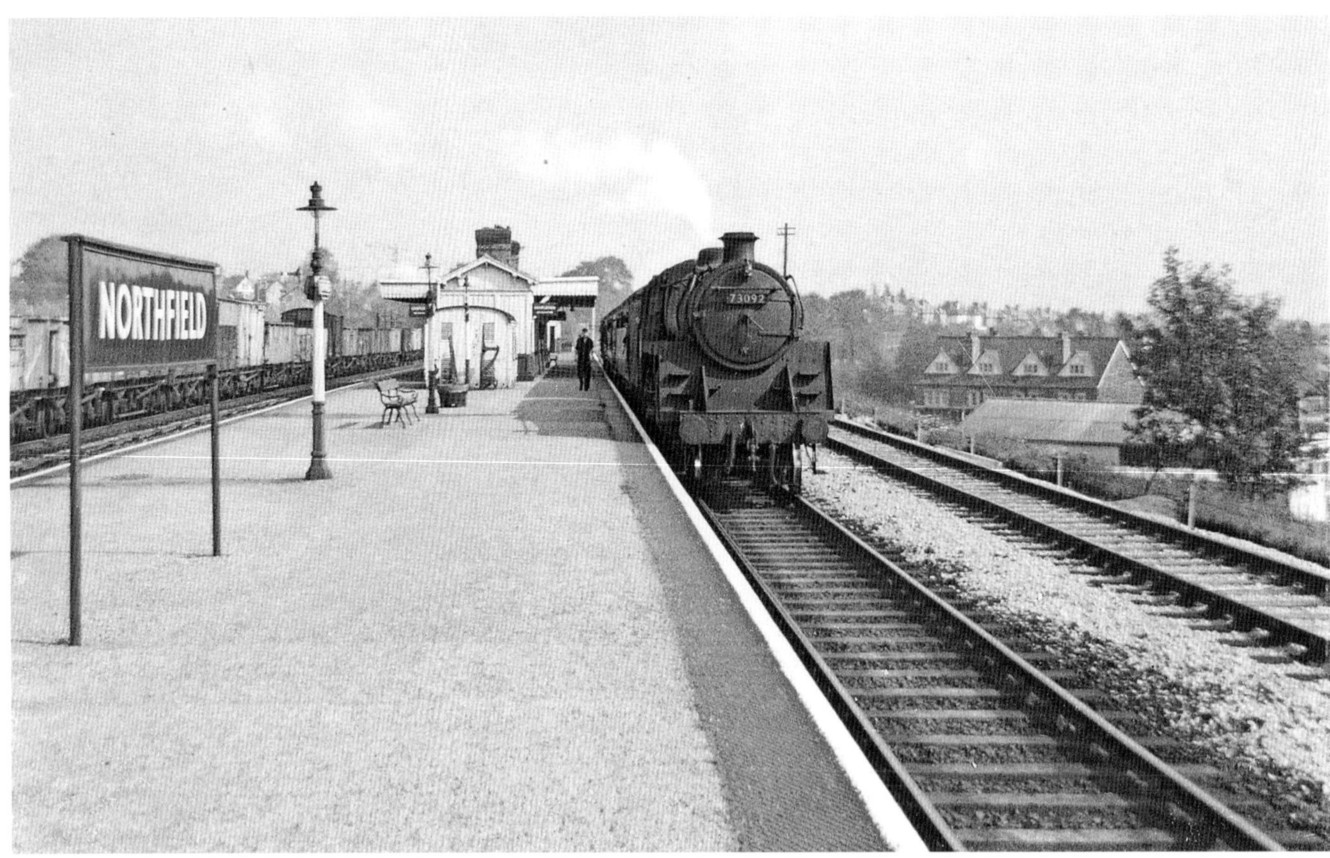

Northfield. When he took this shot of a BR standard 5, 73092, John was working in Bromsgrove signal box. When working, he would cycle the 14-mile round-trip Northfield to Bromsgrove daily on his blue Dawes touring bike, no wonder he could manage a whole Fray Bentos steak & kidney pie, peas and potatoes for supper on a regular basis. *Photo by John Stanford*

Northfield possessed a rail served goods yard until the early 1960s and it was visited by a daily 'trip' working from Blackwell. Here on 4th August 1961, after John had done a night shift at Bromsgrove, he caught a Johnson 3f locomotive delivering wagons of house coal to the Northfield Coal Merchant. *Photo by John Stanford*

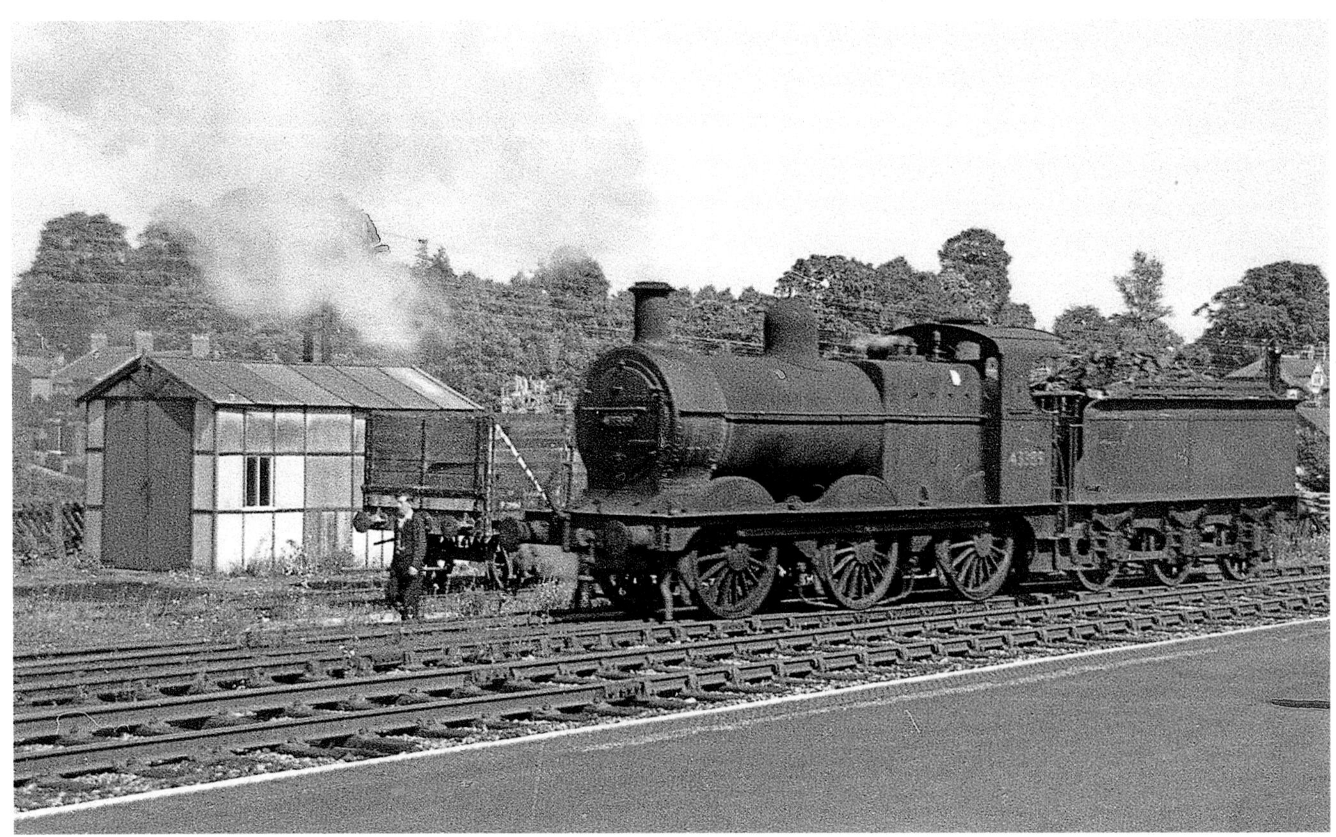

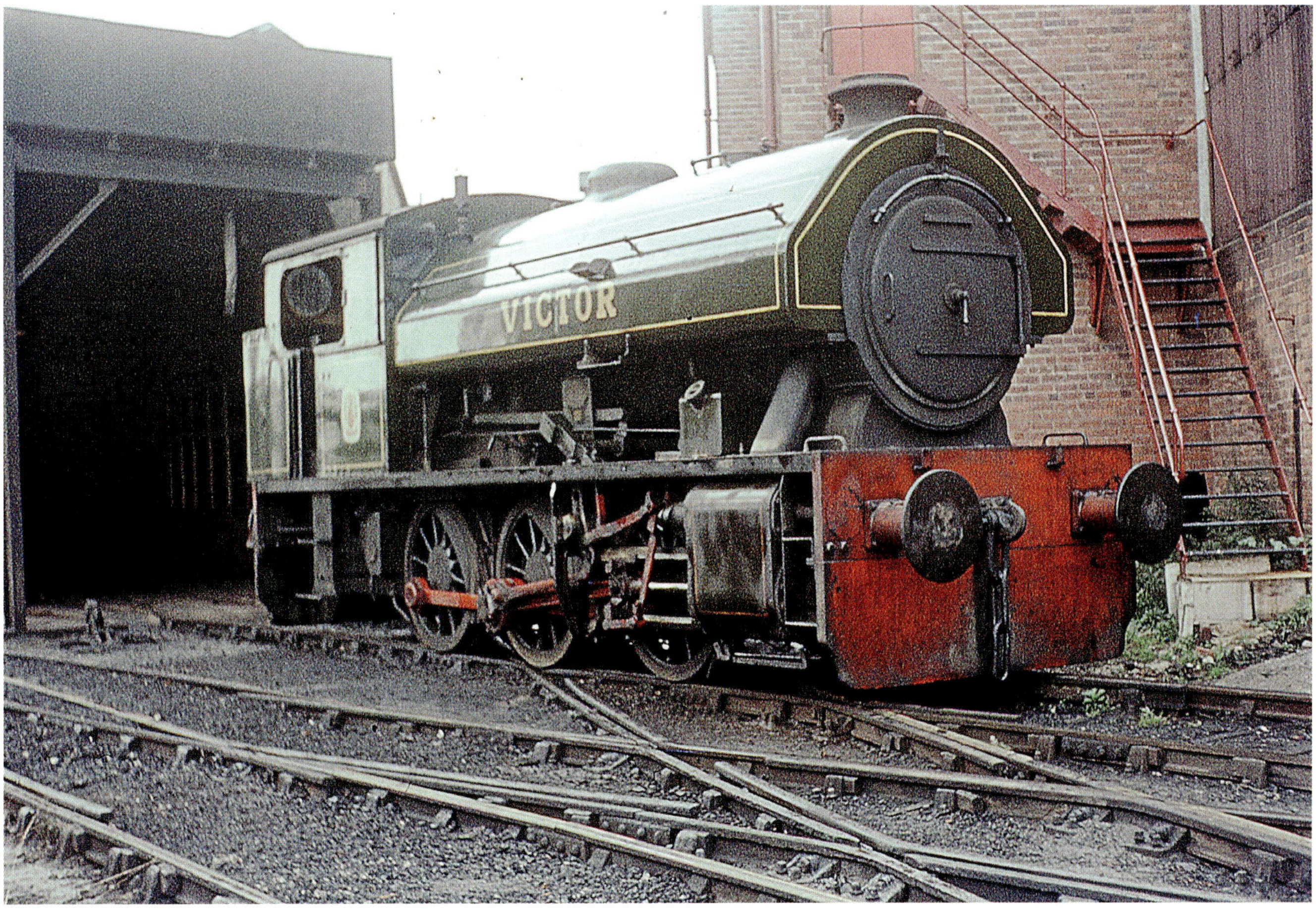

Longbridge car plant hosted steam locomotives until the early 1970s for its shunt needs and this magnificent Bagnall saddle tank rests between duties. John would occasionally see this loco and its sister locos, never imagining they would haul him on the line to Minehead. On the same day Trevor Riddle visited, Austin No.1 built by Kitson was operation. *Photos by Trevor Riddle*

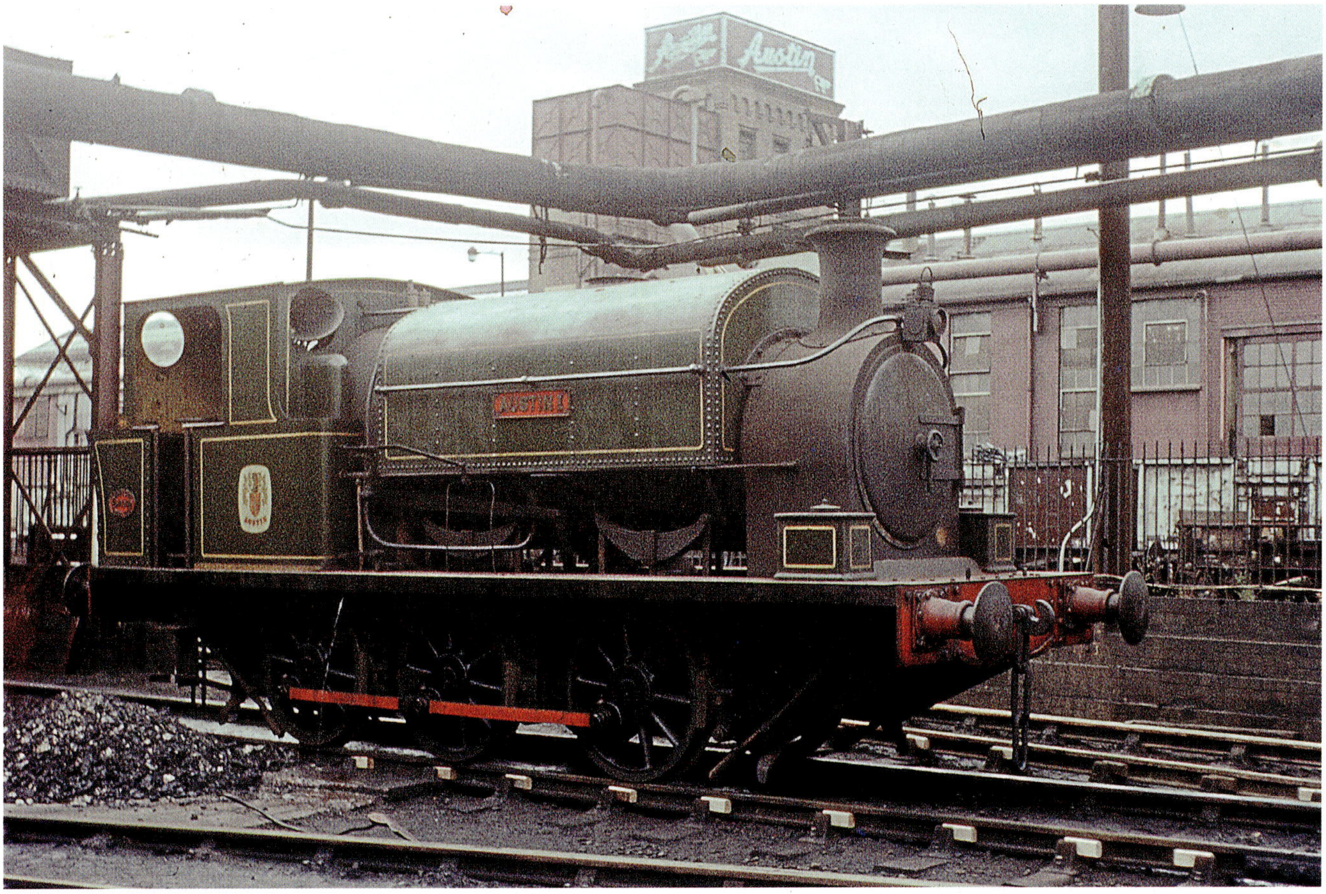

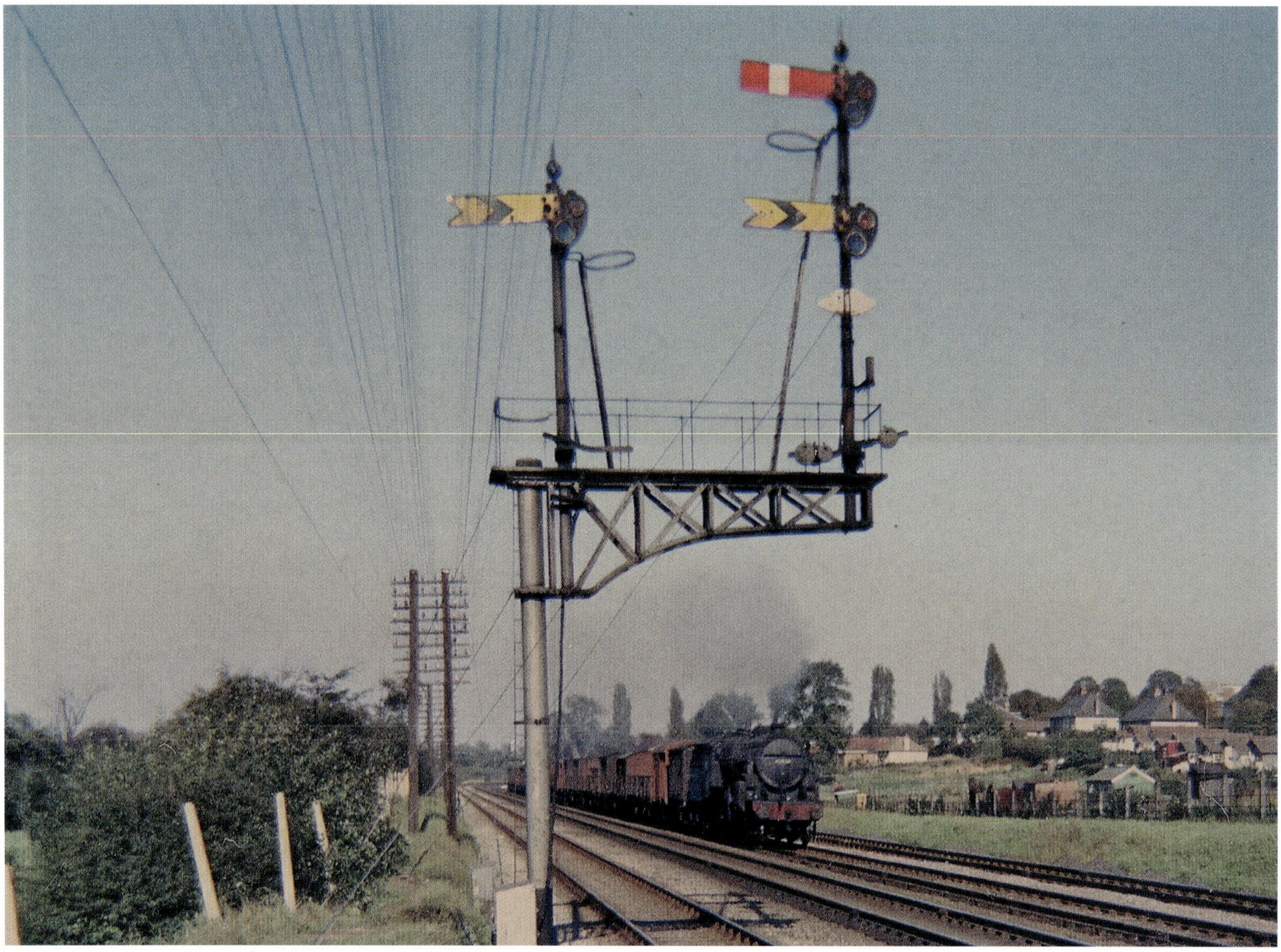

Cofton Park on 25th September 1961 and John caught a Hughes LMS crab, number 42824, hurrying a mixed freight along a down line toward Cheltenham, in this view looking toward Northfield. *Photo by John Stanford*

Lickey Bank and LMS Black 5 piloted by a Midland Railway 4-4-0 was caught by John Stanford during one of family's regular trainspotting trips to the Lickey Incline. This was the summer of 1958; with John, his sister Elizabeth and parents Harry and Betty. So much was to change within a 10-year window on this line, with the elimination of steam, and replacement with diesel locomotives such as Peaks and Diesel hydraulic banking locos, the Hymeks. *Photo by John Stanford*

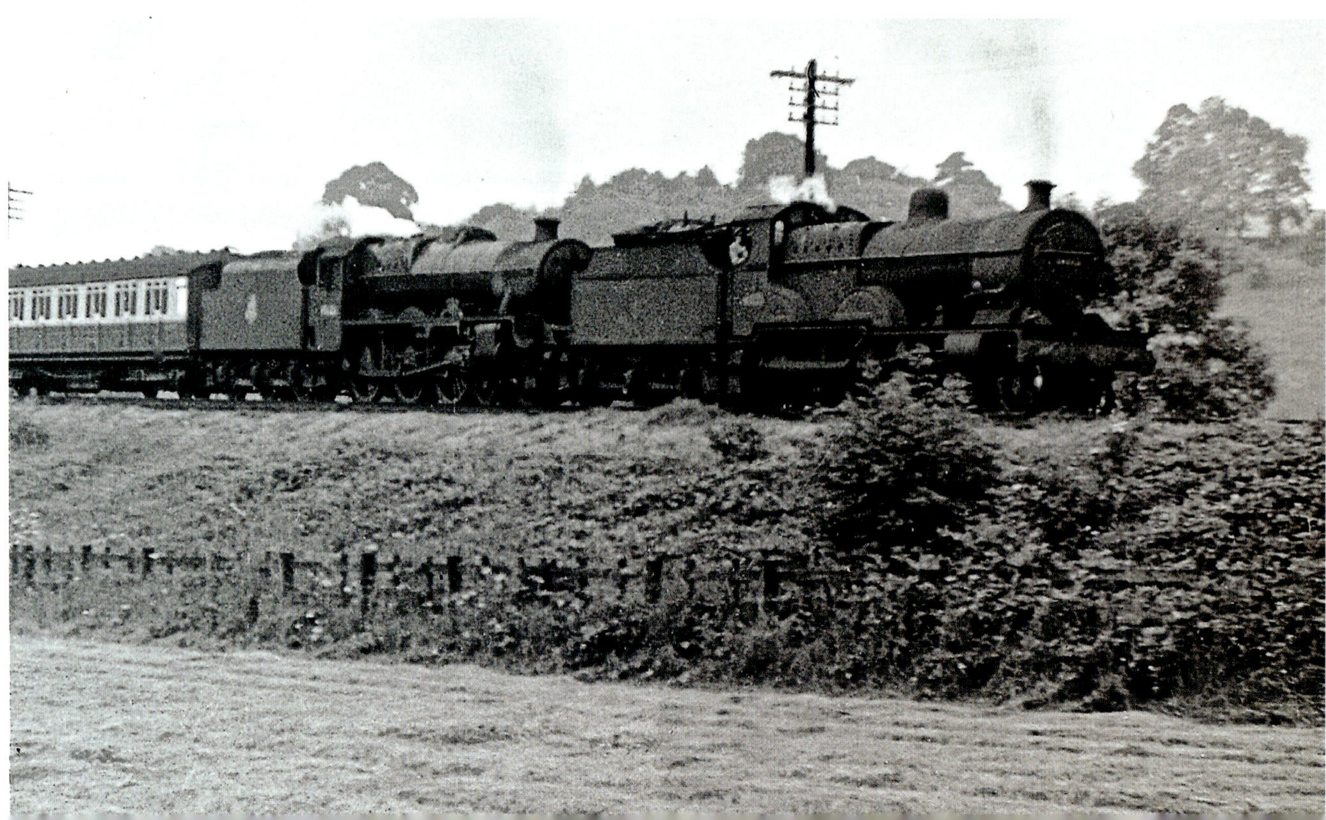

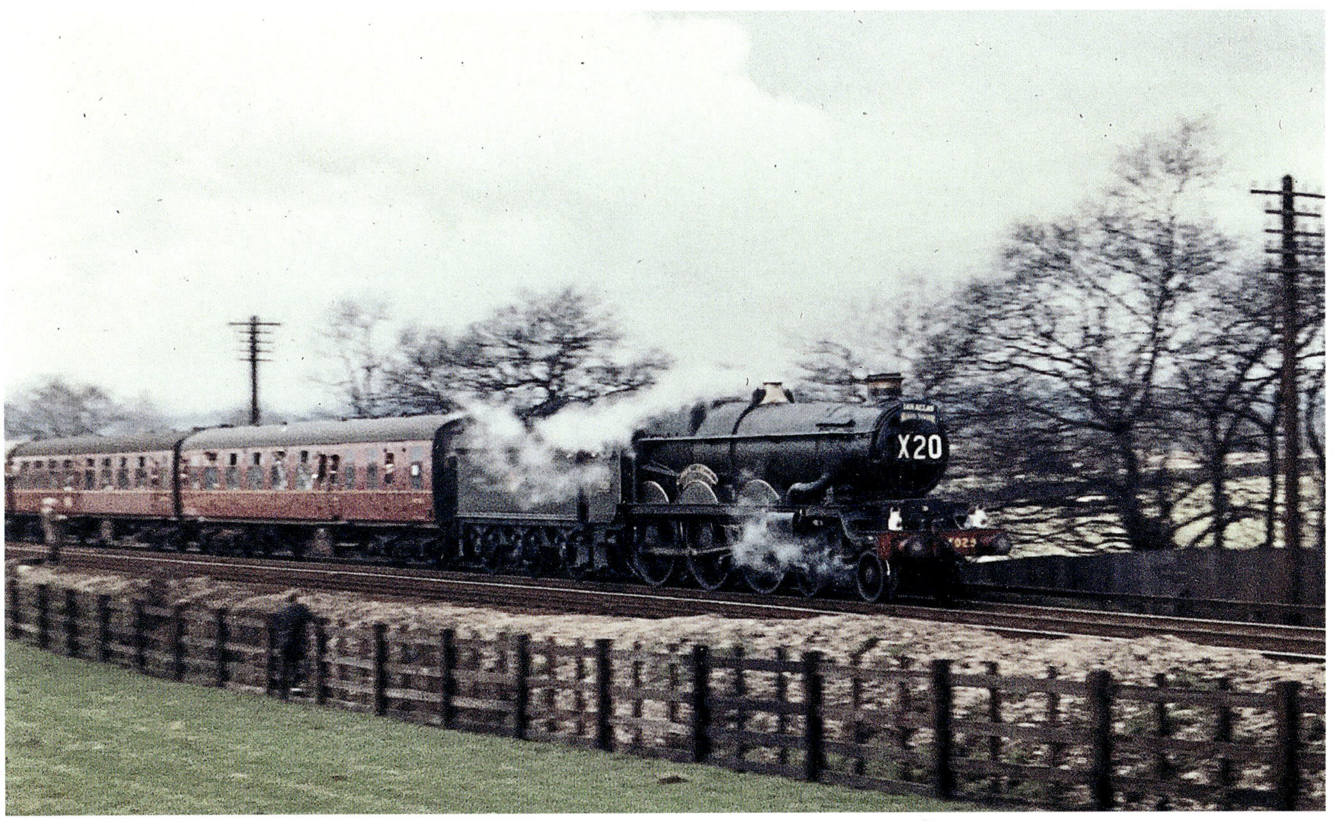

Lickey Bank on 27th March 1965 and John caught 7029 romping up the bank on 1X20 Paddington to Nottingham via Oxford and Worcester. By then the engine had earned celebrity status with some super main line runs. Happily, it is now preserved at Tyseley.

Photo by John Stanford

Lickey Bank and two class 37s (219 and 220) bank an Oakdale to Scunthorpe coal train on 28th May 1985 when the author was working a late shift at Bristol Travel Centre. The class 37s replaced the Hymek locos in the early 1970s on banking duties. The author travelled the 2124 Bristol Glasgow sleeper with Fiona in March 1994, a few days before the sleeper ceased operating with a pair of 37s banking the train, sparks flying into the night sky to his delight. *Photo by Richard Giles*

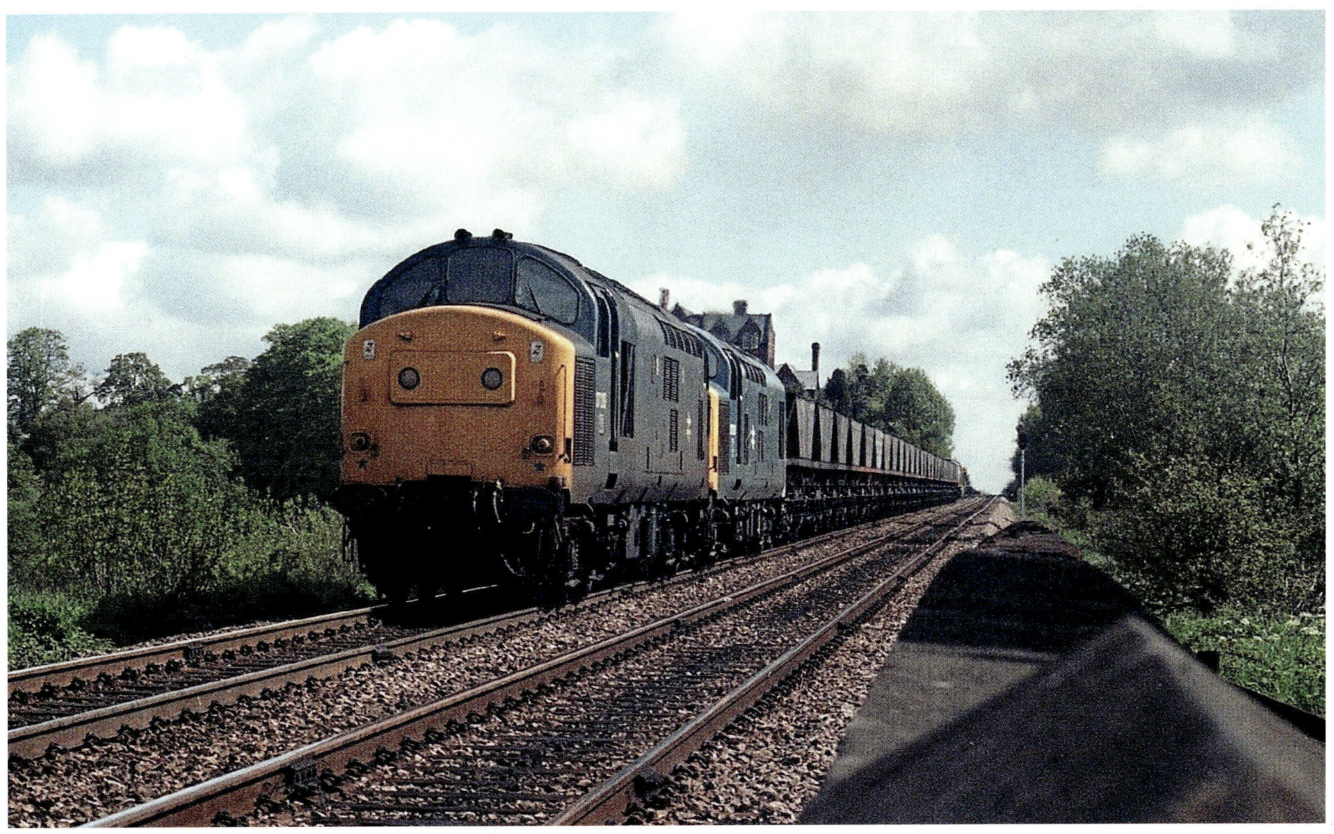

CHAPTER 2

Onward to the West – Worcestershire and Gloucester

John Stanford started his rail career in Bromsgrove signal box, positioned on the station platform in 1960, working early, late and night shifts. He lived with his father and sister in Northfield and would cycle daily to and from the box or take the train. Promotion in 1962 took him away from the area, to Wolverhampton Low Level. Worcestershire however became the family home 1966 to 1969; with John and Wendy living in Worcester where Paul was born in 1967 and John commuting daily to Birmingham.

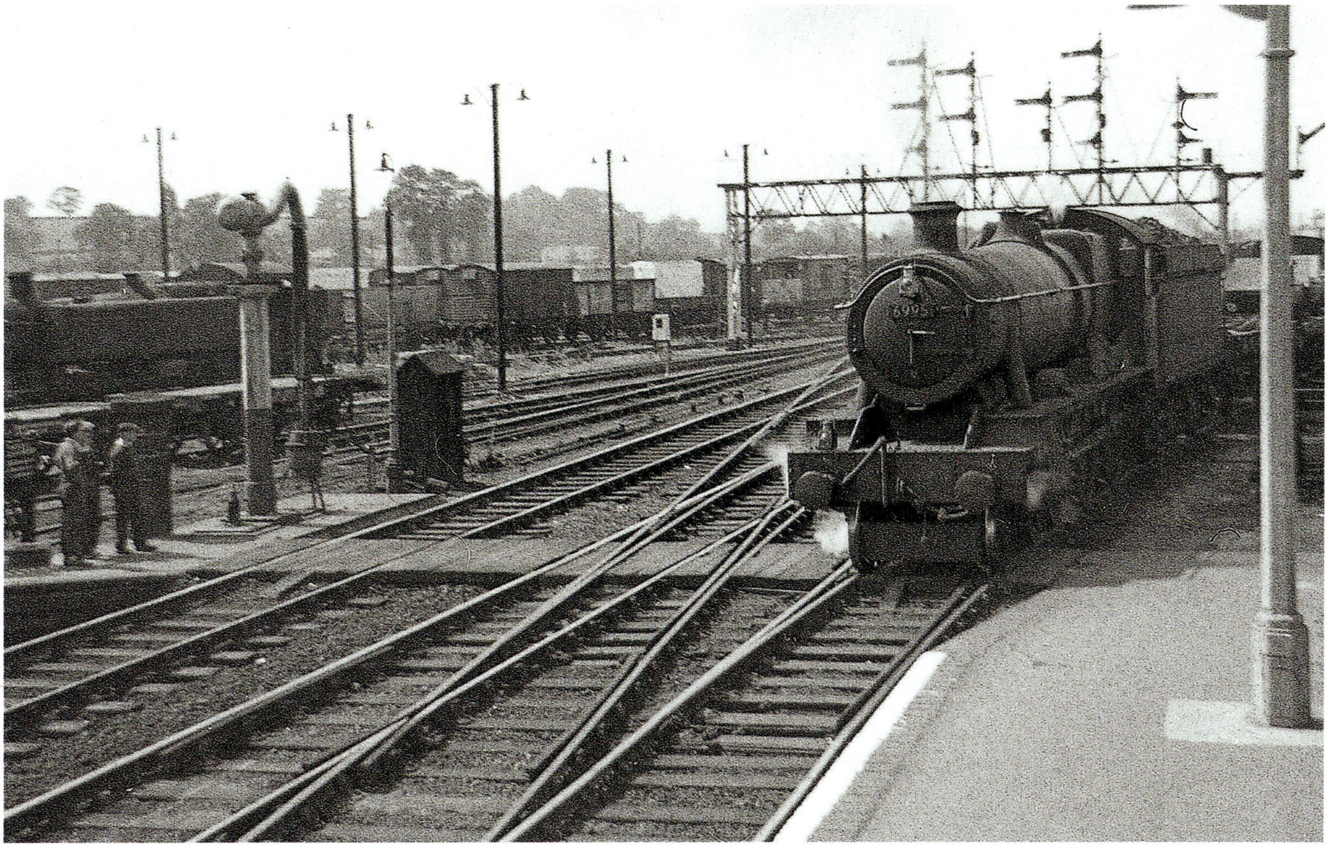

Bromsgrove and GWR Hall 6995 starts the ascent of the Lickey Bank with John photographing the freight train from his workplace, the platform-mounted signal box in August 1961. *Photo by John Stanford*

Droitwich Coal Depot was situated just north of the station. It operated as a rail receiving point for house coal until 1987. On 8th January 1987 we see 37224 coupled to two outgoing empty coal wagons (TOPS code HEA). In the 1980s a loco would operate freight workings in the area, also serving Honeybourne Tip, Long Marston MoD. John tipped off Paul that BR were to cease serving the Droitwich site as part of the cutbacks to the Speedlink Coal network that year, so he made a visit.

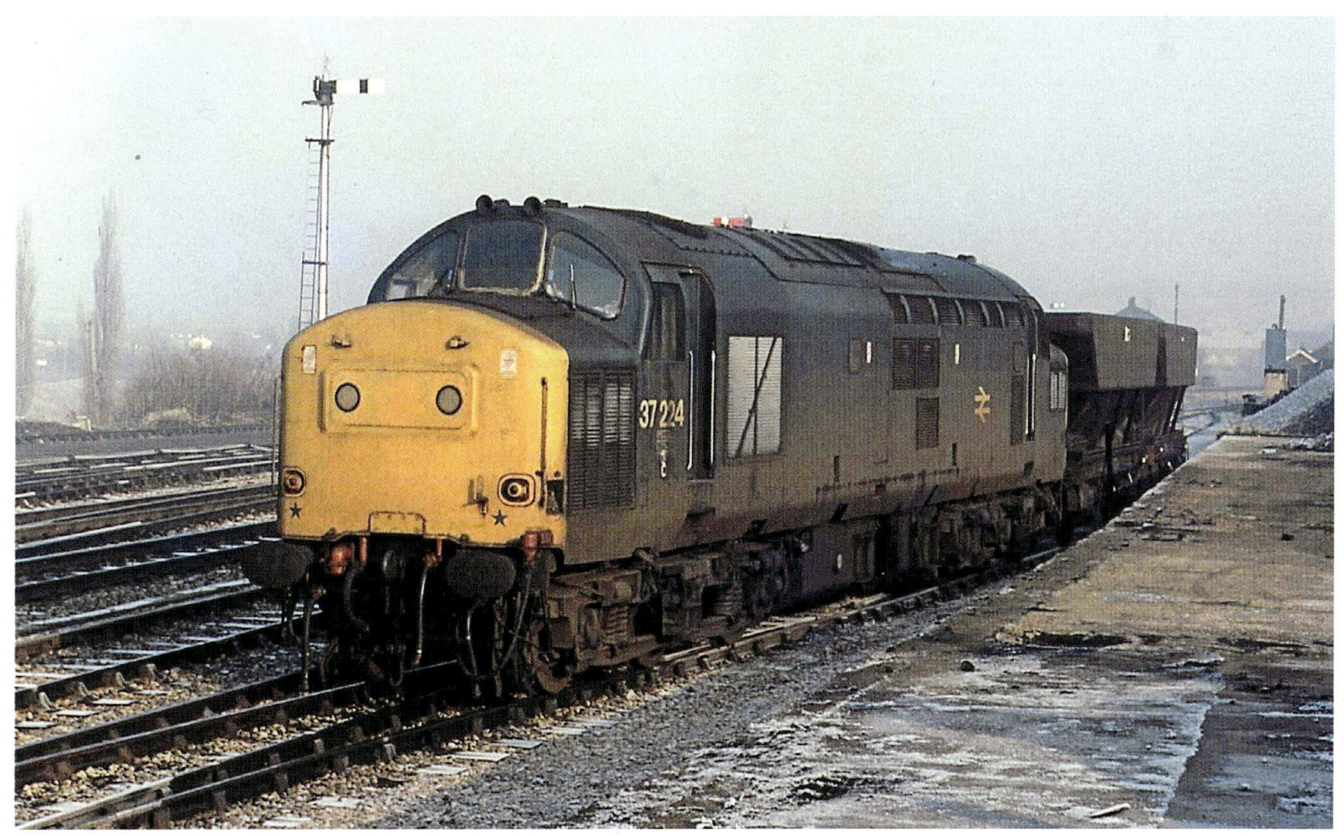

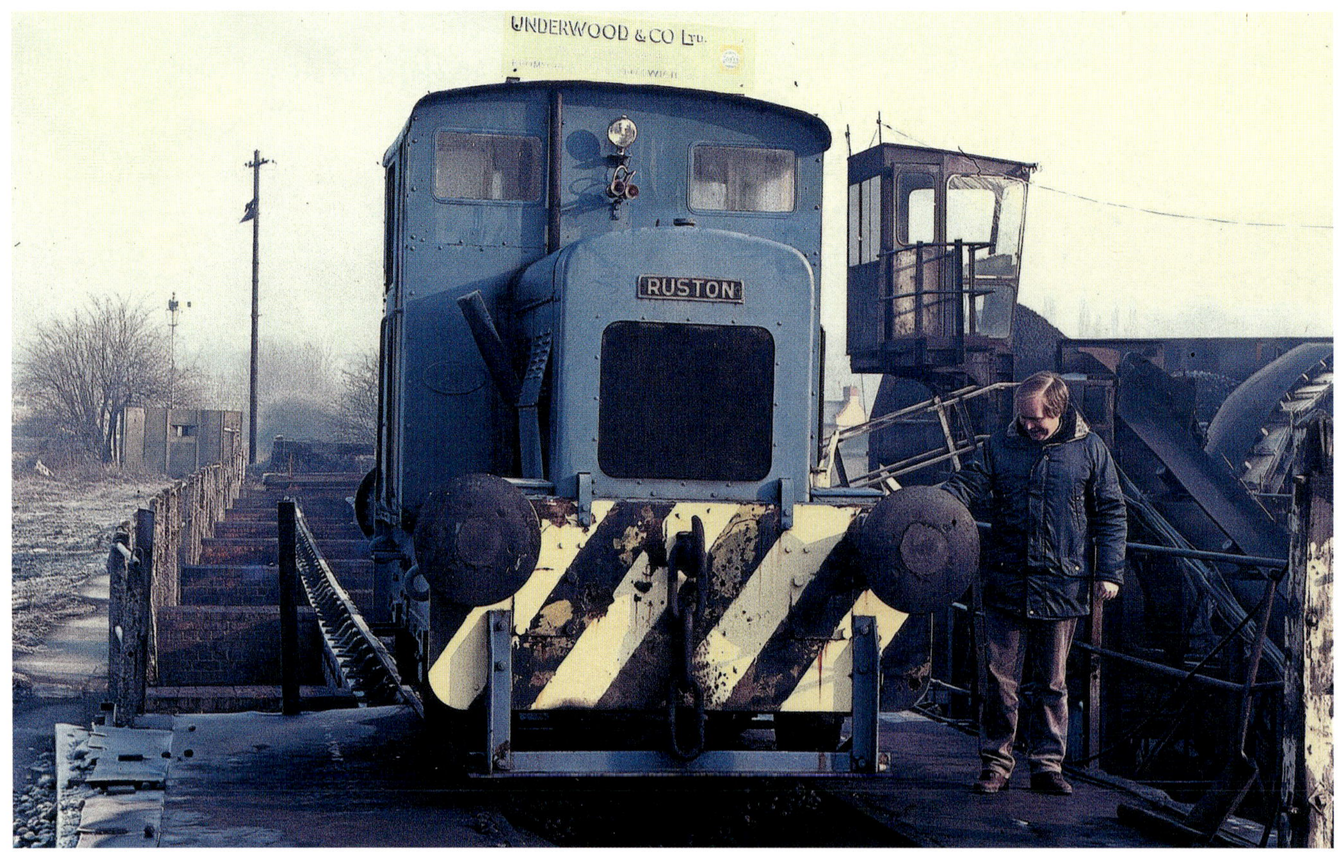

Droitwich Coal Depot had a small Ruston four-wheel diesel mechanical shunter, named *The Sheriff*. Here it is seen on 8th January 1987 with the author's longtime friend and rail colleague Mike Organ. The author used to deputise for Mike through 1987 and enjoyed planning ballast trains, speaking to train-crew depots to arrange the trains with a high degree of autonomy as a 19-year-old.

Worcester Depot seen from Rainbow Hill Tunnel on 12th April 1969. BR organised a public open day. In view are multiple North British D63xx diesel hydraulics, a batch of class 03 diesel shunters, plus 7808 *Cookham Manor* from Ashchurch along with a Peak, The Blue Pullman and a selection of freight wagons. The image was taken during the period John and Wendy lived in Worcester and John commuted daily to Birmingham. *Photo by John Stanford*

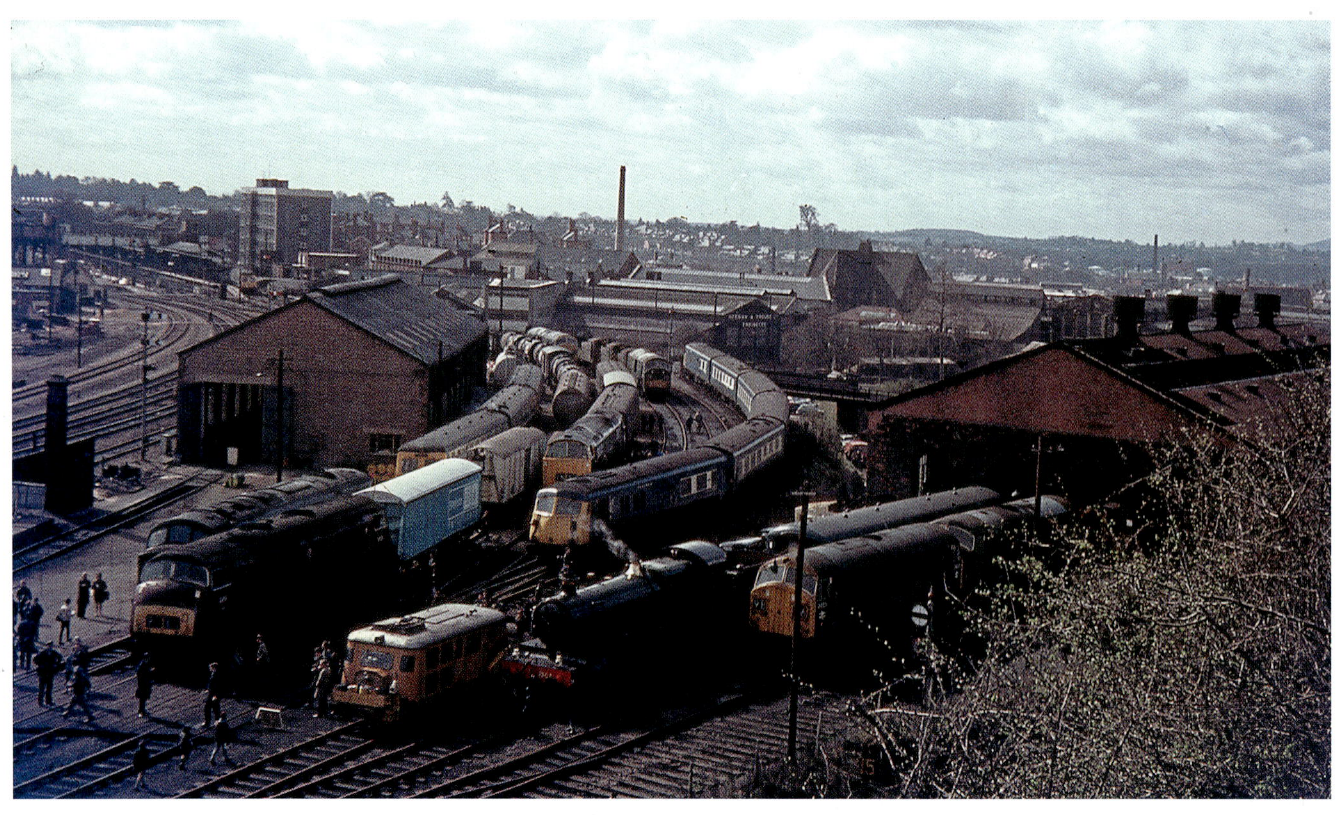

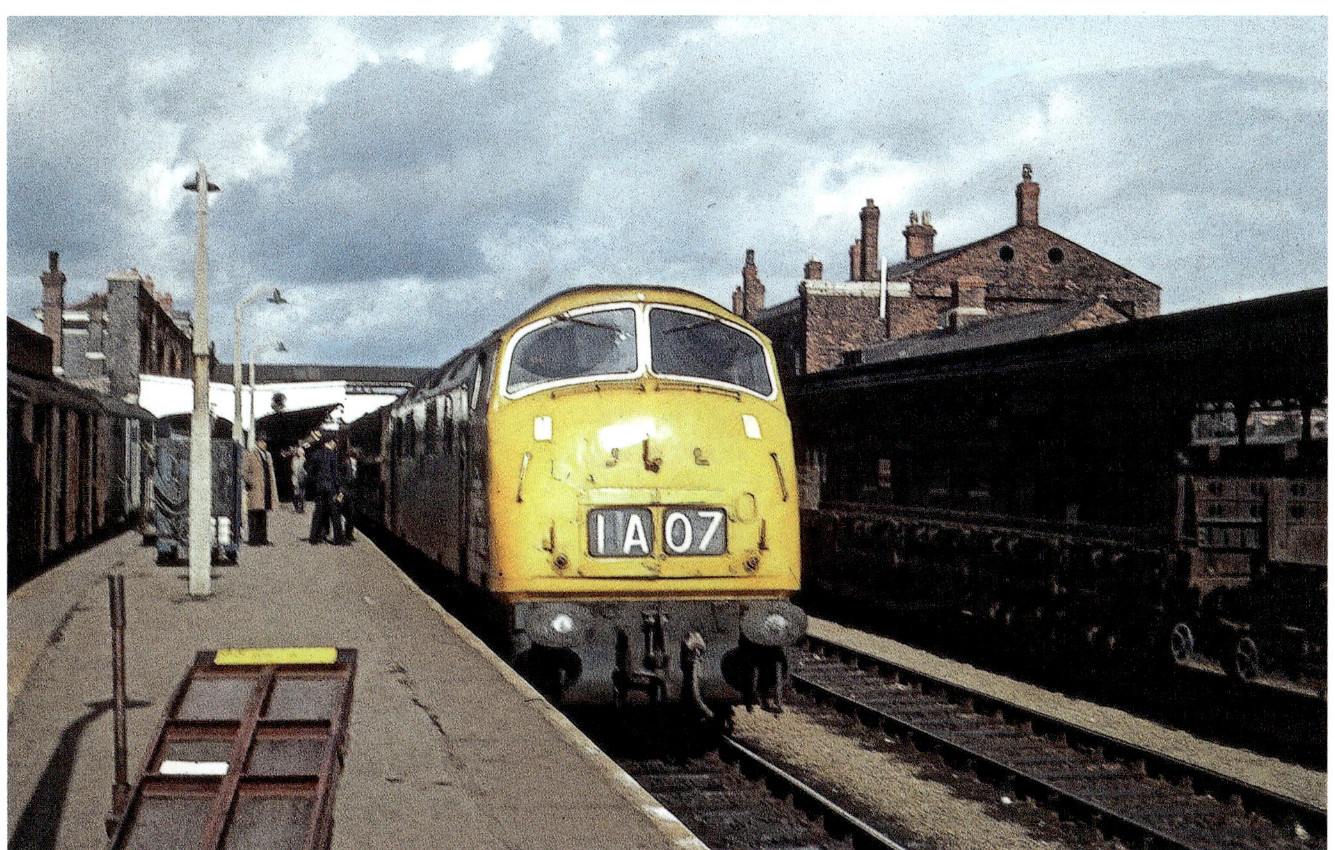

Worcester Shrub Hill and Warship class diesel D859 *Vanquisher* rolls into the station with the 0700 Worcester Paddington bound train in September 1967. The station environs are almost identical in 2025, albeit the station ironwork is beautifully painted. At right of the Warship class diesel is an engineering department wagon utilised for carrying rails. *Photo by John Stanford*

Worcester Shrub Hill on 12th June 1983 and LMS Black 5 is about to uncouple from The Brunel Pullman, which had run Bristol to Bristol via Hereford and Worcester. A BR supervisor in smart BR blue uniform with gold buttons is keeping a watchful eye on proceedings, albeit without an orange vest; this was a regular occurrence until the safety culture gradually changed. At left are BR Grampus wagons, likely destined for Honeybourne Tip. *Photo by John Stanford*

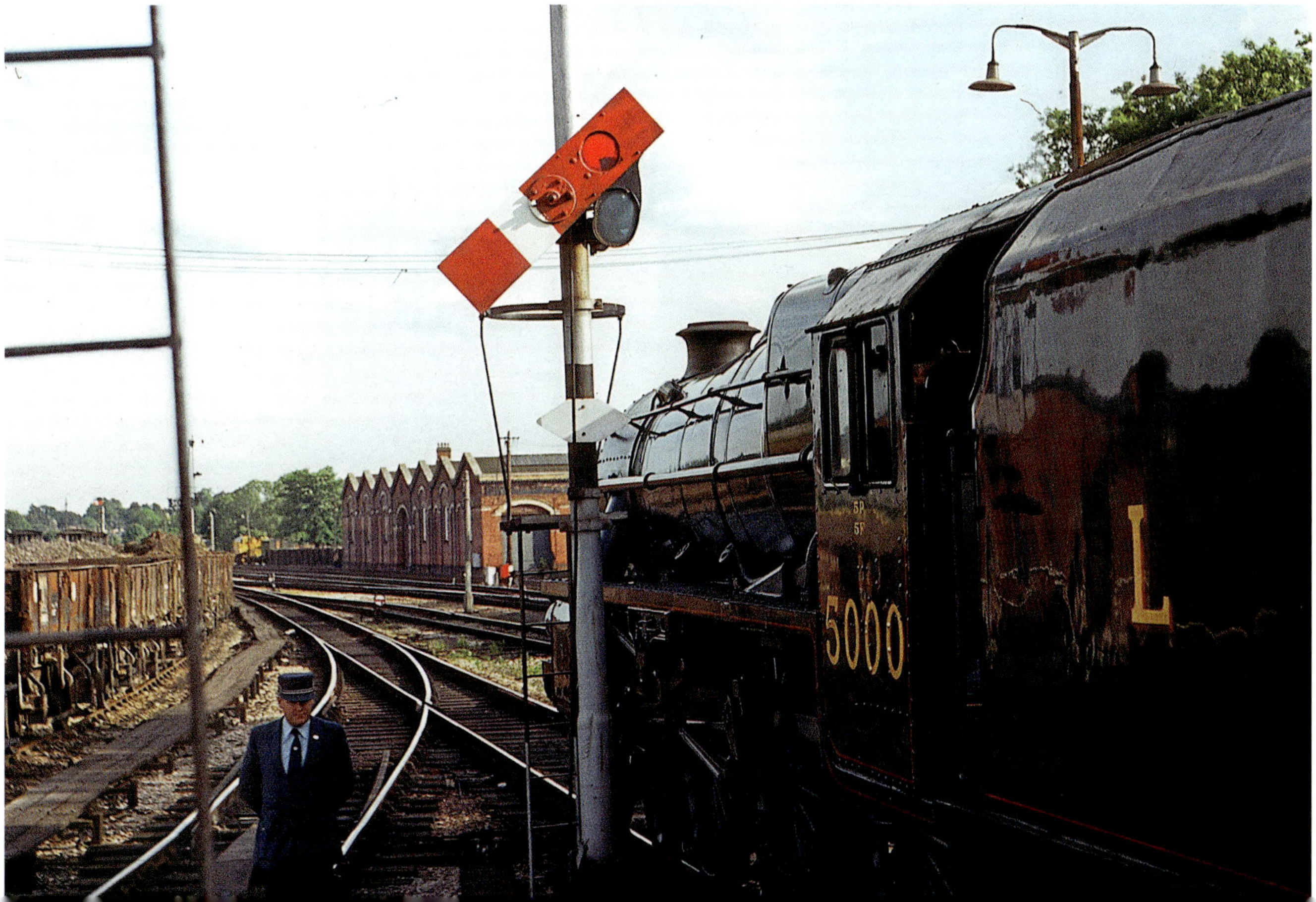

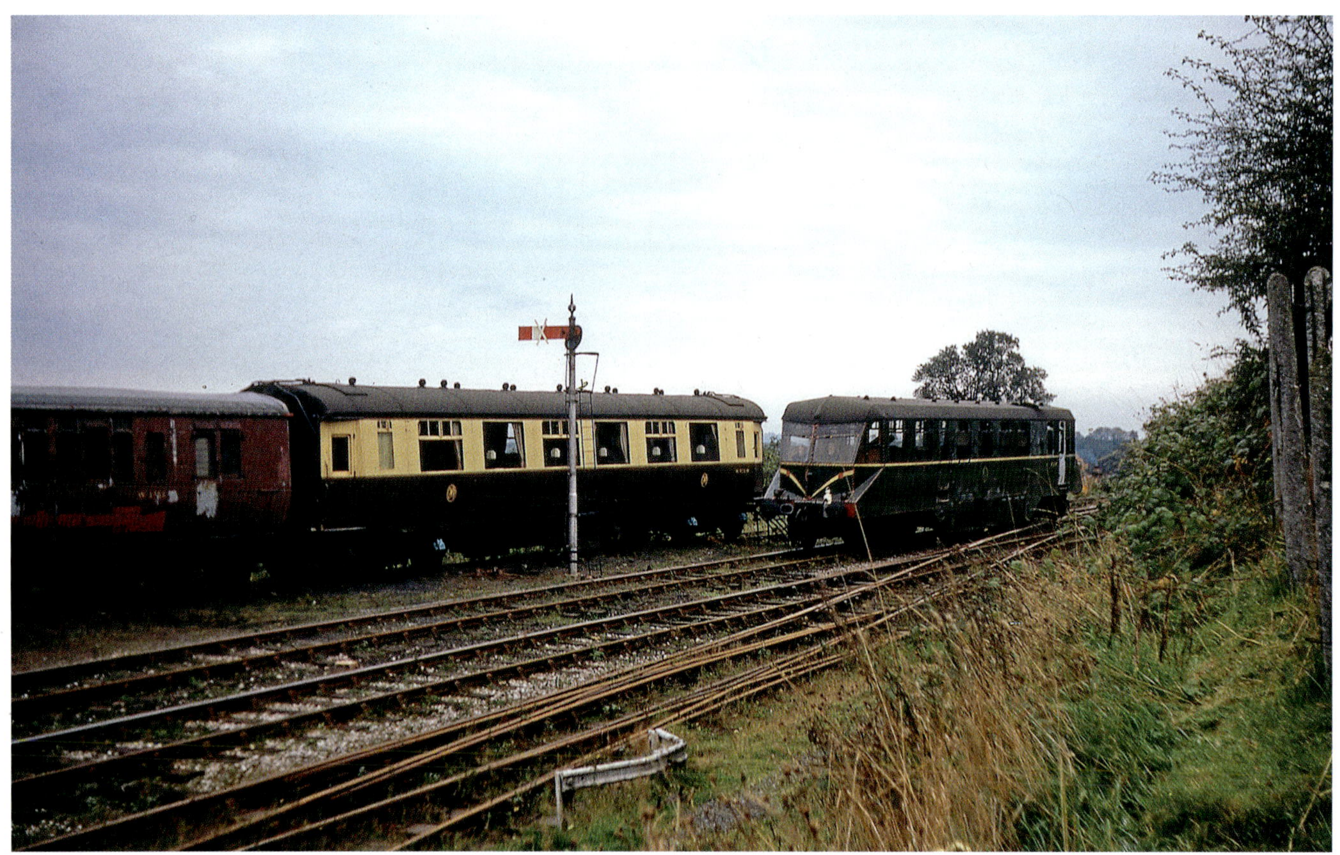

Bridgnorth; a brief deviation as the nascent Severn Valley Railway was regularly visited by John and Wendy when they lived in Worcester. Here on 22nd October 1967 we see GWR Railcar W22 still in BR green, having just carried the author – his first train ride at less than four weeks old. That was when the railway bug bit, according to Wendy. *Photo by John Stanford*

Ashchurch in 1966 when the nascent Dowty Railway Preservation Society was still acquiring rolling stock for preservation. Dominating the view is Cadbury No.1, undergoing a repaint, with the original lettering still visible. In the distance is the Bristol to Birmingham line. *Photo by John Stanford*

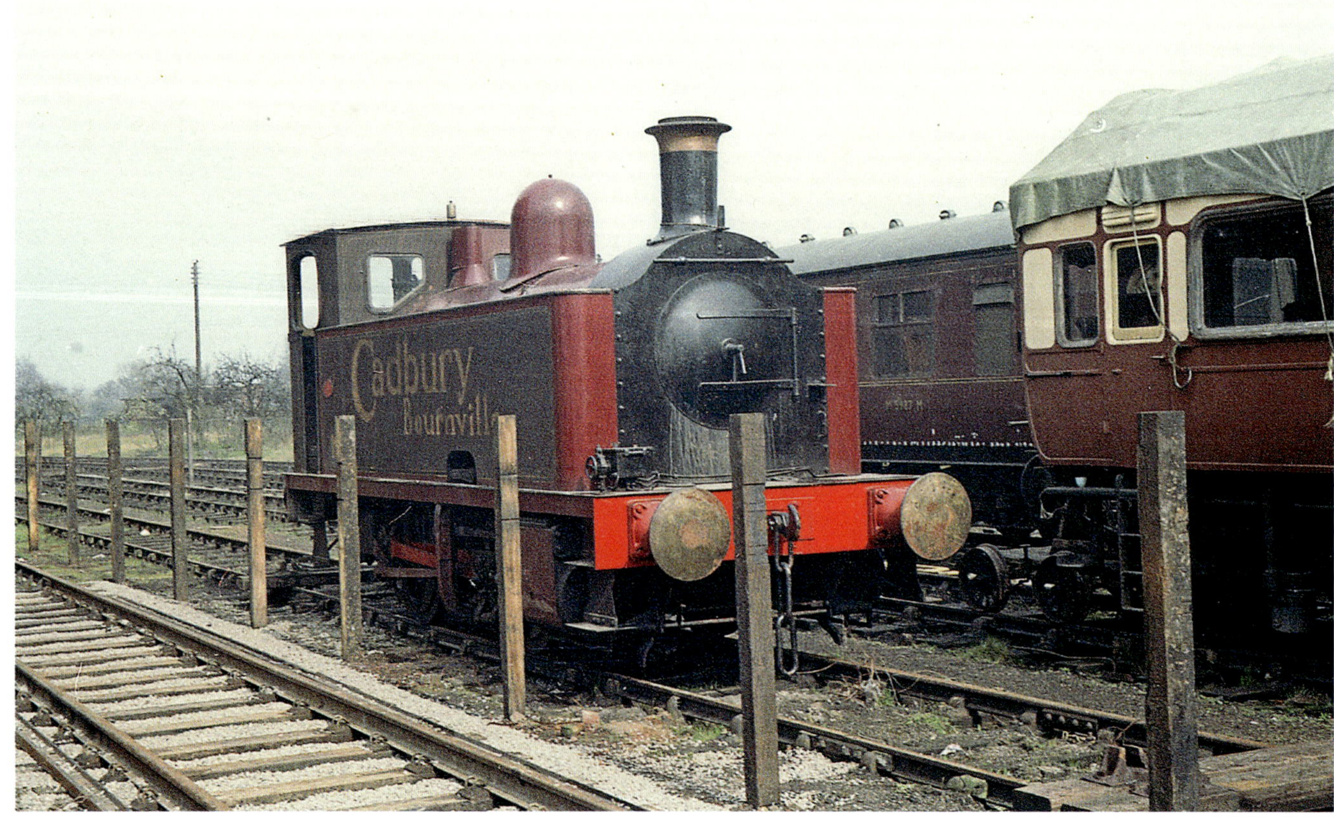

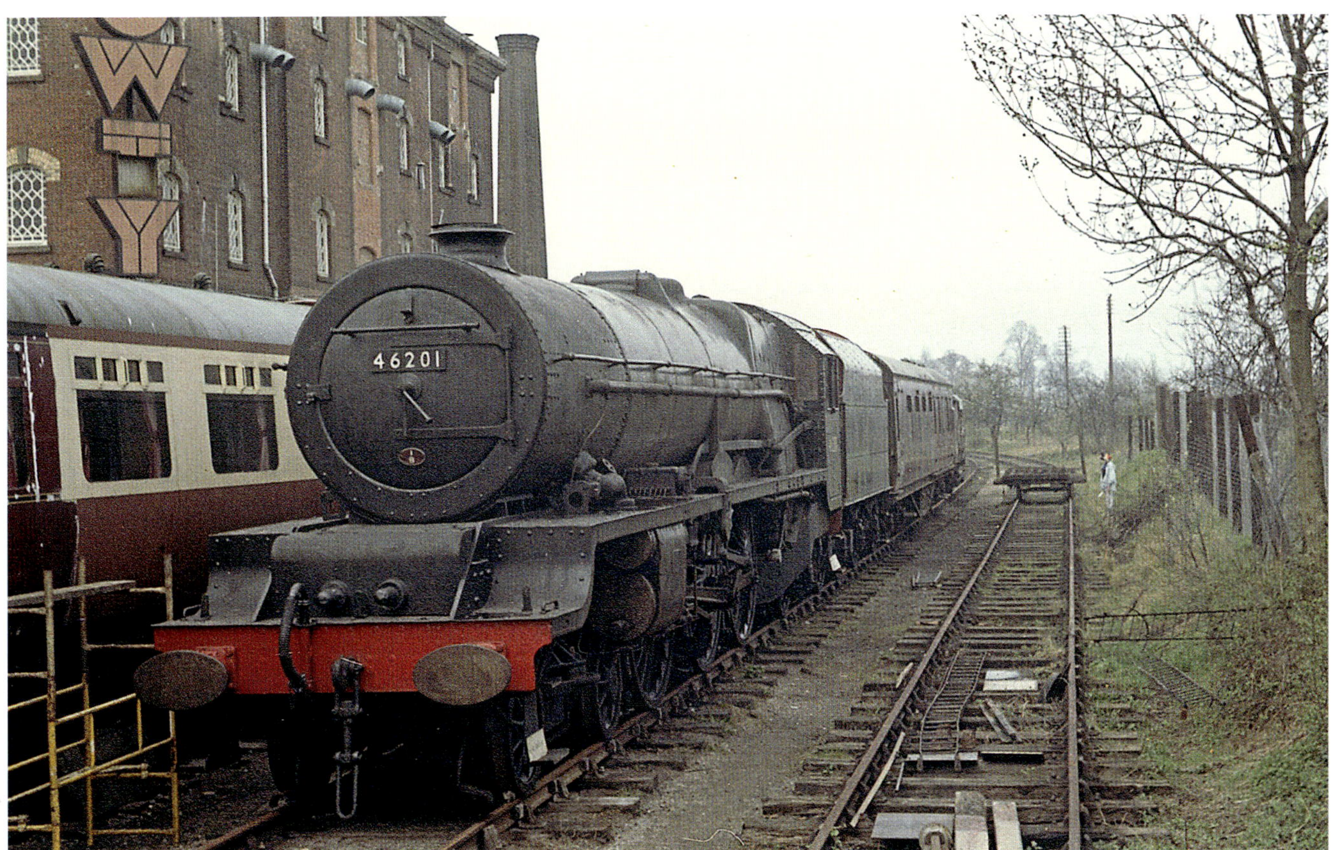

Ashchurch and 6201 *Princess Elizabeth* dominates the scene as the author's mum wanders around the site. The Princess Royal locomotive remained here until 1976; only leaving the site in the meantime to visit BR open days. *Photo by John Stanford*

Ashchurch on 6th May 1967 and 7808 *Cookham Manor* was operating short rides over the sidings when John and Wendy visited. It is noteworthy that the loco still carries the smart BR Western Region livery, as does the Collett coach. The loco was purchased by a Great Western Society member directly from BR and has resided at Didcot since 1970. *Photo by John Stanford*

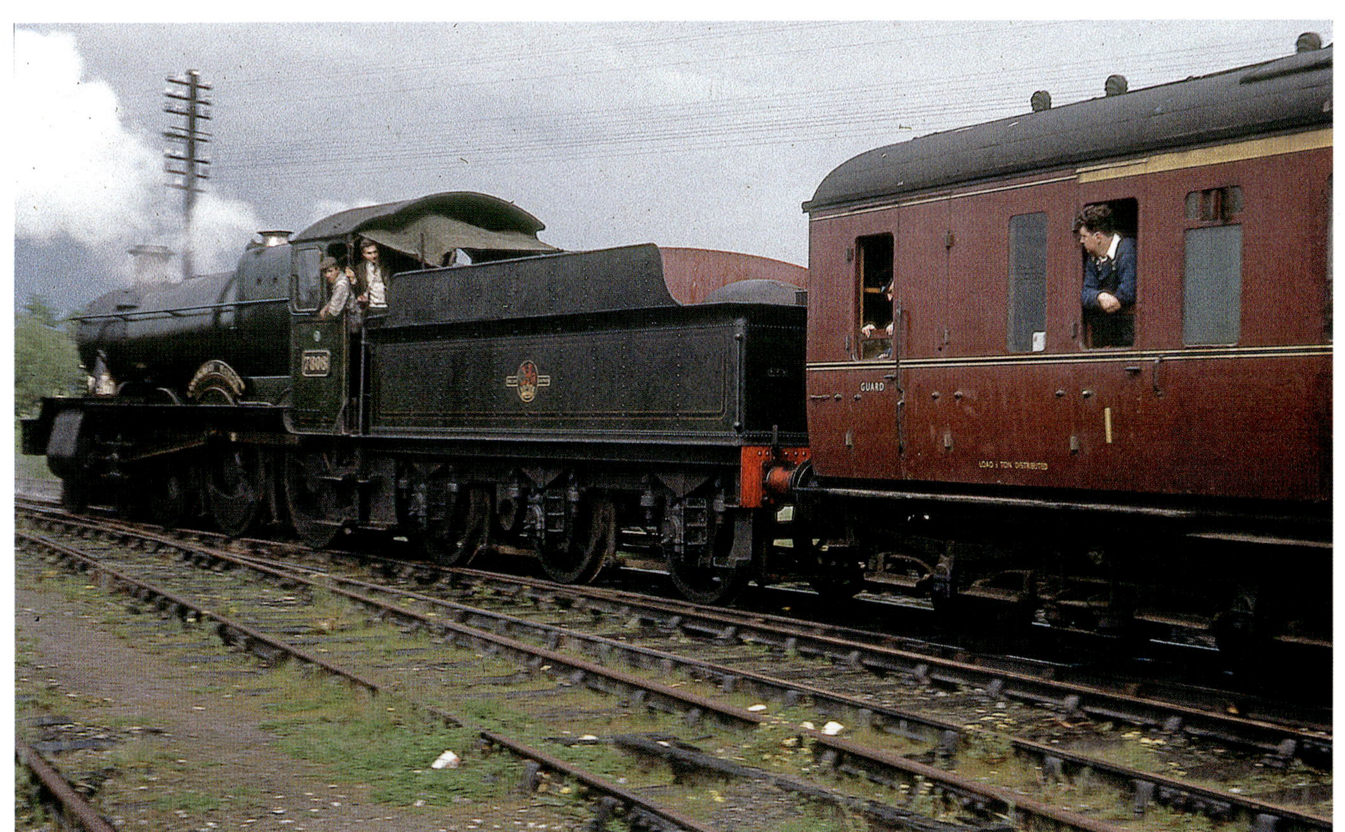

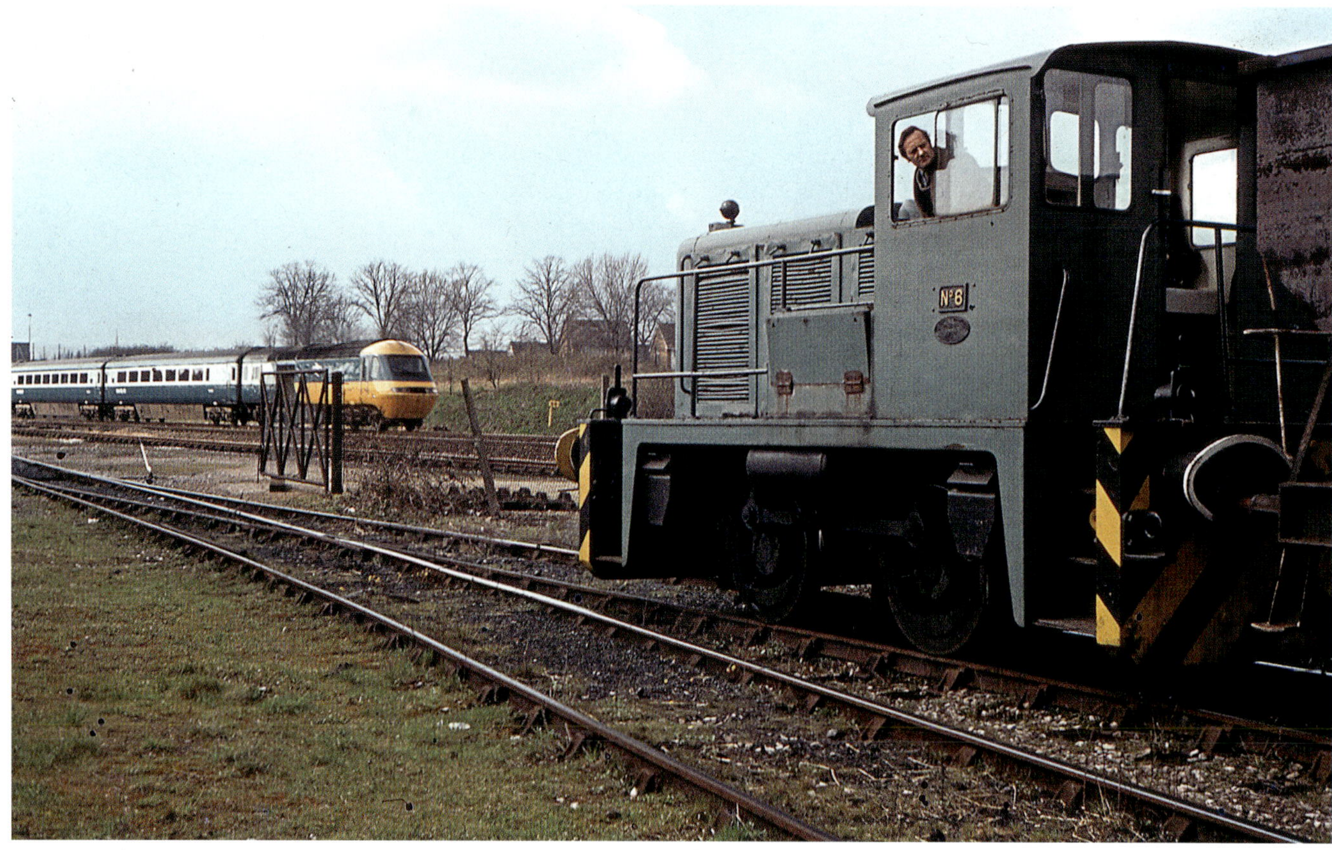

Cheltenham Coal Depot was situated just north of Cheltenham station and was established in summer 1967. It was closed to rail in spring 1985. Here in April 1985 is one of the last trains with coal from Maerdy Colliery planned by John is shunted by a Yorkshire Engine Co locomotive. The wagons are elderly vacuum braked HTV hopper wagons – even then their days were numbered. In the background is the 0912 Bristol to Newcastle train.

Gloucester Depot. Happily, GWR 0-6-2 5637 became the 61st loco to leave the Barry Scrapyard when it was bought by the Birmingham Railway Museum in August 1974 and taken by rail at Tyseley, travelling on its own wheels. This was not entirely successful as 5637's front axle box burnt out during the journey and the loco had to stop here for repairs. The engine is pictured right with 5080 and 4160; they were the last Barry locos to depart by rail. *Photo by John Stanford*

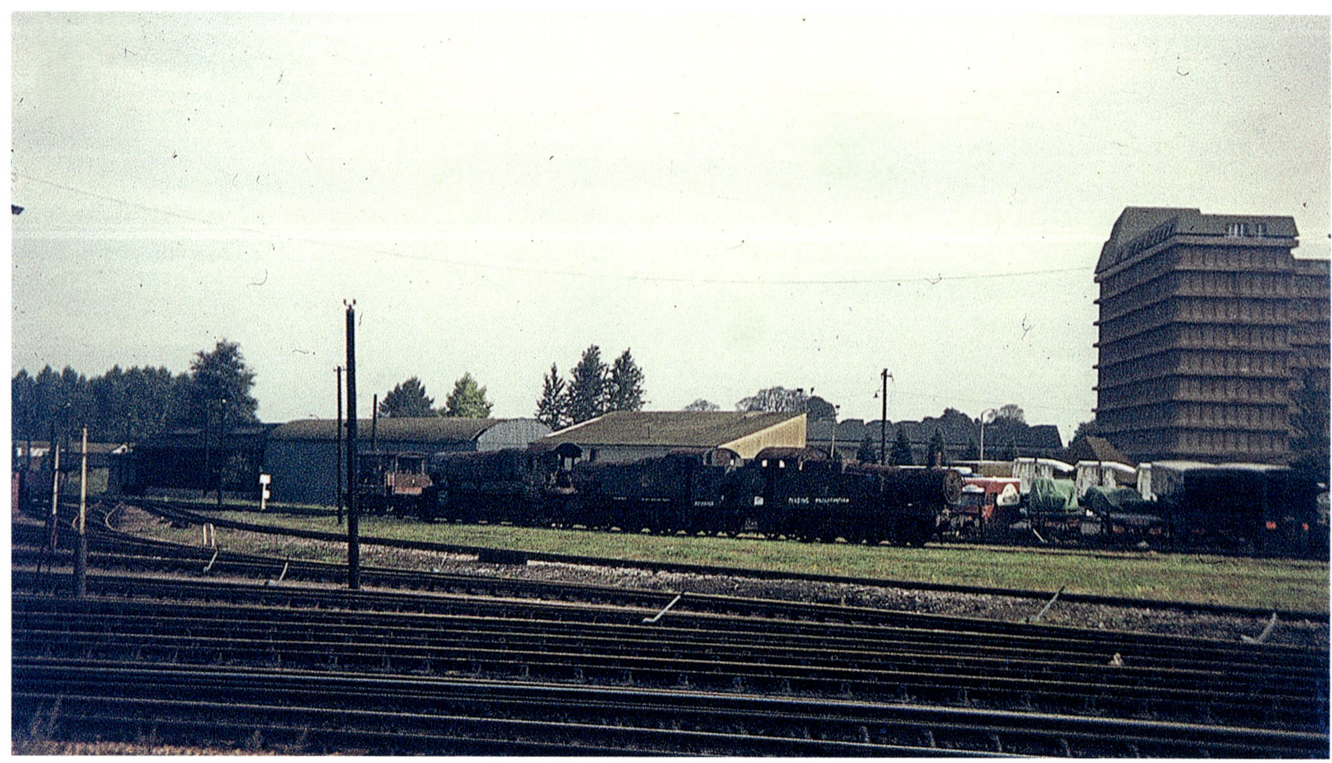

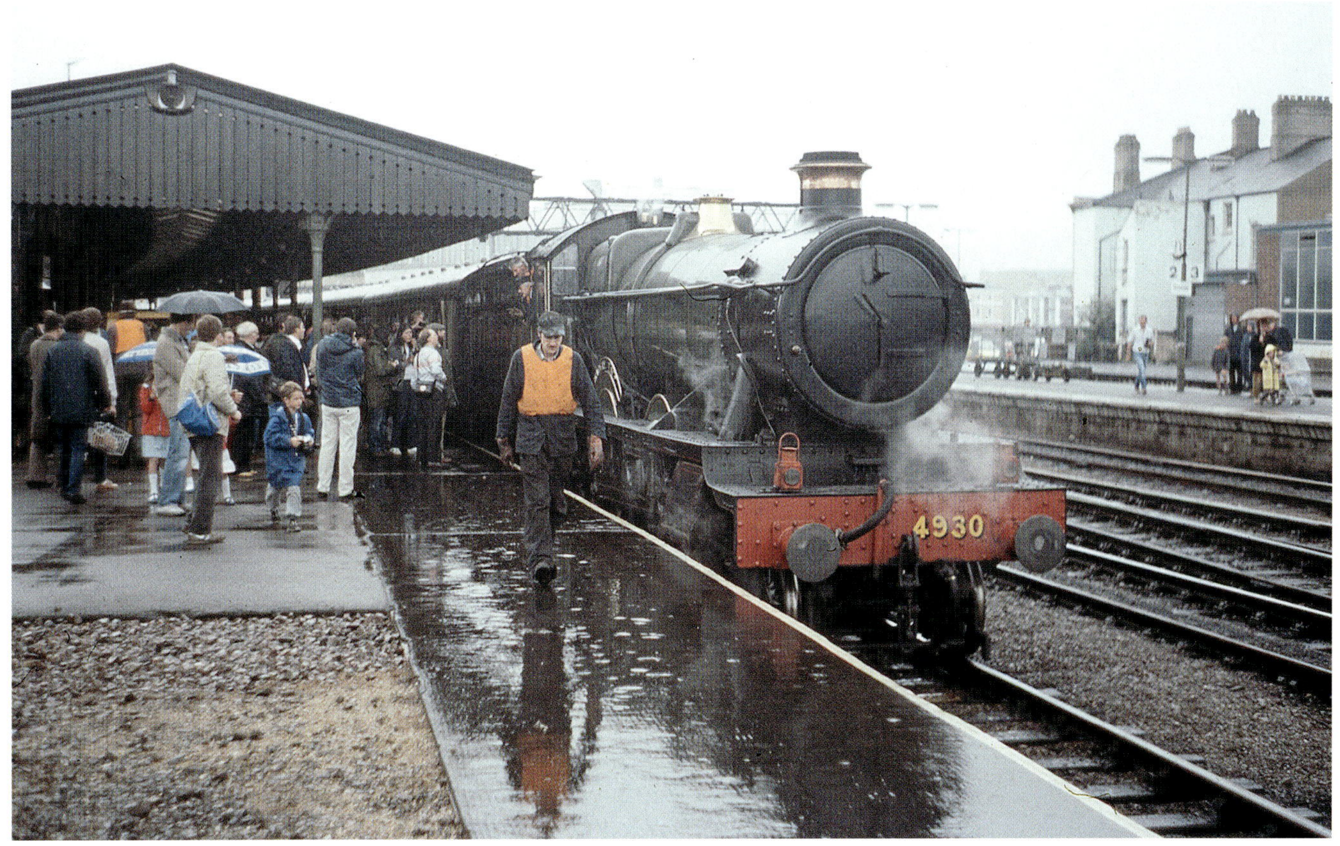

Gloucester was a location that both Paul and John had dealings with in their careers in respect of freight and passenger traffic. Here 4930 *Hagley Hall* is seen during a shocking downpour on 18th August 1985, when Paul had a day off from the ticket office. A cracking run had ensued over Sapperton Bank by the Gloucester train-crew.

Gloucester, nearly 35 years later with a Class 66 on supermarket traffic. The December 2019 timetable change was the biggest such alteration for 40 years on the Western Region. Huge efforts were made by Network Rail and GWR to ensure the changes went smoothly and they did; particularly considering the significant problems that occurred elsewhere in 2018 when timetable changes were made. Some 75% of the timetable changed, reflecting improvements through enhancement works. The author was one of several executives from the Western Route team placed in key signal boxes across the Western Region to support front-line staff.

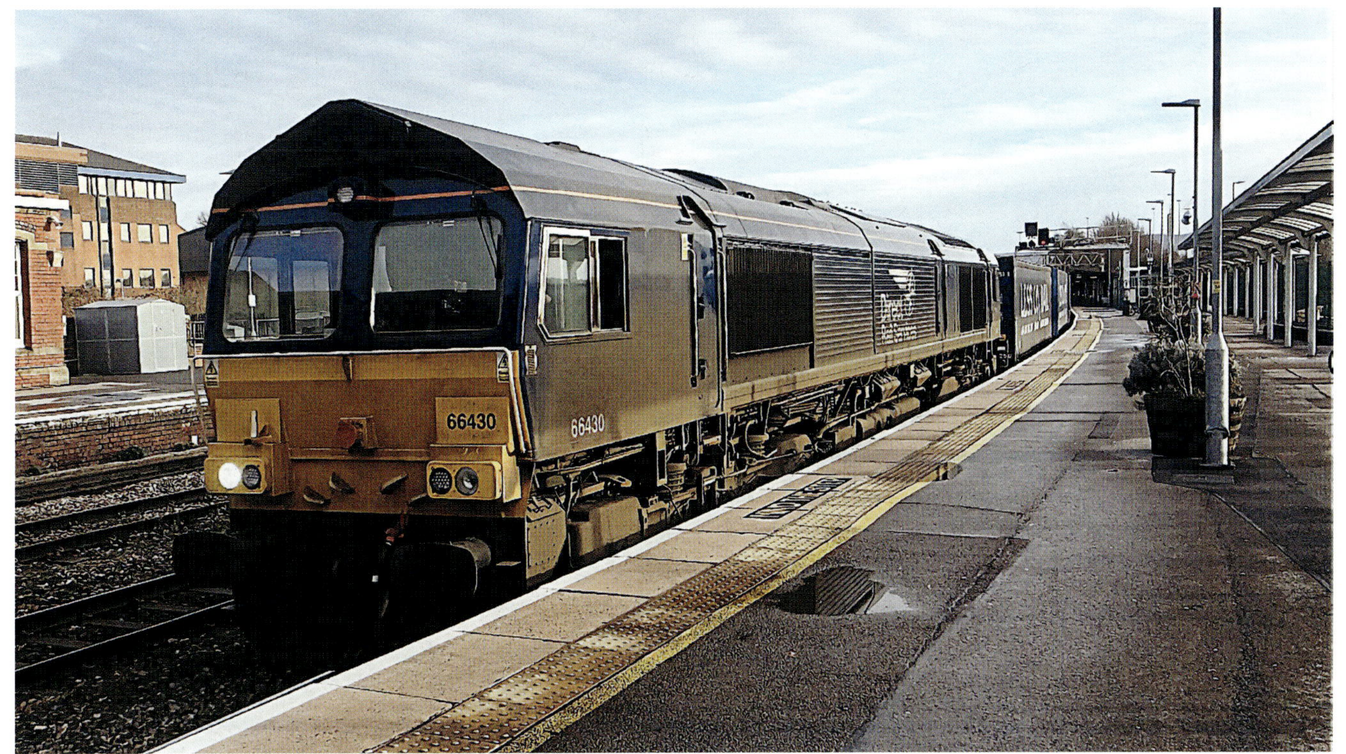

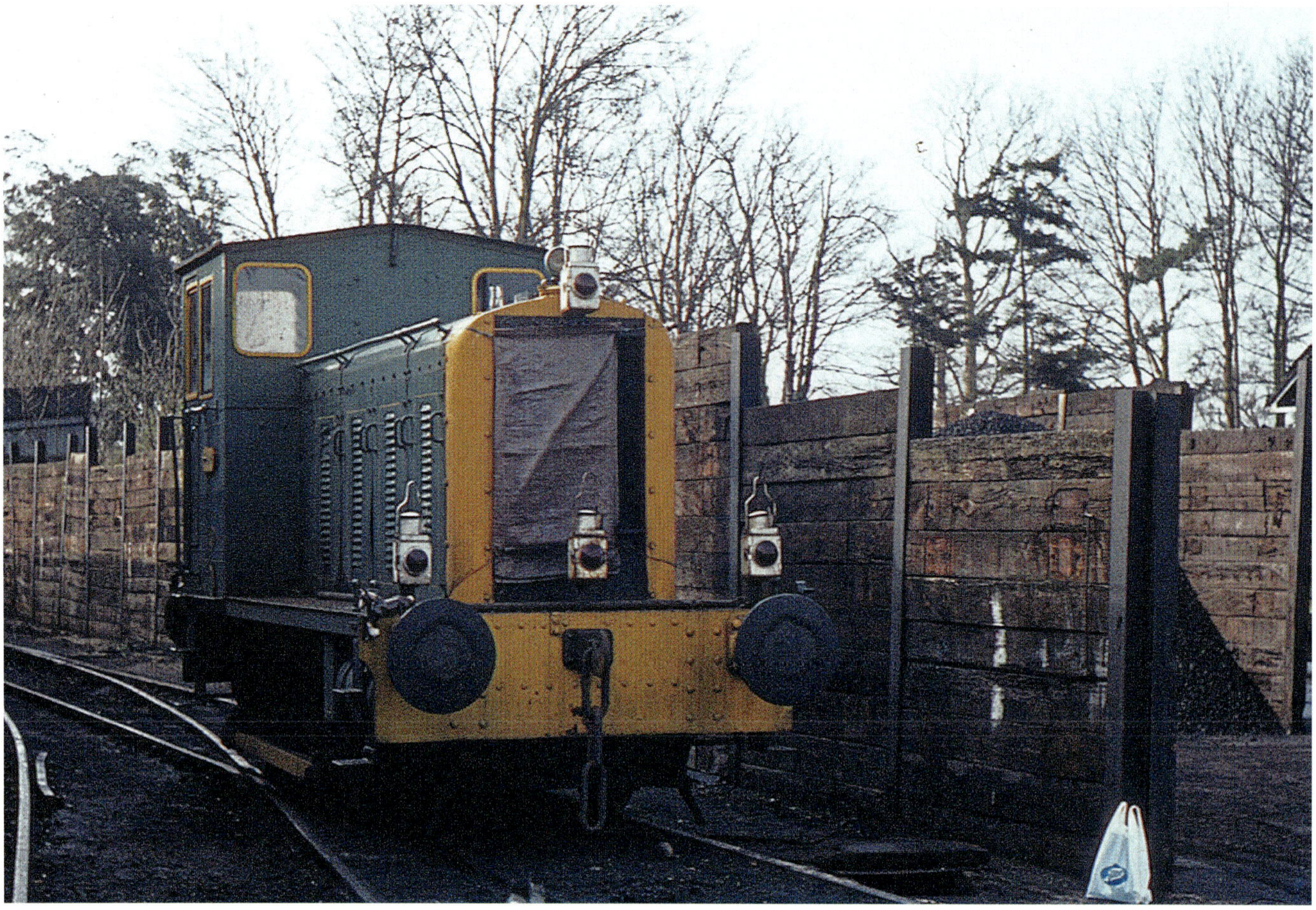

Stonehouse had a coal concentration depot, open from 1966 and lasting until 1989. When the author visited in April 1985, this Vulcan Foundry built loco named *Dougal* was ticking over ready to shunt six air-braked coal hopper wagons loaded with house coal.

Bristol Parkway was opened in 1973 as part of BR's fightback as motorway construction progressed and passenger traffic diminished. It was an instant hit and from the sparse open platforms it quickly gained full length shelters. The buildings are seen here in 1976 when *Princess Elizabeth* left its home at Ashchurch and moved to Bulmer's of Hereford. *Photo by John Stanford*

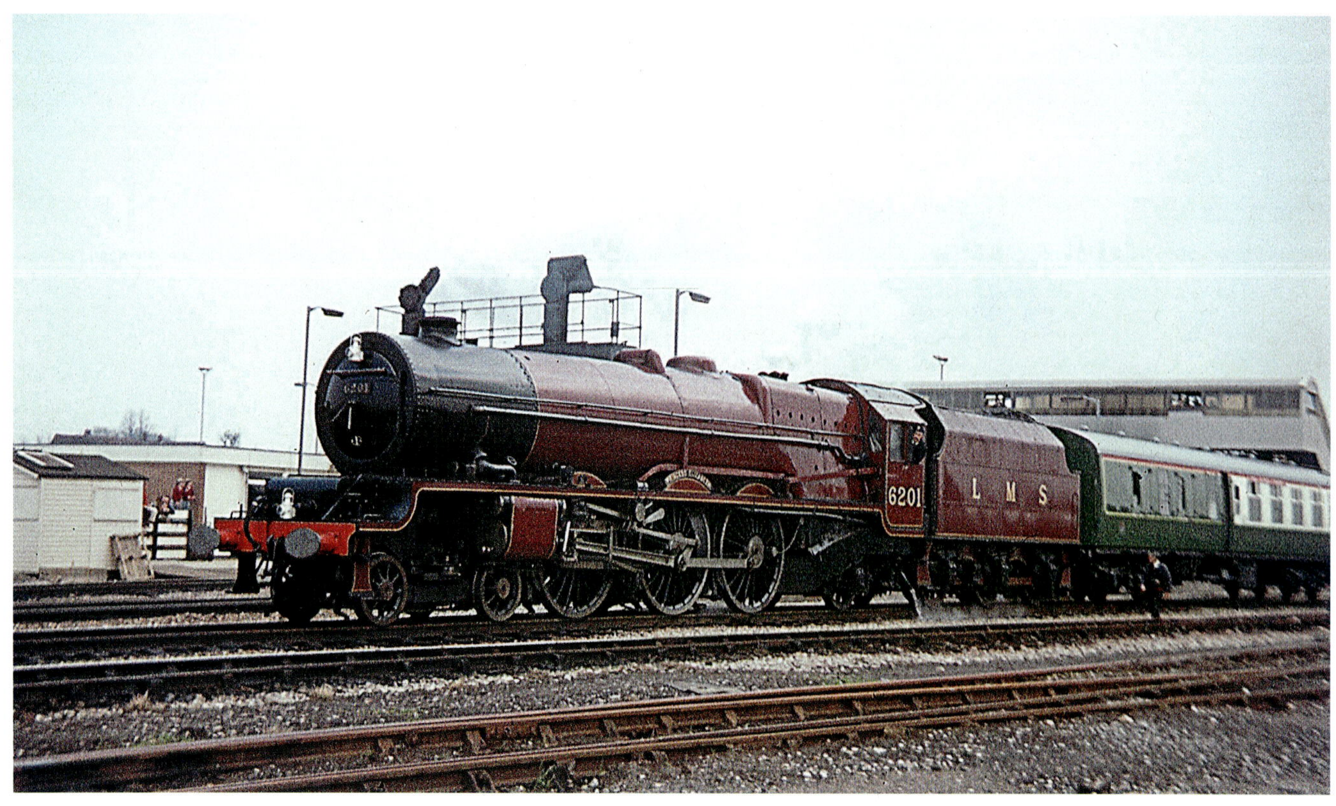

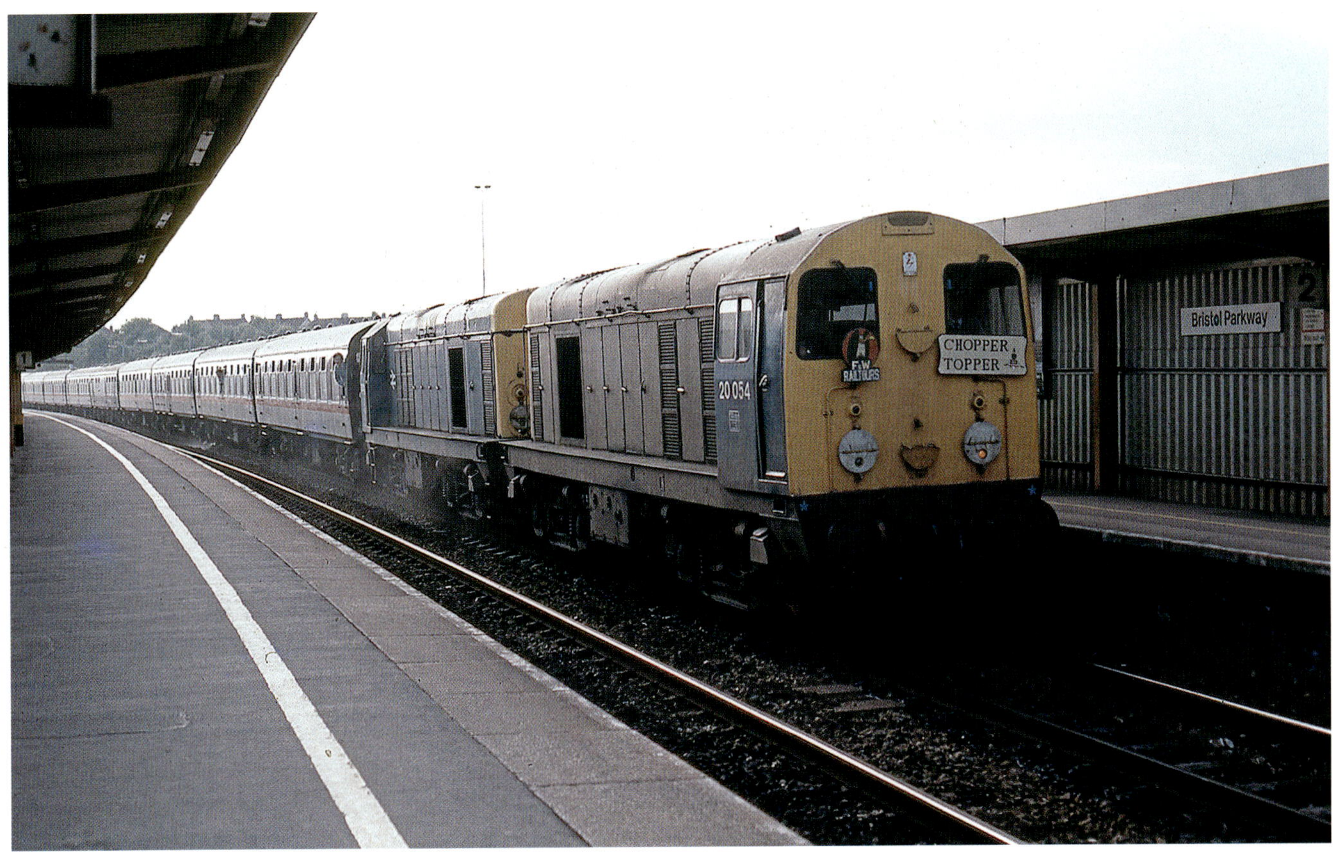

Bristol Parkway on 8th June 1986 as the Chopper Topper Railtour passes through the austere station on its way to Cornwall. The author recollects a 'farce' had played out with this railtour leading to a formal investigation in BR Western Region HQ; linked to a class 37 derailment in Cornwall, preventing the railtour operating as planned. *Photo by Trevor Riddle*

Bristol Parkway Railnet terminal on opening day, 15th May 2000, when the author visited in his role as regional freight manager and sponsor of the rail works. During the terminal construction, £2.6 million provided for a new rail mail station, a new fully signalled bay platform and reversible signalling. Royal Mail funded the construction of the state-of-art building and provision of new handling equipment. Sadly, it only lasted 3½ years, as Royal Mail pulled out of rail.

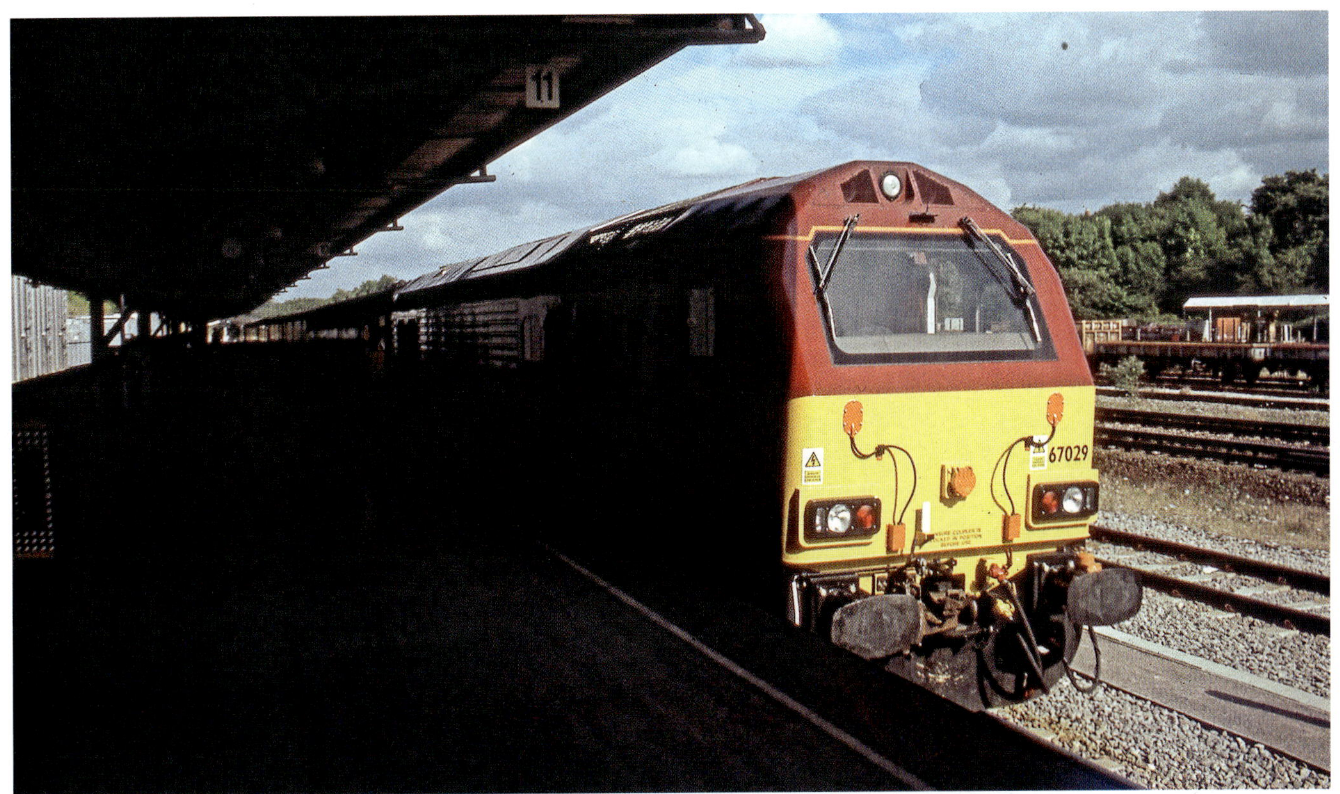

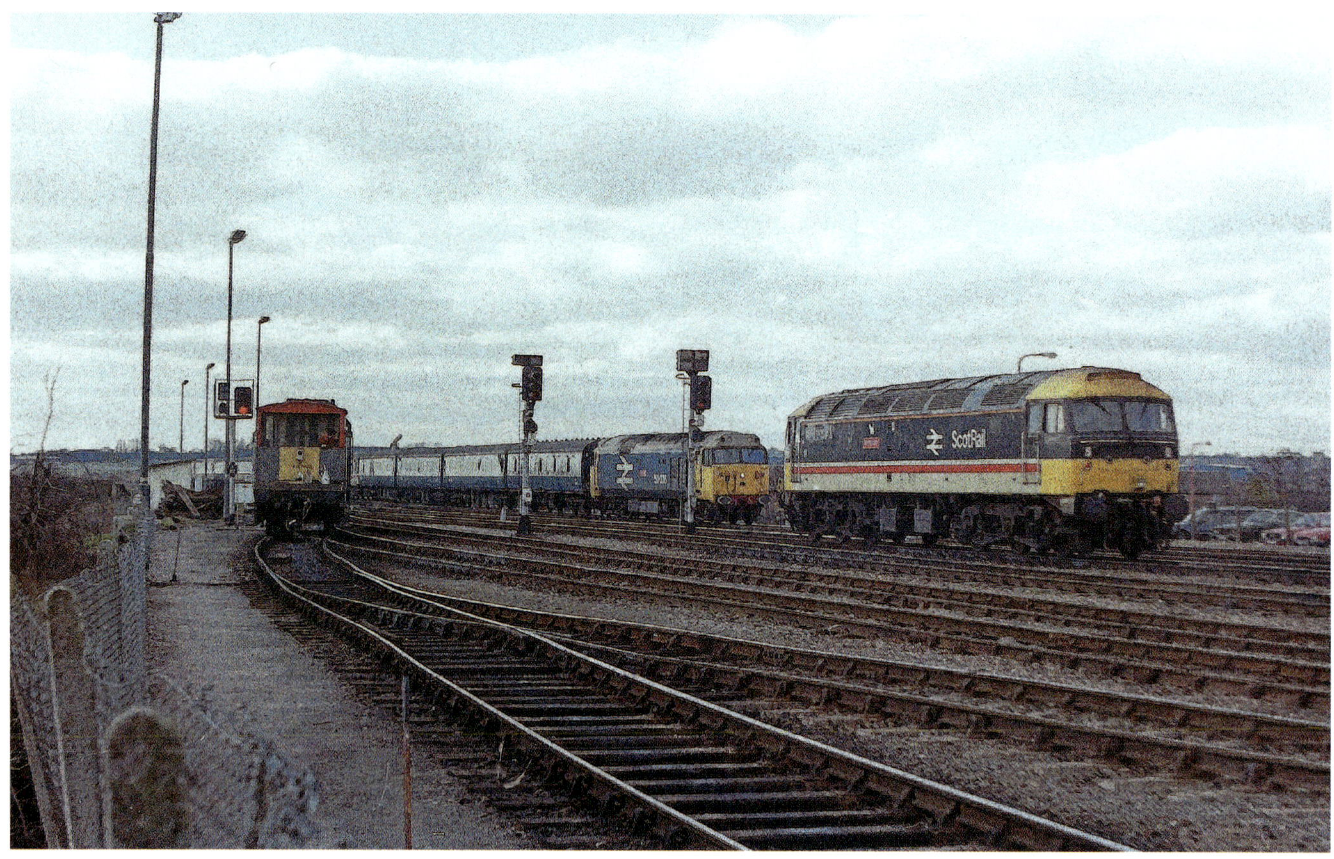

Bristol Parkway in January 1988 as a class 50 heads north with a class 47, just arrived off a parcel train, awaiting its next duty. Meanwhile, a class 08 is busy marshalling wagons of coal for Filton Coal Depot, sulphuric acid from Avonmouth for Puriton Royal Ordnance Factory and cement for Marsh Junction.

Avonmouth Hallen Marsh Jn was a busy railway hub in the 1970s and 80s with a regular passenger service and wide variety of freight. John was involved with this via the Port of Bristol Authority docks traffic. Paul started visiting and working the signal boxes as he undertook BR's Safe Working of Trains correspondence course from the start of 1986. Here on the last day of semaphore signalling (22nd January 1988), the signal-box is seen as a Sentinel diesel shunter leads a train of coke to the smelting works.

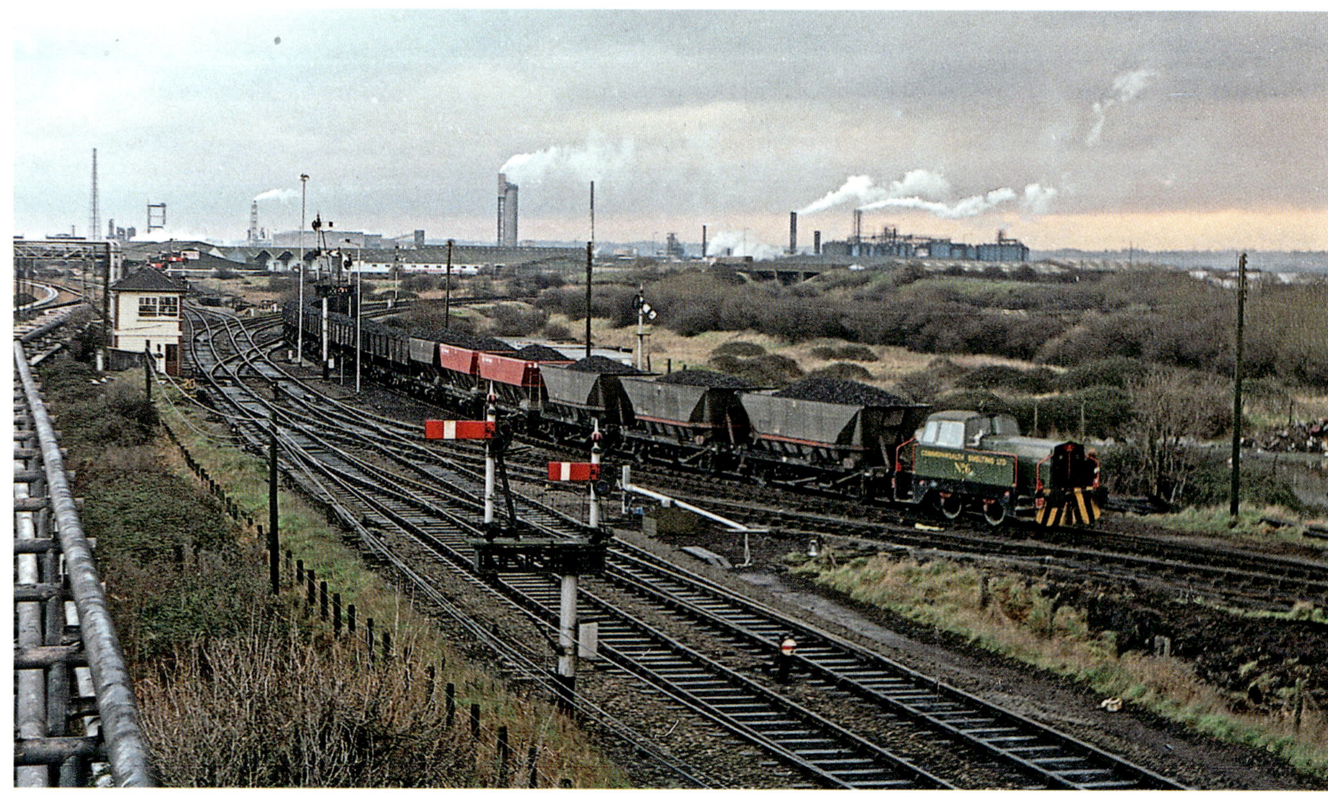

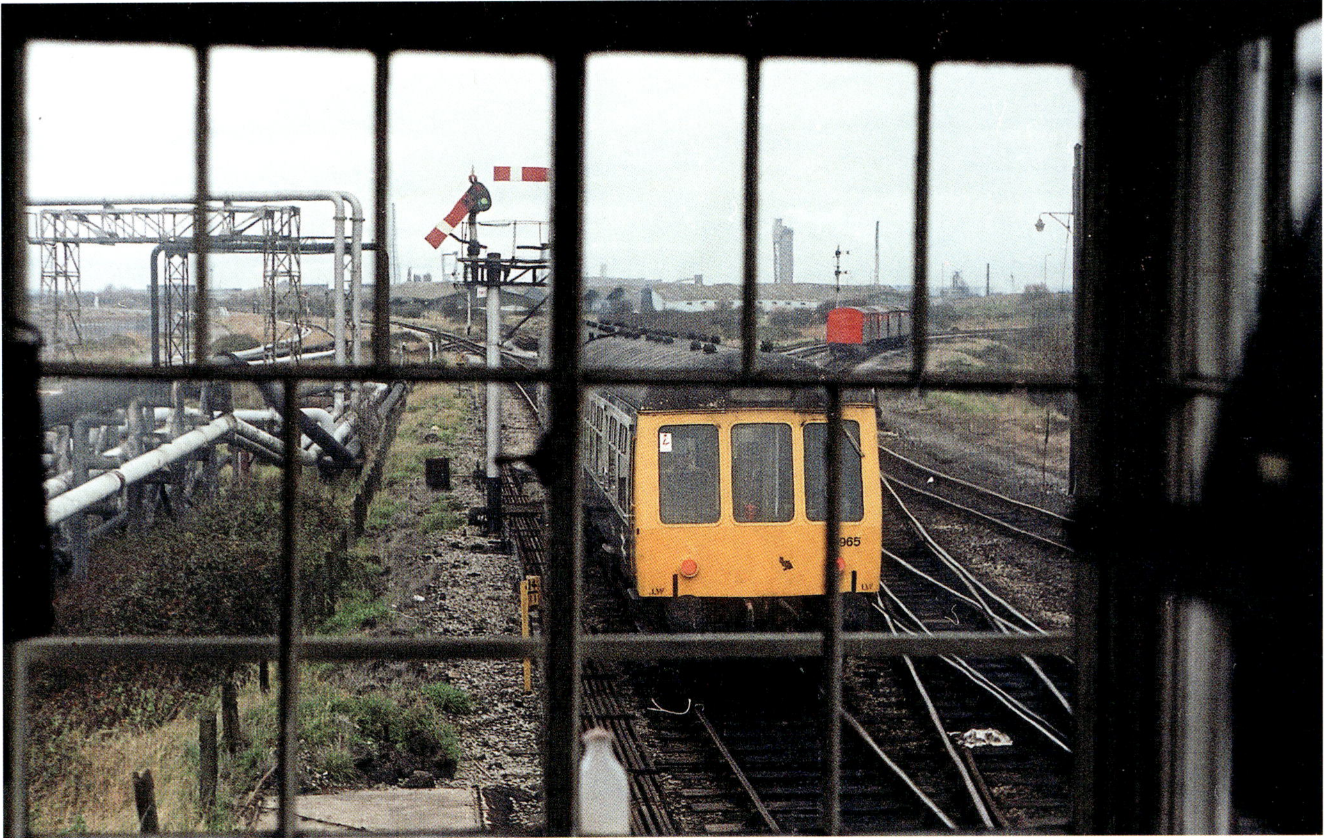

Avonmouth Hallen Marsh Junction Signal Box was an impressive structure, controlling lines toward Bristol Parkway, Severn Beach, to Avonmouth and of course the smelting works. Additionally, it controlled a diamond crossing for the dock railway system to access Chittening industrial estate. Here a class 108 DMU heads to Severn Beach in December 1987, a few weeks before the signal box closed.

Avonmouth Hallen Marsh Jn 35 years later and a very different scene exists. Happily, the line has a high level of passenger service, with freight still heading to and from Severn Beach and into Avonmouth docks – notably cement, stone and containers.

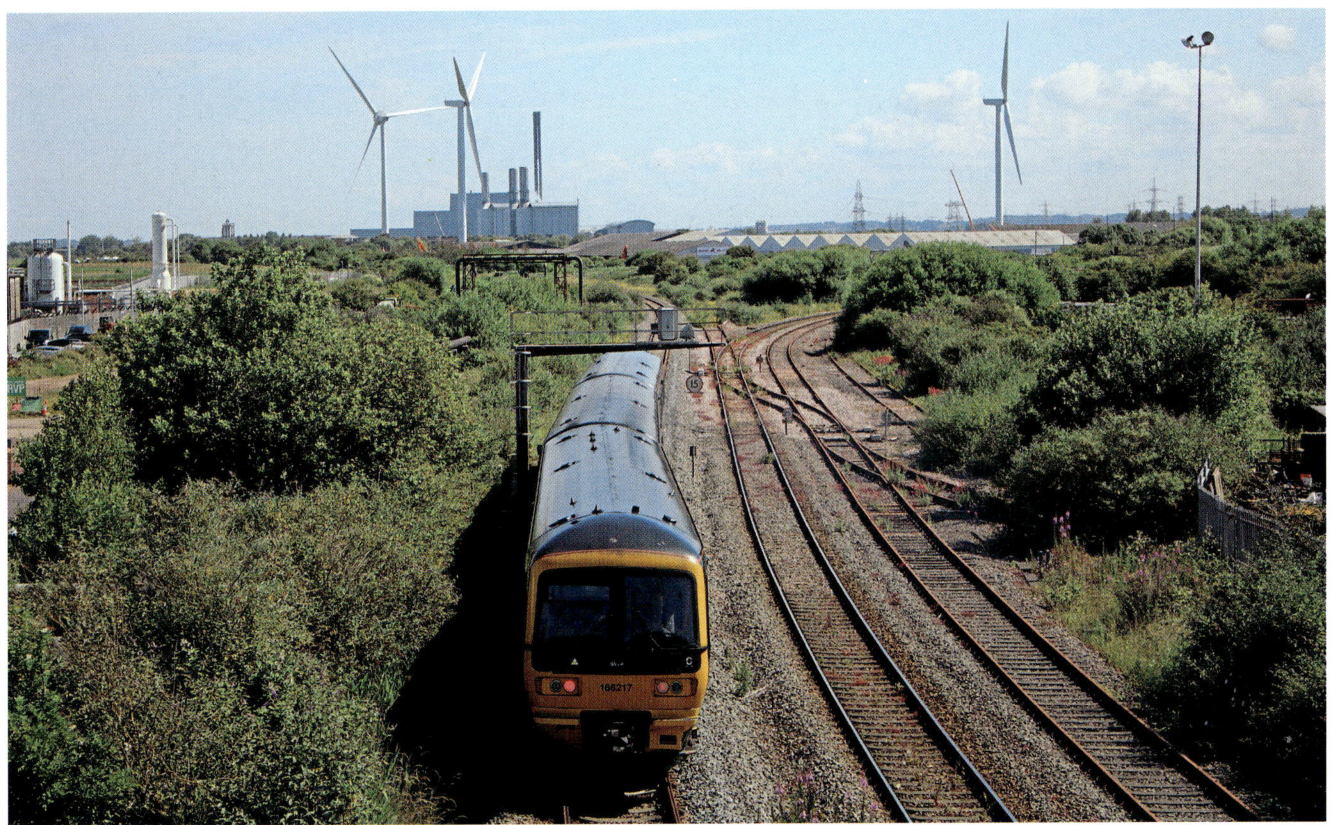

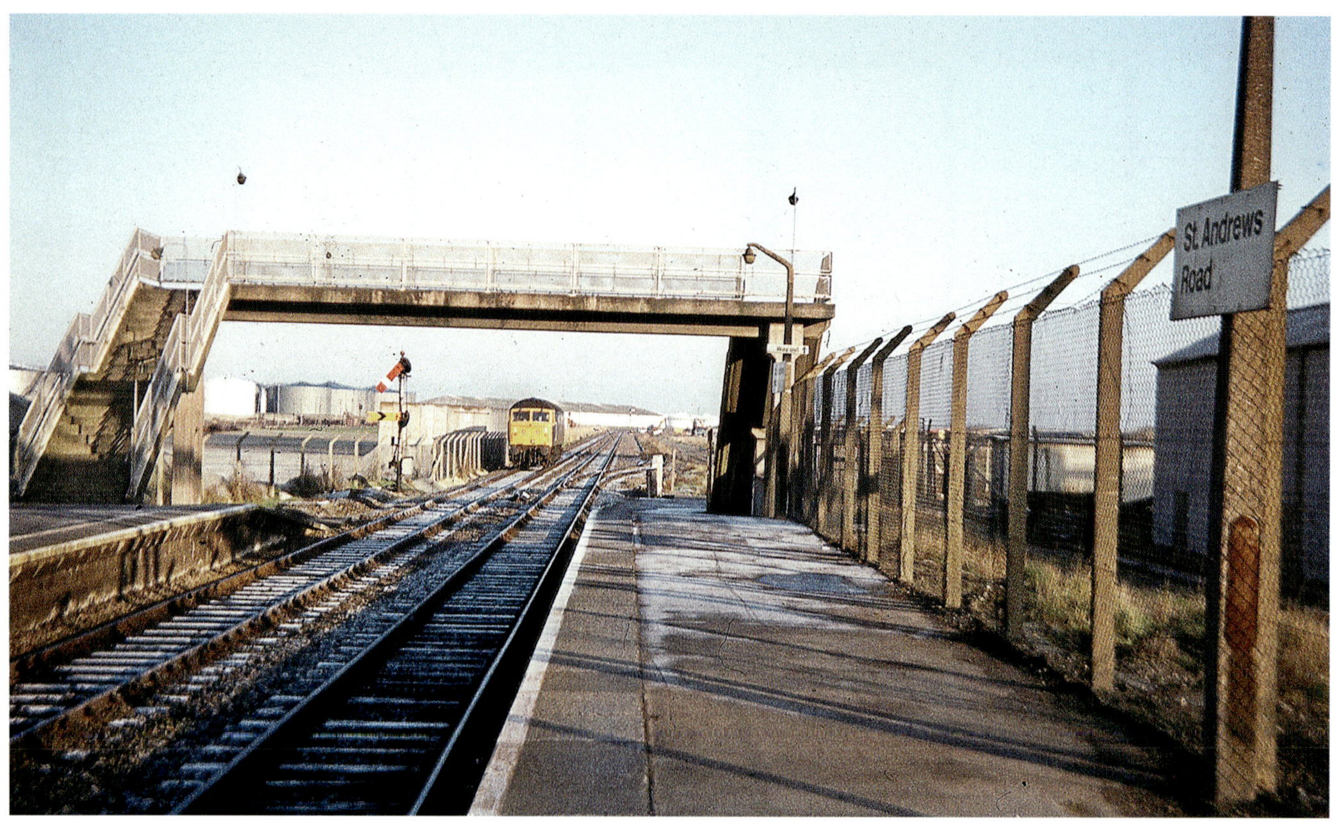

Avonmouth St Andrews Road is seen in January 1985. A few months later the author committed a faux-pas with a telephone train inquiry for St Andrews; he directed the passenger to the single unit railcar in Bristol Temple Meads bay platform for St Andrews. Some hours later the passenger and his family arrived and called to the travel centre perturbed and complete with golf clubs. They wanted St Andrews in Scotland, not industrial Avonmouth! A hasty apology from the author followed and he directed them onto the 12.15 to Glasgow instead, helping carry their bags to the train.

Avonmouth St Andrews signal box in August 1986, looking toward central Avonmouth. Dominant are the now demolished 'art deco' style grain warehouses, once such a feature of Avonmouth.

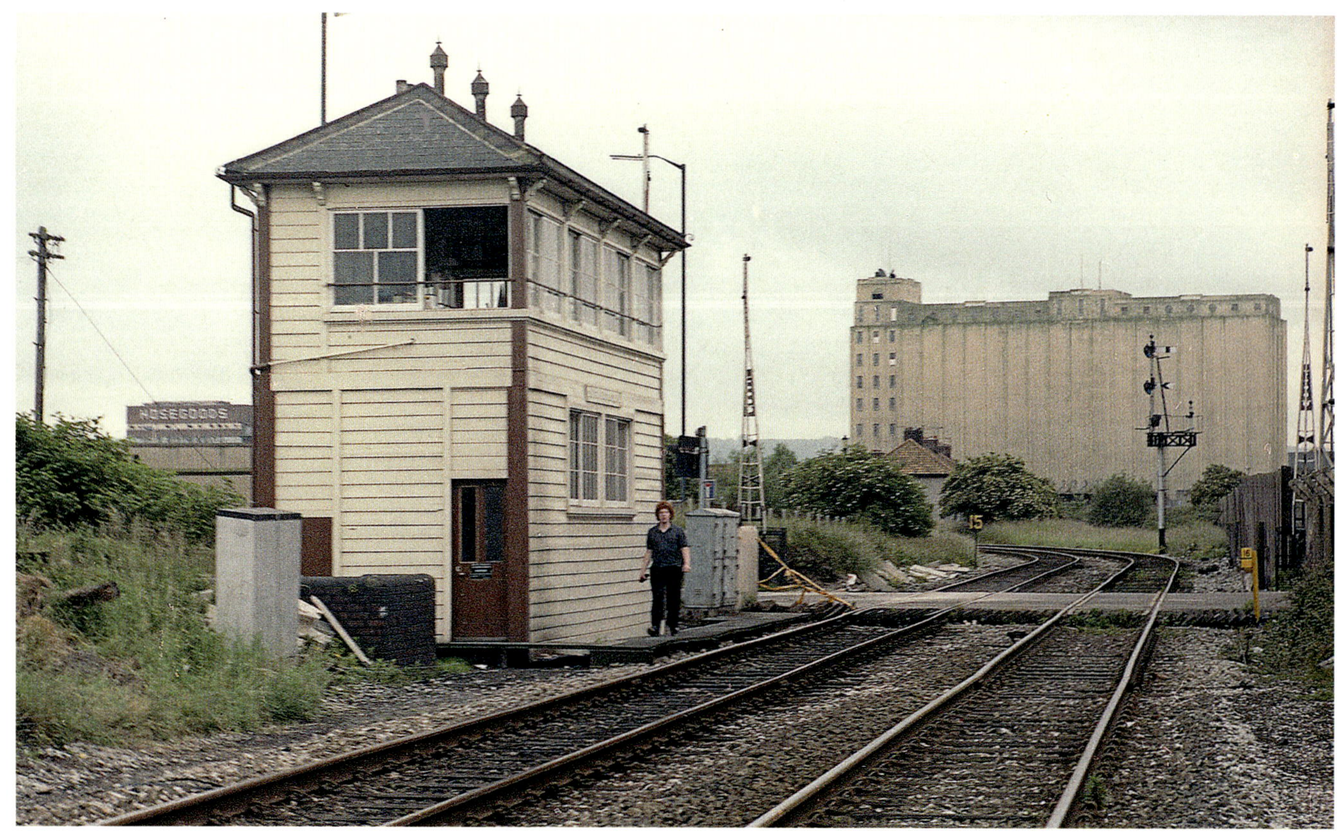

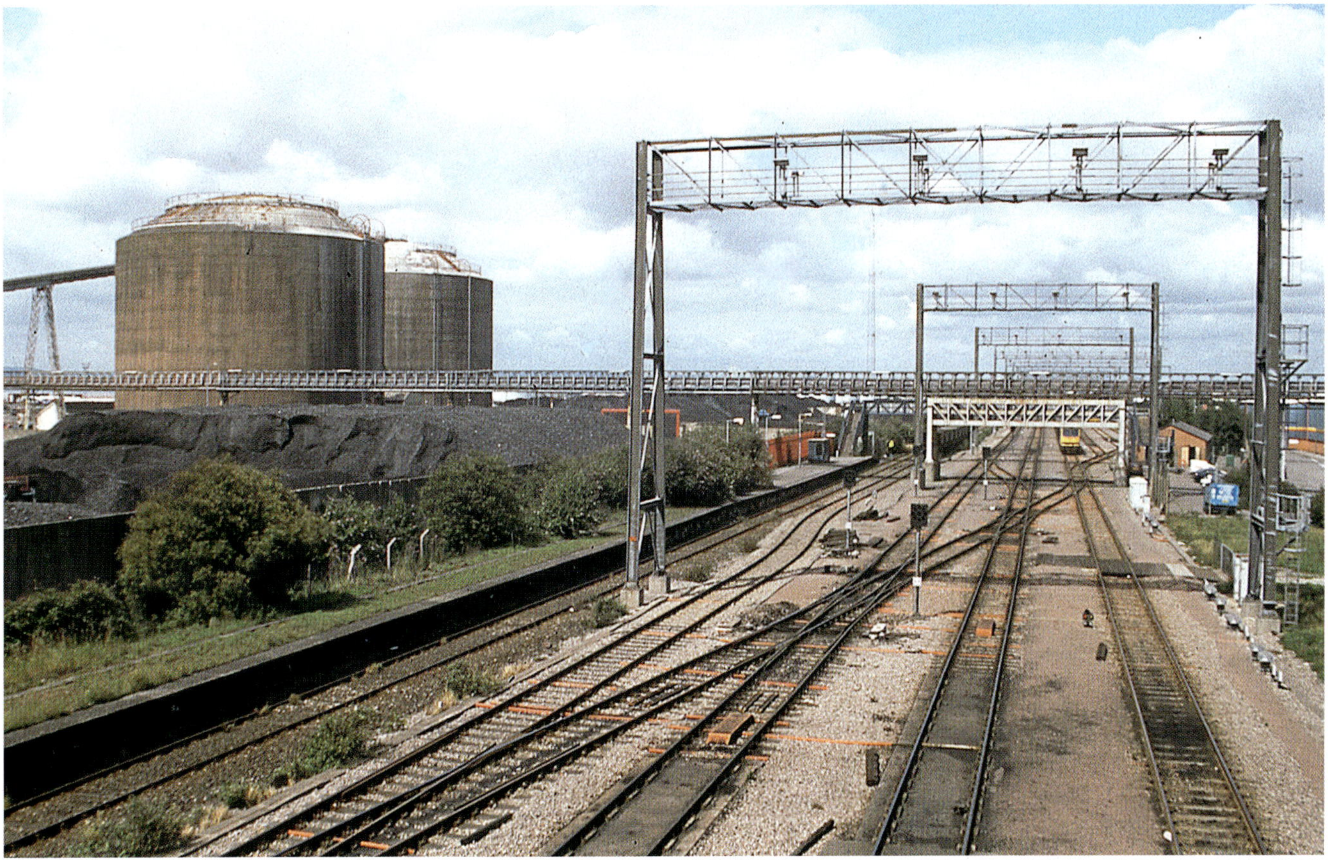

Avonmouth Bristol Bulk Handling terminal in July 2001 was busy with loading coal for Didcot Power Station and other stations. The author was at Avonmouth this day to meet directors of Bristol Port Company for a progress meeting for the reopening of the Portishead branch line to serve Royal Portbury Dock (see page 60). This is the view from the coal silo control room and a view of the yard pilot locomotives.

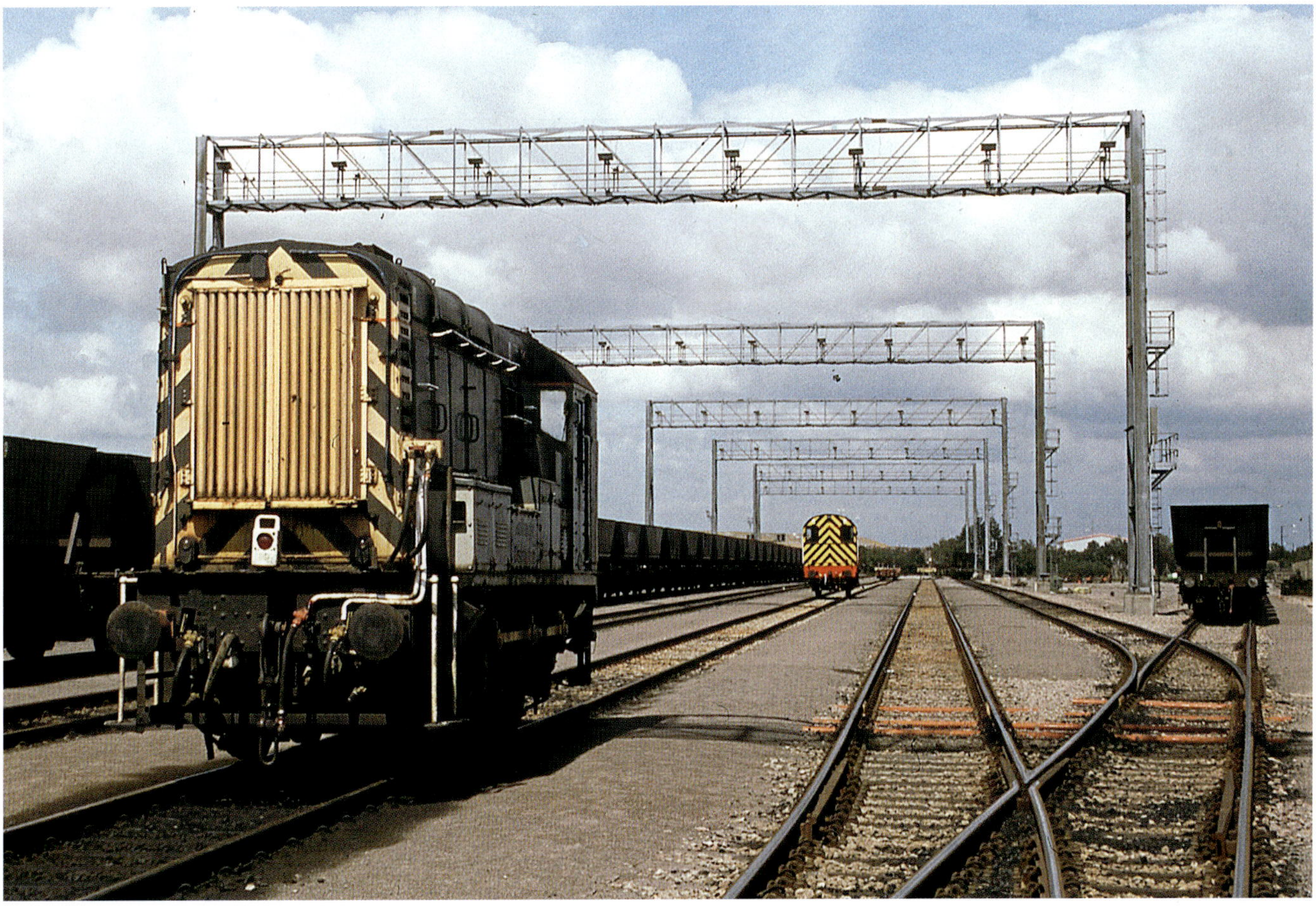

CHAPTER 3

A New Home – Bristol and Somerset

Bristol was in the vanguard of railway establishment in the UK, with the first part of the Bristol and Gloucester Railway opening in 1844 – three years after the full opening of the Bristol to London GWR line. Meanwhile, the Bristol & Exeter Railway opened in 1844 too, meaning a rail journey from Newcastle to Exeter was possible by July of that year.

The Bristol area and Somerset was and is diverse in rail traffic, with both local and long-distance passenger trains running and GWR still operates the Night Rivera sleeper train. Aside from the evolution of the passenger business, a wide mix of freight traffics existed, especially as ports established themselves around Bristol and Avonmouth in the late 19th century; and a wide variety of freight traffics operated through the 20th century. This only reduced post-Second World War, commensurate with the development of the road network.

Rail freight traffics in the area in the past included cocoa beans, bananas, chemicals, timber, coal, lead ingots, fertiliser and oil (all through Avonmouth), wood pulp, coal, chemicals and cement (Portishead). General merchandise in the Bristol area ranged from beer to molasses, to Frys' chocolate. Across Somerset meanwhile, cider, aggregates in huge volumes, explosives, furniture and fertiliser were carried by rail within the author's living memory. Plus, over a longer-term, agricultural produce, house coal and cattle.

So, whilst rail passenger growth has occurred over the last 30 years, freight has reduced following the trend from the 1950s and simplified too, with the loss of mail traffic (2004), wagonload freight (1991) plus of course the loss of coal and chemicals in the past 20 years. That said, containers, aggregates, cement, steel, and some nuclear traffic are still regularly witnessed in 2025 in Bristol and Somerset, along with specialist traffics such as domestic waste (for use in a waste to light power station) china-clay and oil passing through the area.

Returning to the family linkage, post-Beeching report in 1963 the following principal lines closed to passenger traffic in and around North Somerset before the end of the 1960s:

- Yatton to Clevedon and to Frome via Cheddar and Wells
- Bristol to Portishead
- Bristol to Radstock via Pensford
- Bristol to Bath via Bitton 1966 and then via Mangotsfield to Westerleigh three years later

Burnham on Sea to Highbridge to Evercreech plus Chard and Yeovil area lines and Bath over the Mendips out of Somerset into Dorset

In the wake of these closures though, promotion took John to Bristol from Birmingham in

June 1969 and meant a house move for him, Wendy and the author. Yatton became the family home; with John smitten with the area after a trip from Yatton to Frome line, steam-hauled via the Cheddar Valley Line in 1962 and Wendy's aunts living on the line at Winscombe.

He worked on the Bristol re-signalling project in the operations function from 1969, with his work ranging from the production of special operating instructions for re-signalling through to the special train notices in connection with the works.

Subsequently he moved to the love of his life from 1972, the freight-by-rail business, and remained in that world until 1988 when he took voluntary redundancy. He rejoined BR a week later. to work in Yatton station ticket office. Meanwhile, Paul progressed through school and joined BR in September 1984 aged 16, working initially at Bristol Temple Meads, then heading to regional operations in Swindon on promotion in 1986 before returning to Bristol on promotion in 1989 as head of engineering planning.

He then headed to South Wales for five years in frontline operations management, via a three-year spell in Swindon leading on train accident investigation. His younger brother Mark meanwhile joined BR too, starting in 1986, working both at Weston-super-Mare and Bristol Temple Meads ticket offices; his rail career was only to extend to 1992, when he left and pursued other interests. After a 10-year period in railfreight, Paul returned to the Western Region in 2009; managing the passenger business for network rail and then moved into infrastructure projects in 2013; this included leading renewals work and enhancements as delivery director.

John from the 1970s, and then Paul from 1998, were heavily involved with the Mendips aggregates traffic, with both having the privilege of working with long-time family friend Alan Taylor who by 1993 had become managing director of Mendip Rail; a joint venture with, what was then, ARC and Foster Yeoman (now Hanson and Aggregate Industries respectively) to pool their locomotives and wagons to optimise operations. This traffic still runs in 2025; after the 'explosion' in rail-borne Somerset aggregates traffic in the early 1970s; see page 78 for Alan's recollections.

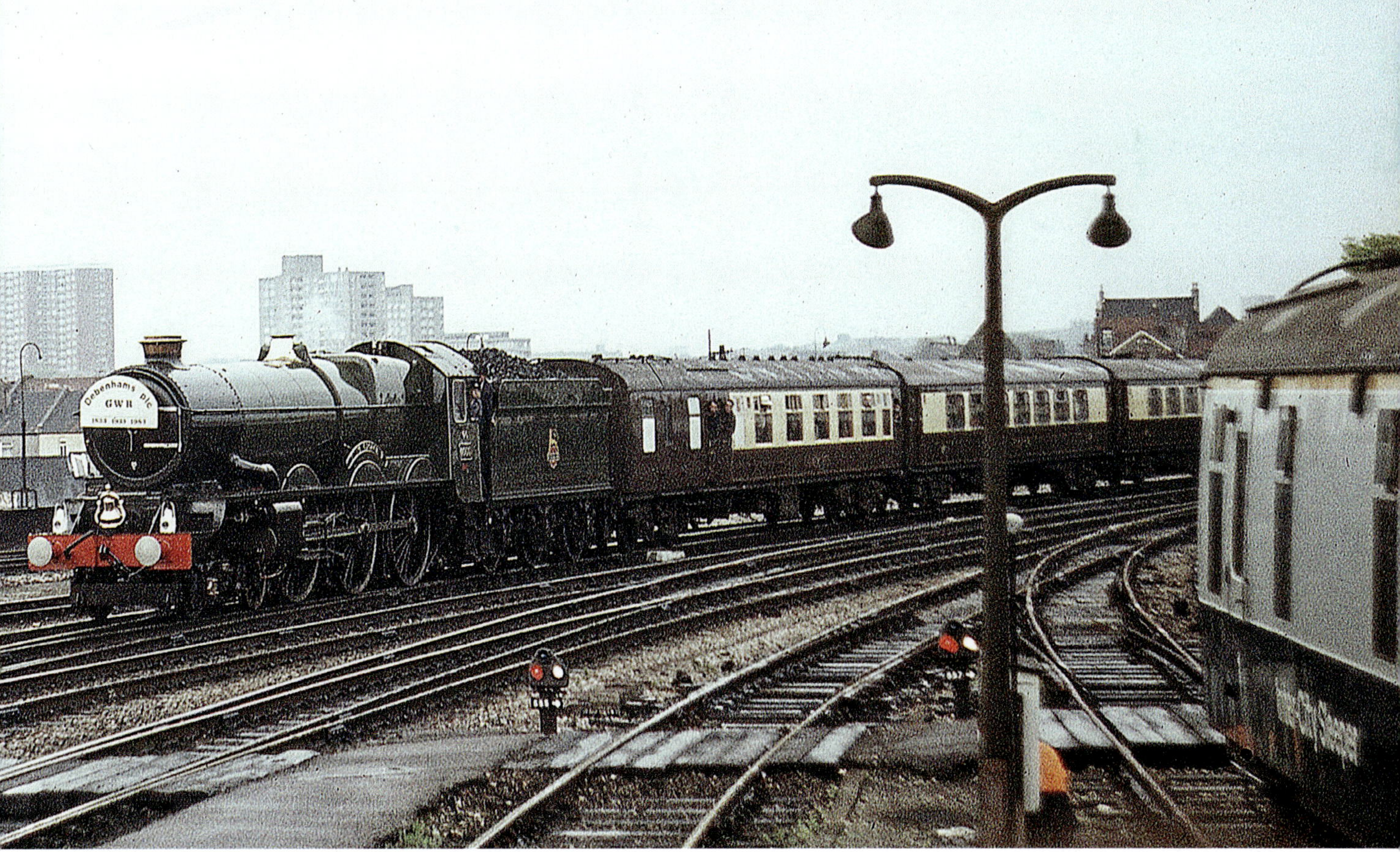

Bristol TM and teatime Saturday 11th June 1983 finds *King George V* hauling a Bath to Bristol TM private charter train. The next day it hauled the Brunel Pullman from Bristol to Hereford via Newport. It was the author's first main line steam trip. Note at right the Mark 1 sleeping car, soon to be displaced by new Mark III sleeping cars. *Photo by John Stanford*

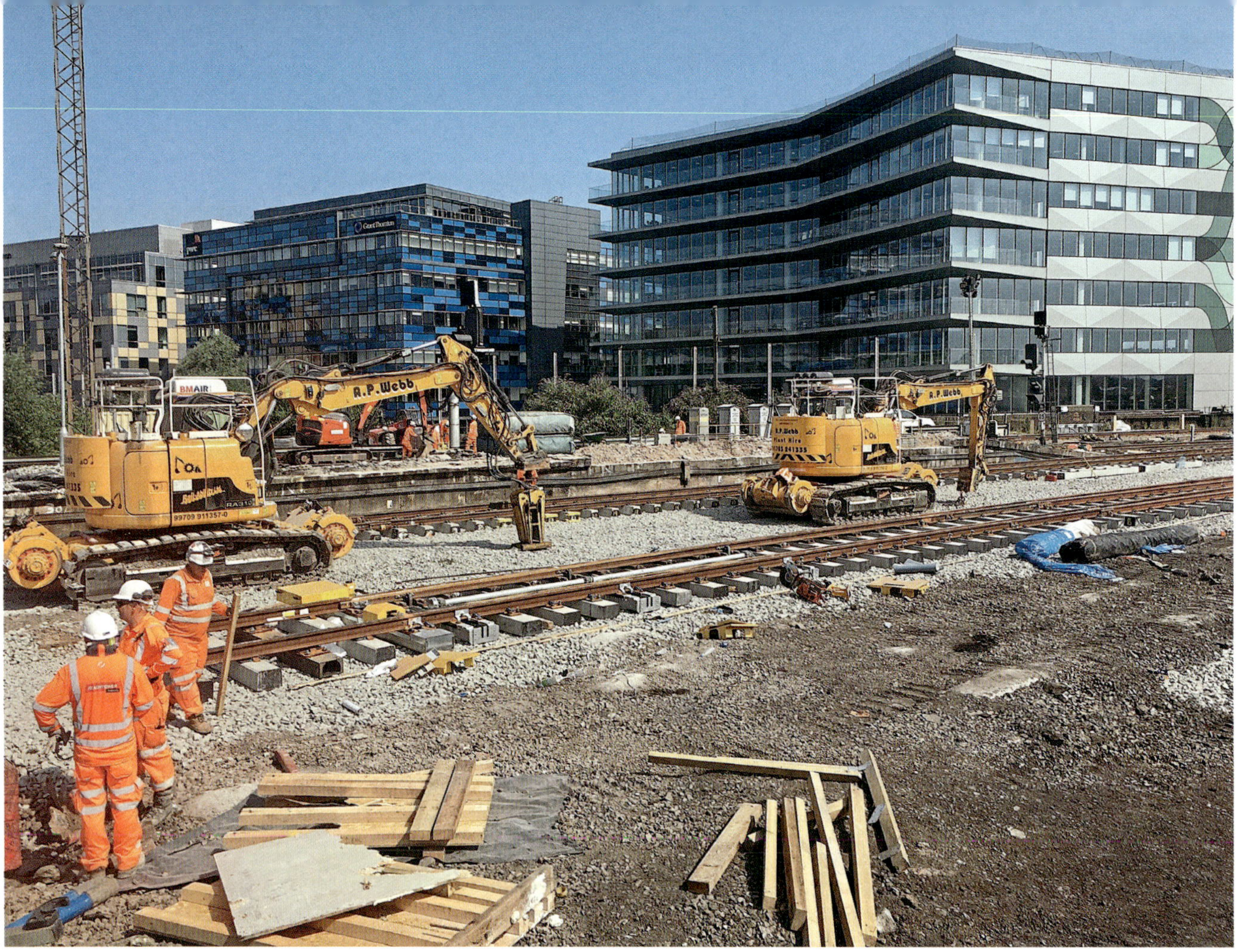

Bristol TM and the same location nearly 40 years later, at the tail end of the author's career as he goes for a walk-out on the Bristol East Junction rebuild project; this followed Bristol re-signalling of 2018. The change in the surrounding area is staggering – the signal at right is in John's shot in 1983 where the King Class loco was captured. The new buildings stand on the low-level rail yard for the Avonside Wharf branch.

Bristol Bath Road Depot adjacent to Temple Meads in 1985 with a real mix of motive power evident. Class 33s in shot would have been used on Portsmouth to Cardiff trains. *Photo by Trevor Riddle*

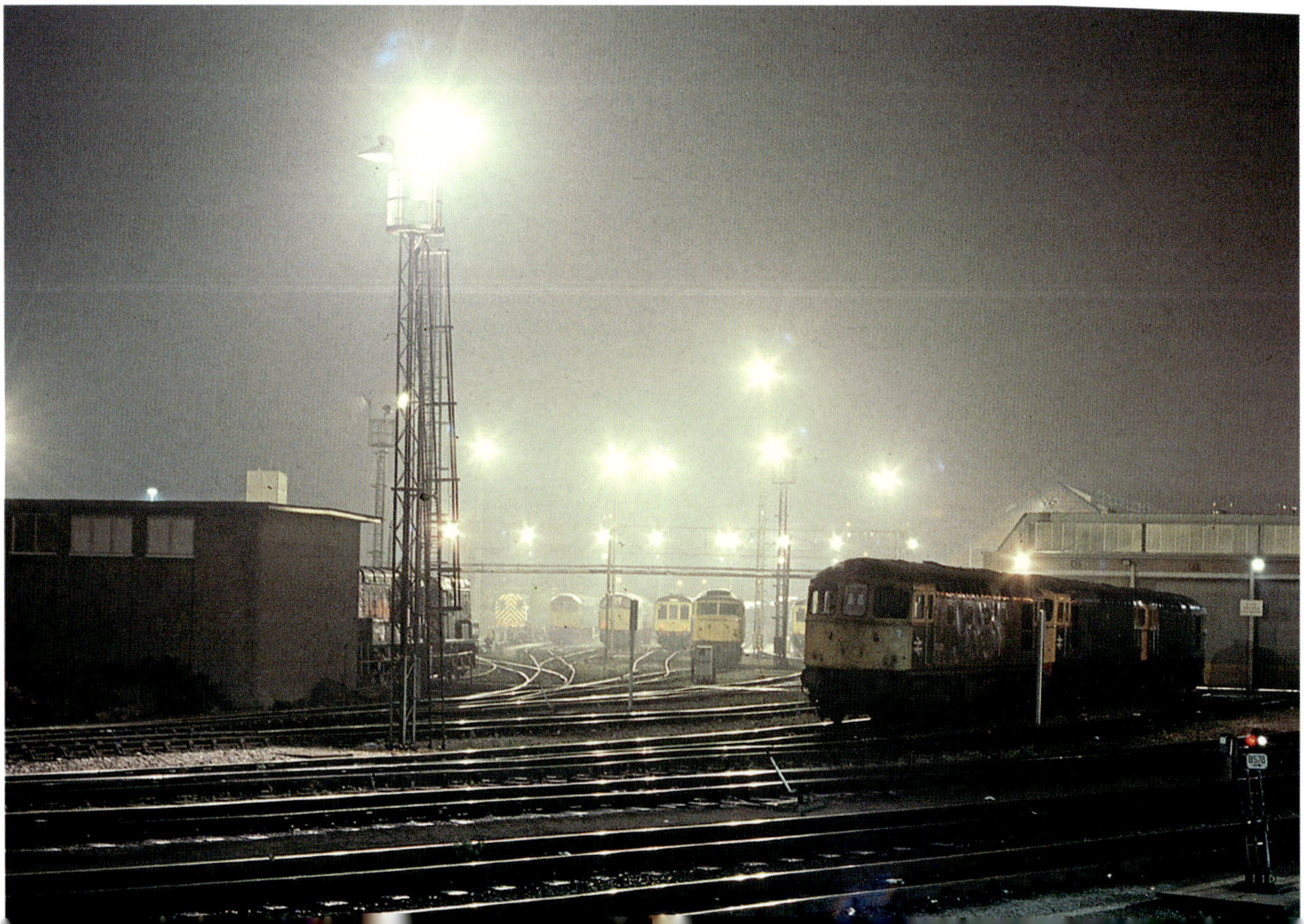

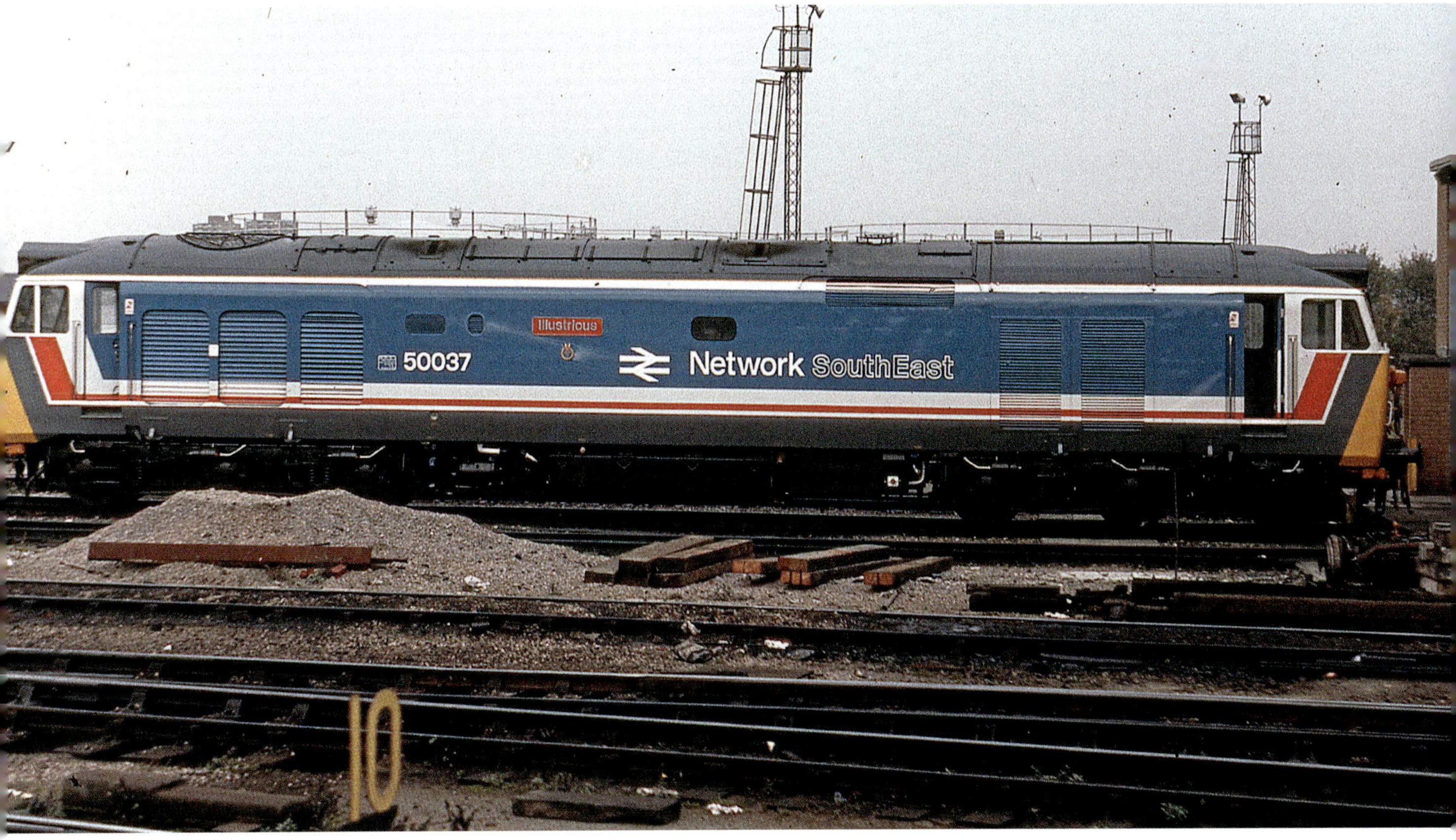

Bath Road and newly painted class 50 *Illustrious* is seen on 17th October 1986; after the author had successfully sat a Safe Working of Trains exam – a BR scheme aimed at helping upskill railway people.

Bristol Temple Meads 5051 *Drysllwyn Castle* and 4930 *Hagley Hall* readying on 7th July 1985 to work the Great Western Ltd to Plymouth. It would end disastrously – John and the author were on the doomed train which slipped to a stand on Dainton Bank.

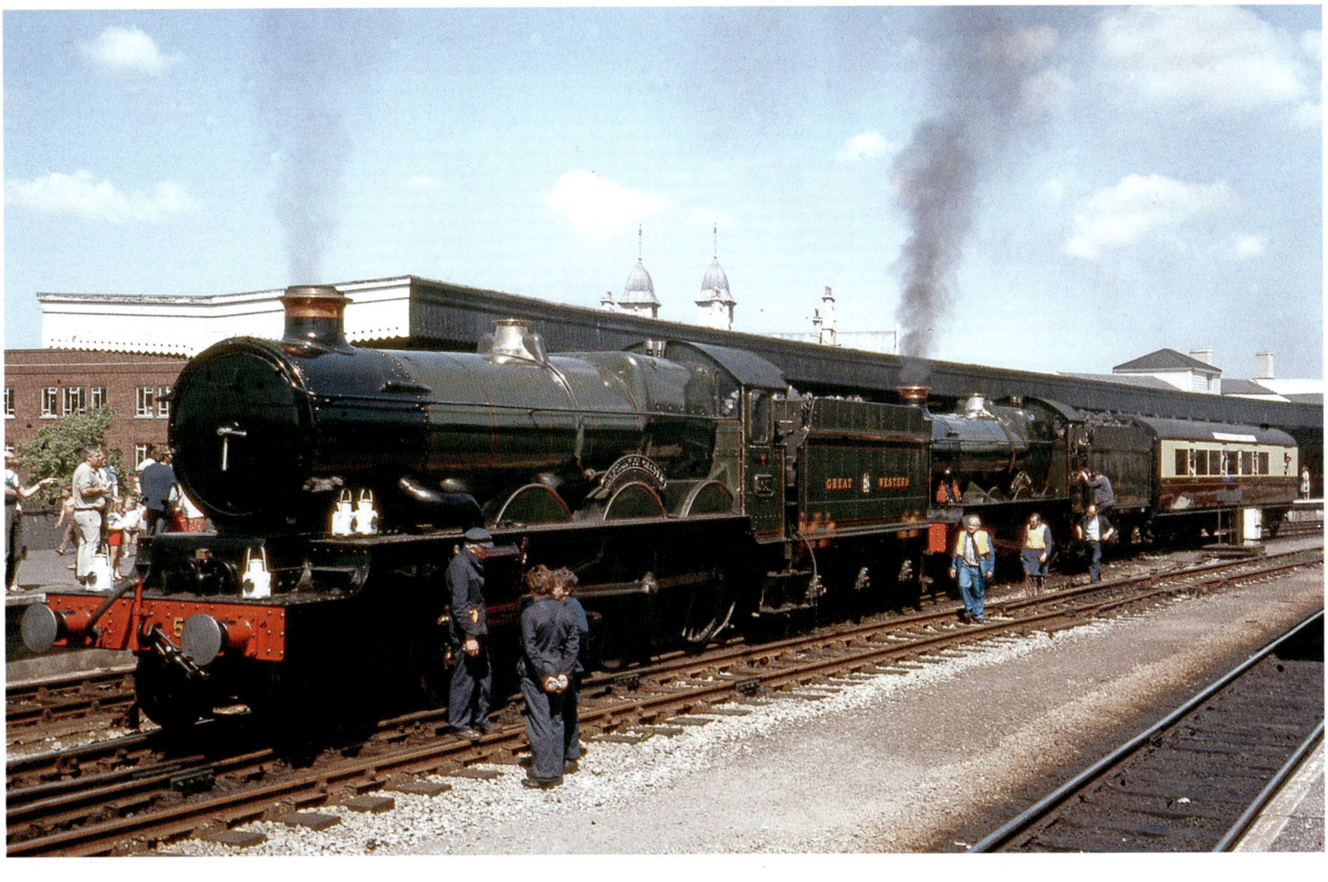

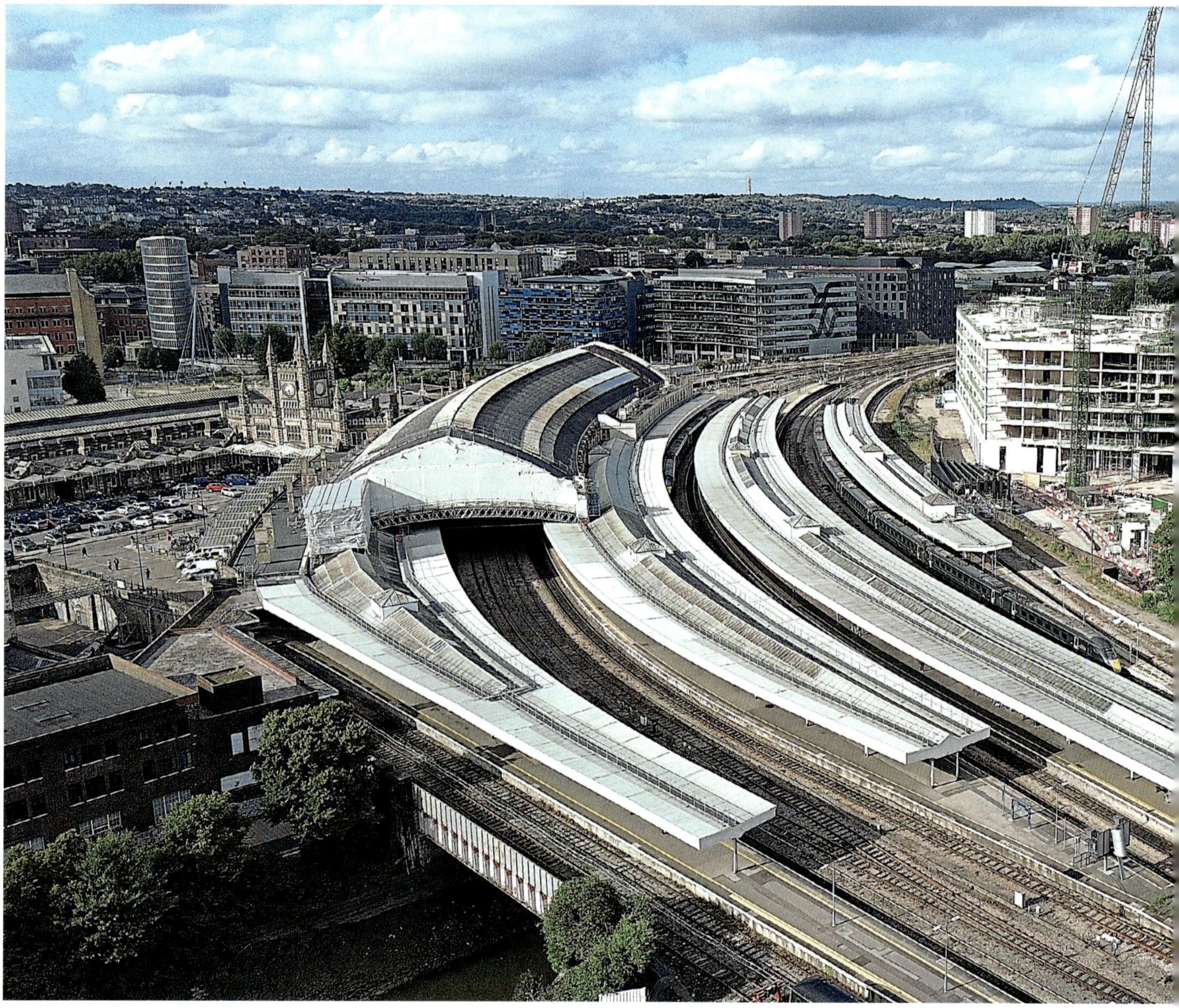

Above: Bristol Temple Meads from the air in September 2024, with the extensive roof work evident. Just out of shot right is B&E House where Paul and John worked. Both Paul and Mark worked in the ticket office by the main station entrance.

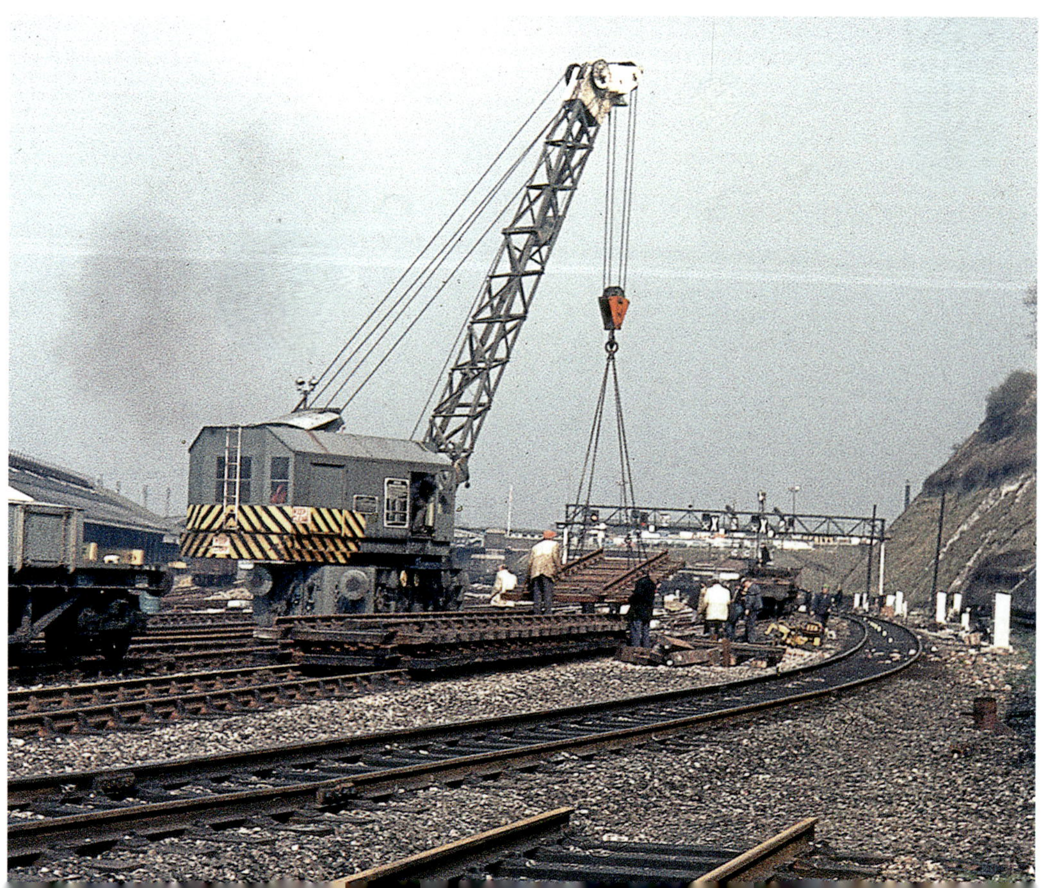

Right: Bristol West. The same week John's notice was in operation he went out on site to see the works and here a steam crane lifts track to reconfigure the layout.

Photo by John Stanford

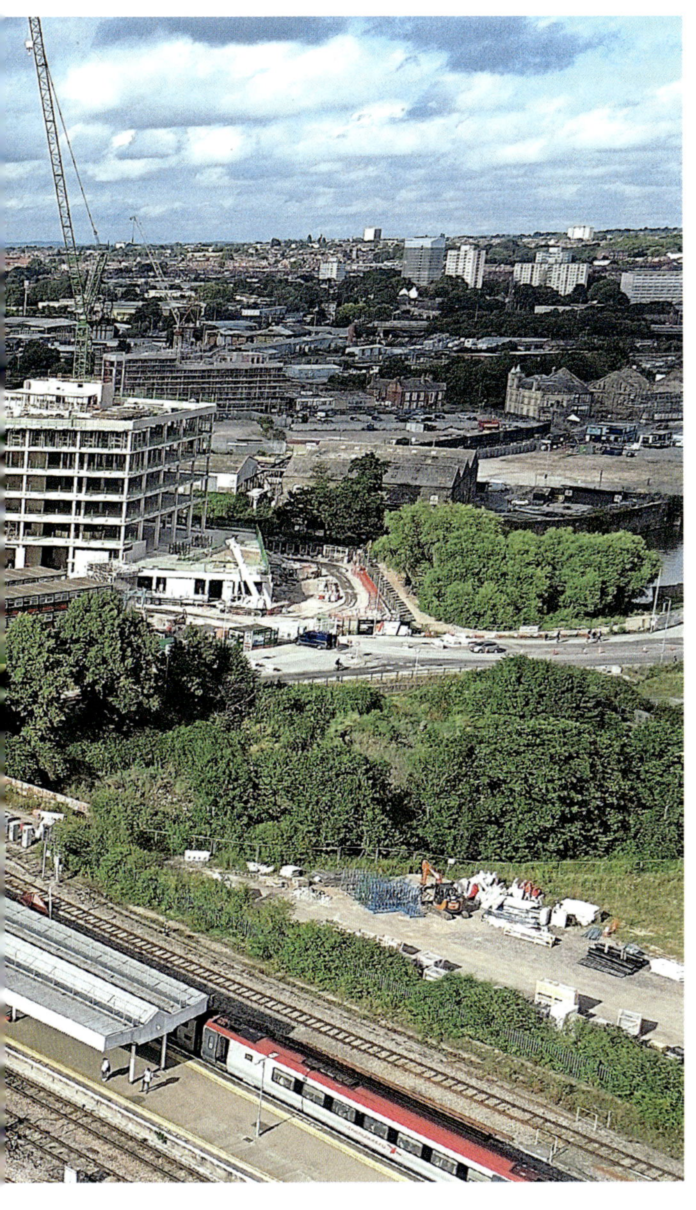

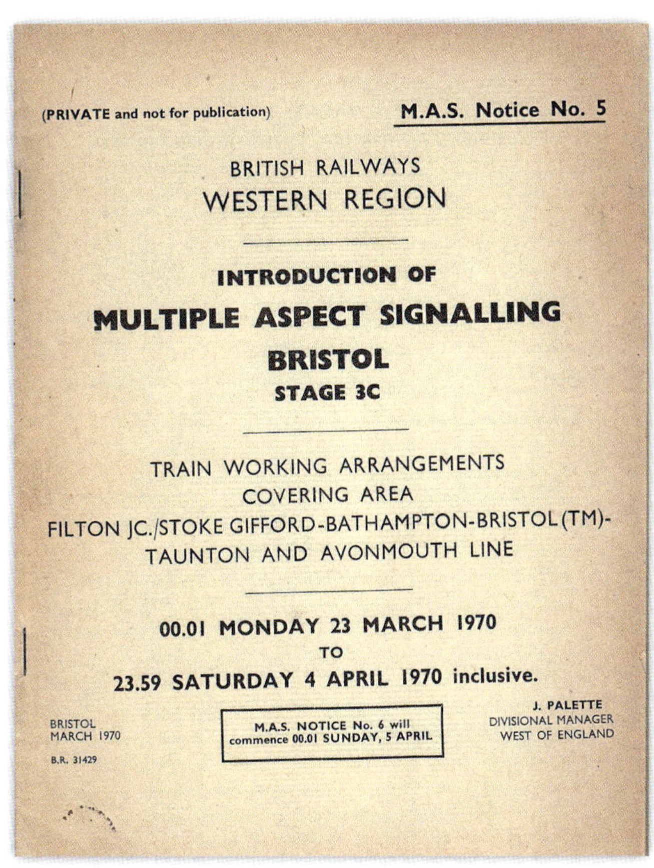

(PRIVATE and not for publication) **M.A.S. Notice No. 5**

BRITISH RAILWAYS
WESTERN REGION

INTRODUCTION OF
MULTIPLE ASPECT SIGNALLING
BRISTOL
STAGE 3C

TRAIN WORKING ARRANGEMENTS
COVERING AREA
FILTON JC./STOKE GIFFORD-BATHAMPTON-BRISTOL (TM)-
TAUNTON AND AVONMOUTH LINE

00.01 MONDAY 23 MARCH 1970
TO
23.59 SATURDAY 4 APRIL 1970 inclusive.

BRISTOL
MARCH 1970
B.R. 31429

M.A.S. NOTICE No. 6 will commence 00.01 SUNDAY, 5 APRIL

J. PALETTE
DIVISIONAL MANAGER
WEST OF ENGLAND

Above: Bristol West Signalling notice, produced by John in his first role upon promotion to Bristol in 1969.

Below: Ashton Junction in May 2001 as a class 66 locomotive pushes a ballast train over the newly relayed level crossing. Work was swift after the author concluded the works agreement with the Bristol Port Company in October the previous year. *Photo by Richard Giles*

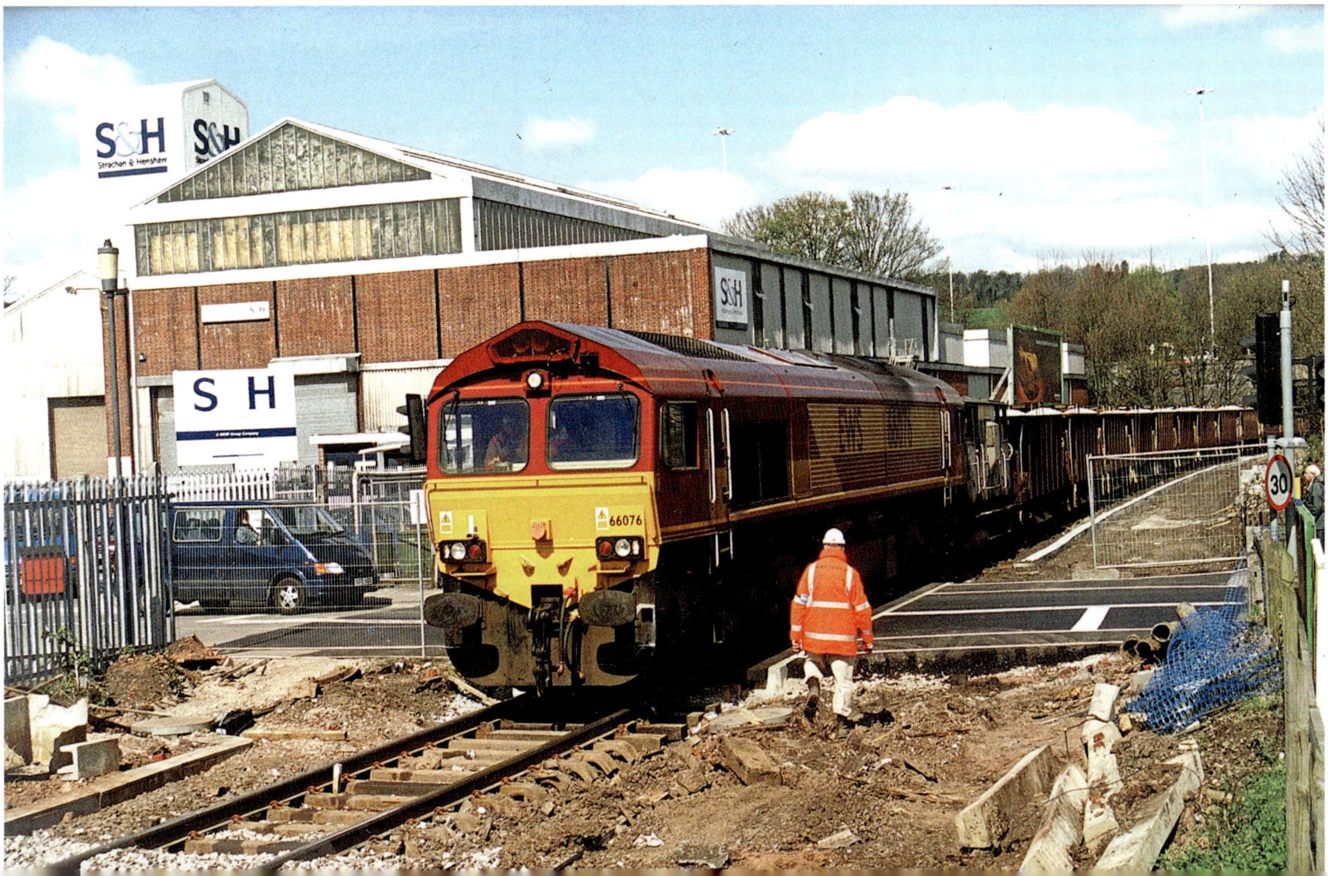

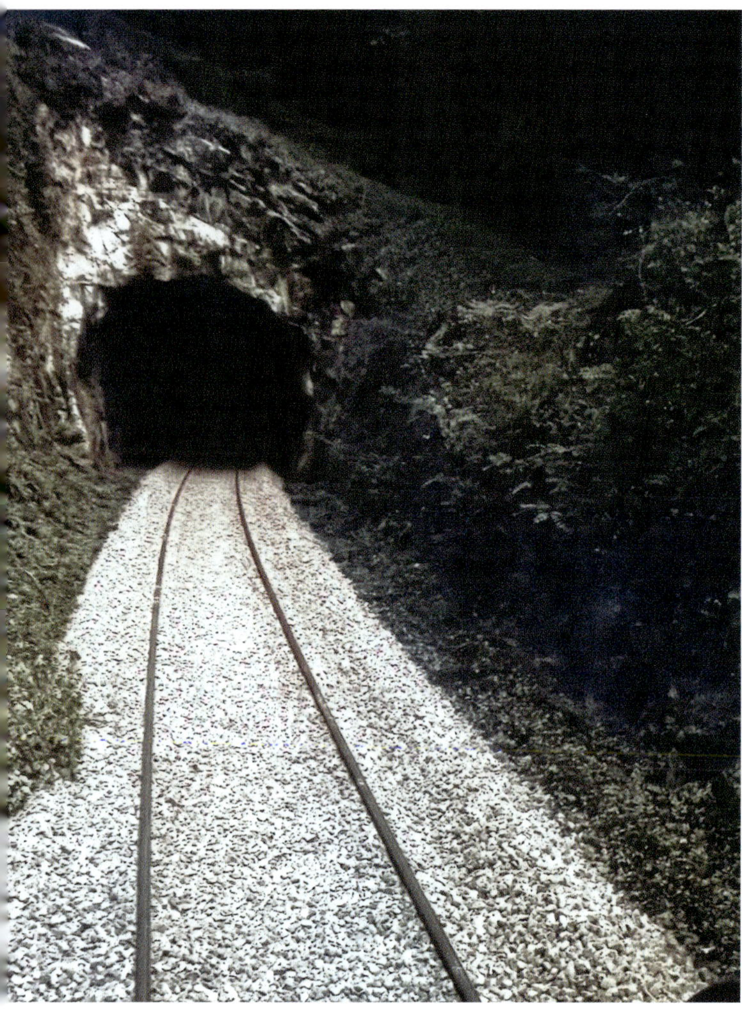

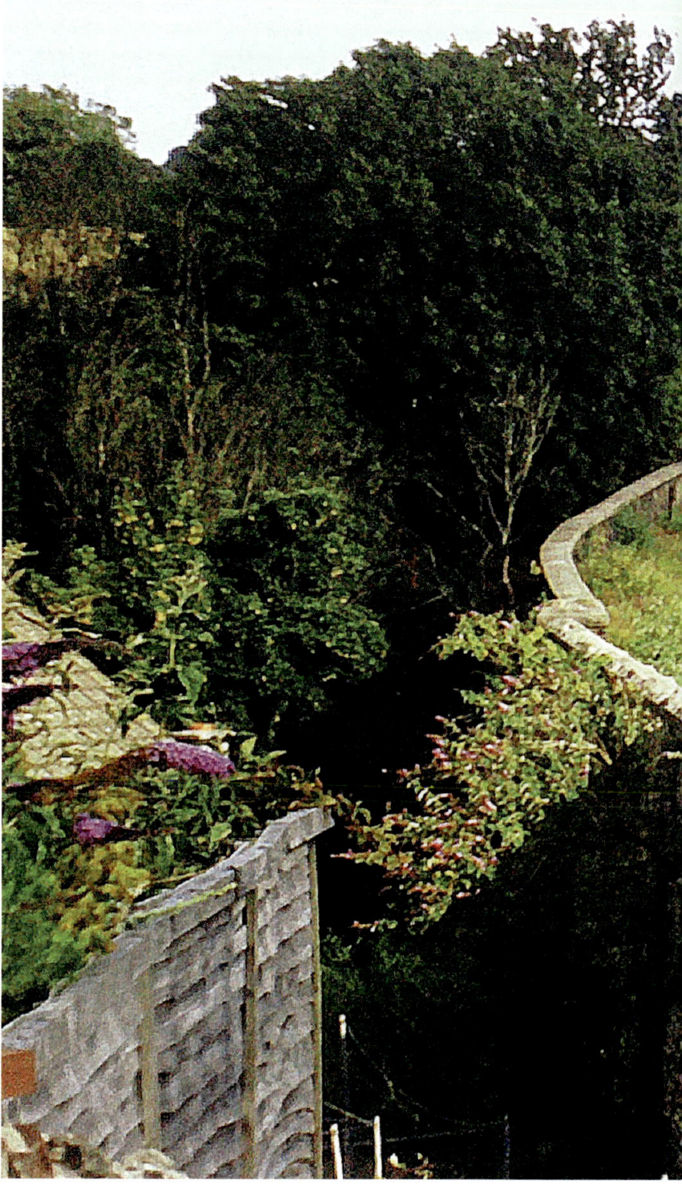

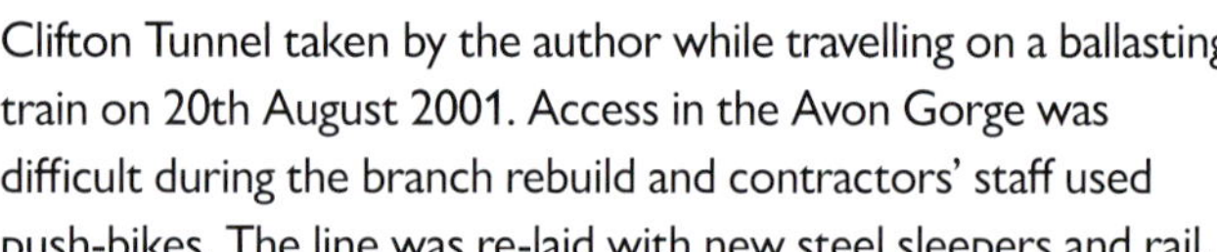

Clifton Tunnel taken by the author while travelling on a ballasting train on 20th August 2001. Access in the Avon Gorge was difficult during the branch rebuild and contractors' staff used push-bikes. The line was re-laid with new steel sleepers and rail.

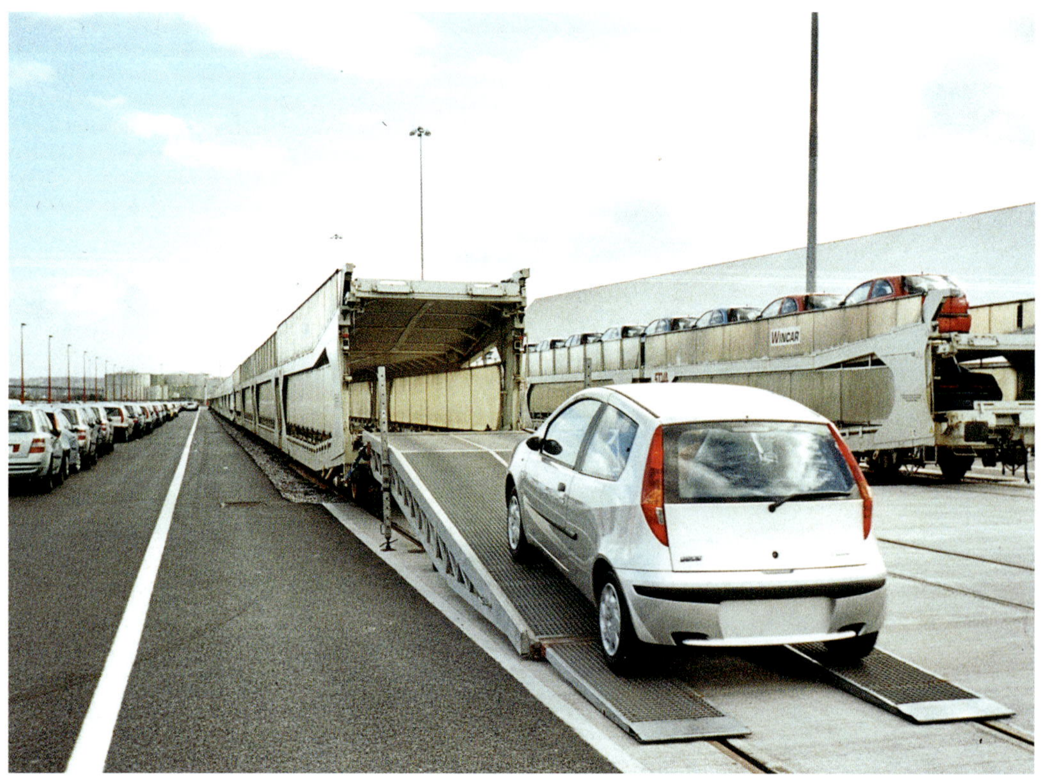

Portbury Dock in March 2002 as the first car train is loaded. Coal trains had started on 7th January 2002, after the branch rebuild. Now in 2025 the line is seeing use for import steel. Since reopening it has seen stone, gypsum and container trains. Hopefully passenger trains may return soon.

Photo Paul Stanford Collection

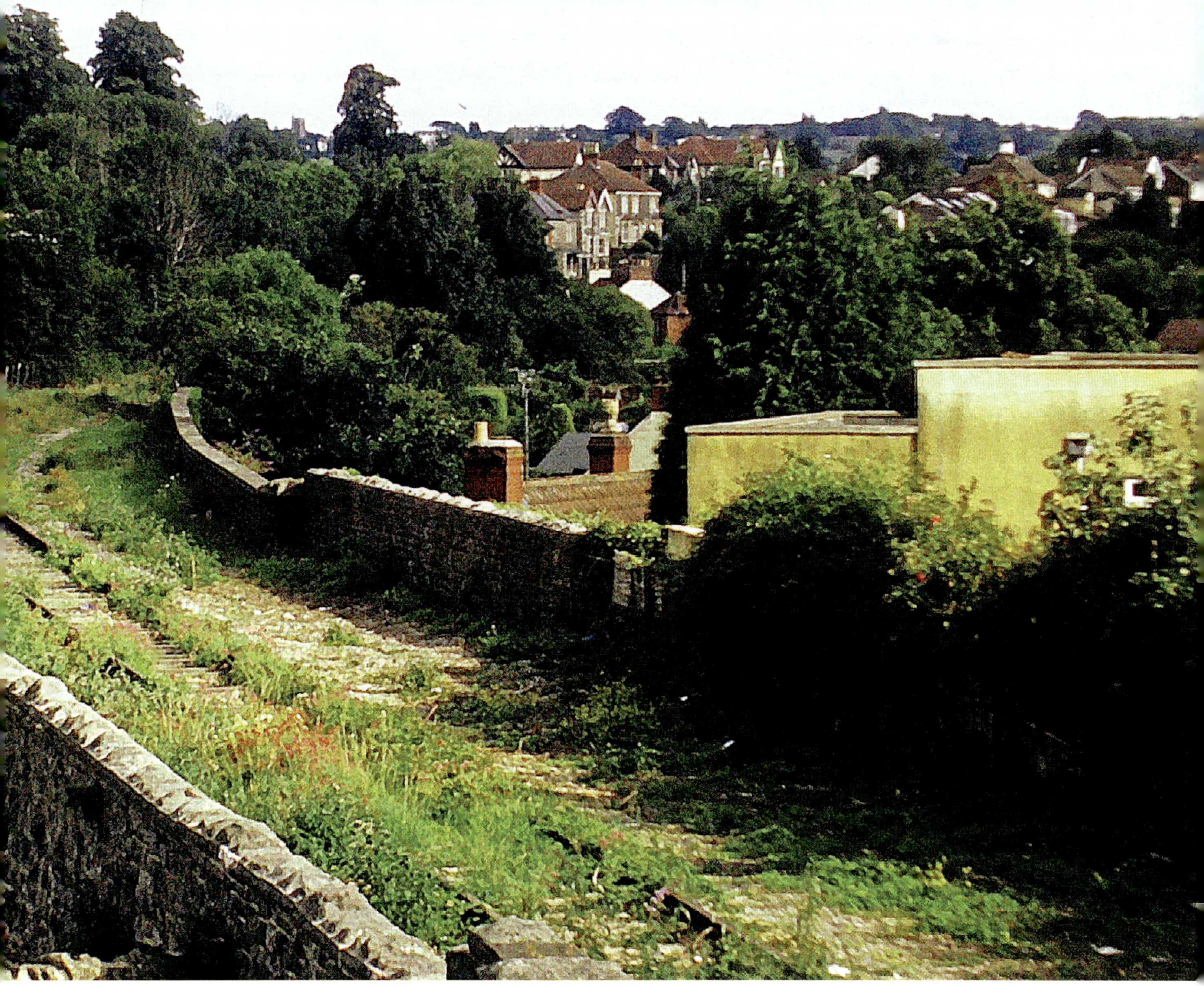

Pill viaduct in July 2001 with soon-to-be-replaced track in view. Track renewals had completed by October 2001, with final track replacement around Parson Street in November 2001, allowing driver training to commence in early December. The author, as regional freight manager, led the work to reopen the branch – one of his career highlights.

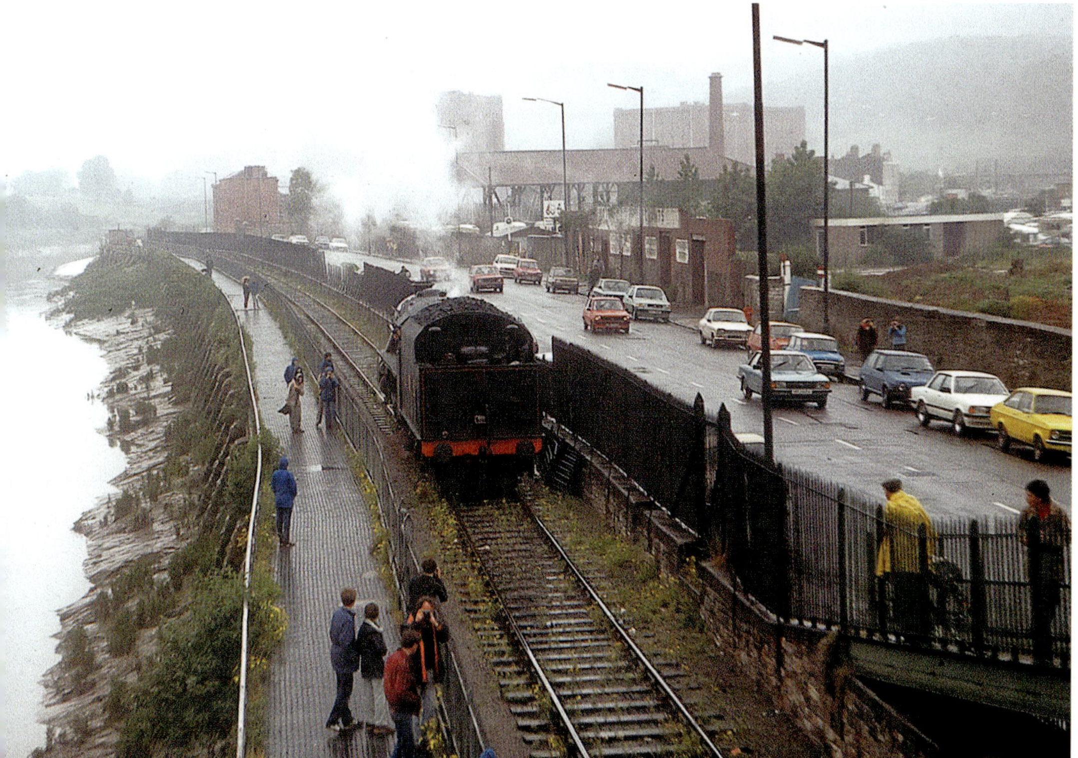

Wapping Branch on 11th June 1983 hosted a passenger train, from the quayside to Bristol Temple Meads hauled by LMS Black 5, No.5000; here is the associated light engine movement. The author and John travelled behind the same the next day hauling The Brunel Pullman from Hereford to Worcester.

Photo by John Stanford

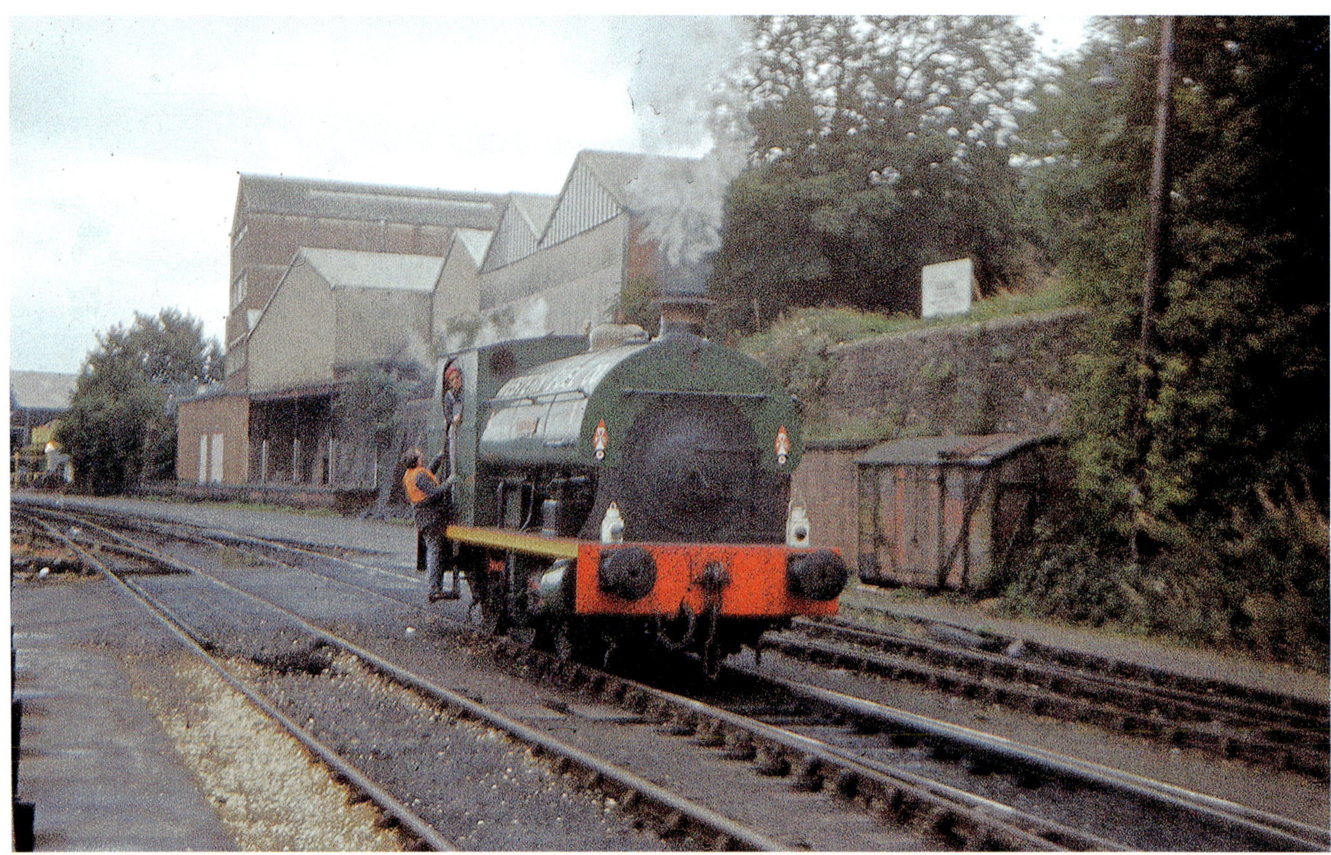

Wapping Wharf locomotive *Henbury* built by Peckett of Bristol shunting in October 1981, working real freight traffic after the depot diesel loco had failed. The area behind the loco has changed beyond recognition now. Coal traffic ceased here in May 1987.

Photo by John Stanford

Wapping Wharf and 0-6-0 diesel loco *Western Pride* is shunting wagons of house coal for unloading on 9th July 1985 when the author had a day off. Scarcely conceivable now that such industrial activity could take place in the centre of the city. St Mary Redcliffe church dominates in the background. Both locomotives, *Henbury* and *Western Pride*, had long careers with the Port of Bristol Authority at Avonmouth Docks.

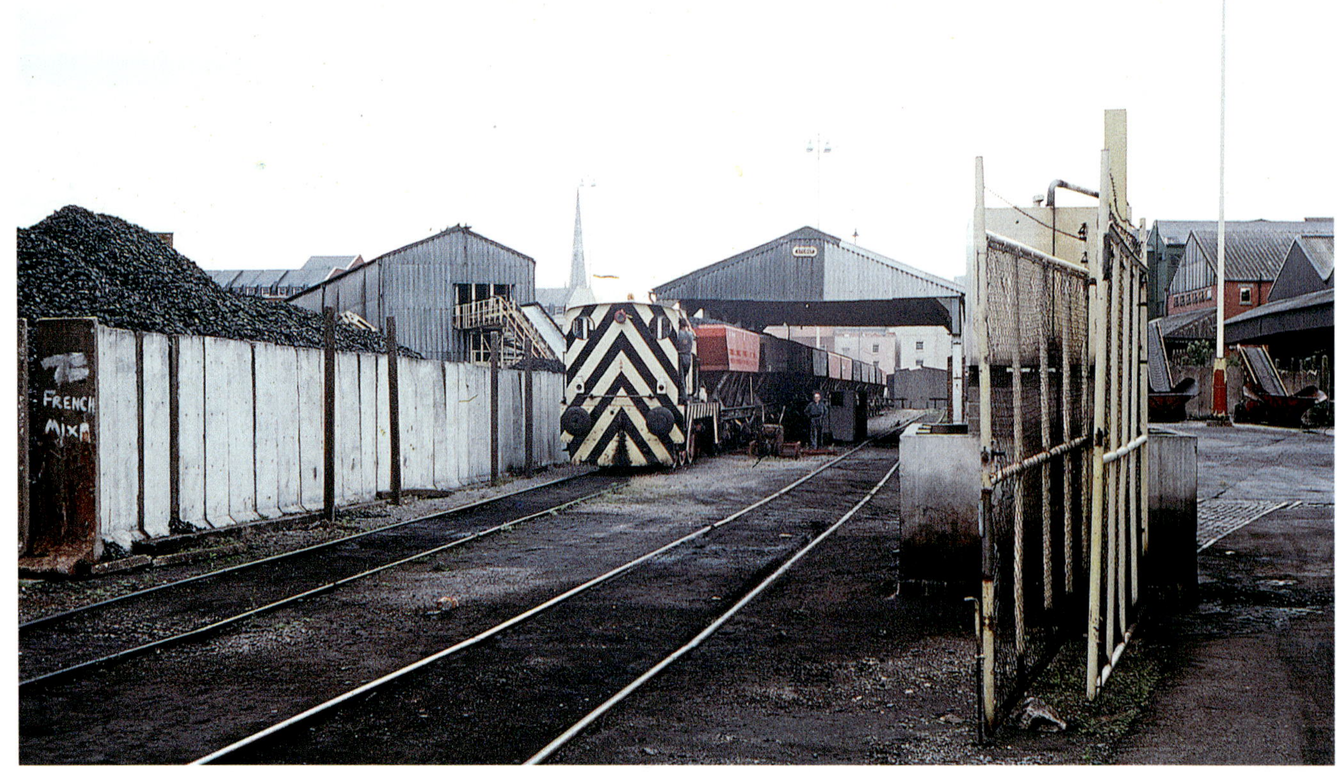

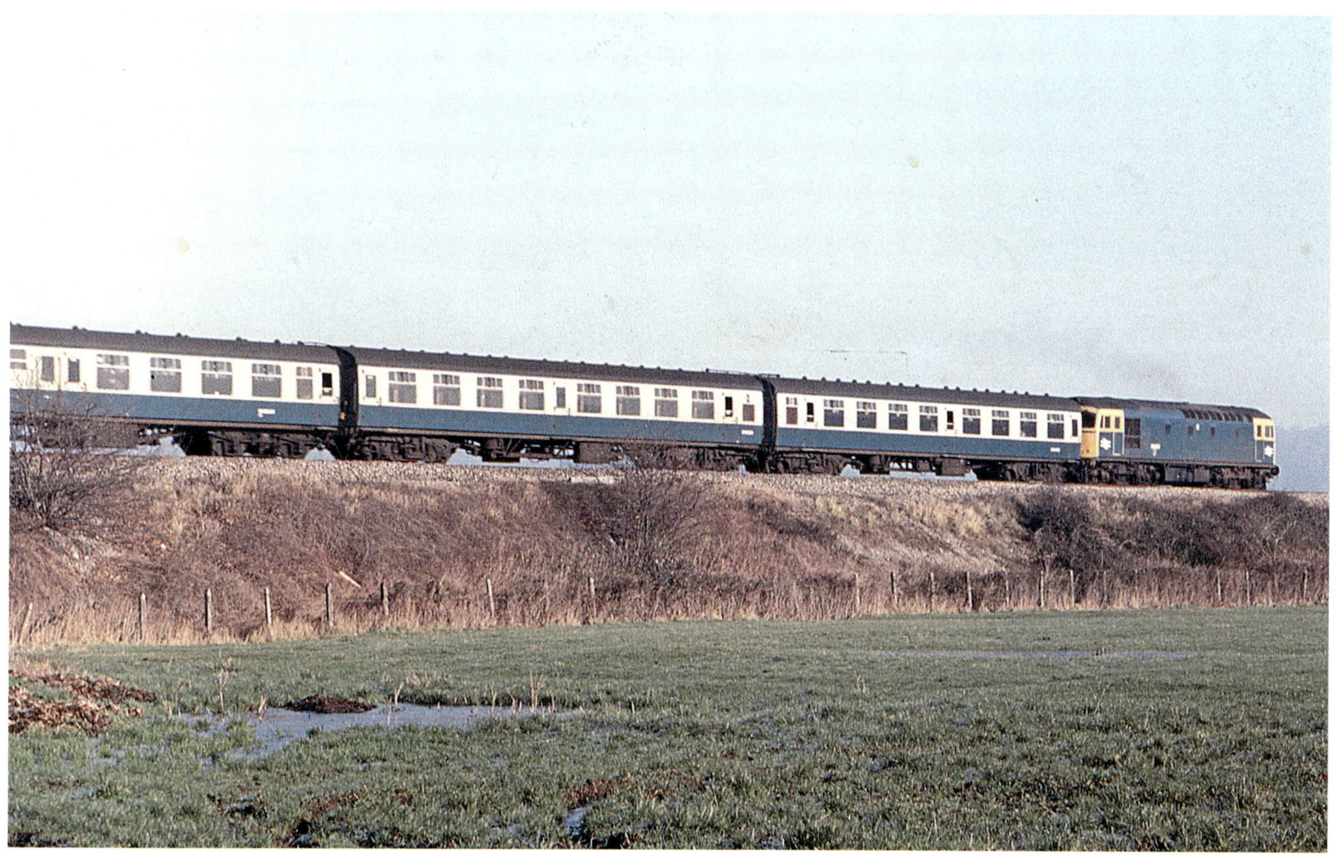

Nailsea on a cold winter's morning on 3rd January 1987 and 33062 gets its train underway for Bristol. Just over a year later Sprinter trains displaced loco and coach trains.

John's first visit to Yatton was in summer 1962 to travel the Cheddar Valley. Here, taken the same summer by John's long-time friend George Jenks, a GWR Hall is seen on a down passenger train arriving at the station. All of John's 1962 Somerset shots were lost in a camera accident, changing a roll of film in Edinburgh.

Photo by George Jenks, with special thanks to the Jenks family.

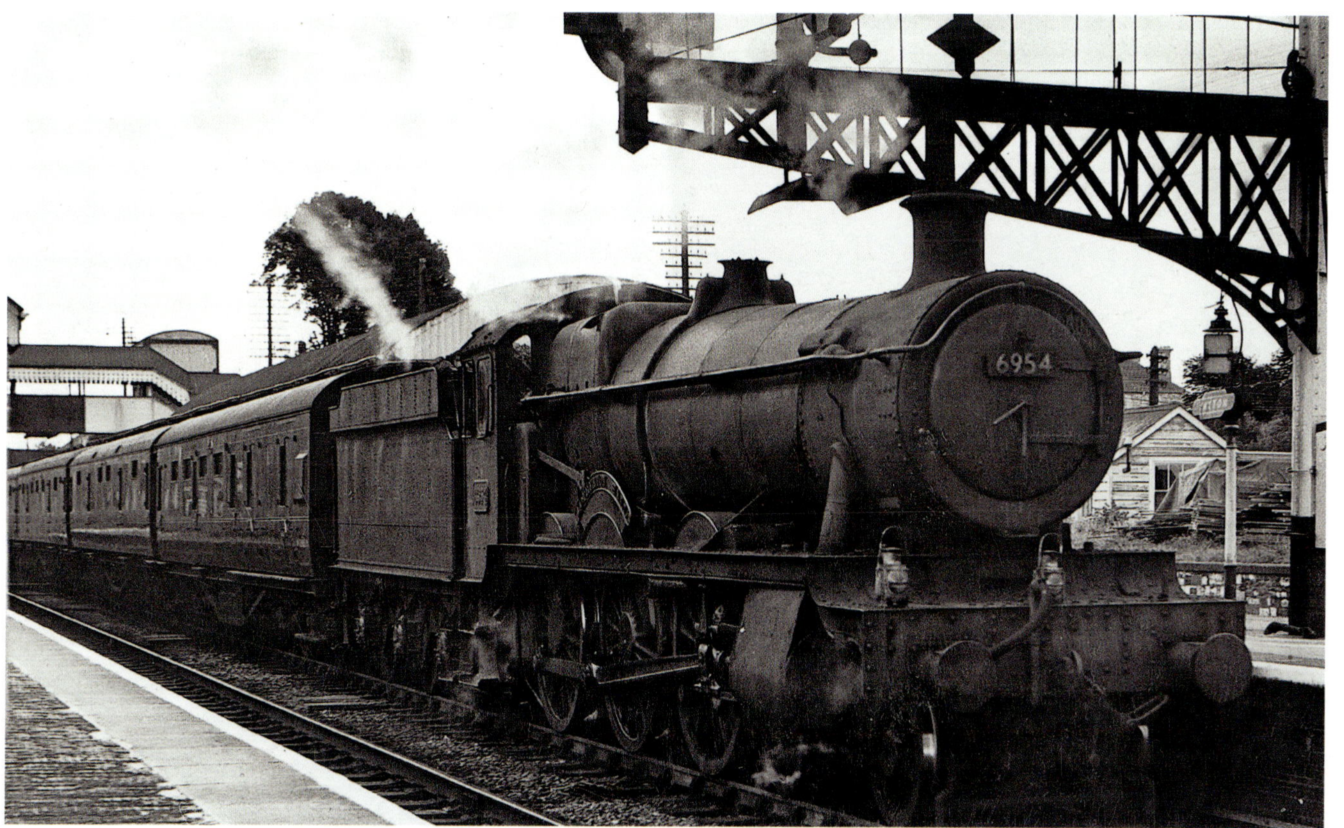

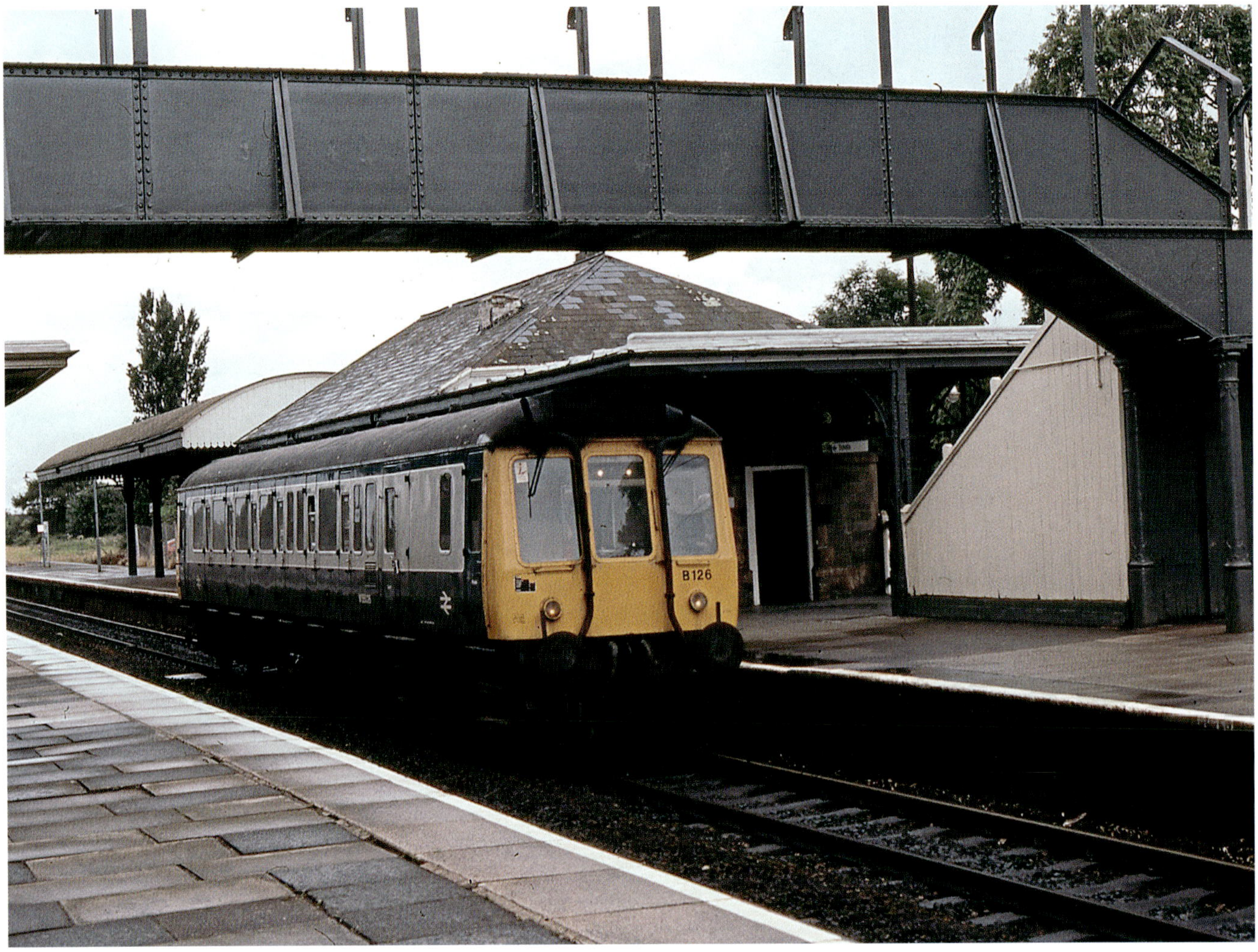

Yatton in August 1986 when the author worked in Locomotive Resources and John worked in the freight office at Swindon. Just over two years later the attractive building in this view became John's workplace. *Photo by Trevor Riddle*

Yatton. The Clevedon branch passenger services ceased in 1966 and John captured this view at Yatton that year when he visited the area. In the distance is the pretty Yatton Church were John and Wendy were buried in 1994 and 2011 respectively. Dominant is the Bristol & Exeter Railway Signal Box, closed in 1972 and then demolished. *Photo by John Stanford*

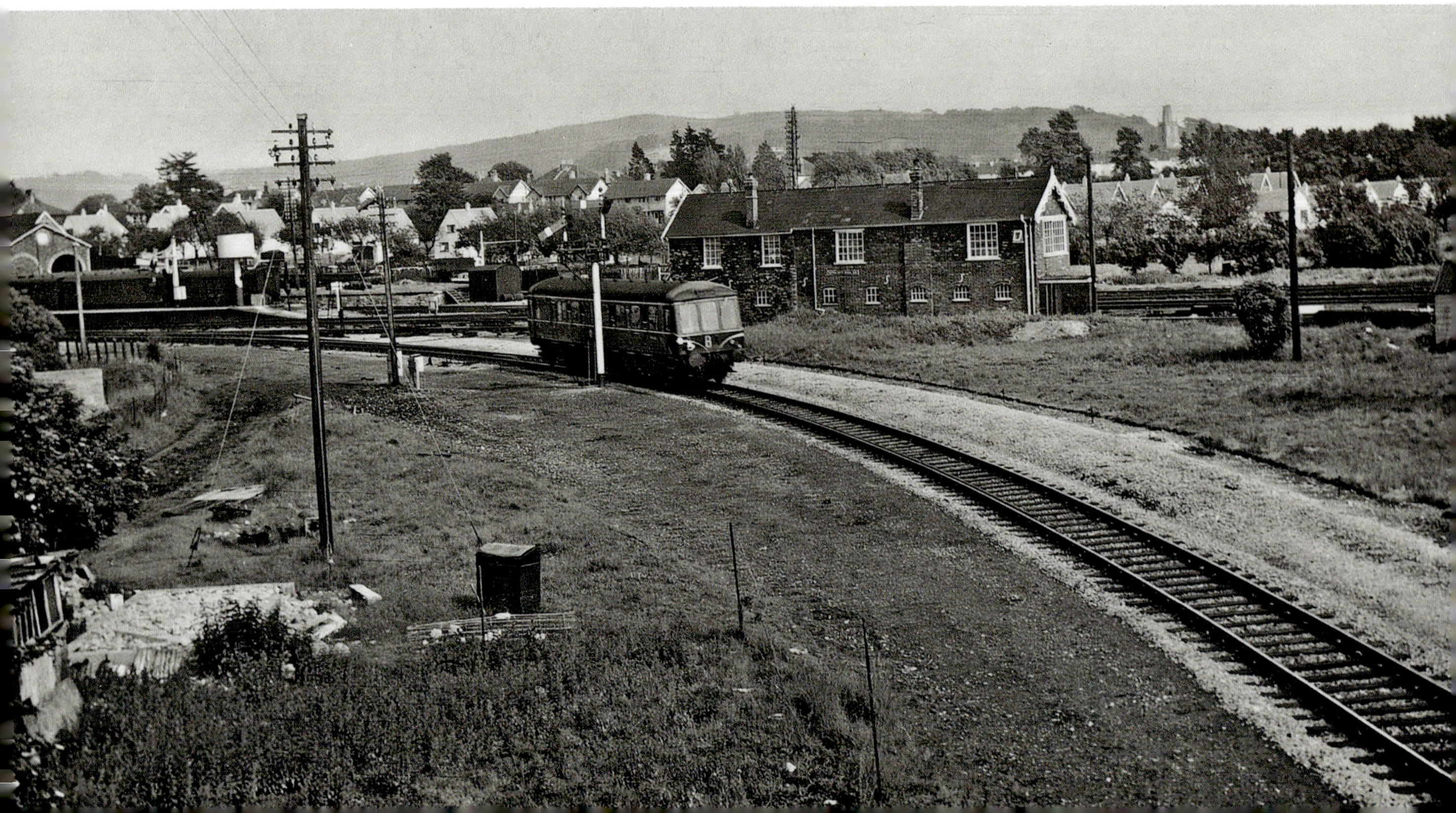

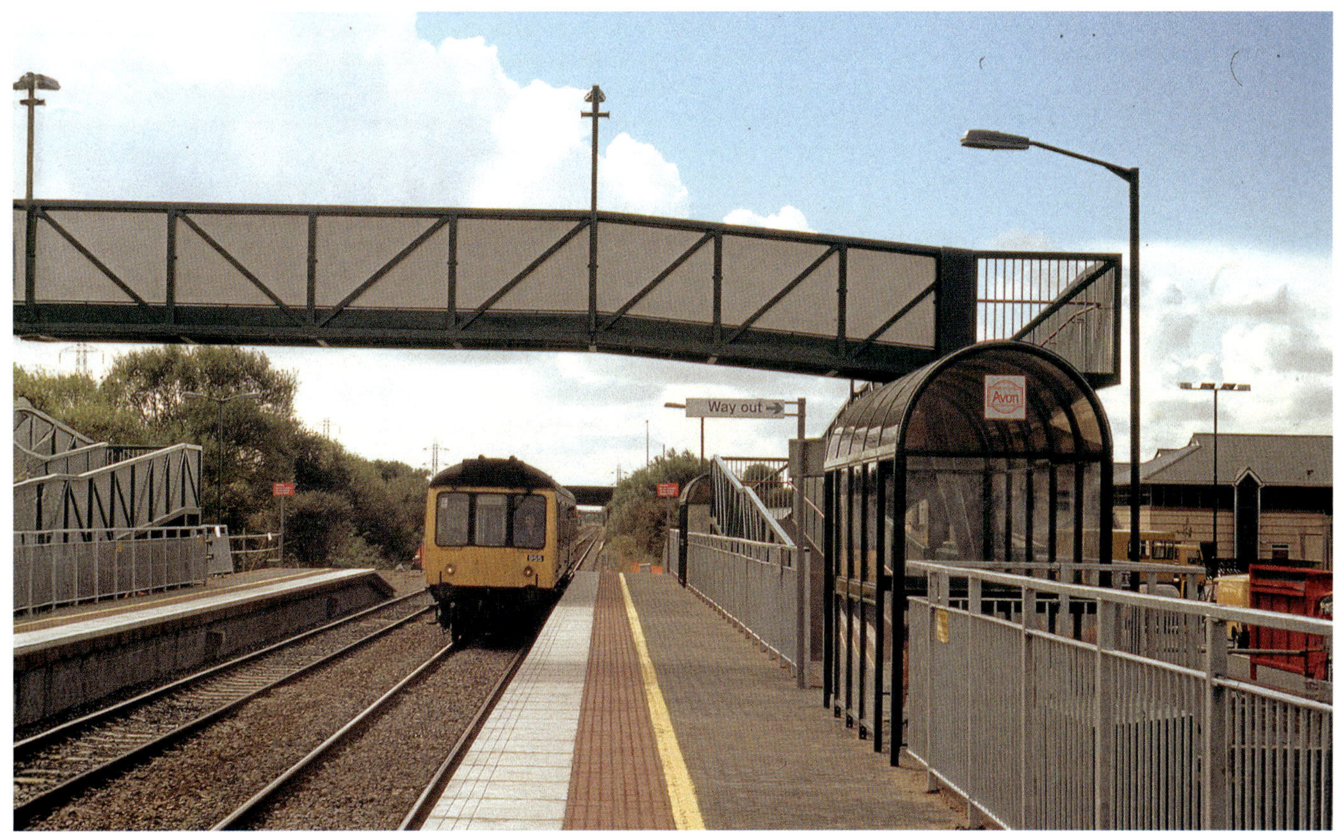

Above: Worle on 17th June 1991. The author commuted from here to Cardiff from 1996 when he was operations manager South East Wales & Marches for three years. On one occasion he had to implement Single Line Working on his way to work from Worle, because track relaying works went awry; borrowing a guard's red flag in lieu of a pilotman armband to wear, to get trains operating in both directions on one line – permitted by the rule book. *Photo by John Stanford*

Below left: Weston-super-Mare and Mark Stanford on the line. When he took up the role of train information clerk in 1987, BR did a press release, and the *Weston Mercury* newspaper ran a feature with a picture; here Mark replete with BR issue white shirt and tie (dark blue with small red BR logos) obliges for the camera. *Photo with special thanks to* Weston Mercury

Below right: Bleadon and Uphill Station had closed in 1964 and the Yieldingtree Railway Museum was established. Here it is 13th May 1967 and Wendy sits in front of former Cardiff Railway Kitson built saddle tank 1338 which had been a long-time pilot loco at Bridgwater Docks and now preserved at Didcot. *Photo by John Stanford*

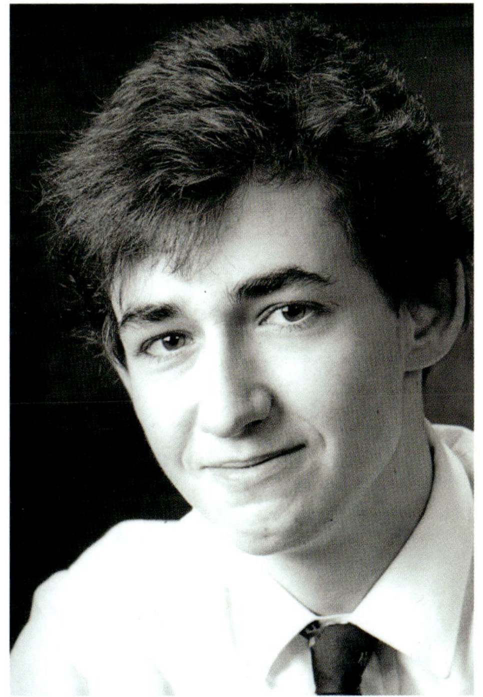

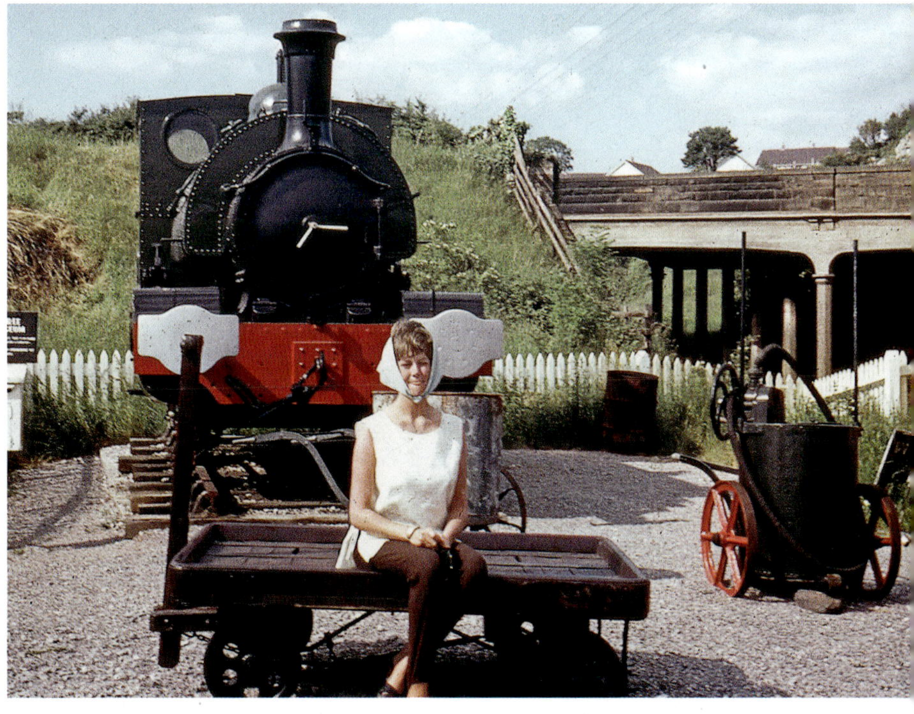

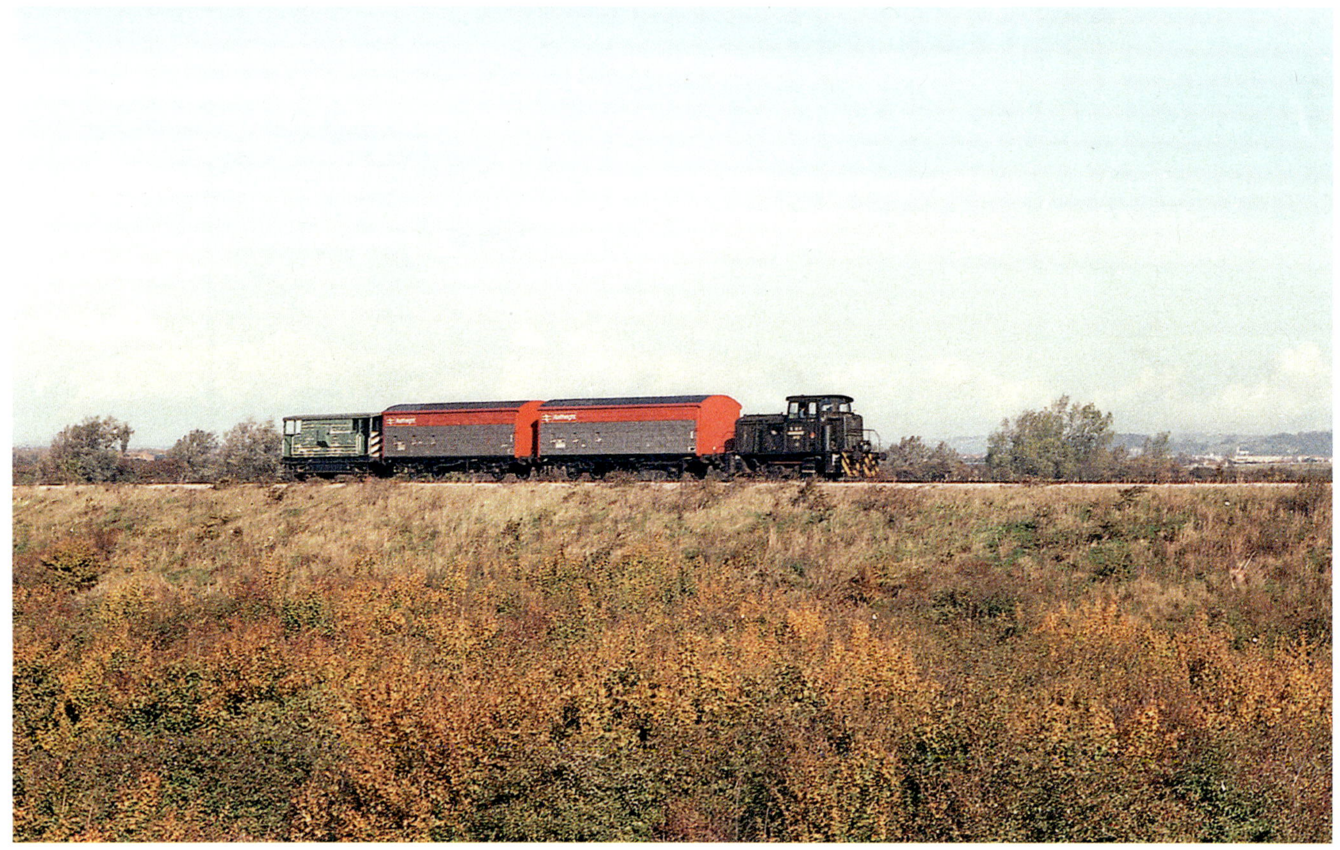

Puriton, 11 miles south of the previous location, and a Barclay 0-4-0 loco crosses the M5 motorway with the daily Royal Ordnance factory train on 22nd October 1987. In 2023 exciting plans were announced to redevelop the old munitions factory site for a car battery production plant with the rail link reinstated. Site works are now ongoing.

Bridgwater Cellophane works saw the first oil train for the works power plant on 15th March 1988. This was the penultimate rail-freight flow John established, working with his Railfreight Petroleum colleague Tony Lovell, before taking took voluntary redundancy. He tipped off Paul about the start of the new freight traffic. No.1 in the pop charts that week was I Should Be So Lucky by Kylie Minogue.

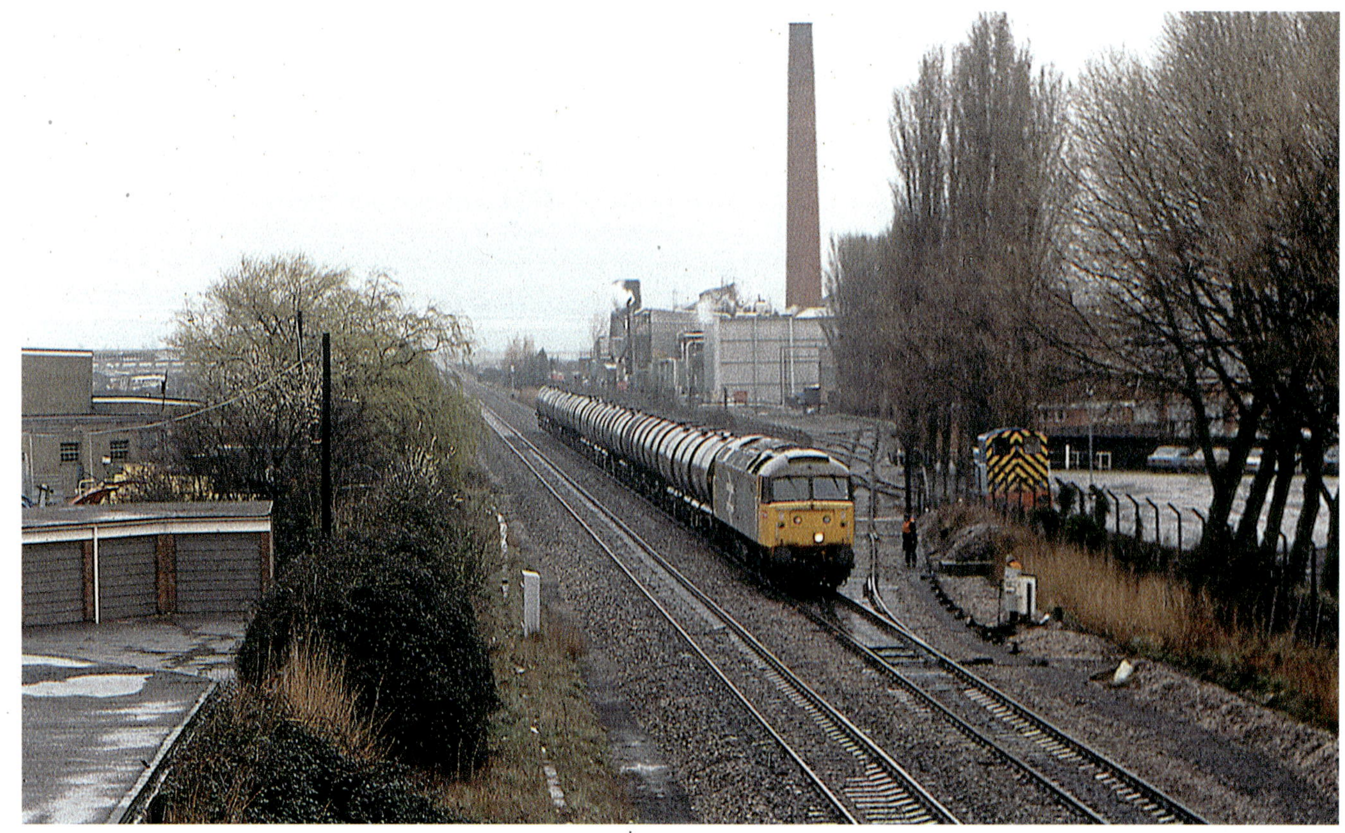

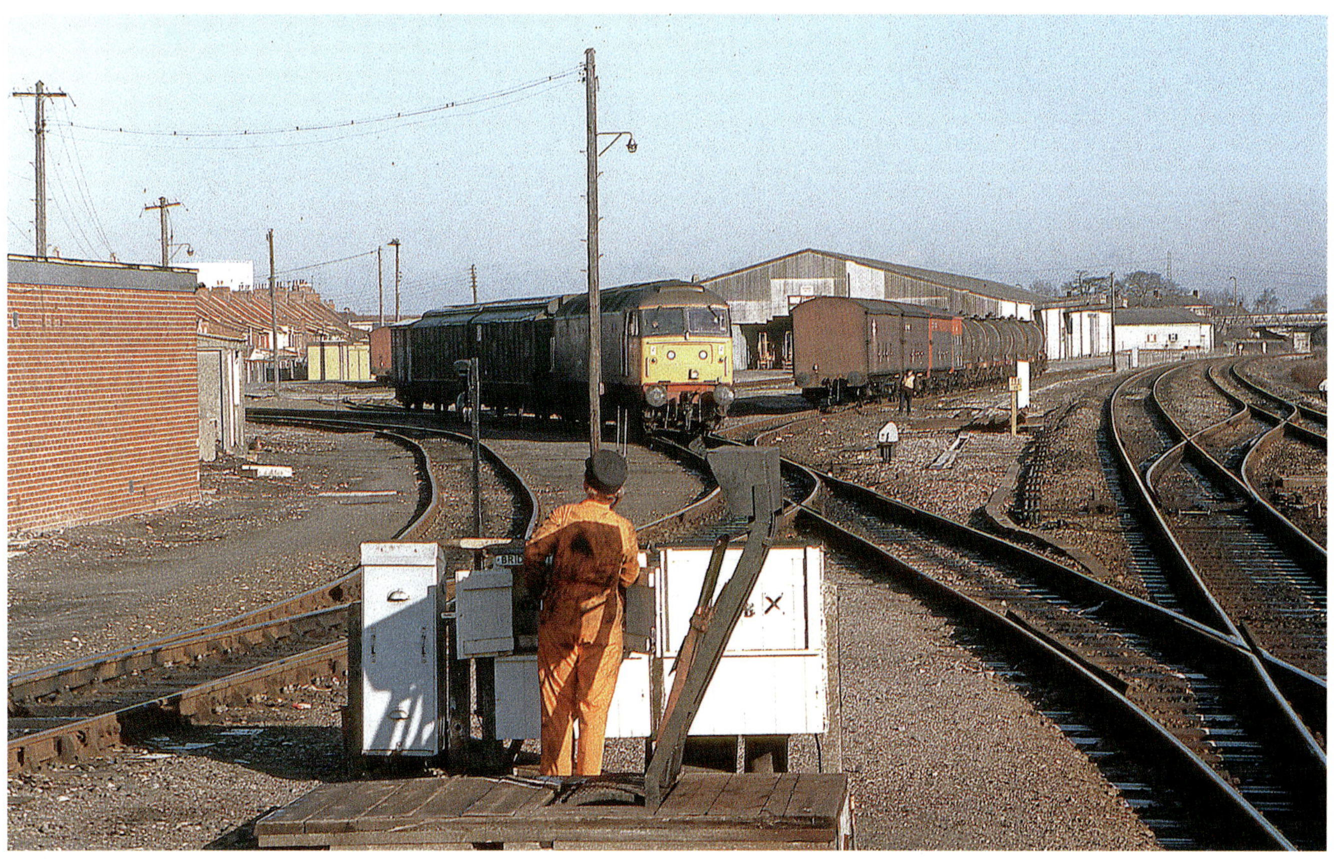

Bridgwater on the morning of Friday 20th February 1987 and Chris the Chargeman Shunter speaks to Bristol signal box to send the class 47 on its way to Taunton cider with box wagons of Spanish oranges. With a girlfriend in the town, meant visiting her gave the author an opportunity to observe activity in the freight yard, driving his love of the rail-freight business, although he never declared that to her – as maybe a little 'uncool' for a 19-year-old to admit!

Bridgwater on 22nd October 1987 and the author caught 31223 on a train ballasting the sidings. In view are cargo vans and VDA box vans for the regular Babycham traffic.

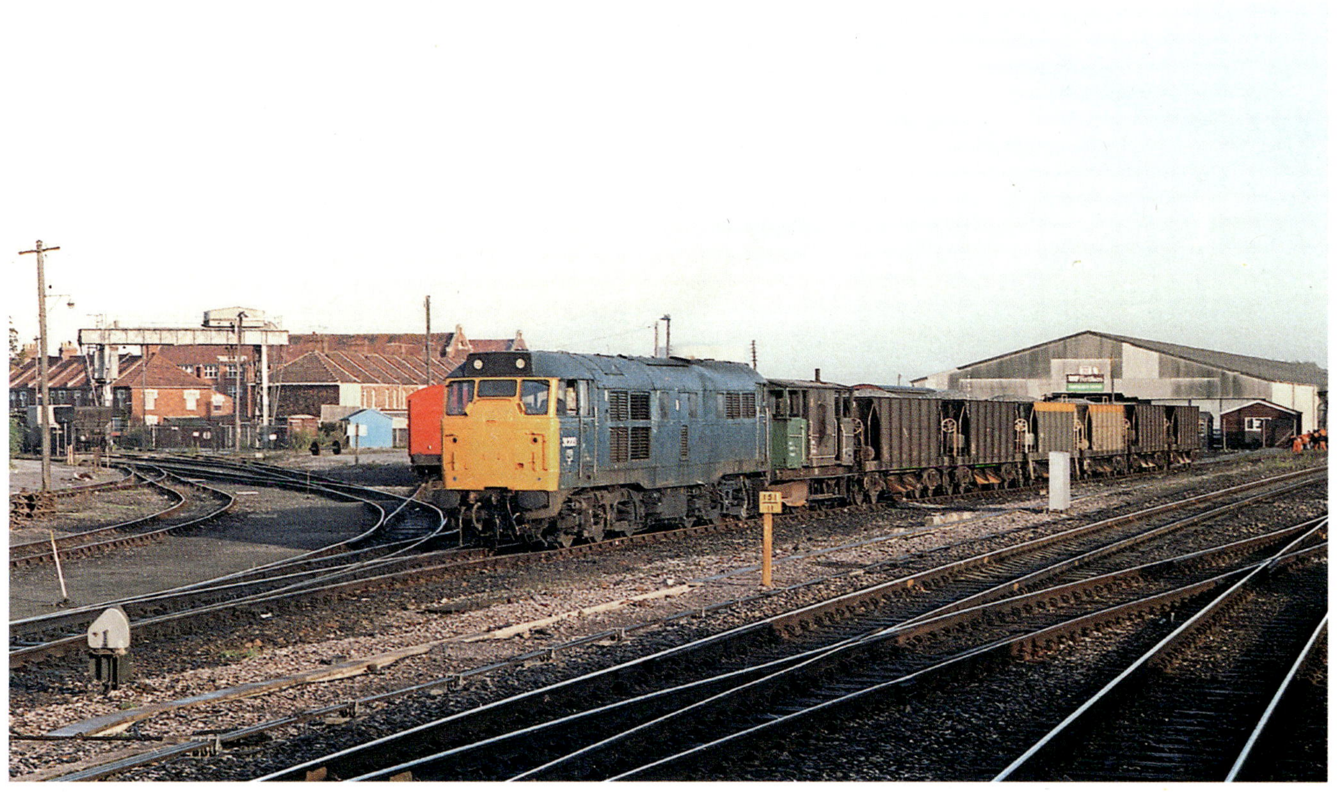

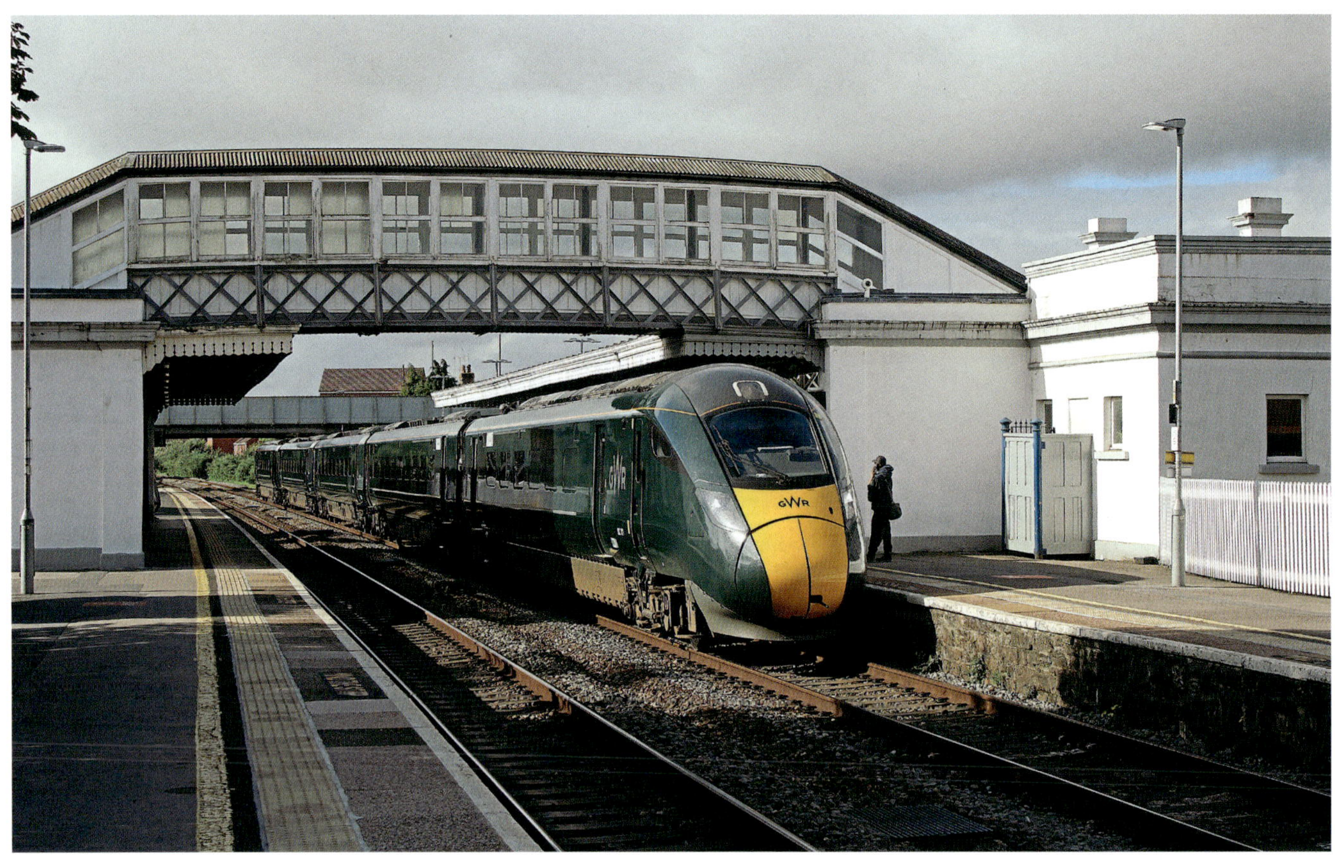

Bridgwater and an IET leaving on 15th May 2024; the level of rail usage has risen and now there are 49 trains a day serving Bridgwater versus 34 trains a day when the author first visited in January 1987. Passenger usage in 2023/24 was 442,000 journeys, compared with 120,000 journeys in 1996/97.

WE NOW TAKE THE ALTERNATE ROUTE TO TAUNTON FROM BRISTOL VIA BATH BRADFORD ON AVON AND WESTBURY; TAKING IN THE SOMERSET QUARRIES

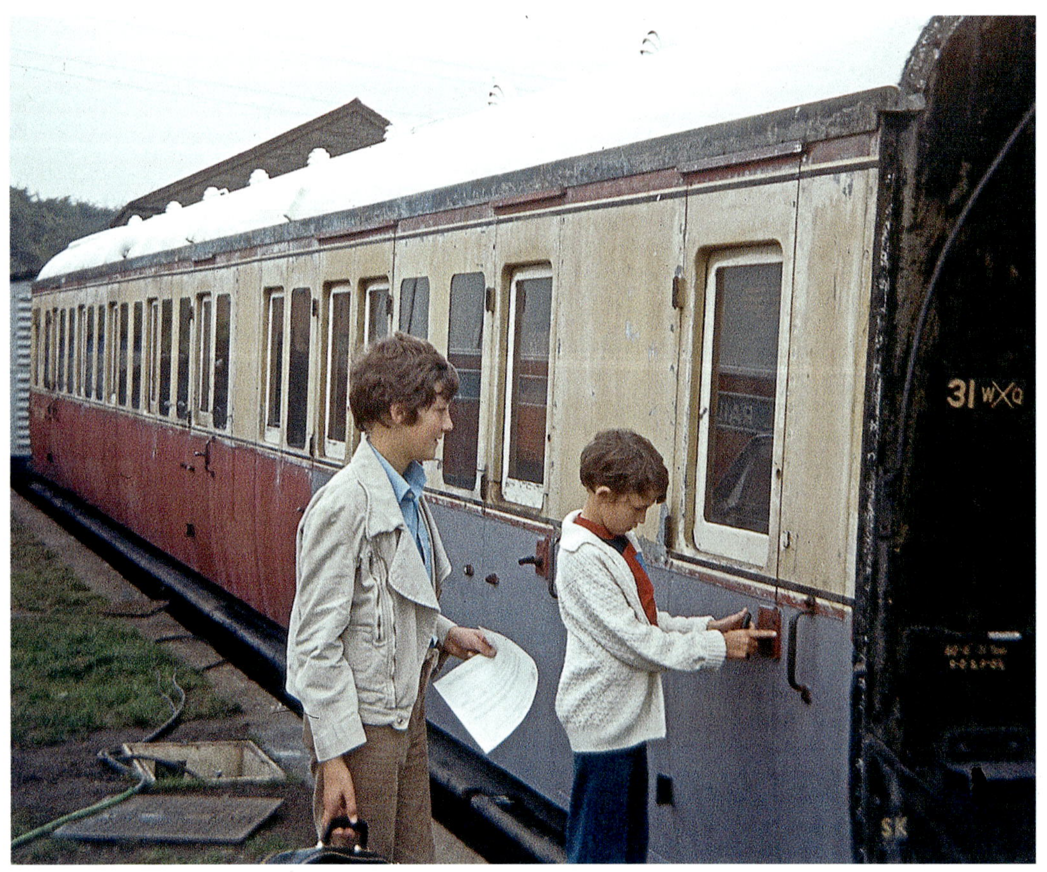

Bitton is the home of the Avon Valley Railway (AVR), born out of the Bristol Suburban Railway Society. Here on 20th September 1980 Paul and Mark examine a recently arrived GWR Collett coach; which originated from Craven Arms. The author recollects his father was fascinated that a vehicle had survived in original BR red and cream colours for so long.

Photo by John Stanford

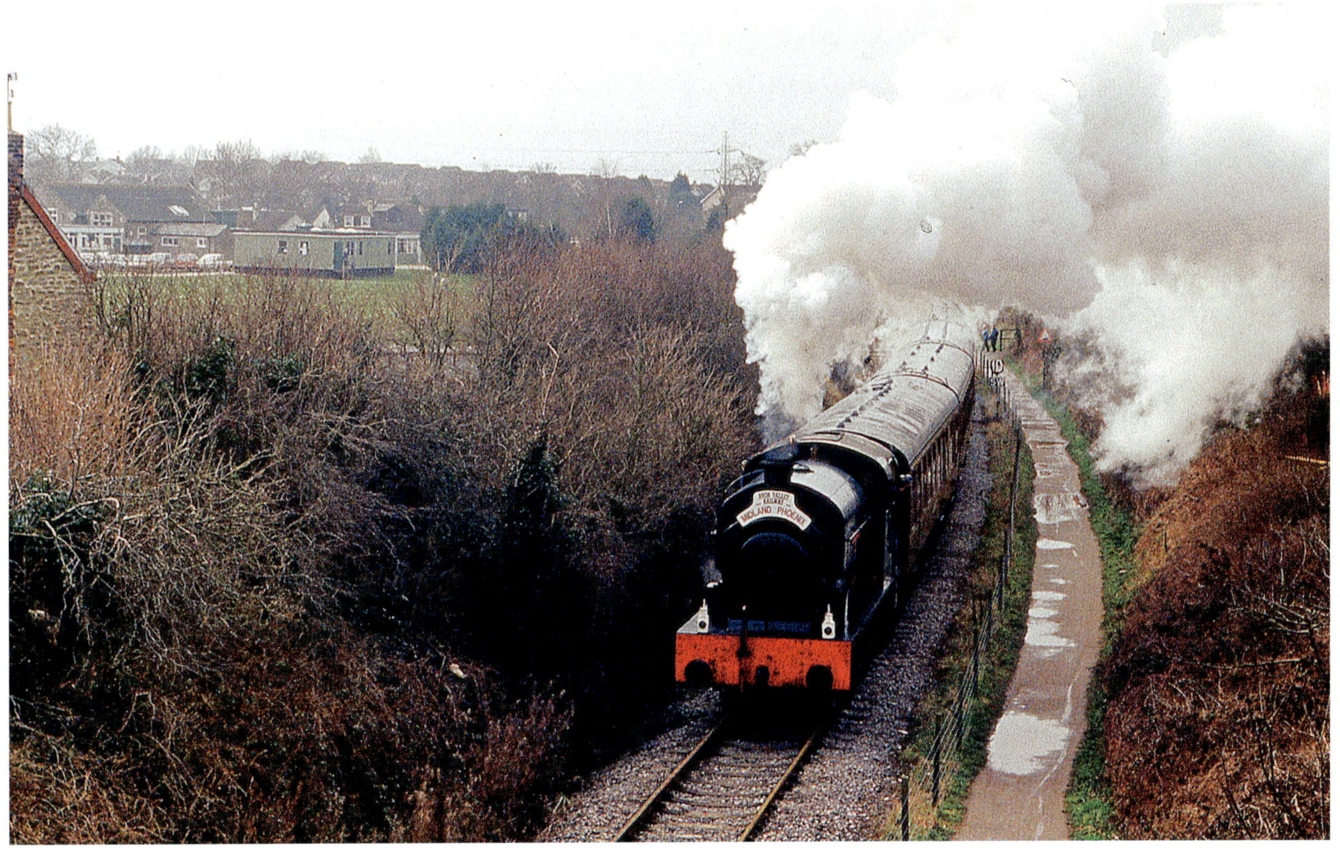

Bitton to Oldland reopened on 6th March 1991, and locomotive Littleton No.5 blasts to Oldland on the very first train. By then the author had been volunteering for 10 years on the railway, qualifying as a guard in December 1988 aged 21 and honoured to be asked to become operations manager for the railway some 2½ years later.

Oldland Common station was rebuilt by volunteers and opened in December 1997. Here Tyseley-based GWR pannier 9600 is seen with a Toad brake van when the author was the guard; pannier locos were synonymous with the Bristol area.

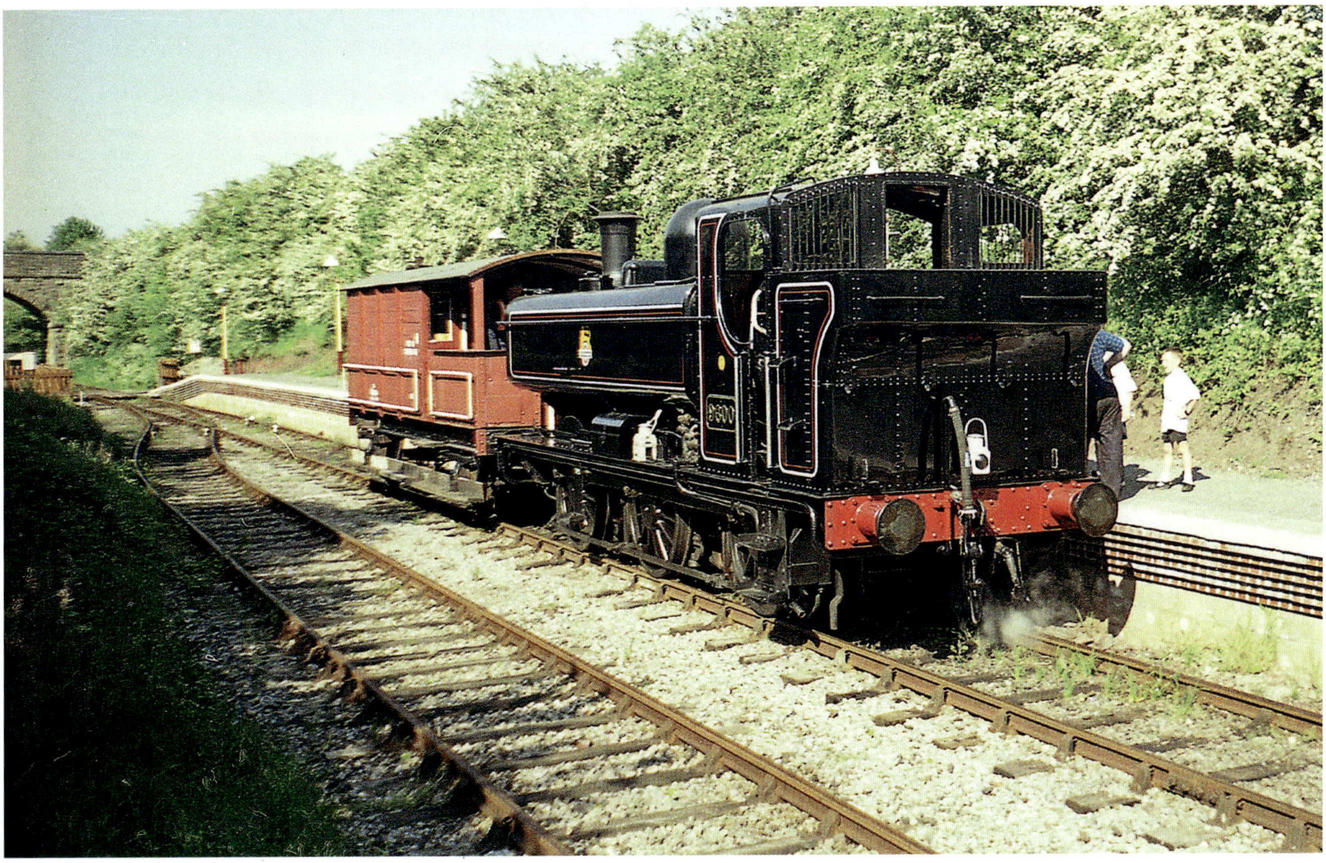

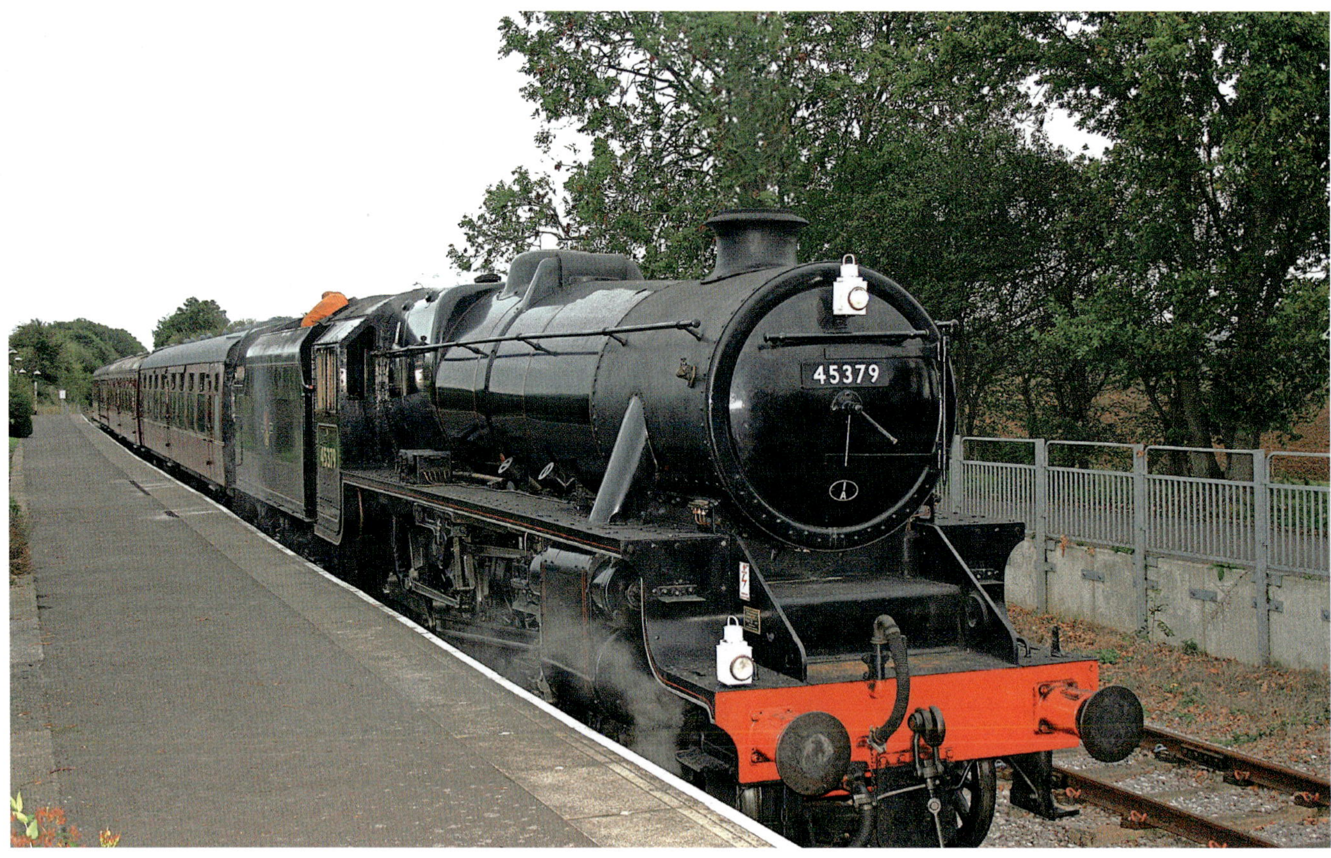

Avon Riverside on 11th October 2011 and Mid-Hants Railway-based Black 5 locomotive, a former longtime resident at Bitton, awaits departure on empty stock. The author and five AVR friends chipped in to pay the bulk of the road haulage and hire costs to bring the engine to the AVR for several weeks. As a thank you, the AVR laid on a day of playing trains for the sponsors.

Bath and 33021 leaving the station with a Portsmouth to Cardiff train on the last day of loco hauled services on the route, Sunday, 15th May 1988.

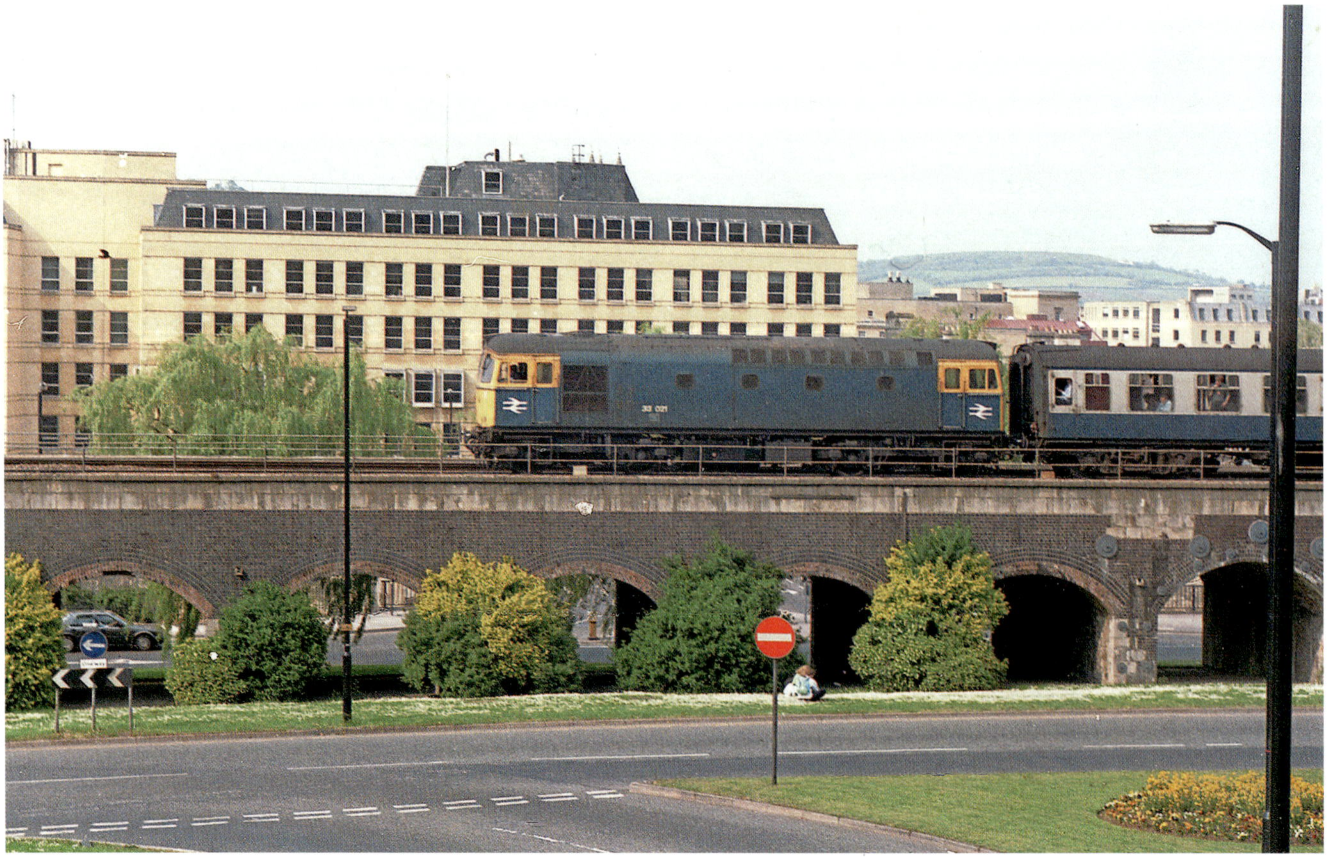

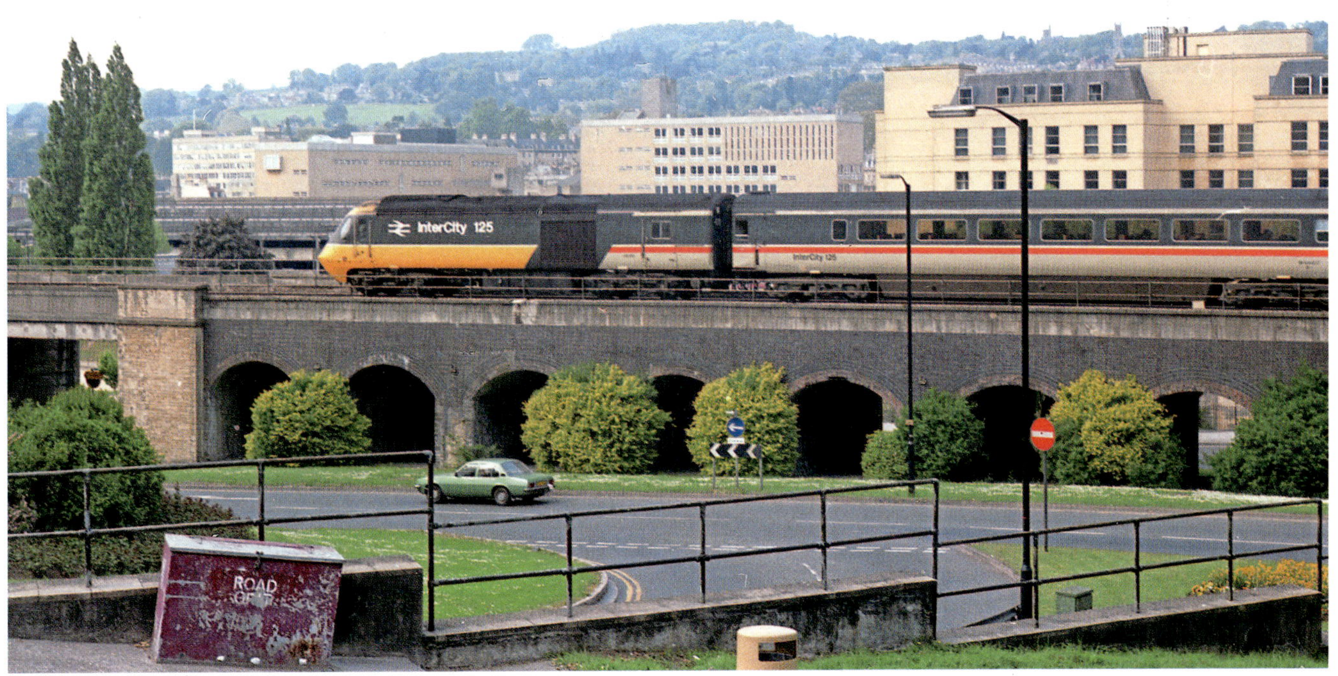

Bath with an HST leaving the station on the same day – 15th May 1988 – and looking smart in the Inter-City livery. A Vauxhall Cavalier is vying for attention too.

Bradford on Avon, class 33 locomotive (33031) passes over the weir with a Portsmouth-bound train March 1988; tree growth makes this scene impossible to recreate in 2025. The trains were only loco-hauled for two more months before new Sprinter trains arrived.

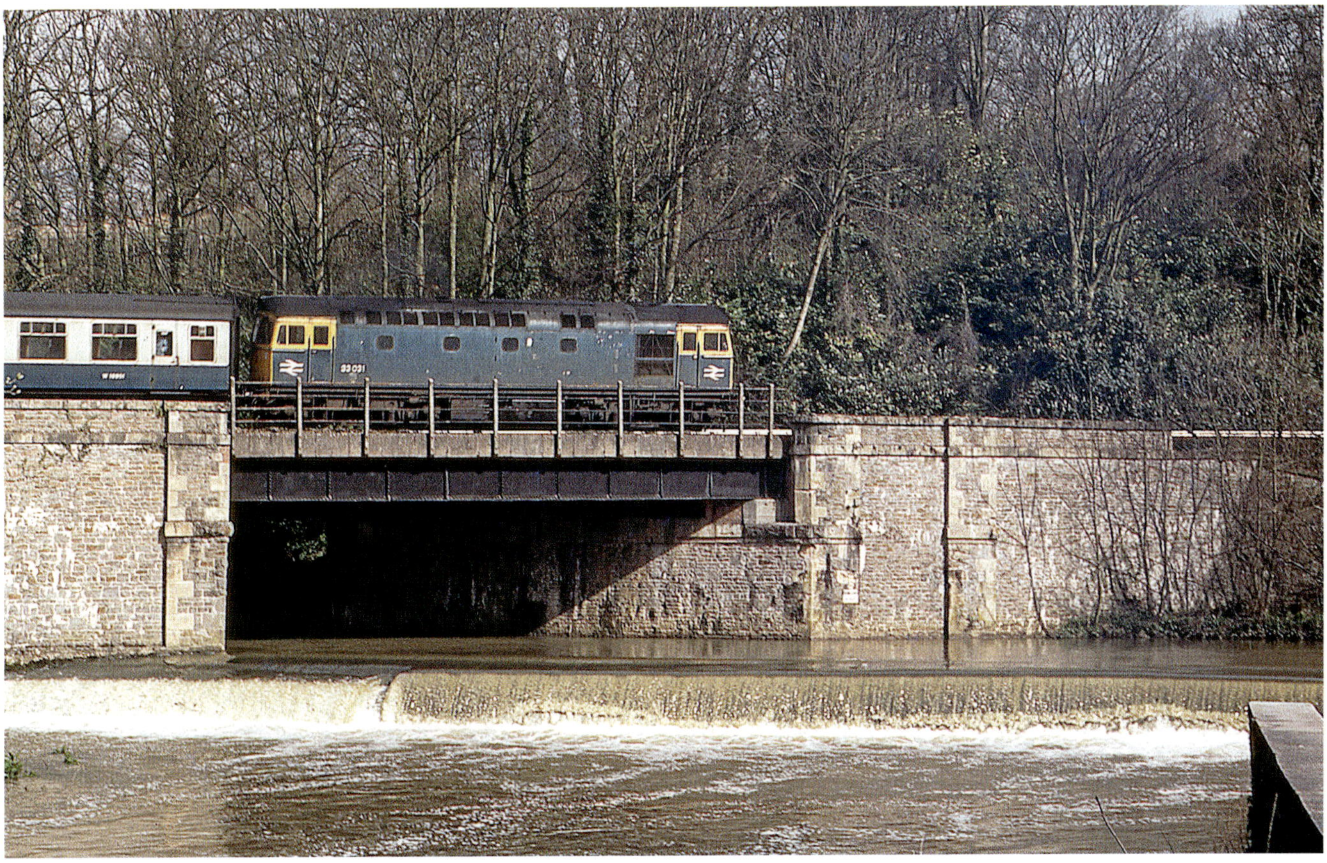

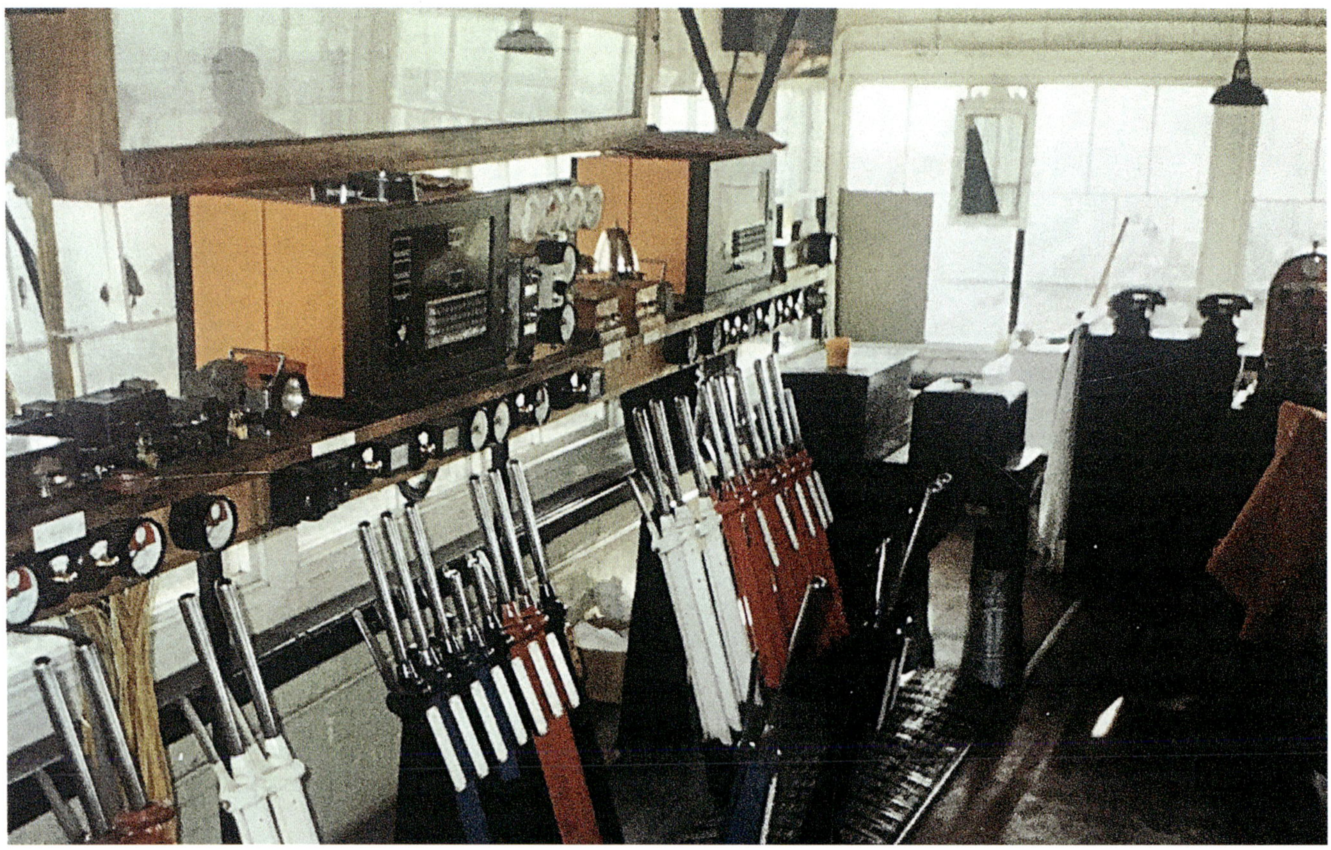

Bradford Junction signal box closed March 1990 and the author visited whilst en route to an engineering planning meeting, in the last week. Railway inspiration Jim Barnes, Area Signalling Inspector at Bristol, is seen in shot as a class 56 loco slowly passes the track lifting crane. He taught Paul to undertake Single Line Working along with many other operational processes. Even in the last week, the signal box was immaculate.

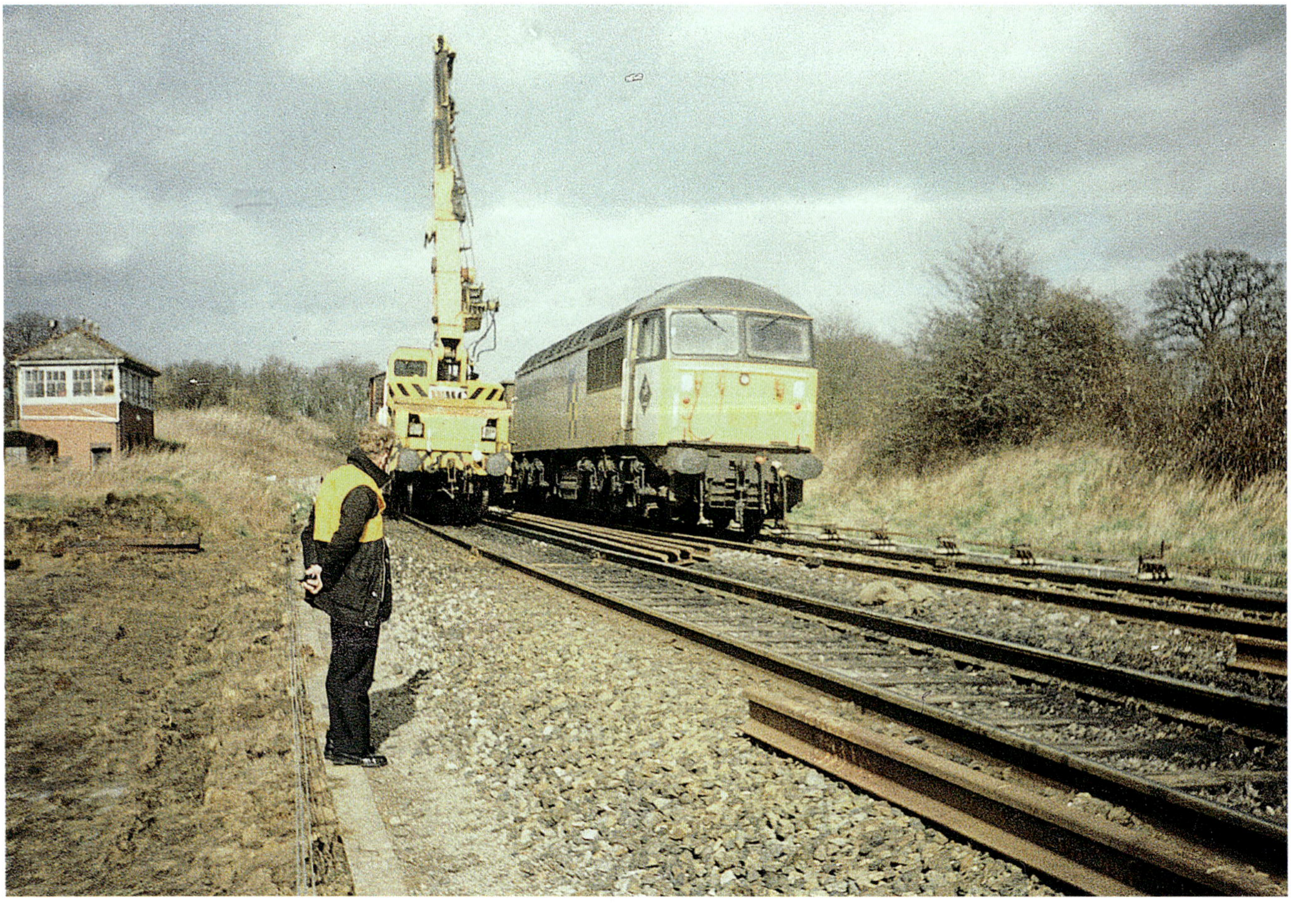

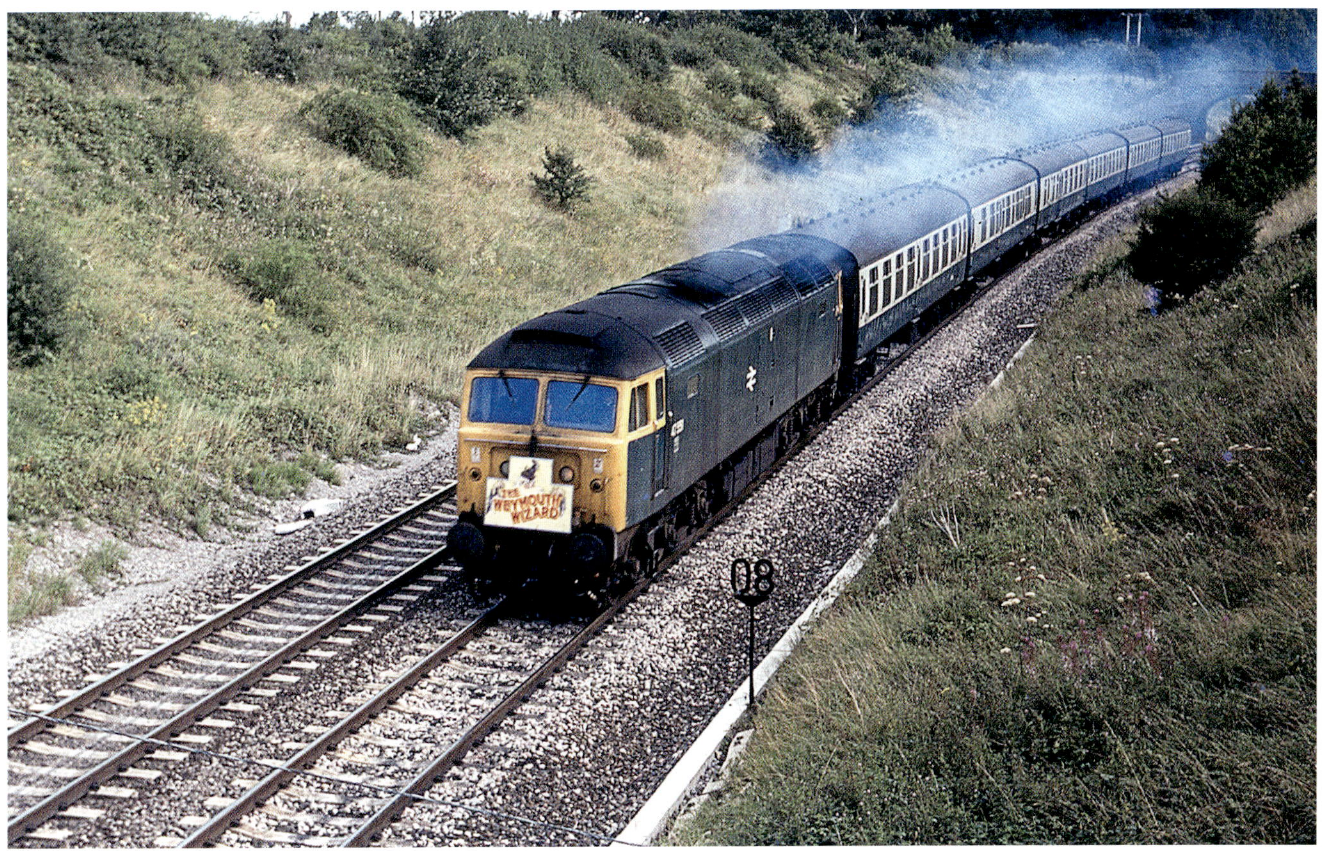

Westbury Hawkeridge Junction and the regular summer-only Weymouth Wizard train heads to Weymouth. These trains in the early 1980s called at Melksham and kickstarted regular trains to Melksham in 1985. To John's amusement, in 1984 the BR press officer dressed as a wizard at Swindon to see off the first train. *Photo by Trevor Riddle*

Westbury North and John captured locomotive *Clan Line* in April 1974 as it prepared to rejoin its train back to Eastleigh. It hauled a significant train, the first daylight steam train since the end of Southern steam in 1967 to head over electrified lines. The train was a success but BR was rightly worried people would trespass on these lines to see it. *Photo by John Stanford*

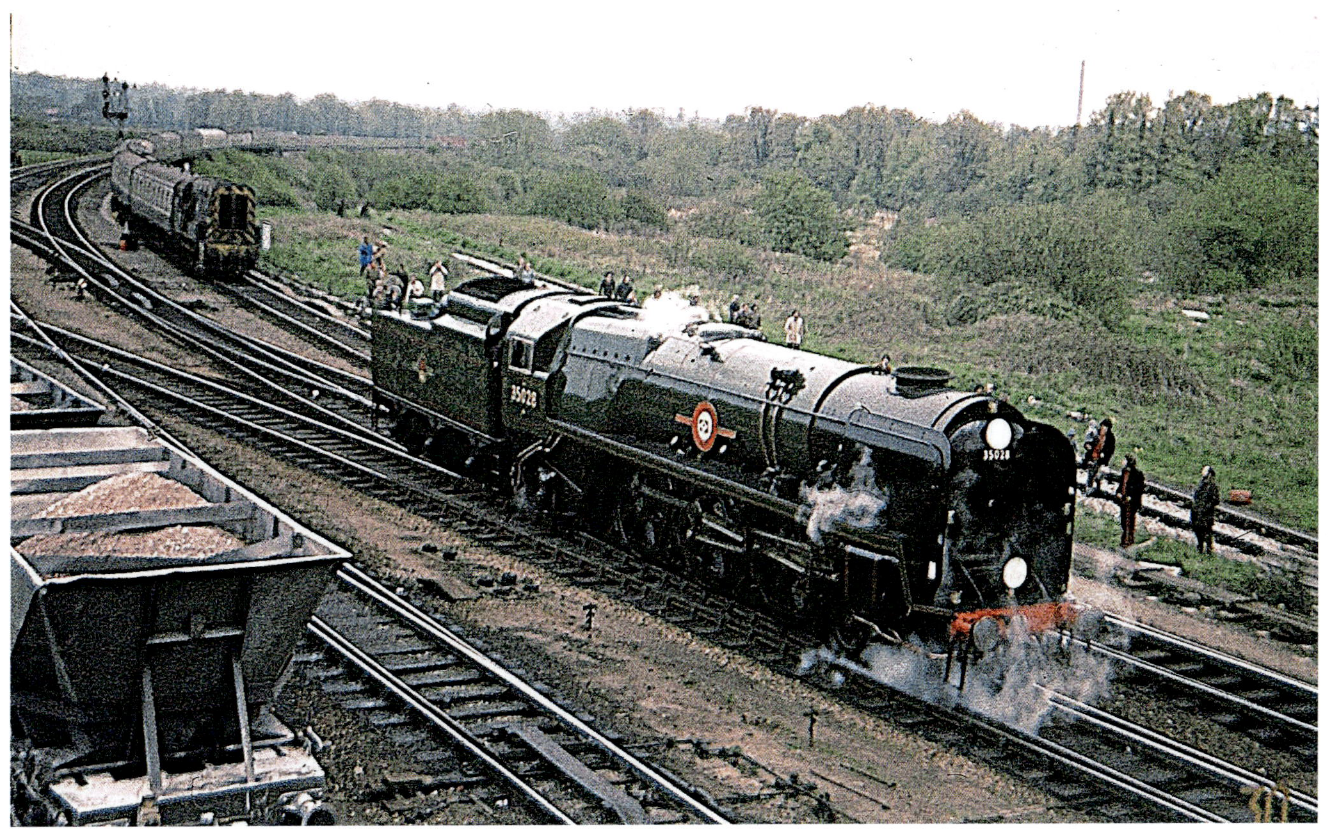

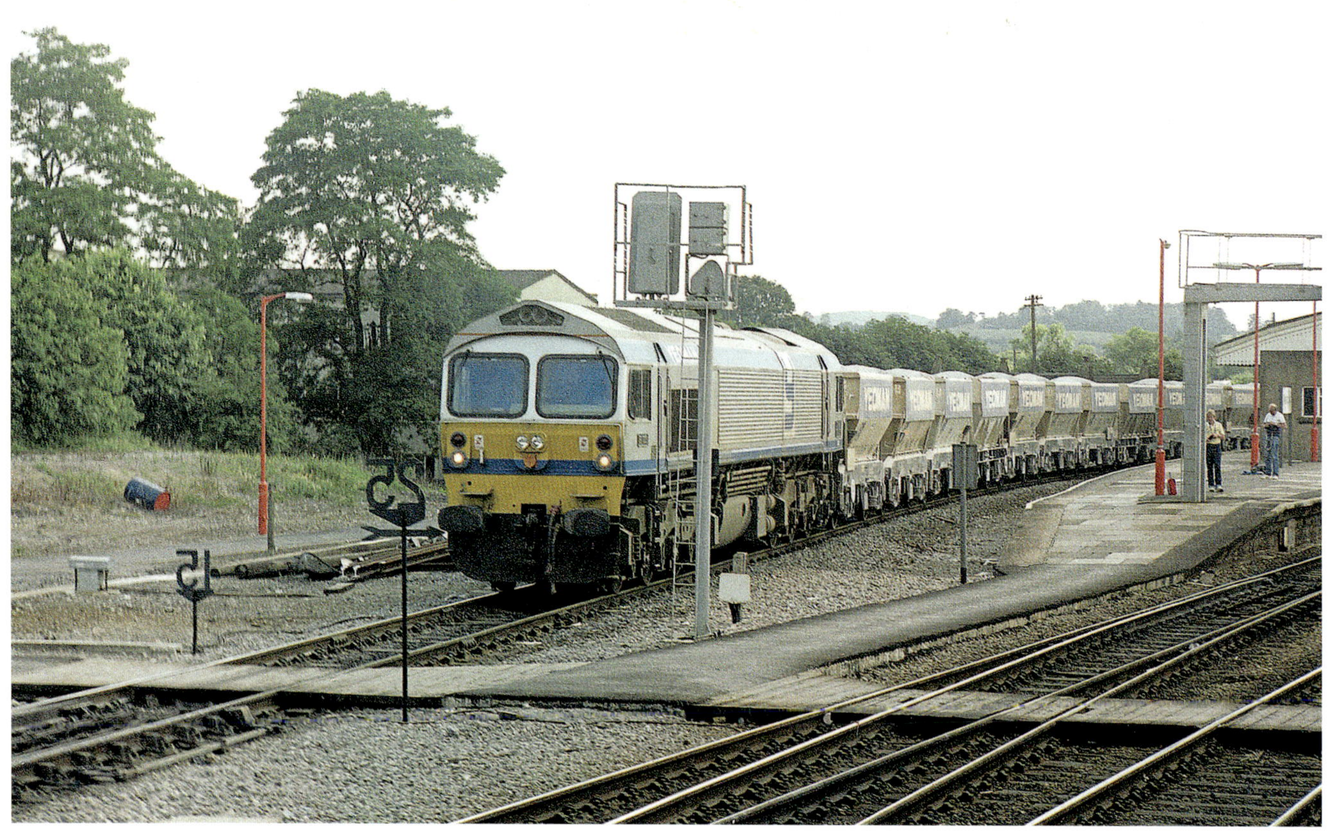

Westbury on 4th July 1986 and new-out-the-box locomotive 59003 waits to head towards London with a loaded rake of PGA hopper wagons. Earlier in the year, Paul had to monitor the performance of the locos in his role at Swindon; they were exceptional on reliability and performance, validating Foster Yeoman's investment in them.

Frome and the daily class 31-hauled trip working operates to Radstock on 28th August 1987. In the background is Frome North Yard which in 1987 saw use as an aggregate loading point. The traffic to and from Radstock wagon repair works ran until closure in June 1988, with the author's friend Chris Woodley, then a Bristol-based guard, somehow managing to work a trip there before closure.

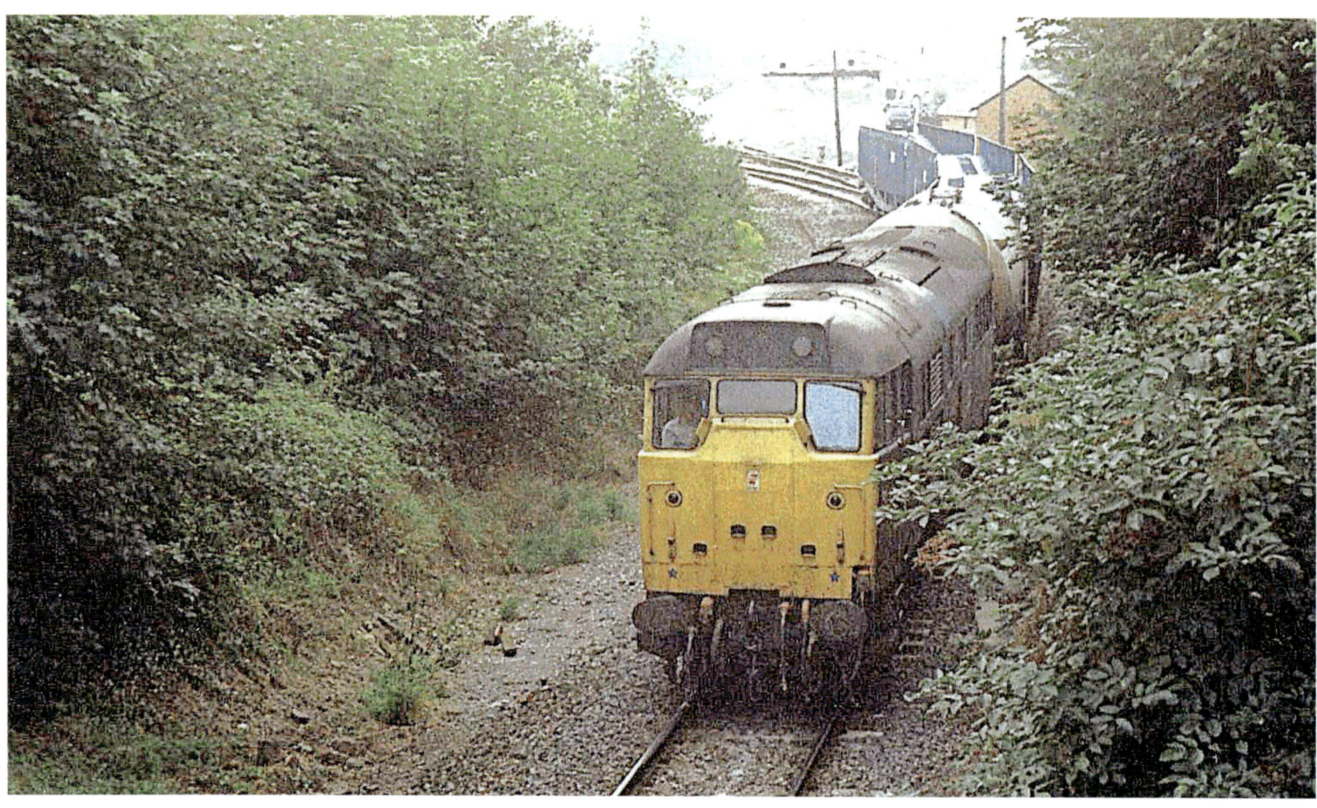

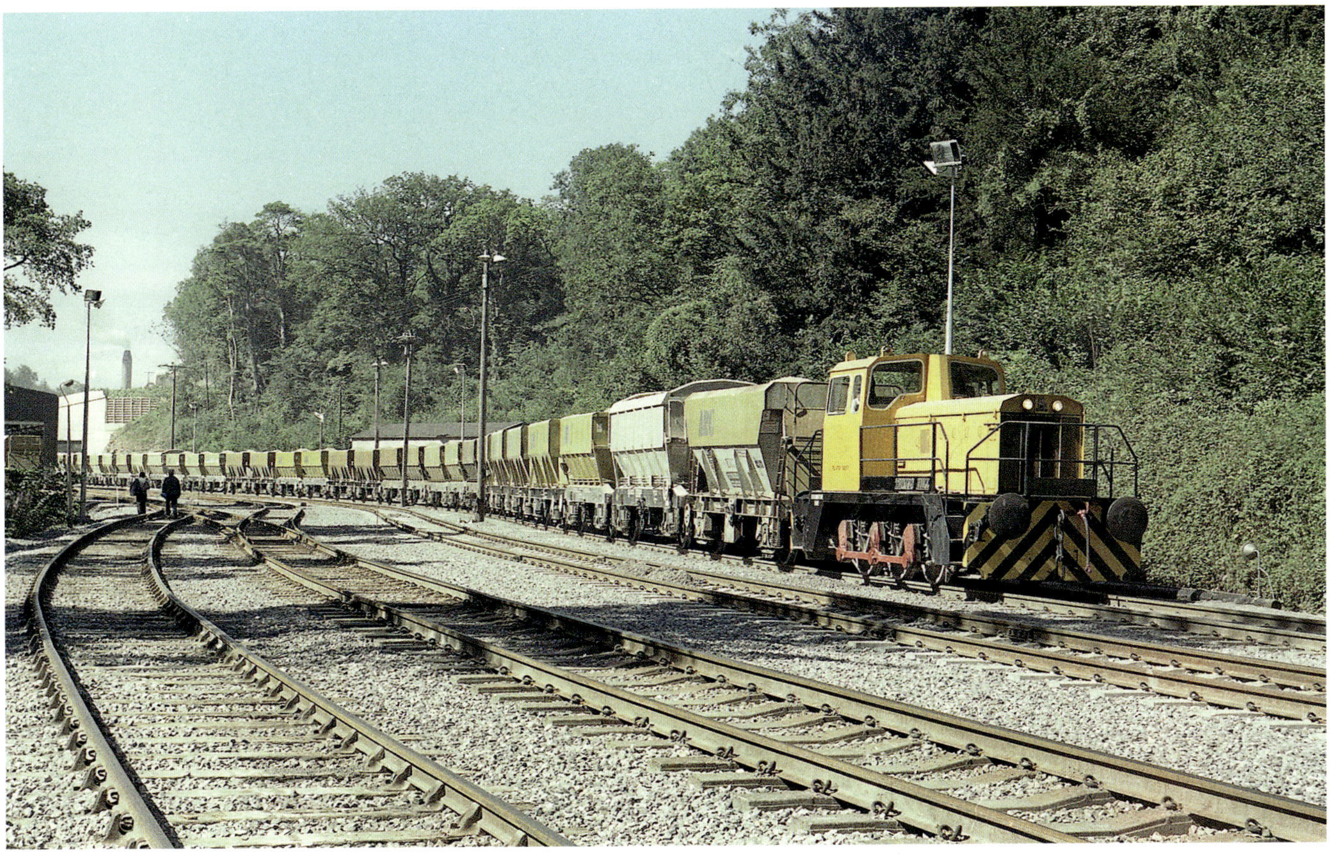

Whatley Quarry rail terminal was rebuilt in 1987 with a Freight Facilities Grant funding the track improvement works and here a Thomas Hill 0-6-0 loco draws a rake of loaded four-wheel hopper wagons (TOPS code PGA) from the quarry on 28th August 1987.

Whatley Quarry and new build Thomas Hill loco *Pride of Whatley* brings empty hopper wagons into the quarry for loading on 14th November 1988. The loco was not a great success, and subsequently class 08 locos were deployed, as well as a class 25, before the quarry settled on an American Switcher loco, similar to that at Merehead.

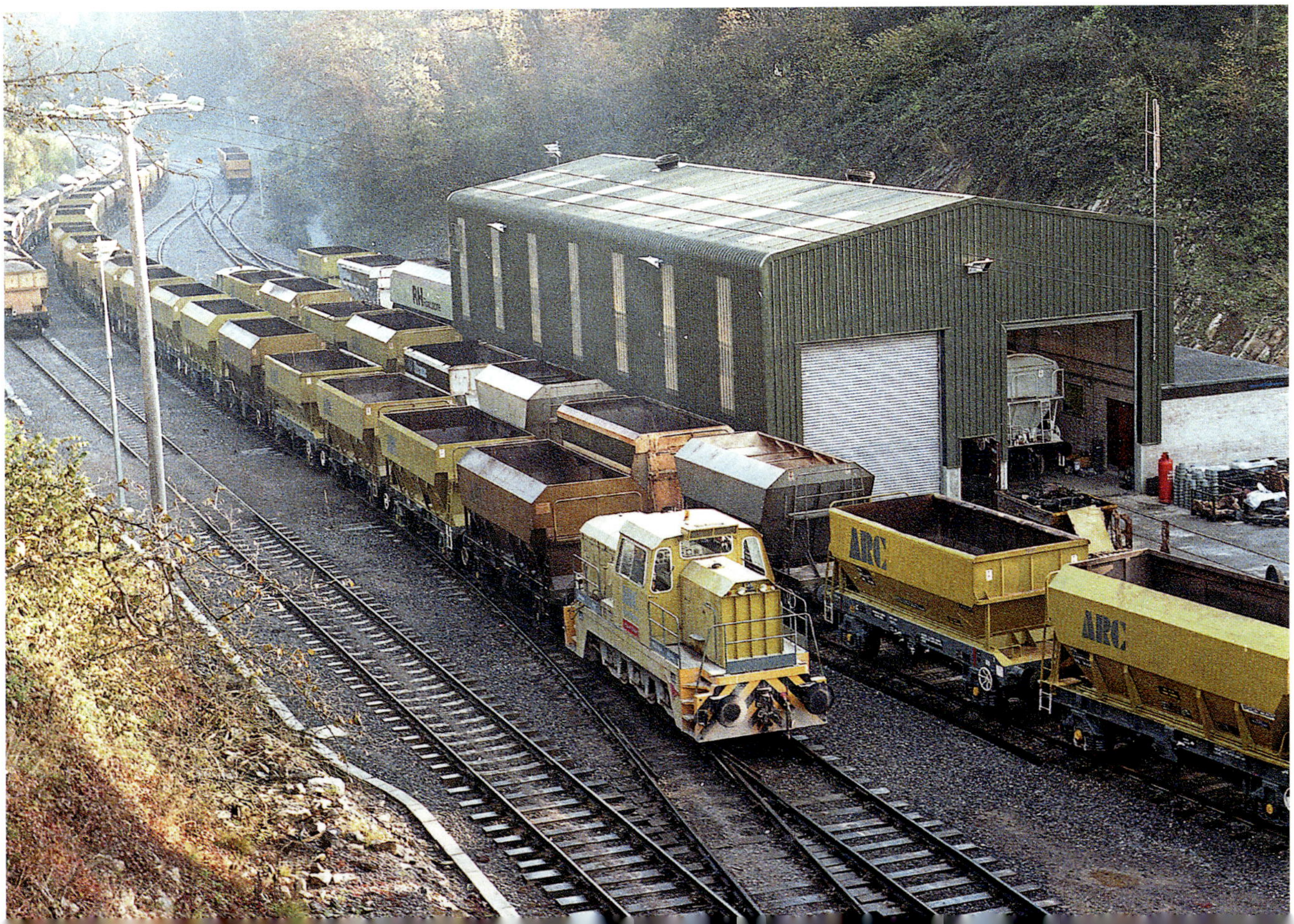

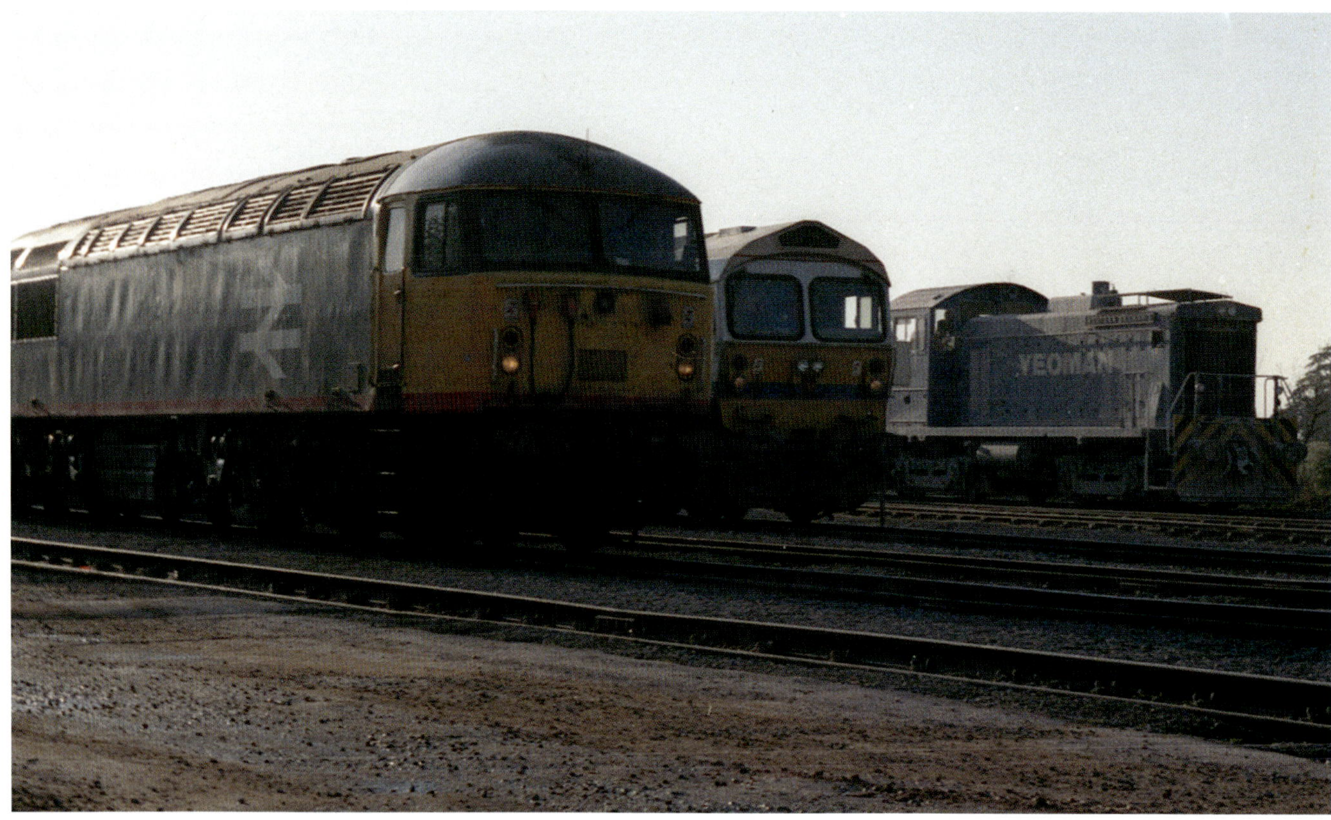

Merehead Quarry on 14th November 1988 finds 56042 and a class 59 alongside the little switcher at right which started the UK American loco revolution, a General Motors (GM) machine. The switcher was such a success that it led FY to order four class 59 locos from GM in 1984, delivered at the start of 1986.

Merehead Quarry the same day, which formed an official visit. The author's longtime railway friends are in shot: Robin 'Horatio' Nelson at left who went on to become head of train planning for Freightliner and Mike Organ, who with his vast rail knowledge was an aid to many people and physical works, right through into the period Crossrail was being built 2010-2018. Both were massively respected in the rail industry.

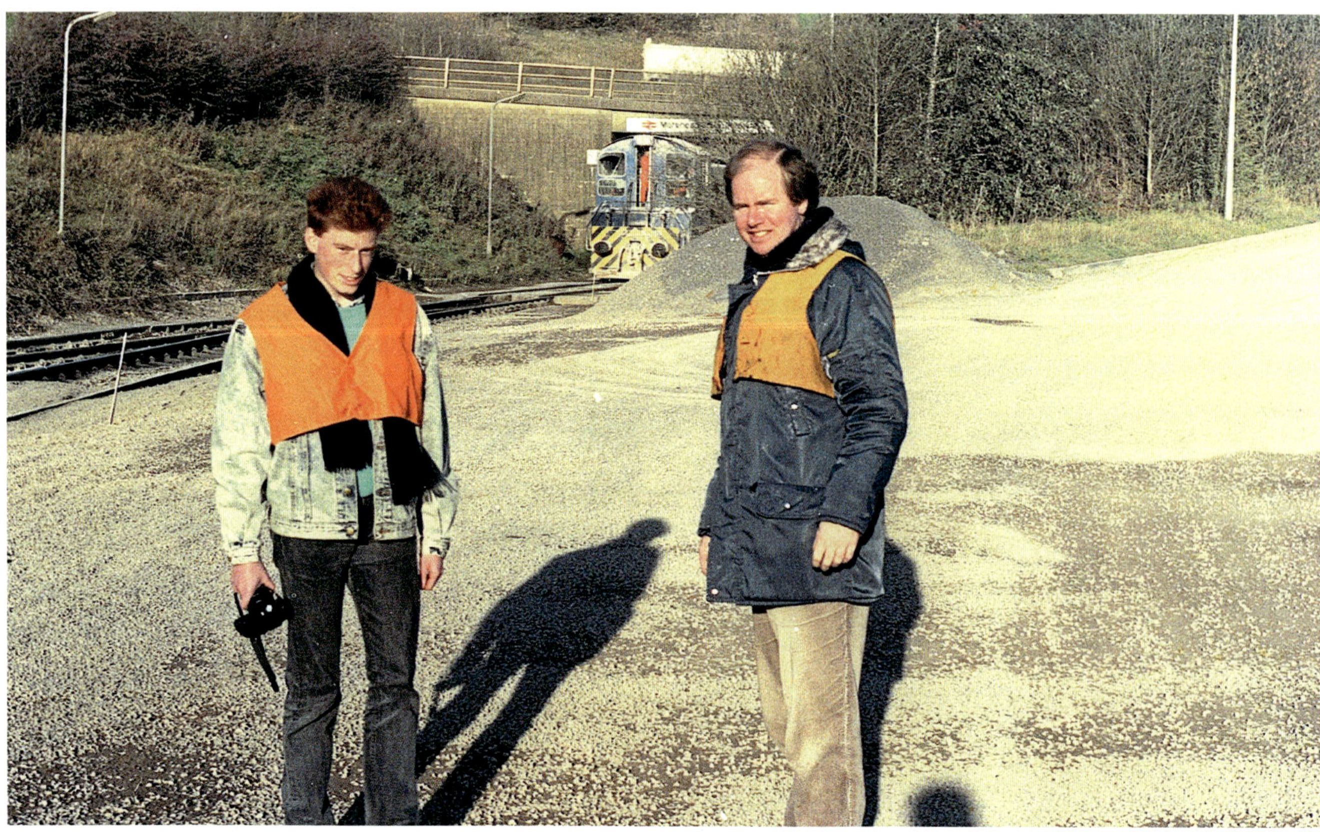

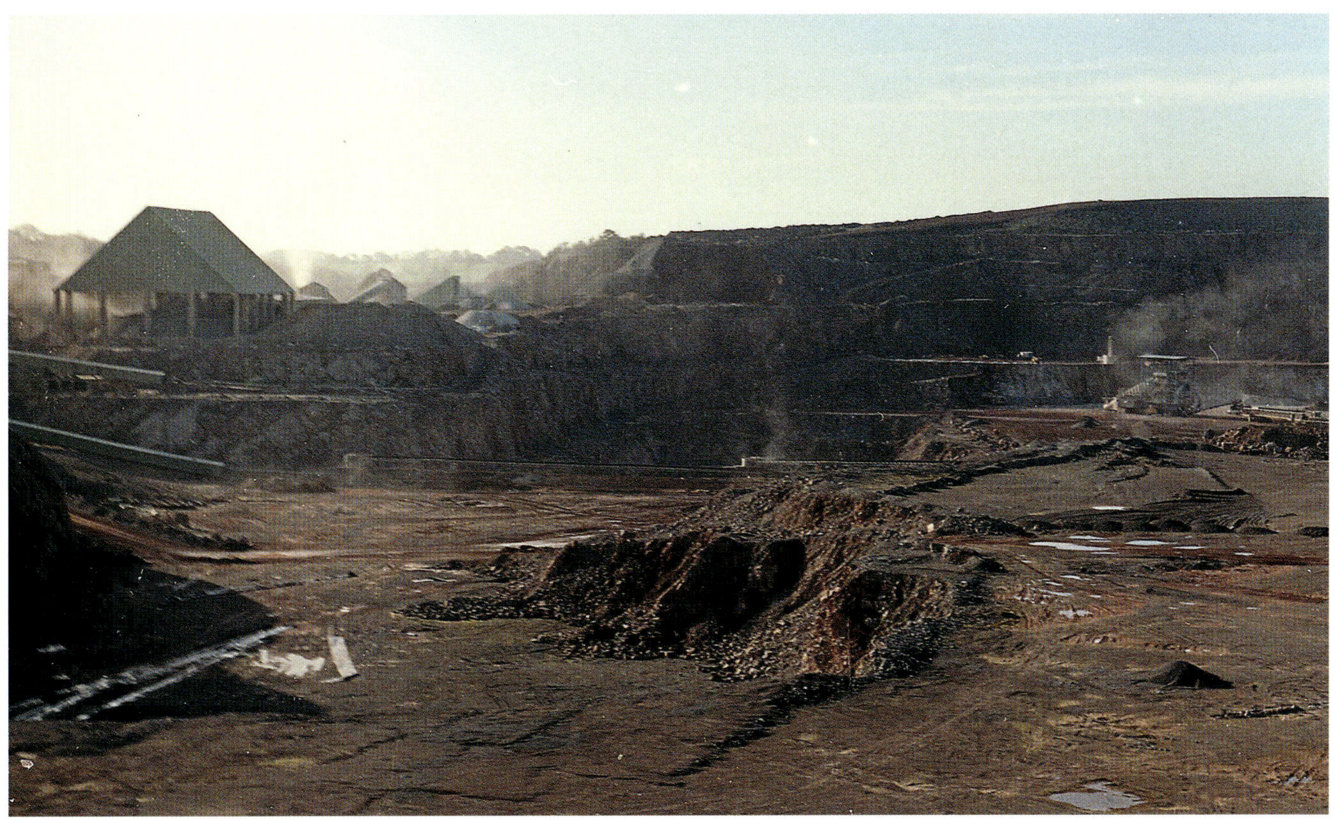

Merehead Quarry in autumn 1988 was and is a significant hole in the ground; and has grown since, providing widespread employment directly and indirectly. The rail terminal is in the middle, left of centre of the photograph. A classic case where rail is absolutely crucial to the manufacturing process for the construction industry.

Blatchbridge Jn south of Frome is nowadays controlled by Westbury panel signal box. On 2nd March 1984 we see a three-car Metro Cammell DMU heading for Weymouth, with Blatchbridge Jn signal box supervising; it closed on 6th October the same year.

Photo by Trevor Riddle

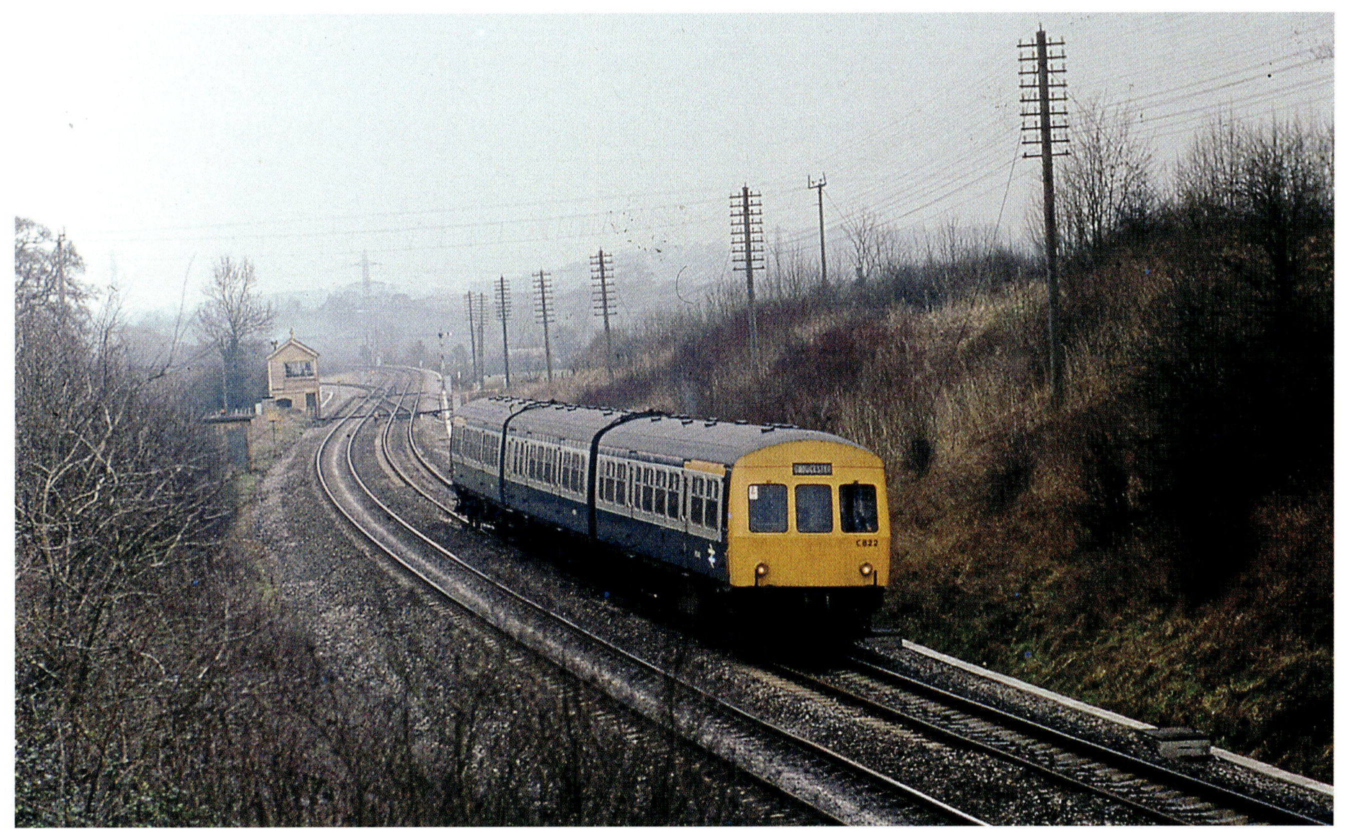

Alan Taylor – lifelong railwayman and former managing director Mendip Rail

My family has over 100 years of railway history, mainly on the GWR, the Western region and latterly the Midland region of BR.

Father retired as operating superintendent at the Birmingham Divisional offices in 1968, that is about four years after I started on the railways – firstly at Birmingham Snow Hill and then New Street passenger enquiry offices. I transferred to the operating department in the divisional offices working in both the passenger and parcels in 1967 and loved every minute of it. I got to ride on special trains as the trains office representative carrying out passenger surveys on trains and at stations. I would work in the control office during major events or incidents such as the commissioning of the power boxes at Birmingham New Street and Saltley, the introduction of electrification of the Euston-Birmingham-Wolverhampton line and as a consequence the ultimate demise of the GWR mainline to Snow Hill. They were great days and great people to work with and this is when I met Paul Stanford's father John and subsequently Paul, who was a baby recently born.

John and I worked together and but also did many trips to places like Carlisle to witness the demise of steam and various branch lines which were now feeling the effects of the Beeching modernisation plan.

John got promotion to Bristol in 1969 and it wasn't long before I joined him in the Bristol divisional manager's parcels train office dealing with milk, special van loads containing anything from corpses to general parcels traffic and divisional BRUTE control. These were special trolleys designed to convey parcels and could be loaded into parcel rail vehicles. It was about ensuring certain areas which had a shortage and taking from others with a surplus, so a job that ensured a ready supply at the main stations existed for each day's business, including Royal Mail, which was virtually 100% by rail.

I moved to the commercial side in Bristol but didn't enjoy it as much as the operating side and in 1977 decided to look for pastures new and met an old boss from Birmingham, Ken Painter, who was a director at Foster Yeoman in charge the railway development side. He offered me a job part time. I knew very little of the stone business but readily agreed to the challenge and it involved railways, which was a bonus.

I started as temporary cover for the rail supervisor, Bill Vivash, on 1st January 1978 at Torr Works or Merehead as the railway called it and my temporary job soon became full time and I became the rail manager, dealing with the daily rail plan, looking for new depots, planning the train plan and managing the wagon fleet which included helping the wagon companies design new wagons.

There was many a proud moment seeing a train comprised of a new wagon design. I was responsible for track maintenance, procuring shunt engines and many other things. Strangely I was more involved in railways than I ever had been from day to day

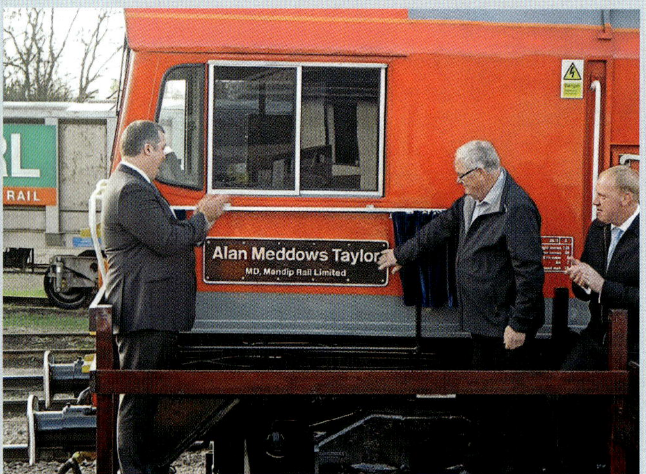

Alan at his loco naming ceremony.

to future planning. I was involved in major projects such as the Channel Tunnel construction, Second Severn Crossing, building of motorways and bypasses, Heathrow airport development, the Thames barrier, the Olympic Park, Crossrail and many more, even West Somerset Railway and building sea defences at Minehead. It was so varied and a key part of the development in the UK.

The best thing of all was, I was still a railwayman, and I had daily dealings with railwayman and railway engineers many whom I had known for 20 to 40 years.

My proudest moments were in 1986 when the Class 59 locomotives arrived from General Motors in America, and we introduced them on our daily operations from Merehead having been party to the design and testing of these locomotives and the ongoing operation in service was amazing and filled me with pride. It was teamwork from a truly remarkable group of people which included engineers, maintenance staff from Westbury and Old Oak, drivers, traction inspectors and train planners – too many to mention and the locos are still going strong today. The commercial agreement for the operation of privately-owned locomotives on BR was a major achievement of hard work and dedication which took many hours and days to complete from a BR and FY perspective but we finally got there in February 1986 and the first commercial train departed Merehead with a class 59 at the head and a rake of aggregate wagons.

Following this Foster Yeoman and ARC decided to merge the rail operations of each company, and I was honoured with being made managing director of Mendip Rail; a very proud moment. It was during this period that I met Paul in his official capacity as Railtrack regional freight manager, which in my mind brought me full circle and kept the family links complete and that is something all railway personnel are always very proud of.

I am truly thankful for my time involved with the railway industry and the all the people I met and worked with. Thank you.

Alan Taylor, February 2025

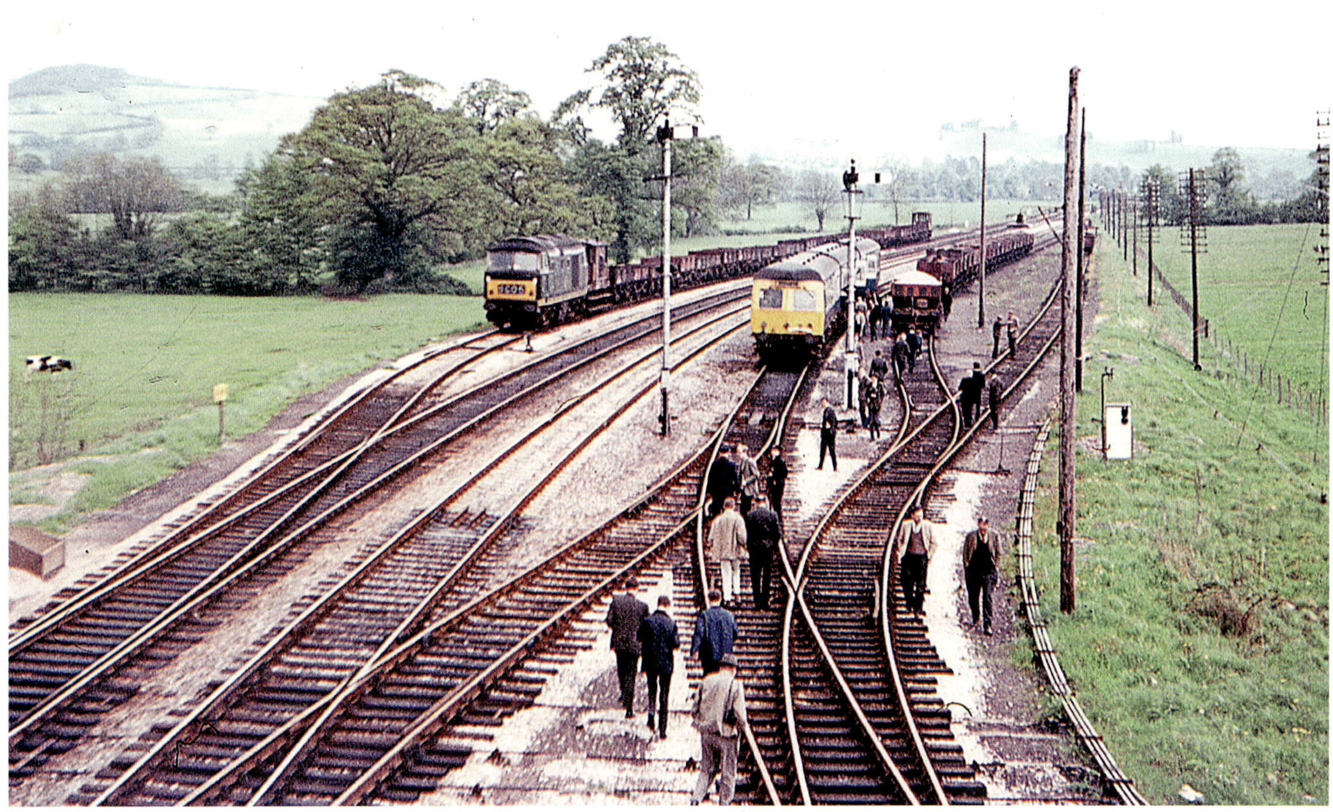

Castle Cary looking toward Westbury. John was a great supporter of railtours and on 17th May 1969 he grabbed this shot of a DMU tour he travelled on which visited Minehead, see page 84. Note the Hymek locomotive on Engineering Department Grampus wagons.

Photo by John Stanford

Castle Cary on 17th May 1967 and John is backed by the wartime signal box; constructed as a replacement after a German plane bombed the previous box in 1942, killing the signalman and wrecking a goods train. The rail route behind John is set for Yeovil and John and Wendy are en route for a holiday in Devon and Cornwall, taking a break from railway work.

Photo by Wendy Stanford

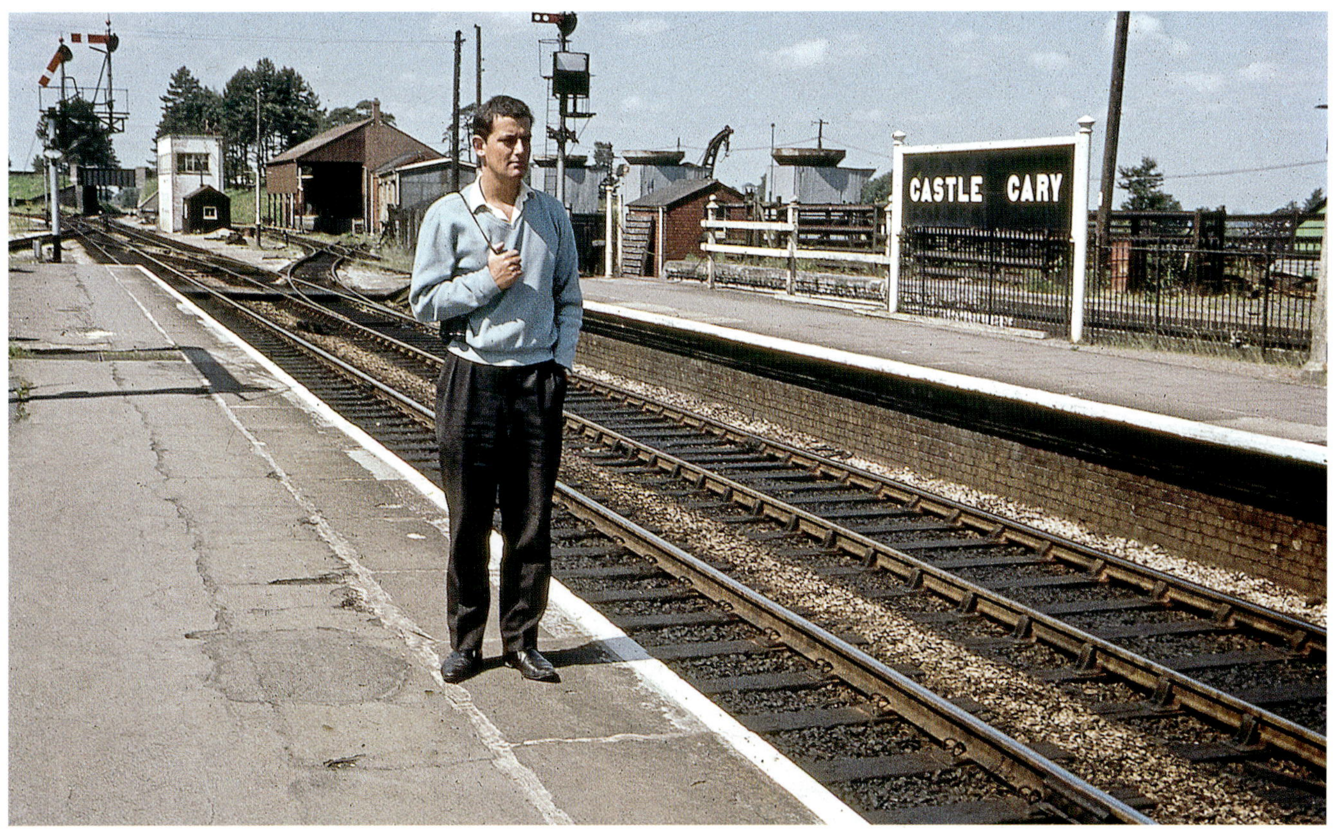

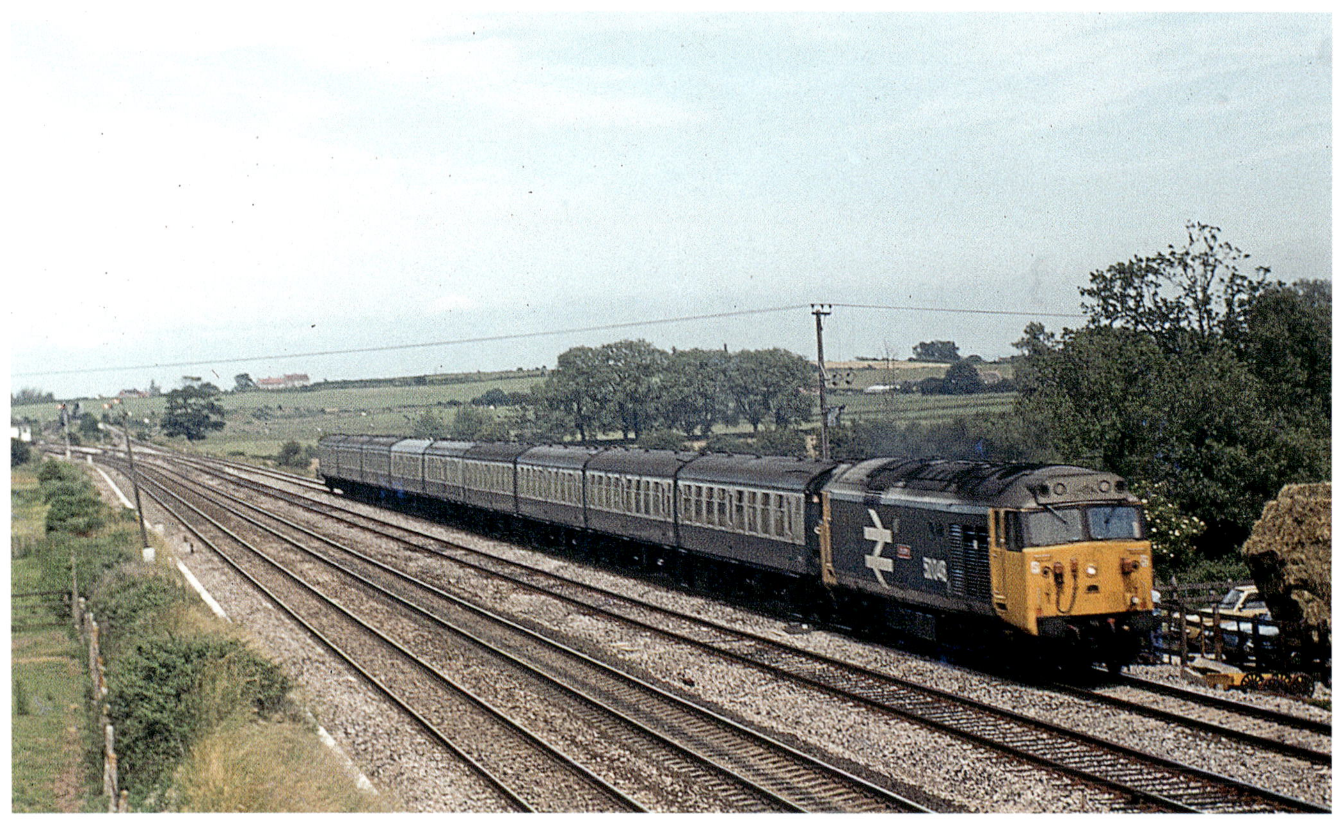

Cogload Junction is where the line from Bristol direct meets with the line from Westbury. In this summer 1983 view, a class 50 locomotive heads westward at speed, looking towards Bridgwater and Castle Cary. The signal box is evident far left – now preserved at Coleford in Gloucestershire following closure a few years after this photograph. *Photo by Trevor Riddle*

Taunton and D1015 has just uncoupled from a retirement train for main line steam supremo Bernard Staite, for locomotives 6024 and 7802 to takeover to Paignton on 28th February 2005. The author was flattered to travel on this train, arranged for him by his manager Barbara Barnes as a thank you for arranging 'on the day' gauge clearance for GWR Manor locomotive 7802 to get the locomotive to Shrewsbury, before it operated a special train over the Cambrian Coast in October 2004.

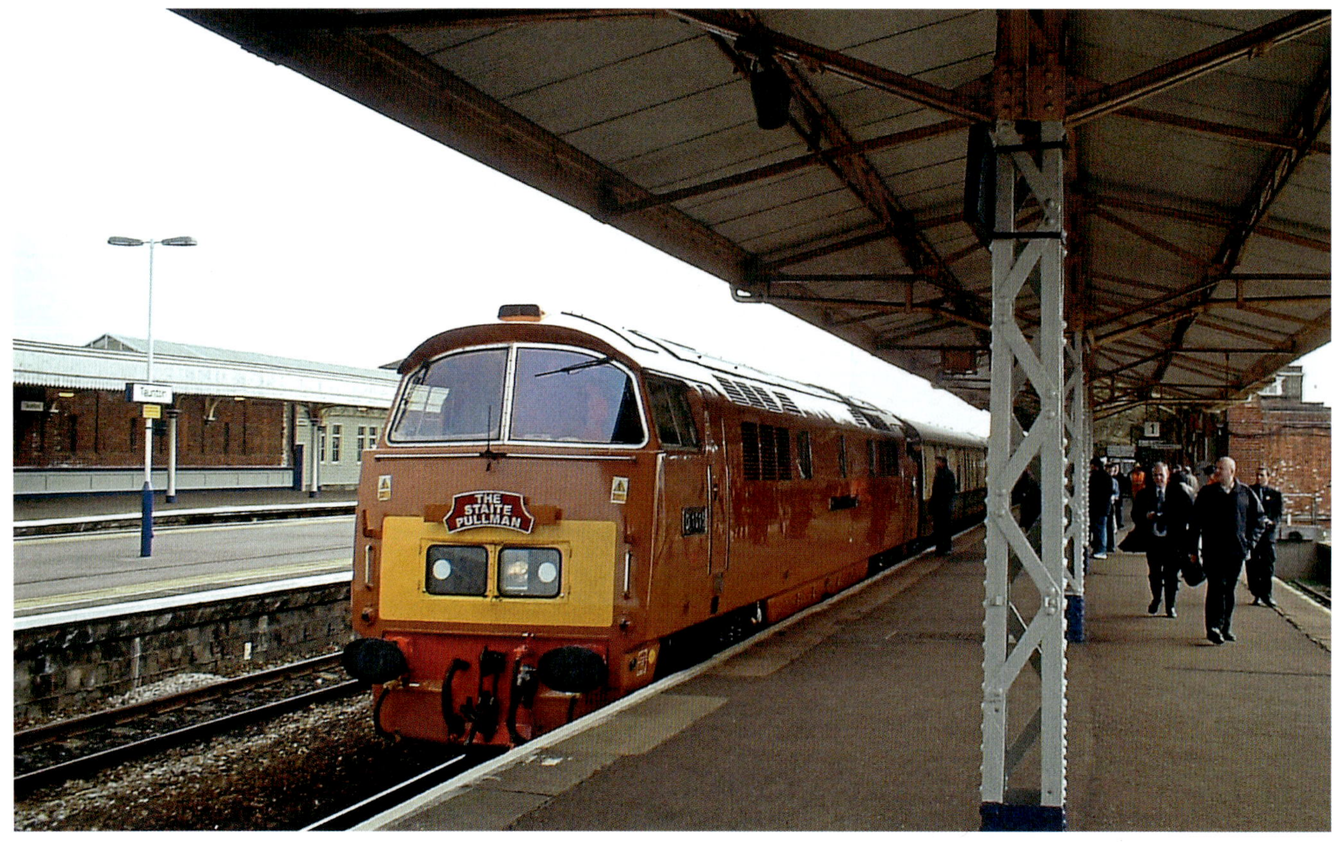

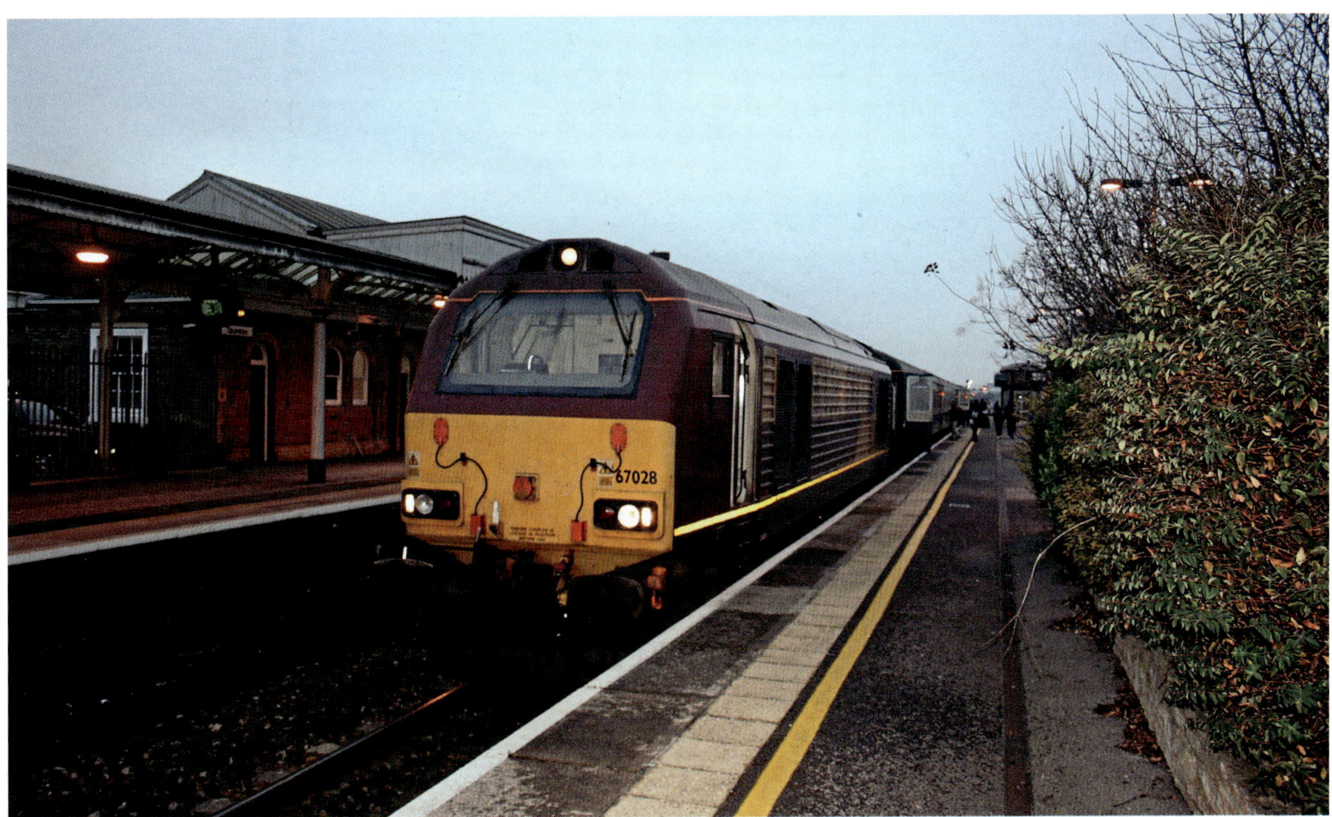

Taunton on 30th December 2008, as the author was about to restart work on the Western Region after seven years in a national railfreight roles. At the time Bristol Taunton local trains were loco-hauled, operated by First Great Western (FGW). Coincidentally the author became the Network Rail account executive for FGW from January 2009 and had the pleasure of working with FGW managing director Mark Hopwood and his team after seven years in national rail freight roles.

Taunton shed was opposite the extreme end of Taunton station and Super Bagnall locomotives *Victor* and *Vulcan* are awaiting transfer to Minehead on 26th April 1975. Note *Victor* still carries the magnificent livery applied at Longbridge. It was subsequently painted a dour black livery, although this became a firm favourite with the author. *Photo by John Stanford*

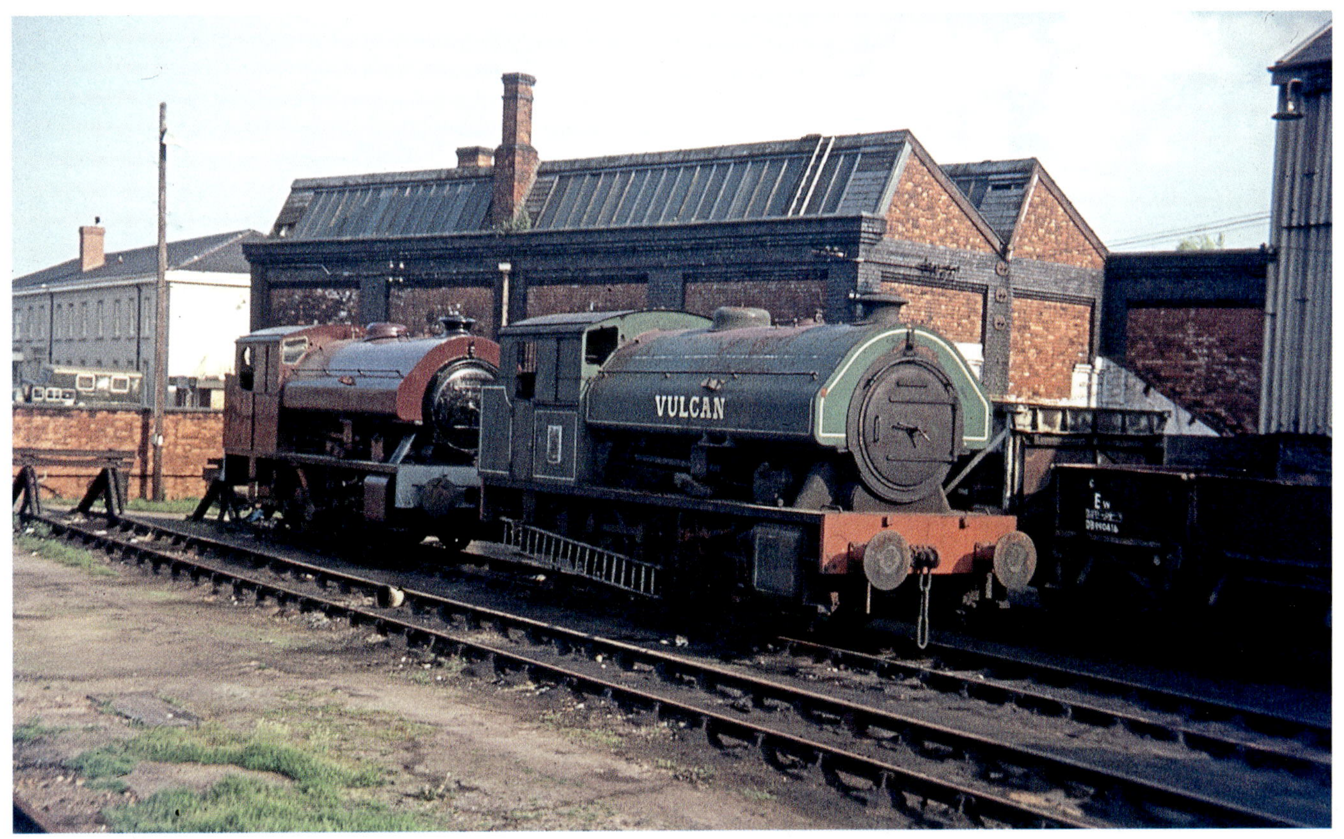

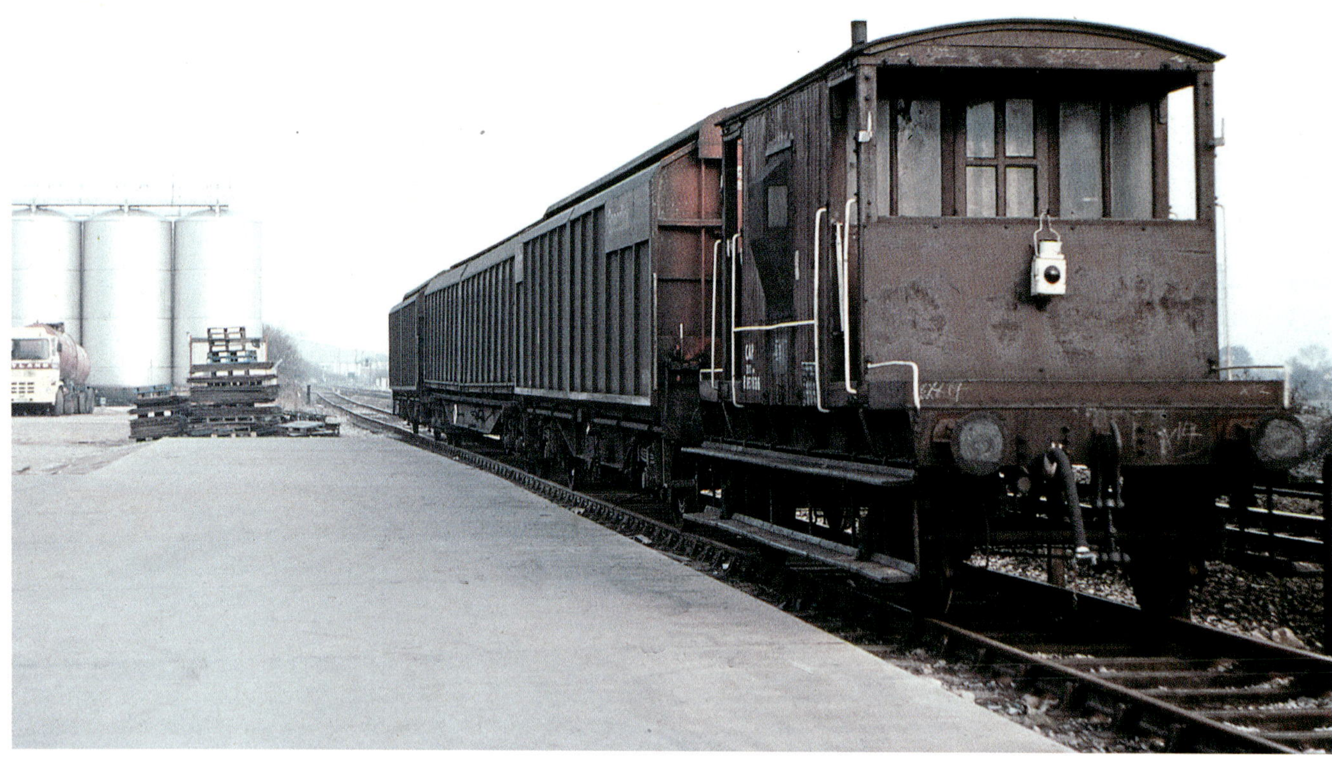

Taunton Cider at Norton Fitzwarren started using rail in 1983 and on Wednesday 12th March 1986 John and Paul visited the factory with the Chartered Institute of Transport. The brake van was used for propelling the empty cider vans from Taunton Fairwater Yard. Initially traffic was loaded on the Minehead branch line. However, by summer 1986 a series of sidings had been laid to deal with the growing traffic. *Photo by John Stanford*

Williton in summer 1973. On 15th July and the author and his brother play trains, as Grandad Harry takes on the role of station master, telling them to go and deal with trucks in the goods yard! The line had been out of use for two years by then, with a few more years before rebirth as the West Somerset Railway, Britain's longest heritage railway. *Photo by John Stanford*

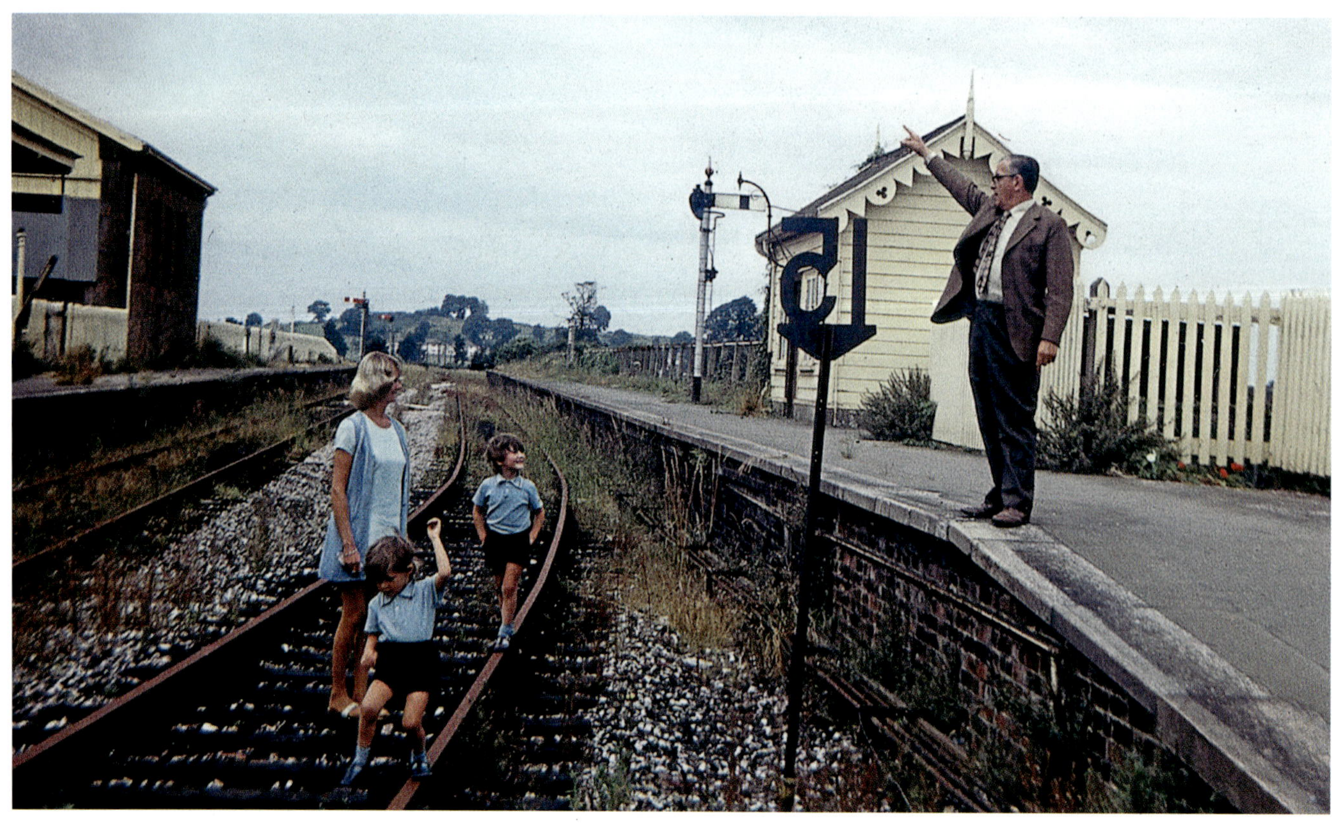

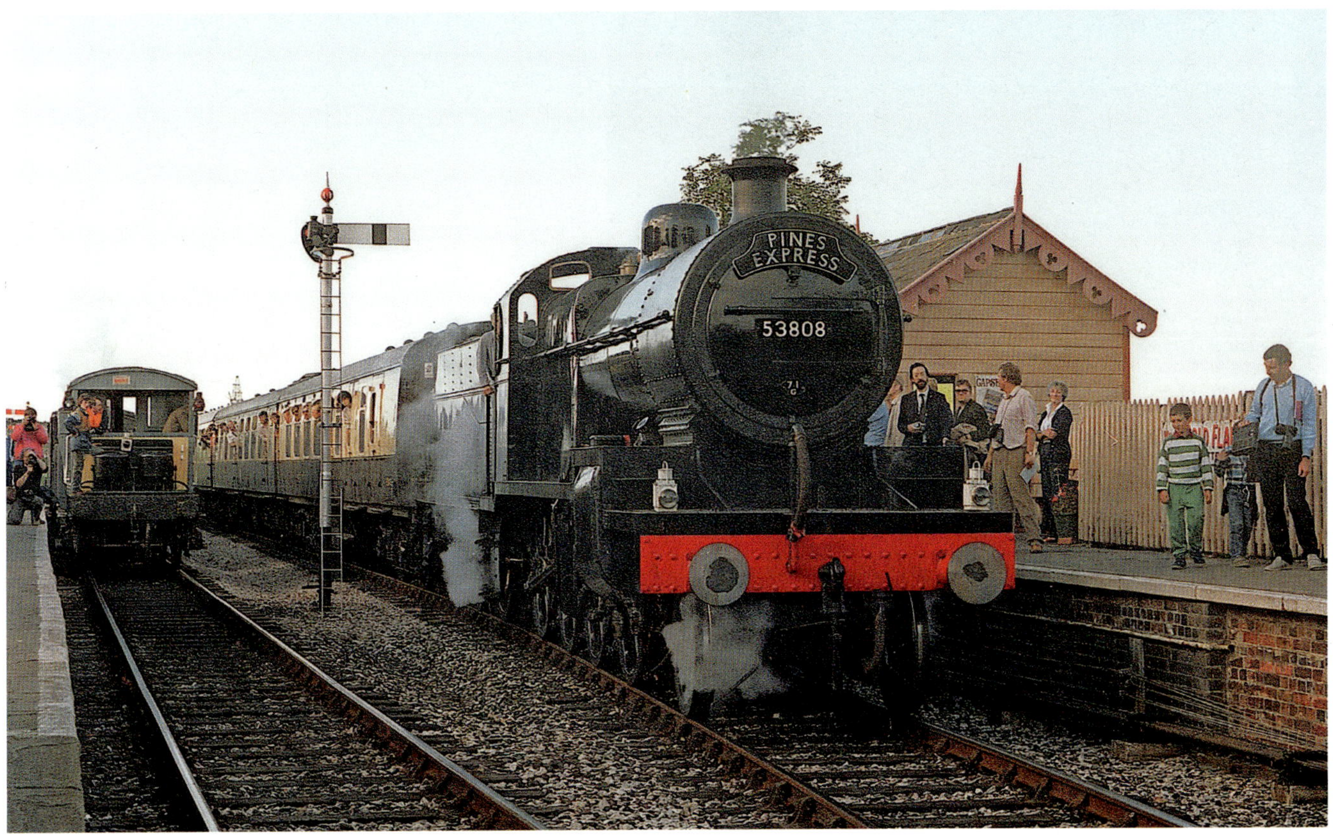

Williton and splendid Somerset & Dorset Railway 7f loco is pictured during the month it started hauling trains in its preserved life – September 1987. The author and John had just travelled from Minehead in the leading coach, beaming as the magnificent loco romped up Washford Bank. The loco has since left the WSR, although the upside is its new home is the steeply-graded Mid-Hants Railway.

Minehead in July 1976, the year that the West Somerset Railway opened, with heritage trains initially running to Blue Anchor, then extended to Williton the following year. Pannier loco 6412, purchased from the Dart Valley Railway, stands at the head of the train as Paul and Mark look on nervously. *Photo by John Stanford*

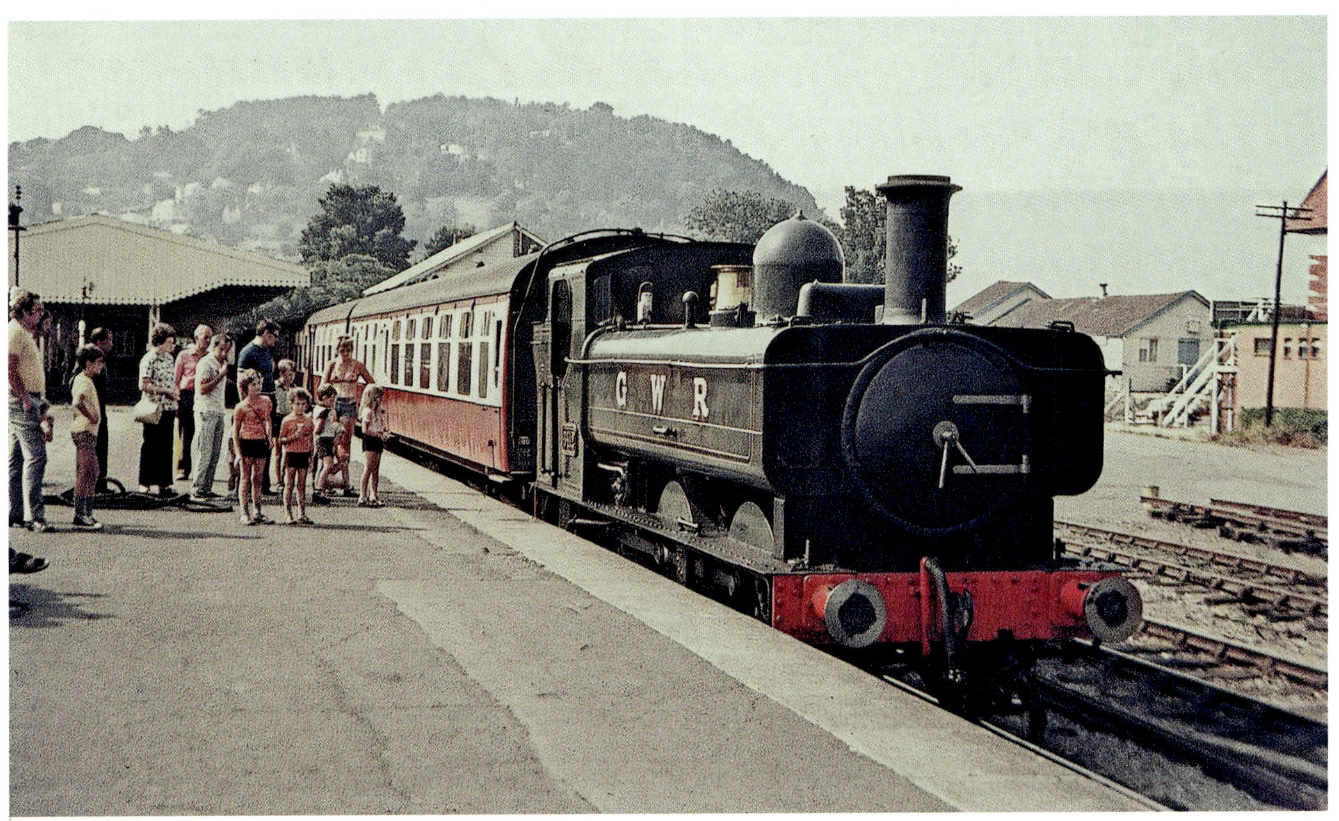

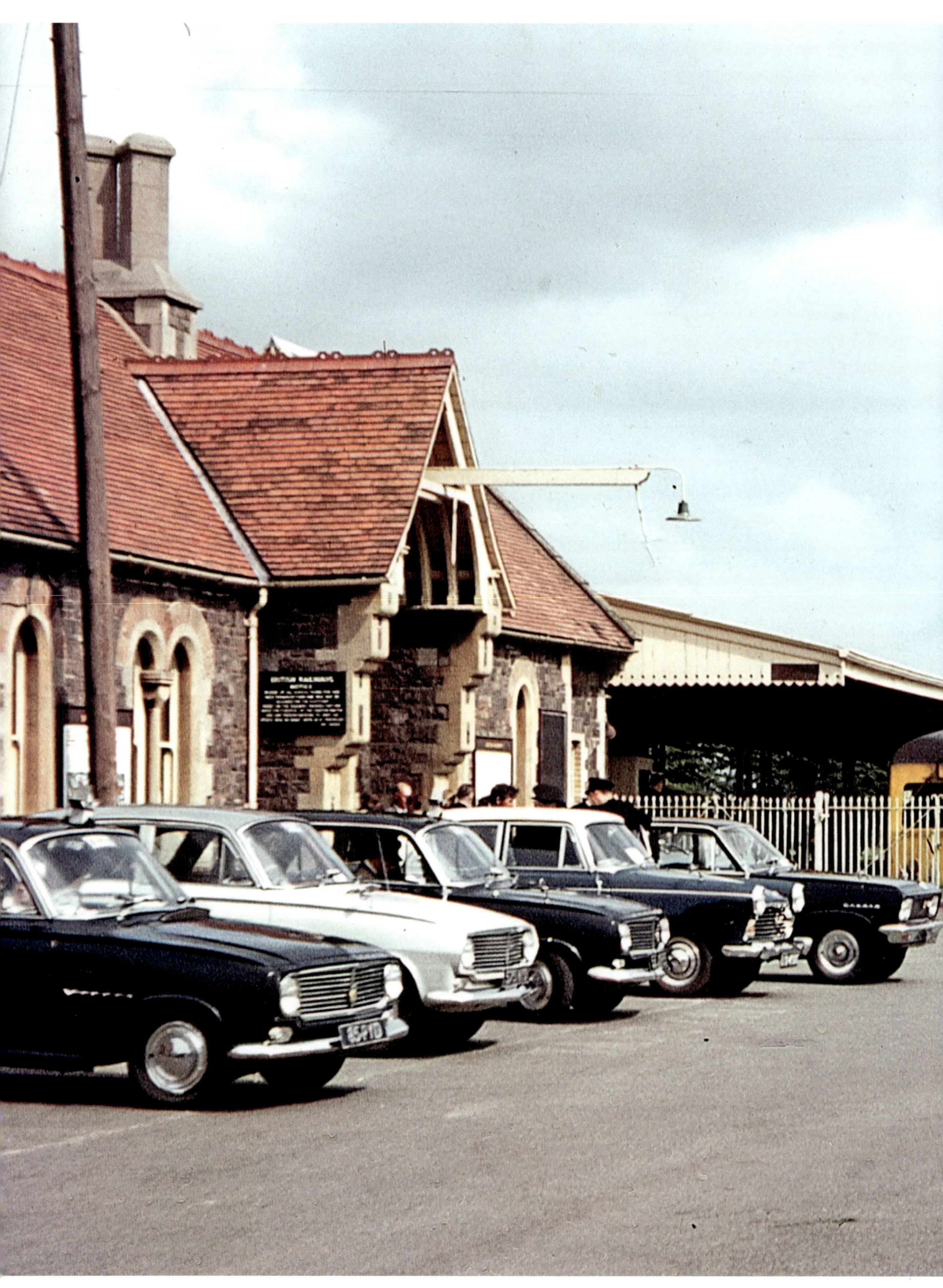

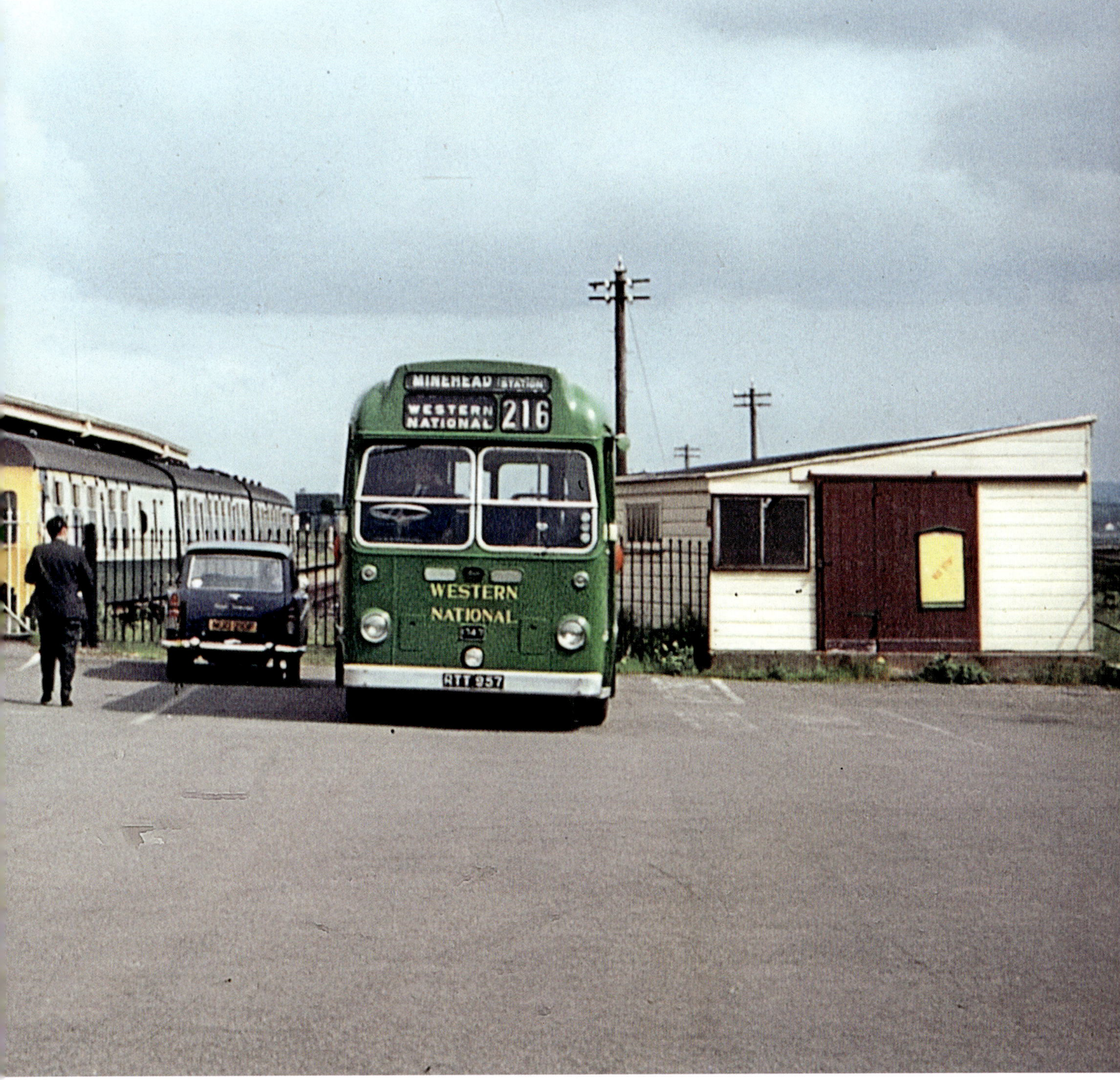

Minehead on 17th April 1969 and John visited by special train in the knowledge that the line did not have long to go under BR before closure. All British-built cars prevail in the car park, and a Bristol LS bus, with ECW bodywork stands ready – almost to taunt the DMU!

Photo by John Stanford

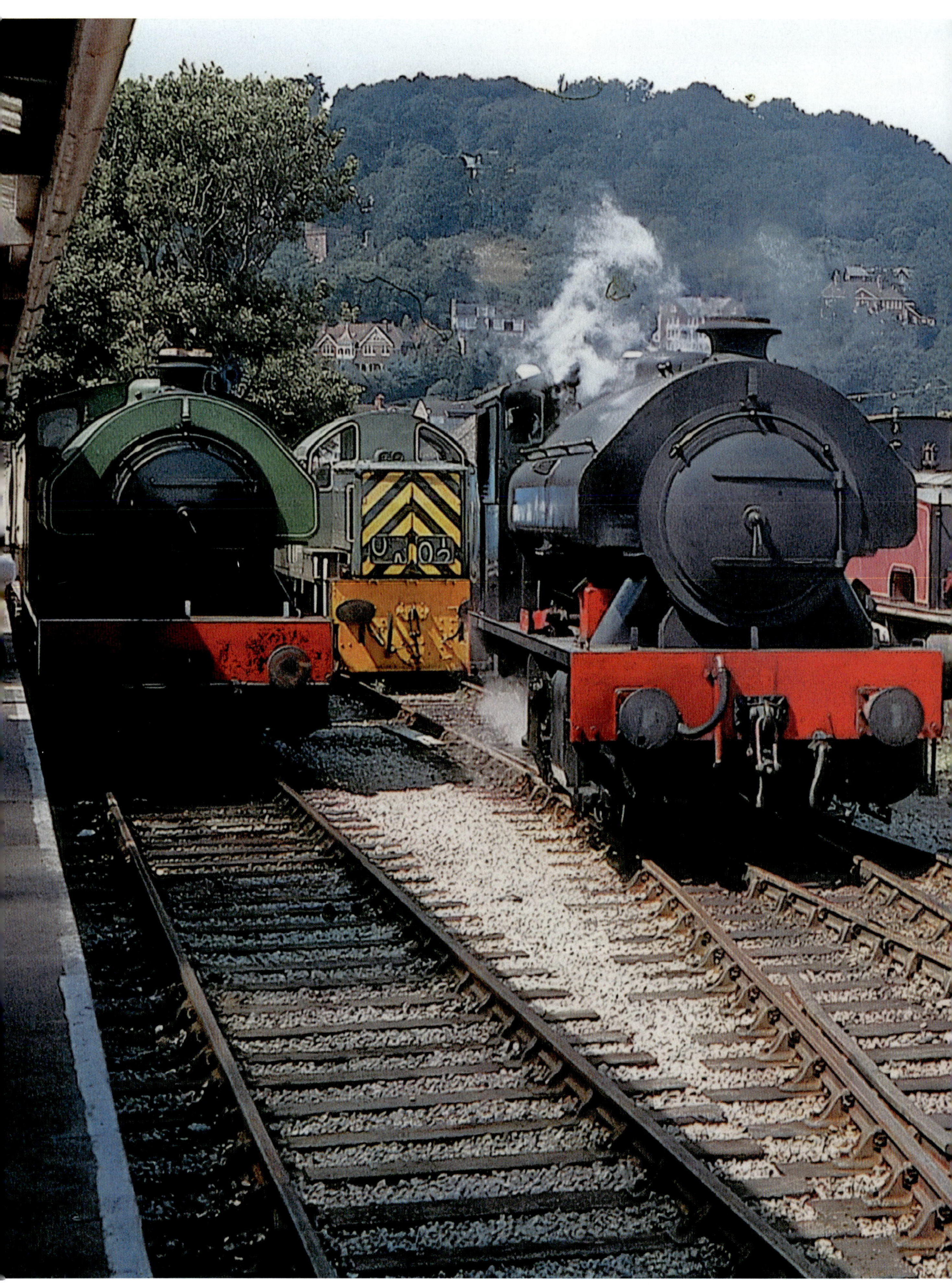

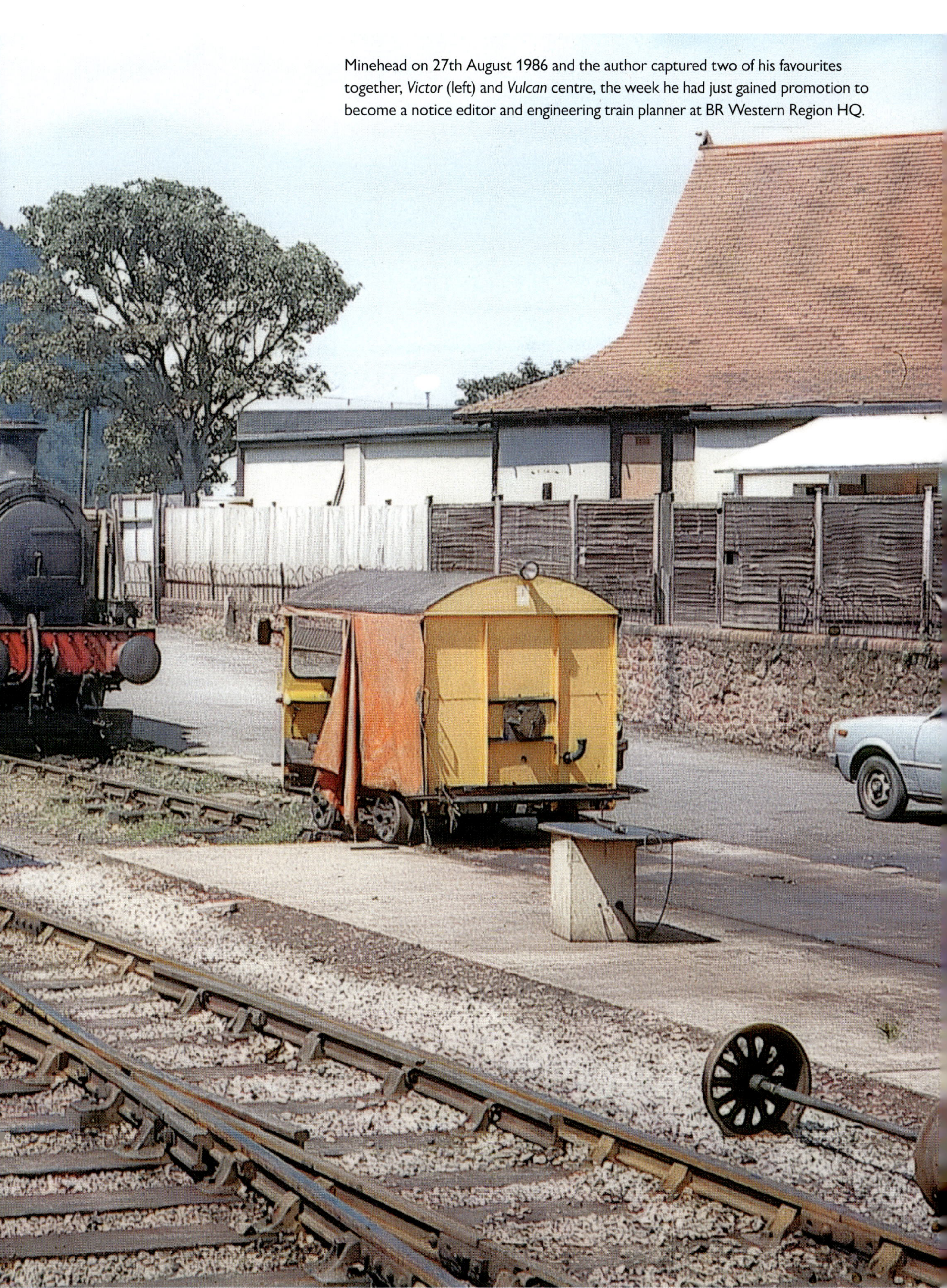
Minehead on 27th August 1986 and the author captured two of his favourites together, *Victor* (left) and *Vulcan* centre, the week he had just gained promotion to become a notice editor and engineering train planner at BR Western Region HQ.

CHAPTER 4

West is Best – Devon and Cornwall

The railways of Devon saw the opening of the line to Exeter from Bristol in 1844 and the LSWR opened to Exeter in 1860. Cornwall however was quite in the vanguard of railway development with the rich minerals needing movement in the country, beating those dates, with the Bodmin & Wenford Railway in 1834 and earlier still the Redruth and Chacewater Railway in 1826.

The railways in these counties played a key part in John and Paul's career and interests. John first travelled the Taunton to Kingswear line when he holidayed with his mum and dad in 1955. He subsequently started travelling the railways of Devon and then Cornwall, once he had gained his rail staff travel facilities in 1960.

In his position in the BR Divisional Office at Bristol, John was involved with the freight by rail business, from 1972 embodying Somerset, Devon and Cornwall. This involvement continued until 1988, ranging from parcels, milk, and clay from Devon and Cornwall through to special nuclear flask movements to and from Devonport Dockyard. Thereafter he would extol the delights of Devon and Cornwall when working in Yatton Station ticket office to his customers. Paul's first involvement came in 1987 when he was planning engineering train movements in the counties. Subsequently he investigated operational incidents in Devon and Cornwall, and the wider Western Region during the later days of BR in the early 1990s, and was routinely involved in the two counties as he rose to senior management positions within the privatised railway era on the Western Region from 2009. He worked for Network Rail until his early retirement at the end of 2021.

As an aside, John was involved with heritage railway movement in Devon from the early 1960s, with the abortive scheme to preserve the Moretonhampstead line, but most notably the sale and takeover of the Paignton to Kingswear line in 1972. He would supply information to the Dart Valley Railway Company about the capability of the line and the state of infrastructure. Typical of John's modest approach however, this only became evident as the author undertook research for this book some 30 years after John's passing and found correspondence between him and the Dart Valley Railway, as part of the due diligence process by the latter before buying the line from BR.

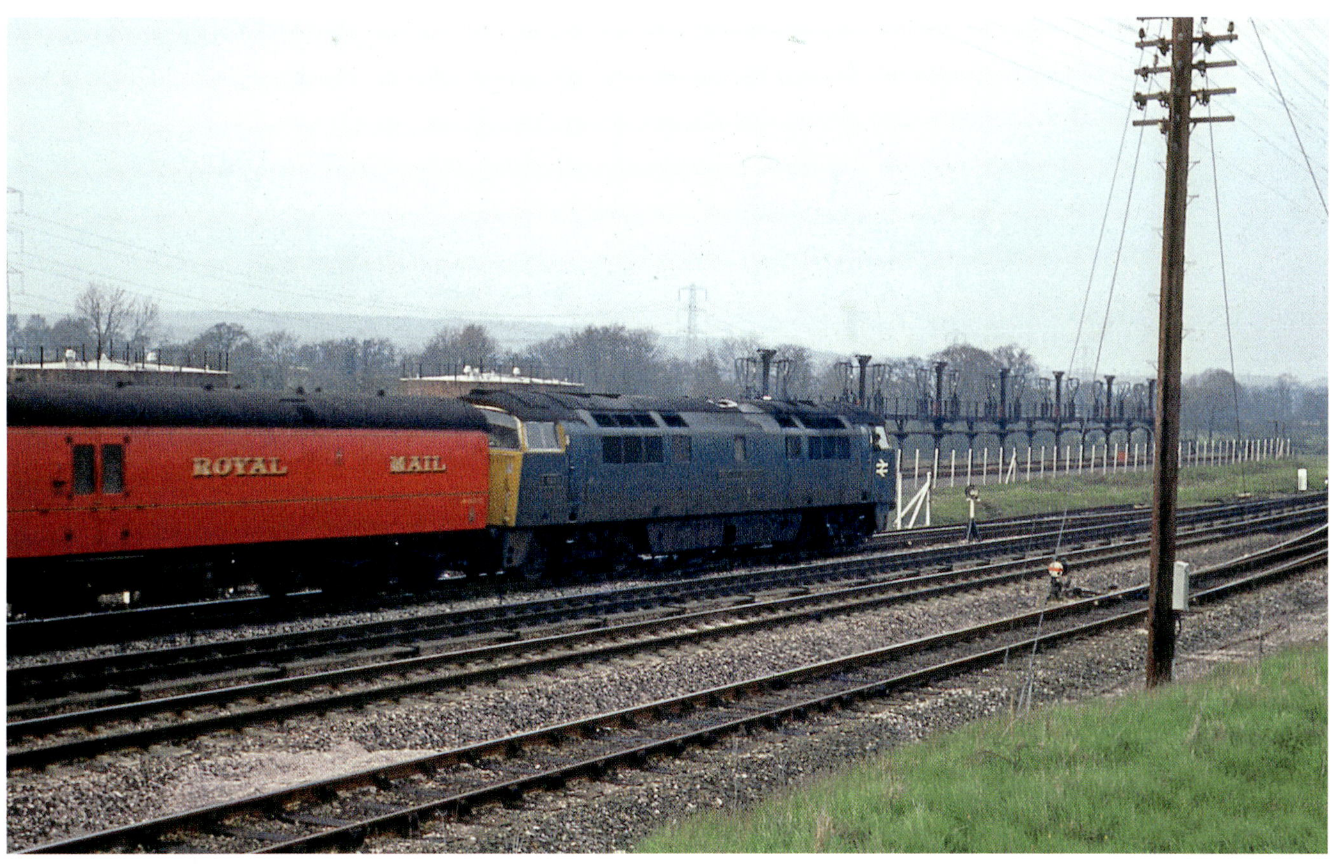

Tiverton Junction in April 1968 and a Western Class loco heads a Taunton-bound Travelling Post Office train. The bright red vehicles certainly made it clear they were carrying letter post. John photographed this scene from the brake van of a milk train he was travelling.

Photo by John Stanford

Hemyock was served by a 7½ mile branch from Tiverton Jn, opened in 1876. In April 1968 John obtained a brake-van pass and travelled with his friend Alan Taylor (see page 78) on the daily milk train. Here D6348 is seen atop of milk tanks just outside the creamery.

Photo by John Stanford

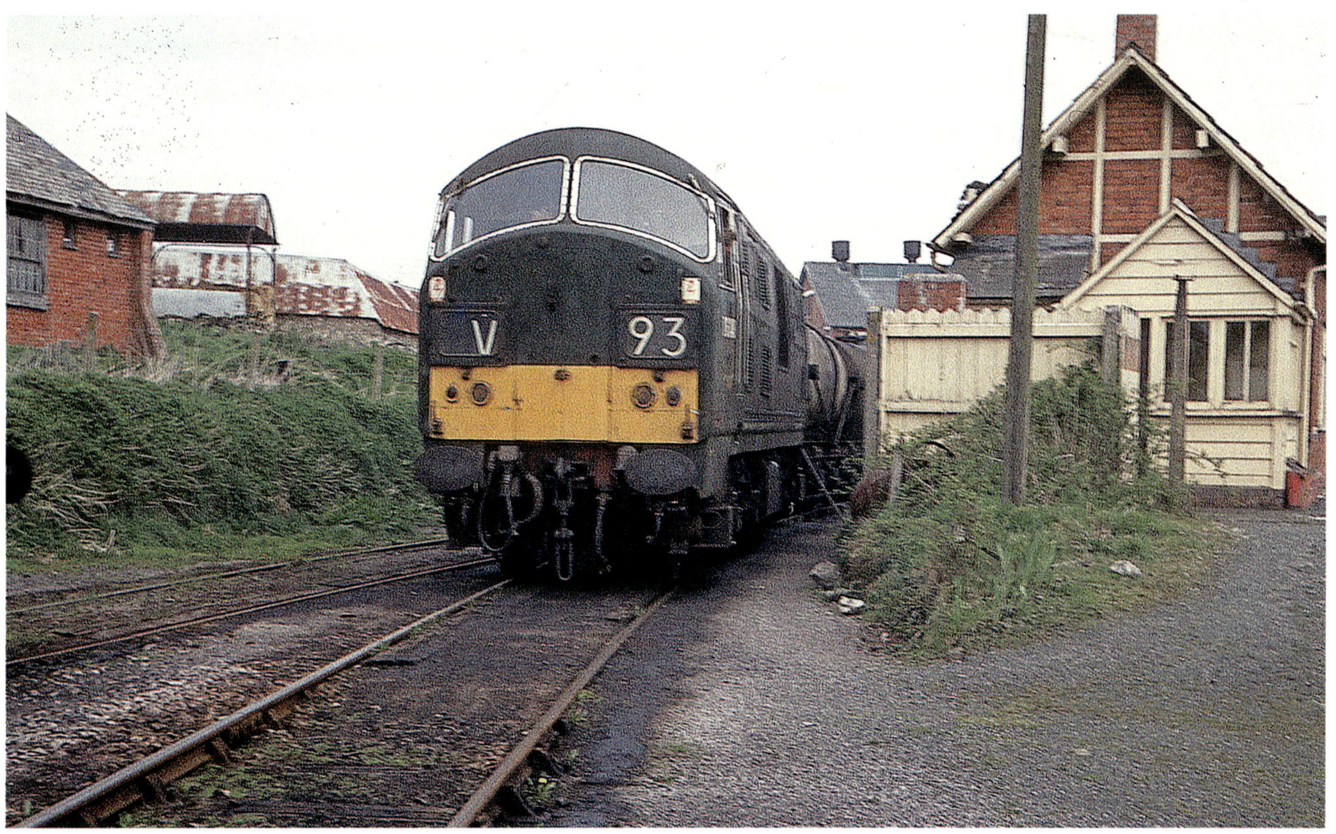

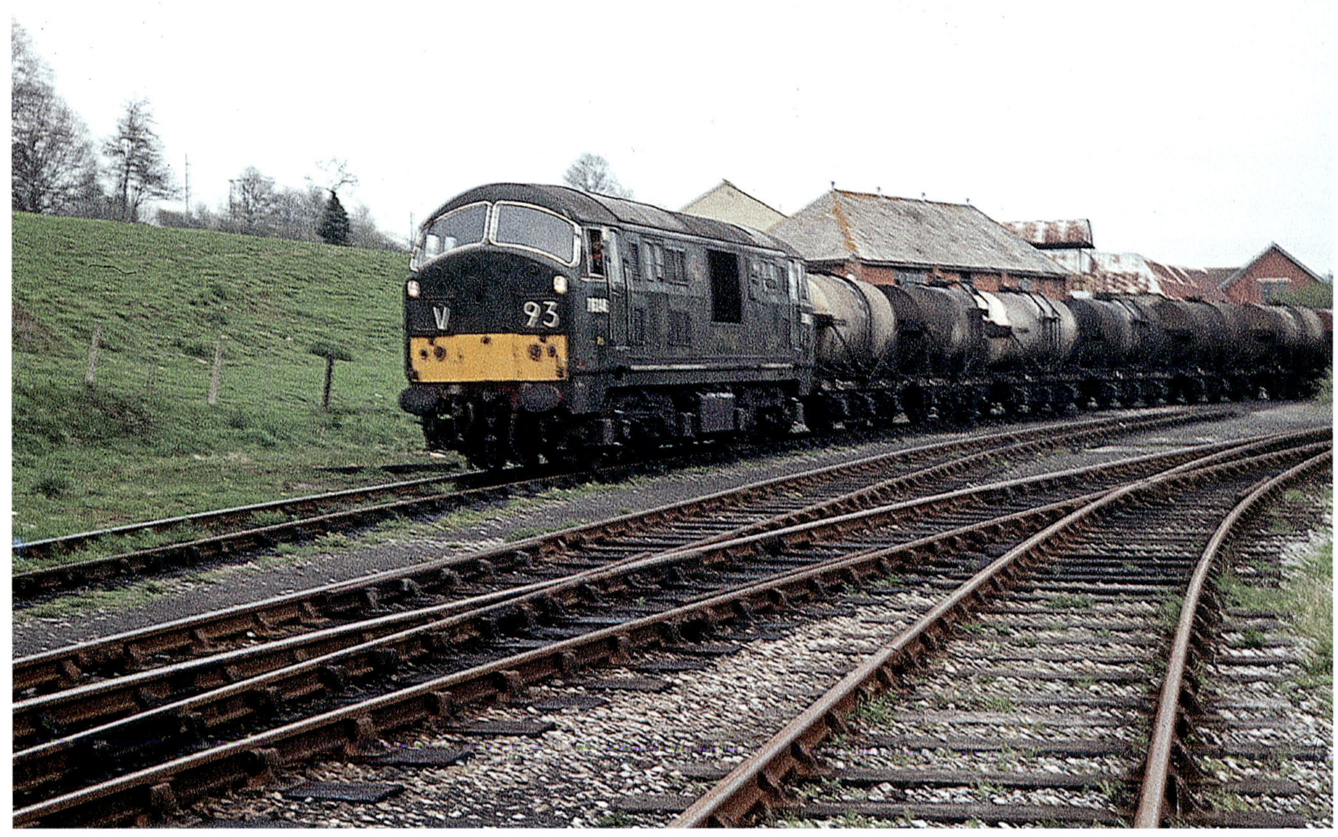

Hemyock. Although the line lost its passenger service in 1963, the station buildings survived. Here D6348 is seen shunting its train. It was a Laira-based loco at the time. The branch finally closed in 1975; at the end it was served by class 25 locomotives following withdrawal of the ill-fated North British-built D63 locos in 1972. *Photo by John Stanford*

Exeter St Davids in July 1962 and John caught West Country Pacific loco *City of Wells*, subsequently preserved, leaving for London Waterloo, as John headed for his holiday at Goodrington. Exeter is one of the few places trains to London depart routinely in different directions, to Paddington and Waterloo respectively. Plymouth was the other in the West Country. *Photo by John Stanford*

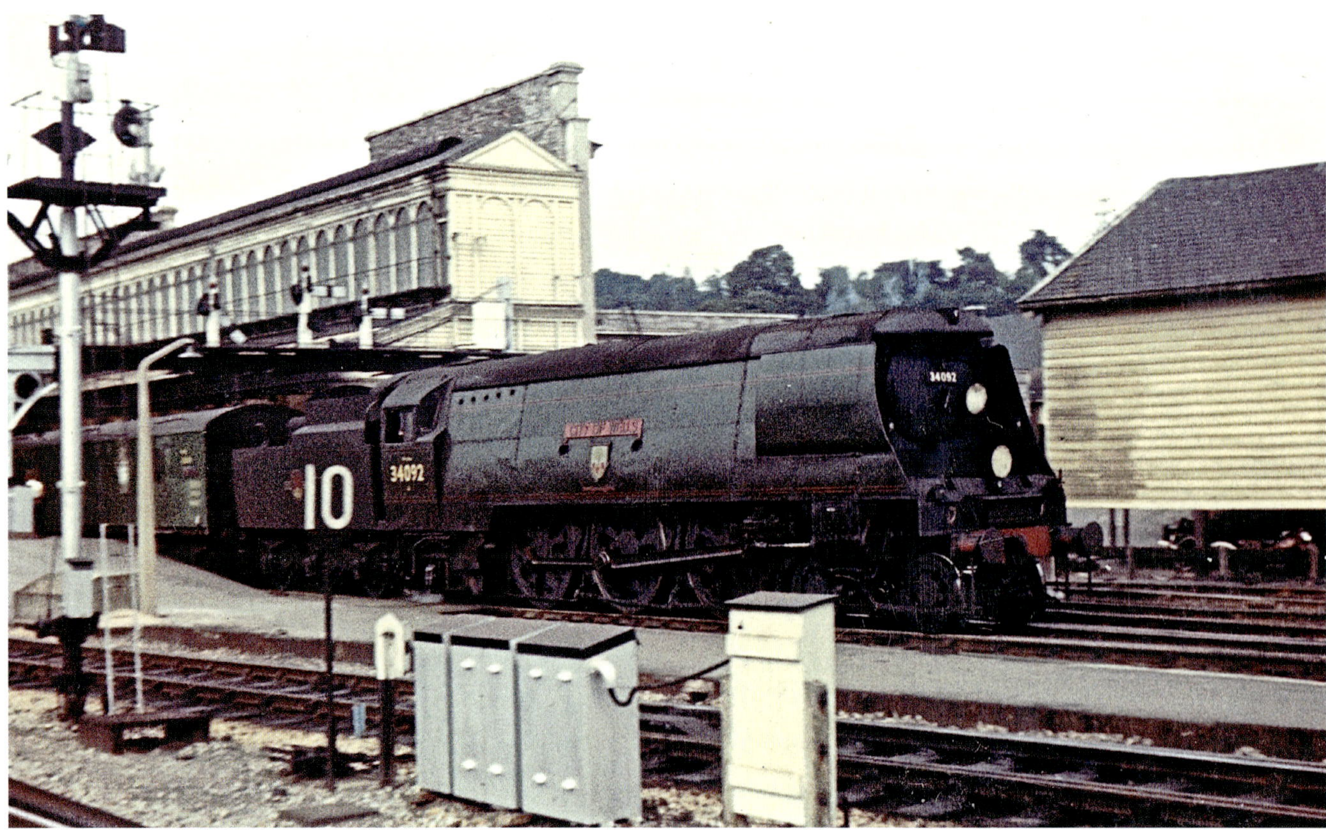

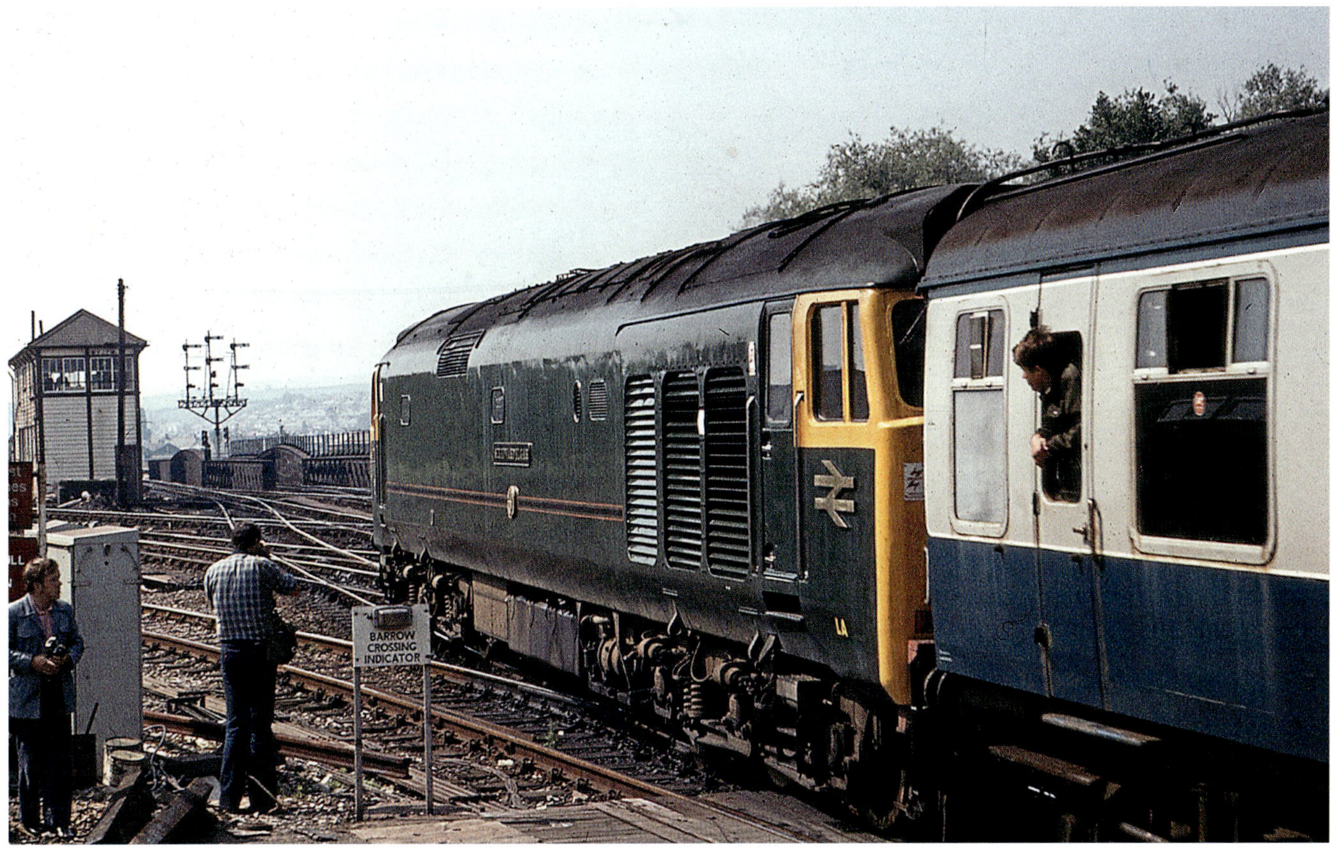

Exeter St Davids on 16th June 1984 and the author caught newly-repainted class 50 named *Sir Edward Elgar* heading south. The loco, 50007, was formerly named *Hercules*. On this day John took Paul to North Devon with his BR friends to walk the closed Peters Marland to Meeth railway, where track lifting had just begun.

Exeter Central on a hot June day in 1984; looking towards St Davids when John had a meeting at the BR Civil Engineers offices. A class 47 stands with freight vehicles as cement wagons are unloaded in the small freight yard, now built upon. *Photo by John Stanford*

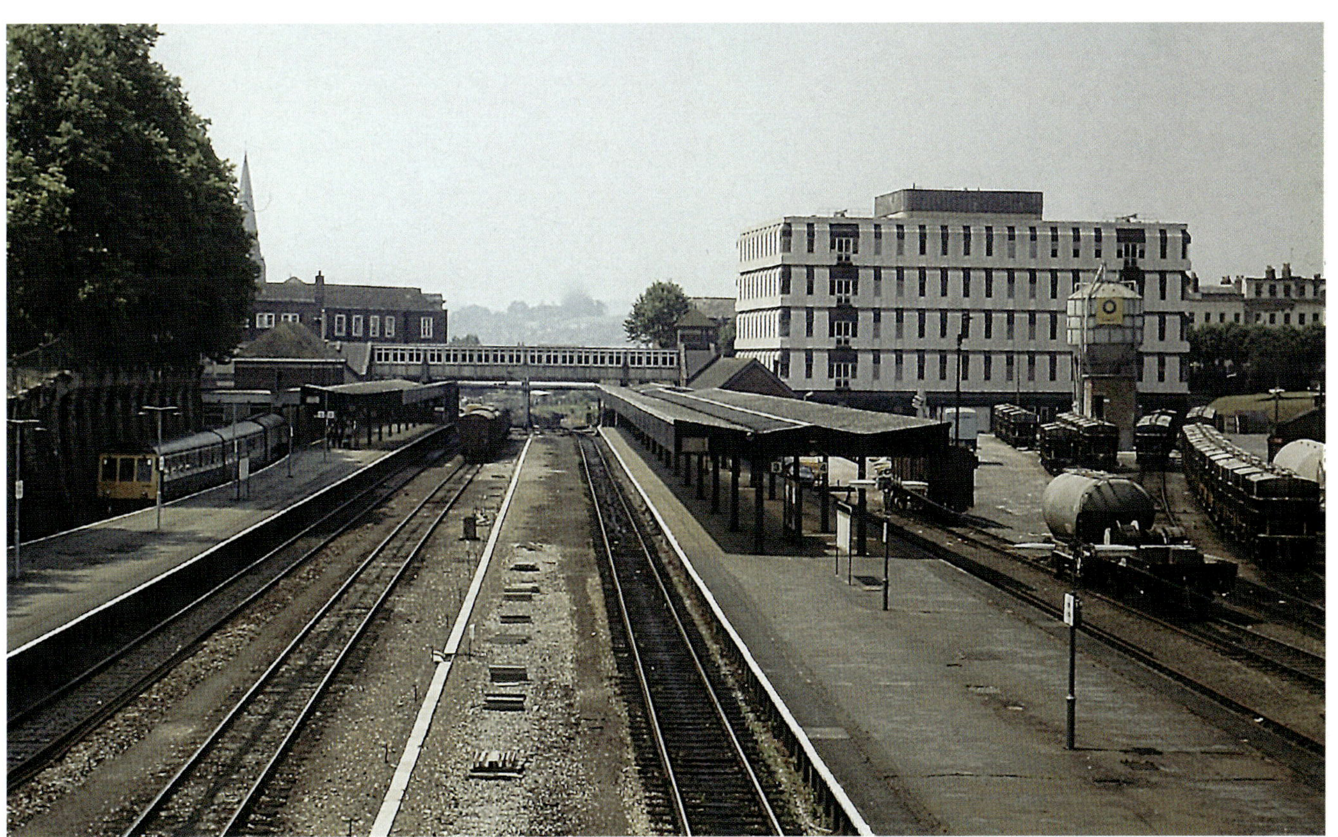

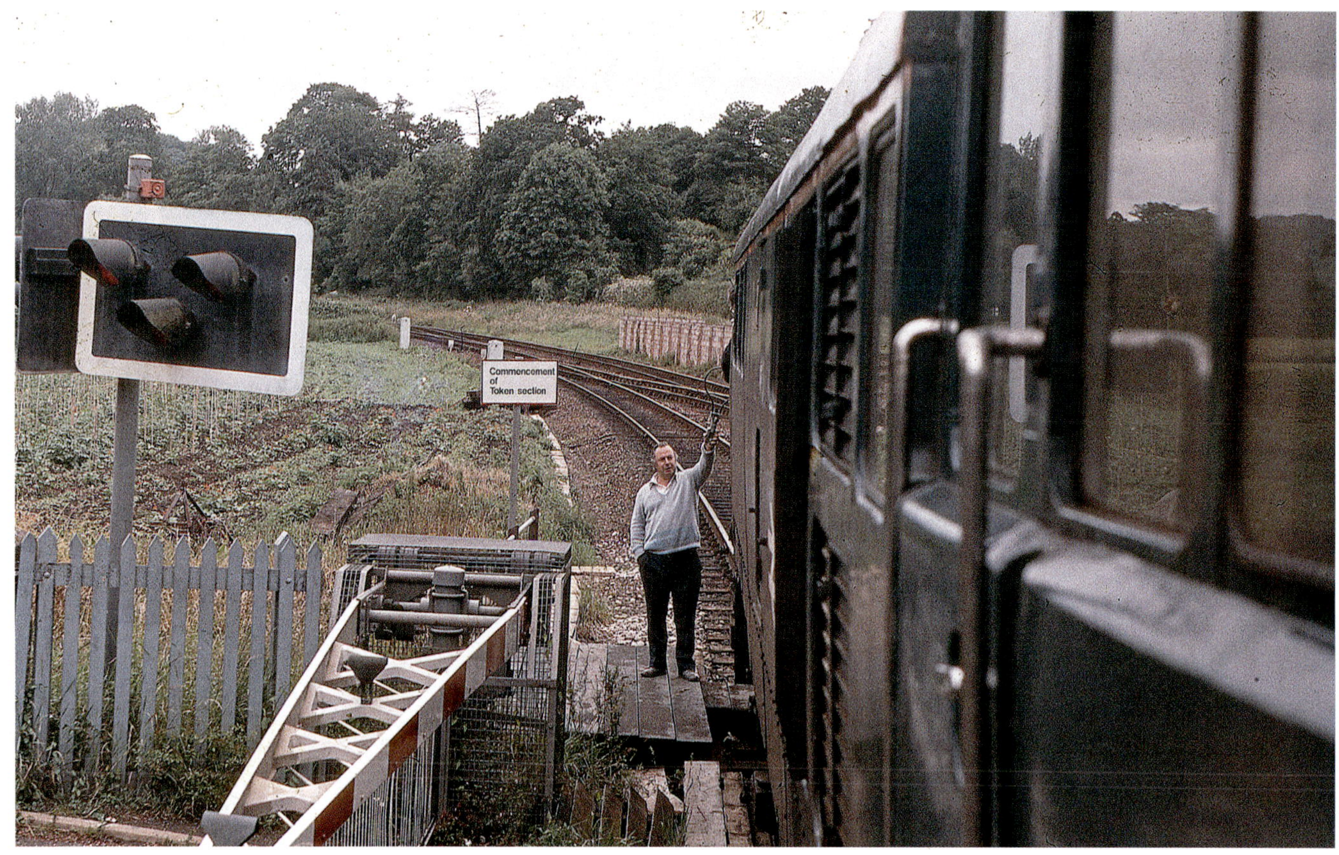

Crediton on 12th July 1986 as the signalman hands the single line token to the driver to proceed to Eggesford. Loco 31405 is in charge but it later failed and 33062 replaced it for that day.

Eggesford is an important point on the single line from Exeter to Barnstaple. Here on 16th June 1984 John captured a class 33 waiting patiently as his DMU-formed train enters the loop. Resident signalman Billy Butt then kindly let Paul and John into the signal box upon their arrival.

Photo by John Stanford

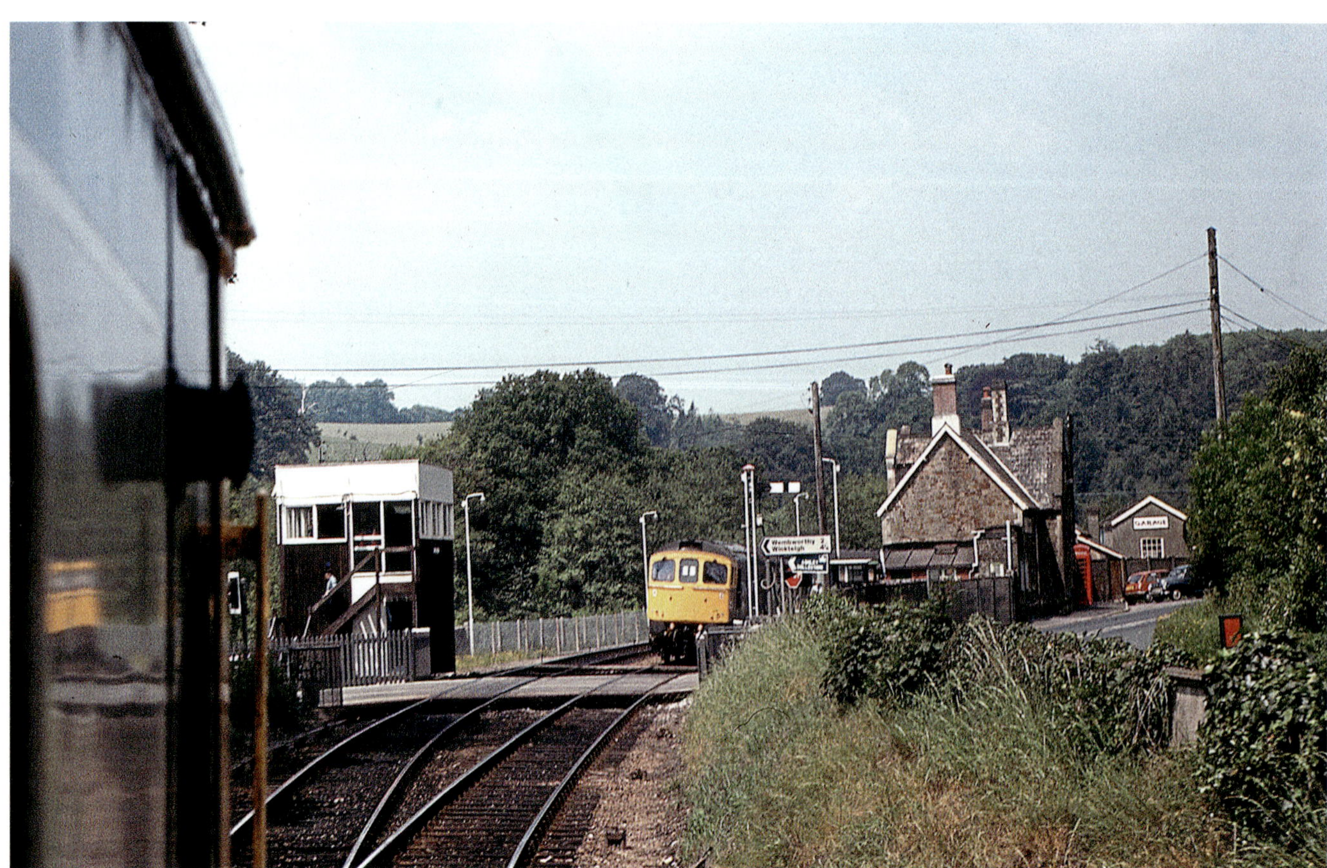

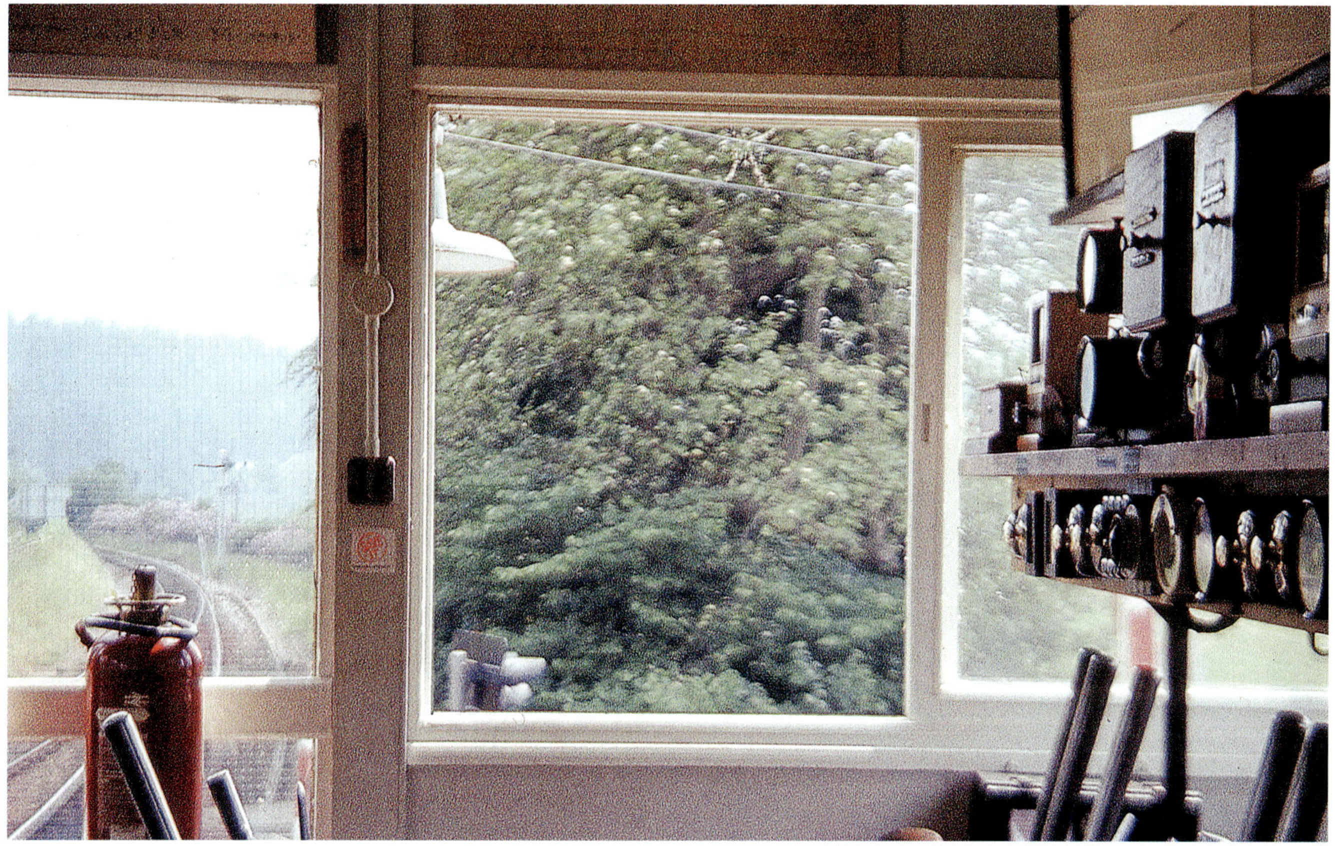

Eggesford Signal Box looking smart on 16th June 1984 in a view toward Exeter. Below the signal box was the River Taw, which flooded in 1967, wrecking the box. The final box, seen here, was opened in 28 September 1969 and lasted just under 20 years.

Eggesford was a favourite location during the author's career, and here on Saturday 12th July 1986 we look toward Exeter, when he spent the day photographing here and hiking. Loco-hauled trains ran until 1991, even after freight ended to Barnstaple in 1987. The beautiful station building is listed.

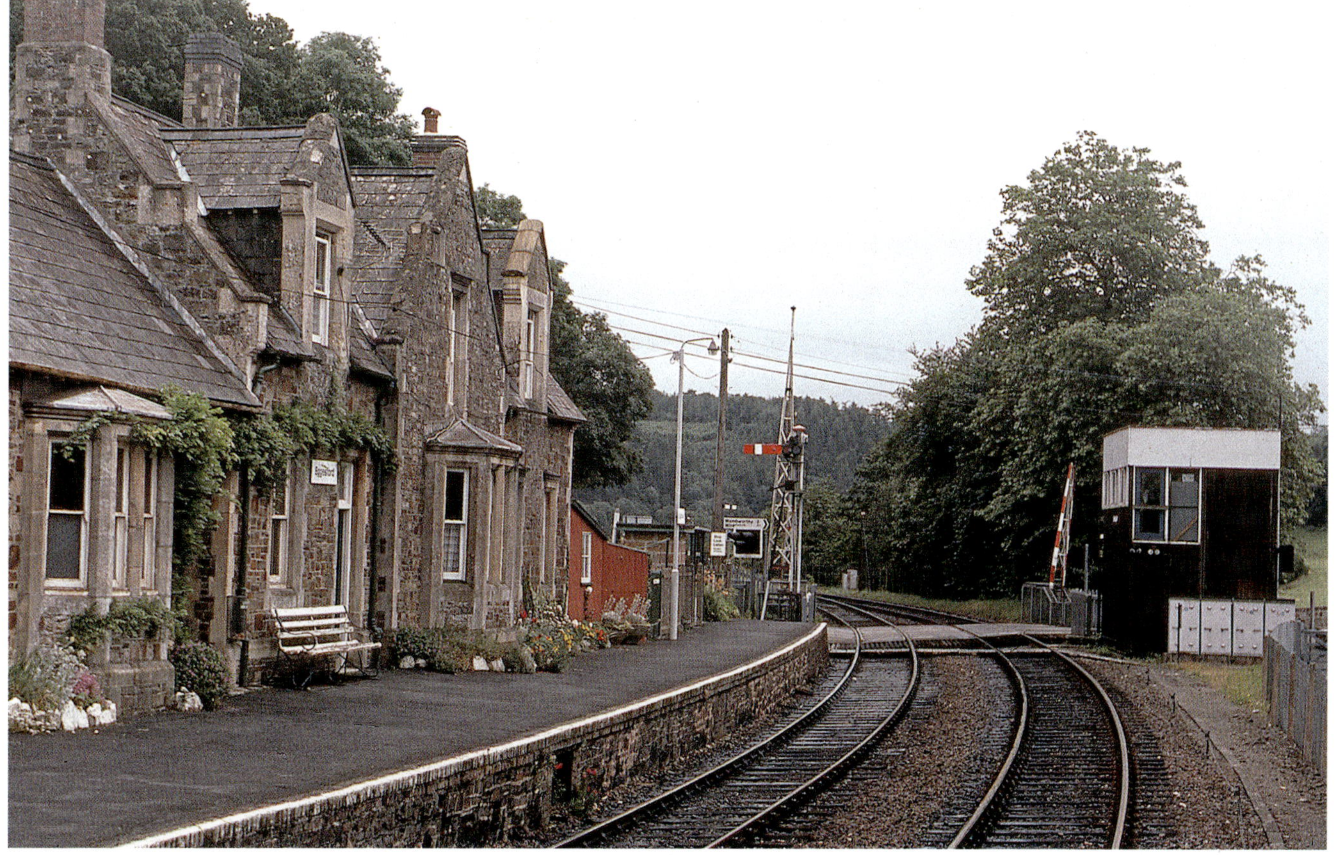

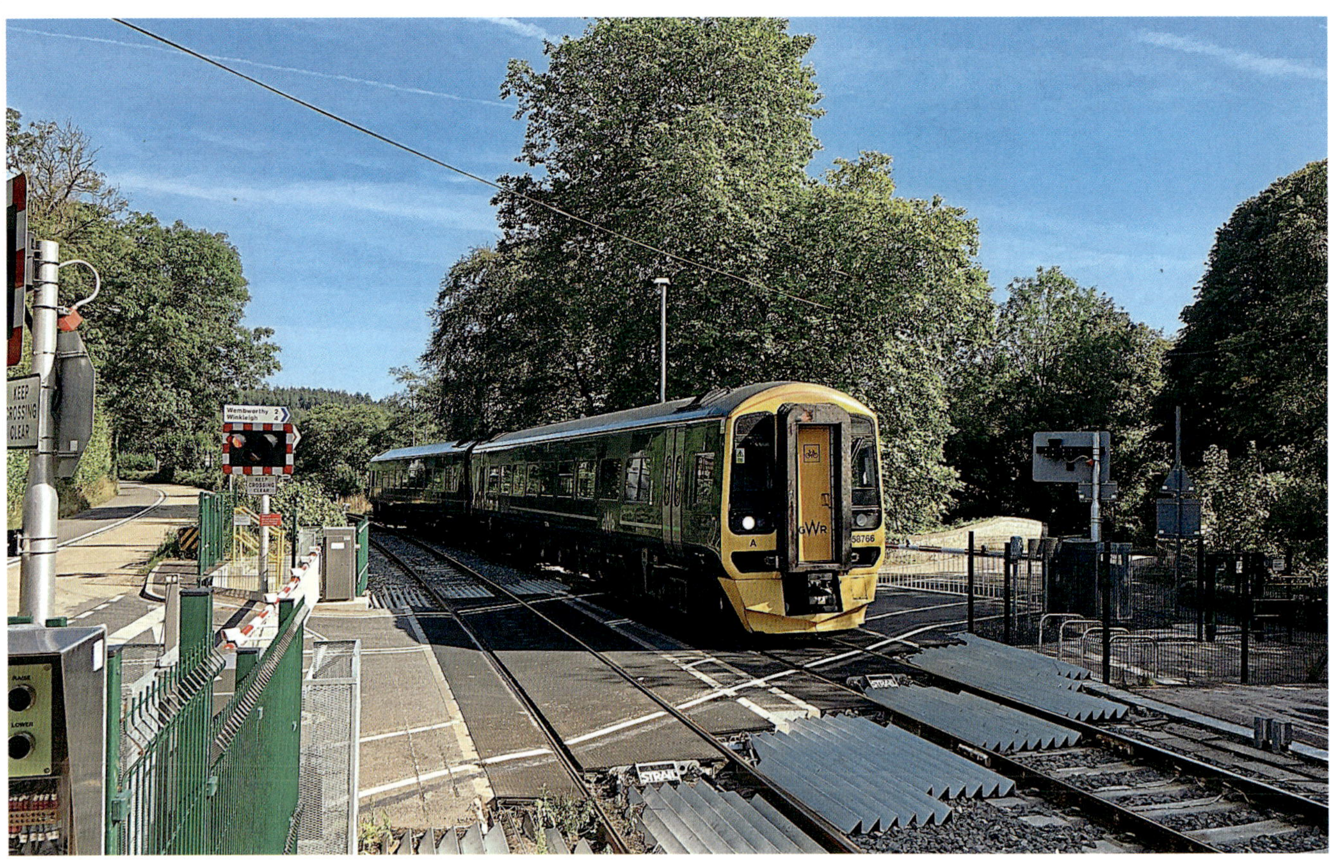

Eggesford and we see newly gauge-cleared class 158 unit entering the station on 14th September 2019. Gauge clearance occurred in 2019 by Network Rail as part of the winter 2019 timetable change. This was the biggest change on the Western region since the start of HST operation in 1976 with 75% of train services altered and enhanced frequencies, including clockface hourly Barnstaple service operated for the first time.

Barnstaple Goods Yard in April 1985, with another two years before closure to freight. John and his BR colleagues chat to the rail chargeman about traffic. In the background are cement wagons (TOPS code PCA) for unloading. *Photo by John Stanford*

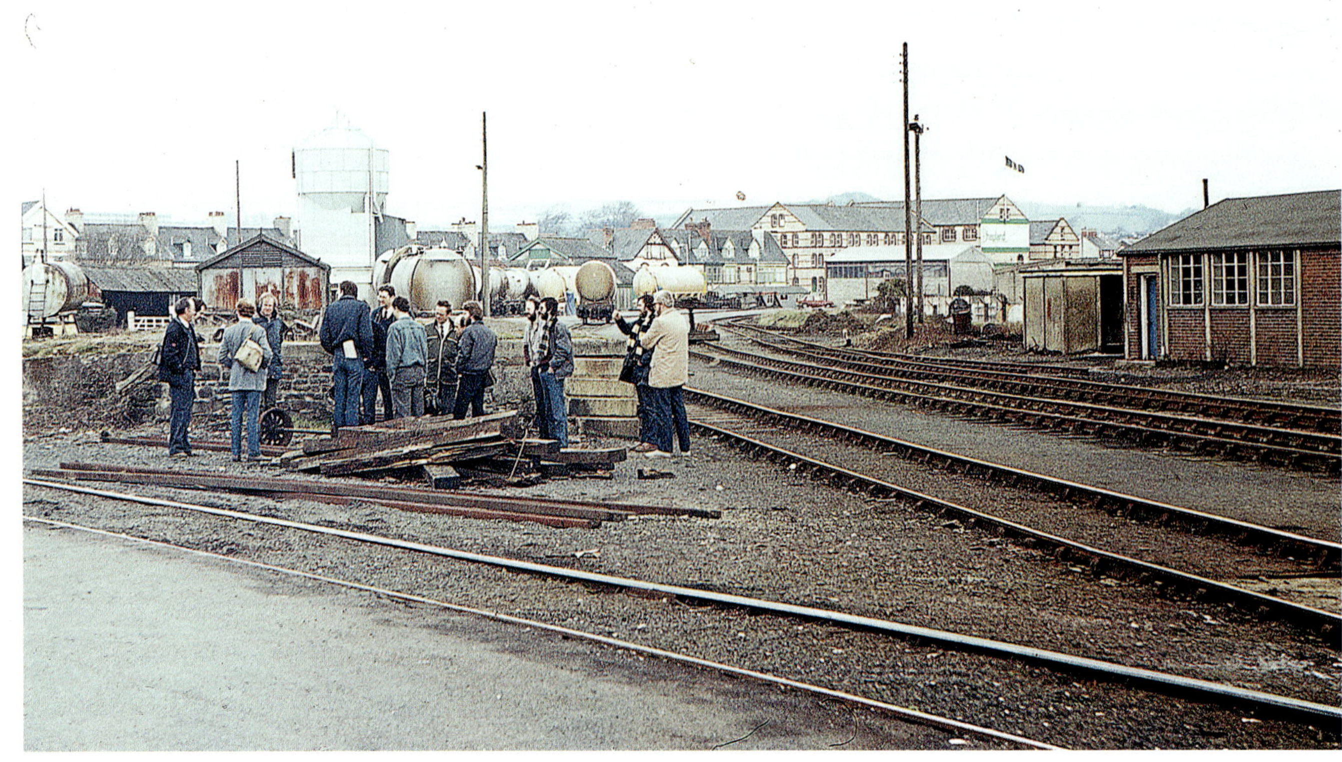

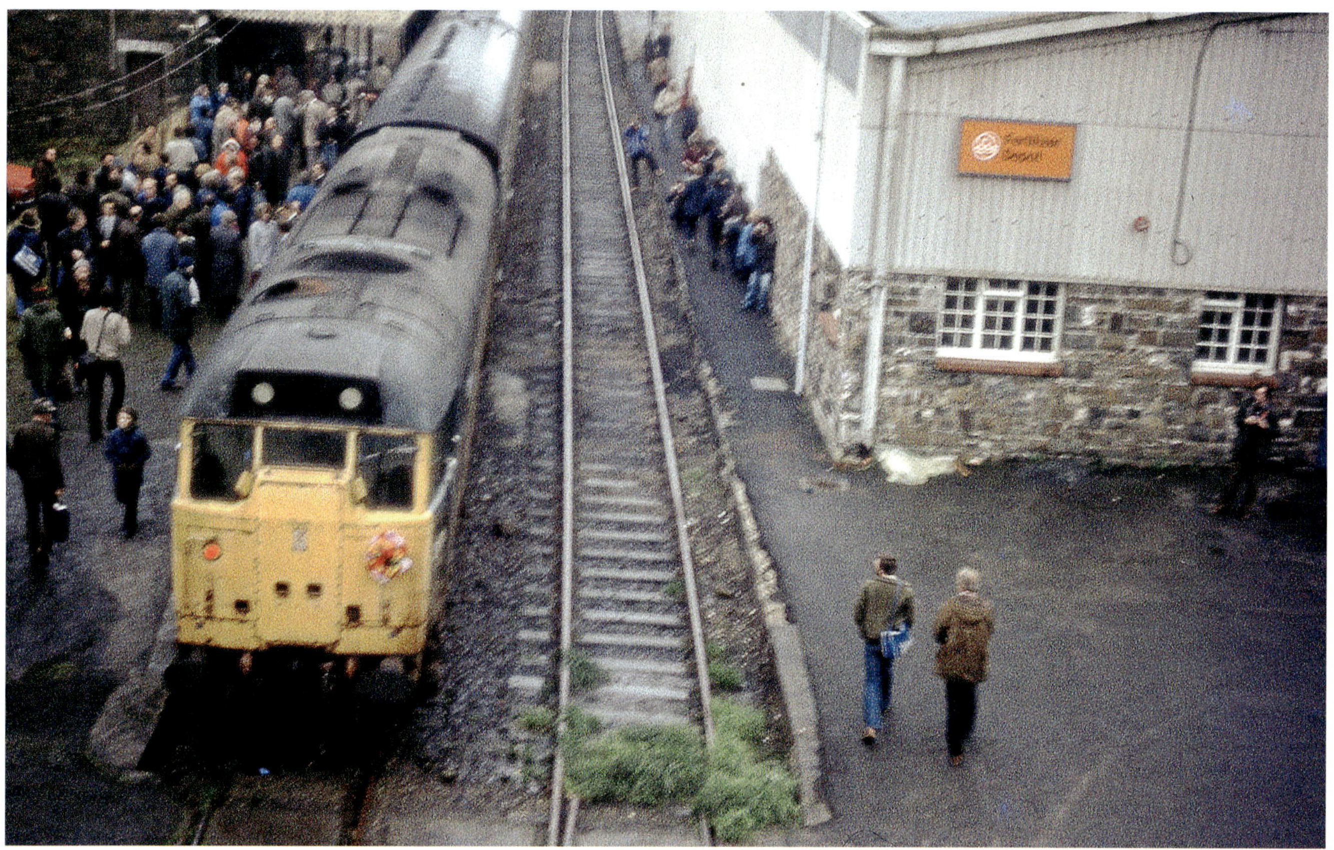

Torrington beyond Barnstaple was a freight-only destination when John arrived on Western Region in 1969, beyond Barnstaple and serving the town plus the clay mines around Peters Marland and Meeth. That lasted until September 1982 when all traffic ceased. The station building was home to Torrington's last rail worker, Harry Beer. John would routinely speak to Harry during the 1970s about incoming and outgoing freight, when clay, milk and fertiliser operated. Harry met the last train on 6th November 1982 and John met him for the first and last time. John and Paul travelled on the train and this trip cemented the author's love of North Devon railways. *Photos by John Stanford and Trevor Riddle*

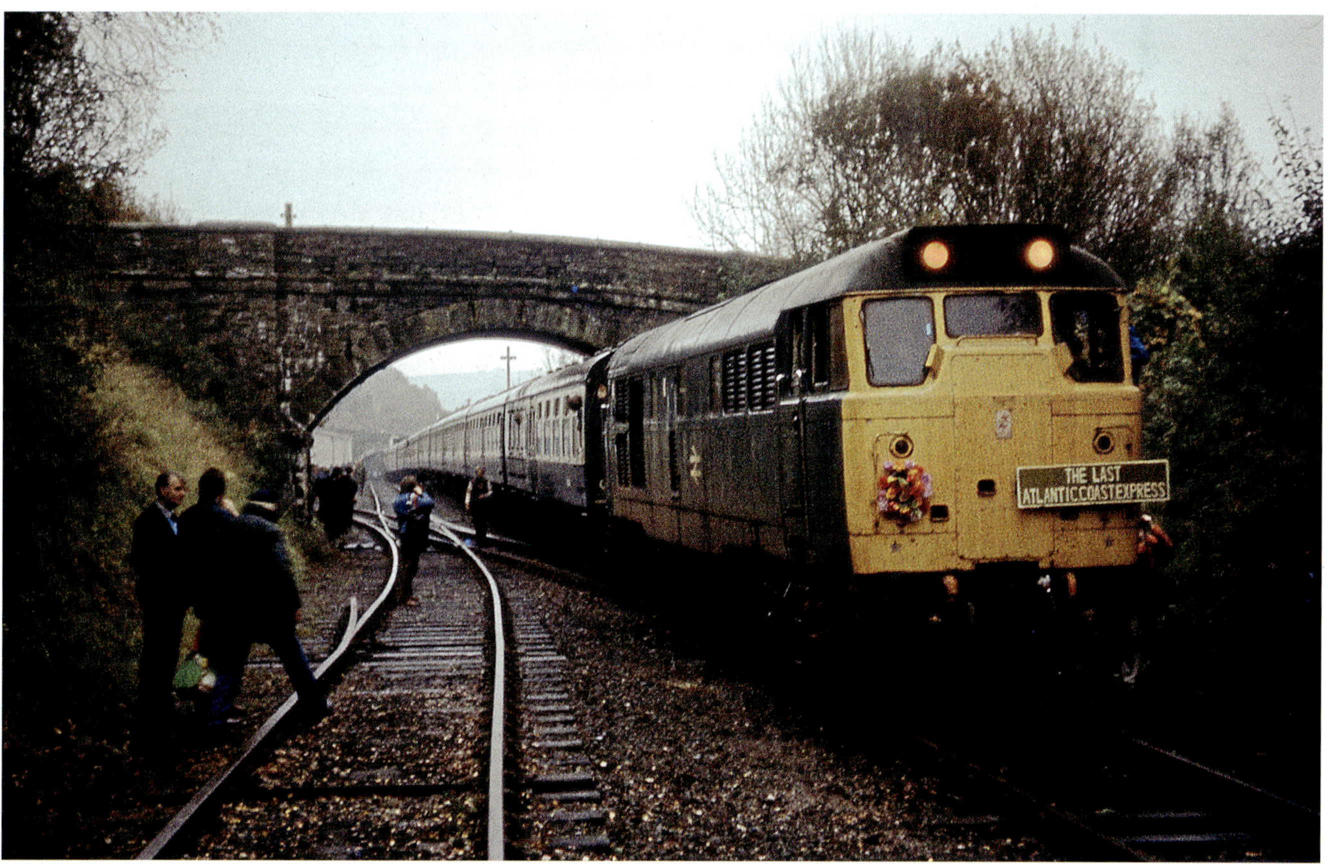

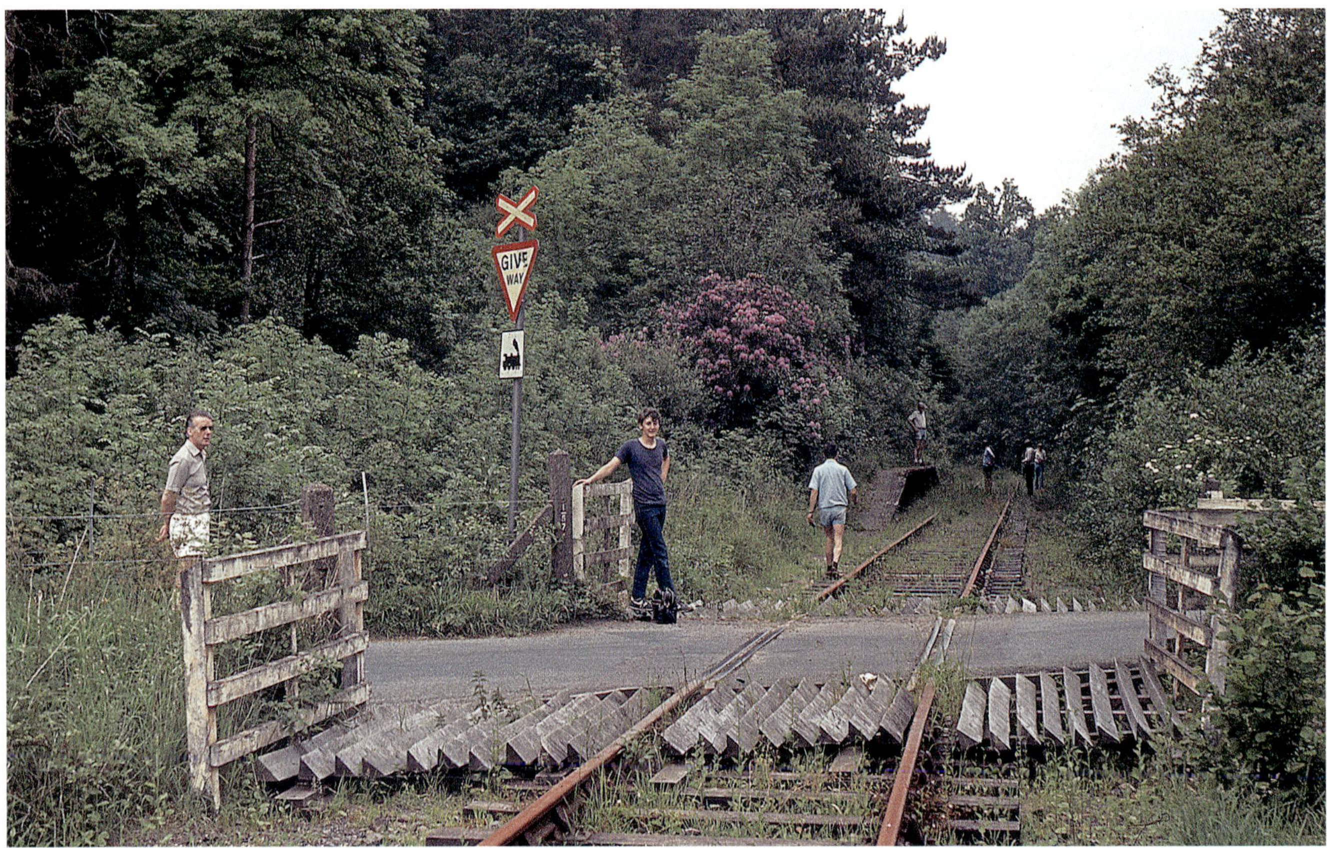

Watergate Halt; beyond Torrington the character of the line changed completely on a section of railway that only opened to standard gauge in 1925. Here John has captured the halt and the author, nearly two years after the last clay train. *Photo by John Stanford*

Okehampton in August 1986 presented a forlorn sight. John was involved with planning trains of military tanks here during the 1970s and Paul did the same with ballast trains from nearby Meldon Quarry in the late 1980s, after the loss of the remaining passenger service in the early 1970s.

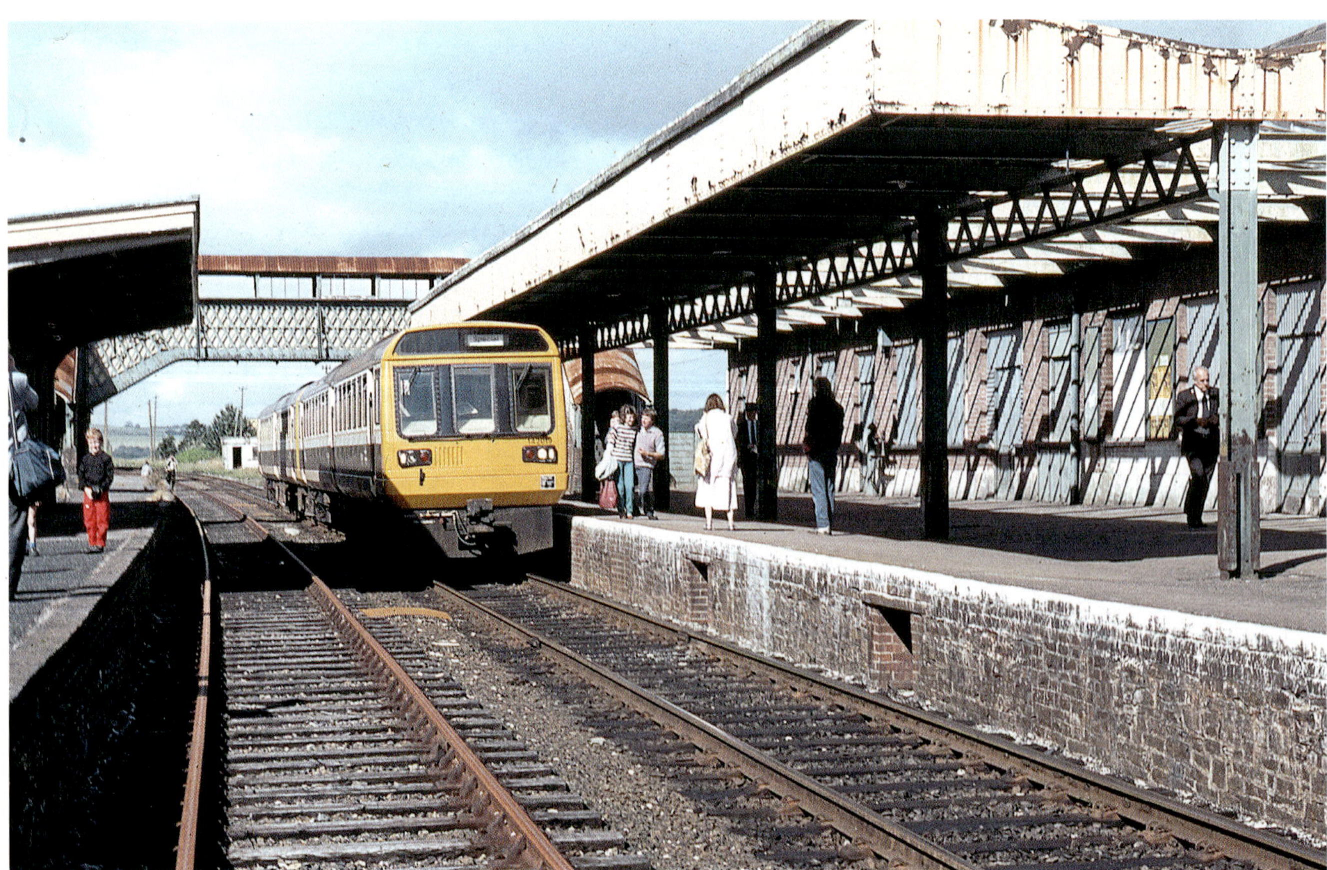

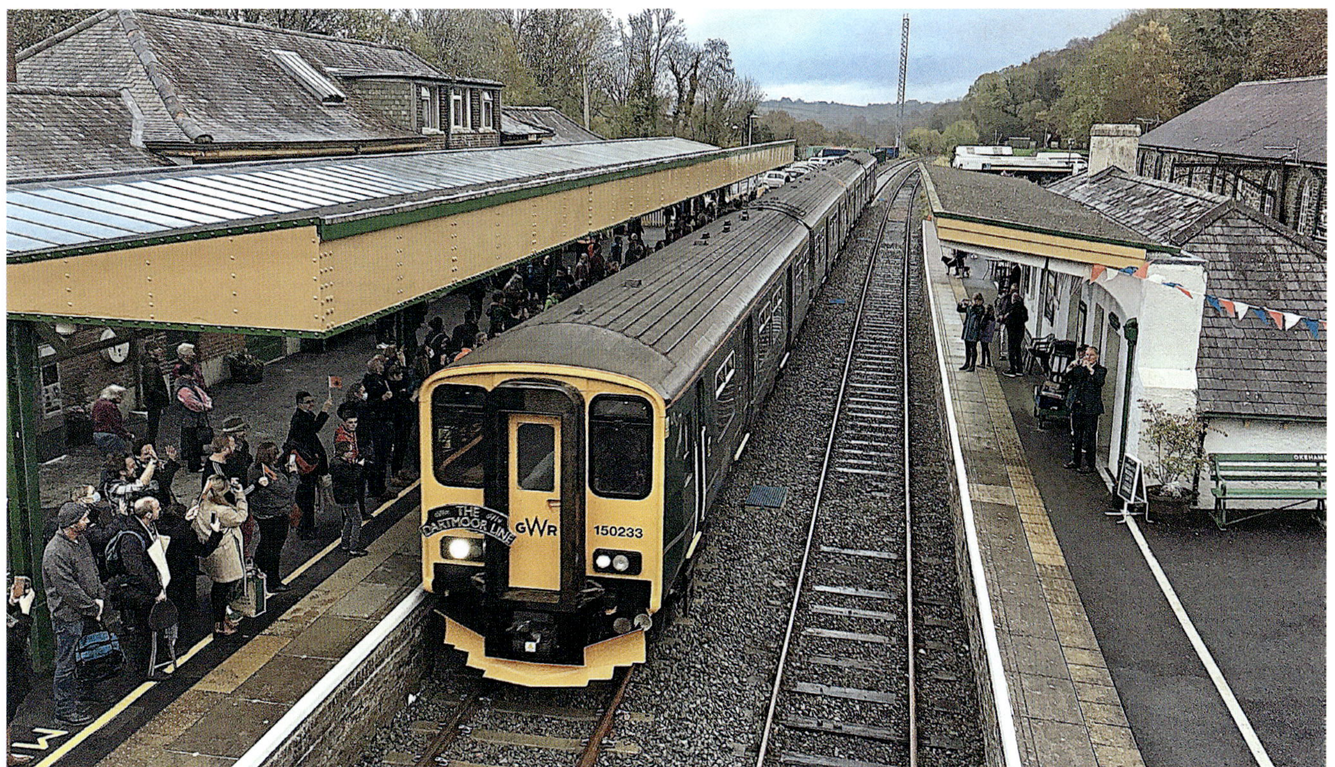

Okehampton was the scene of much excitement on 21 November 2021; with the first days of regular trains, in nearly 50 years. The author's friend and colleague Christian Irwin led work to refurbish the line, on a scale inconceivable when the author visited 35 years earlier. This involved new track and a beautiful restoration of the SR station.

WE NOW RETURN TO THE MAIN LINE AND HEAD SOUTH OF EXETER AND TO PAIGNTON

Dawlish Warren in July 1989 when Paul had a day off from the Rules & Accidents office and a mixed Speedlink train heads south to Plymouth and Cornwall. This just shows the diversity of wagon types prevalent in the West until the end of the Speedlink freight network in July 1991. For example, the last wagon is a gas tank vehicle for Plymouth, followed by a German Railways box van for bagged clay from Par Docks.

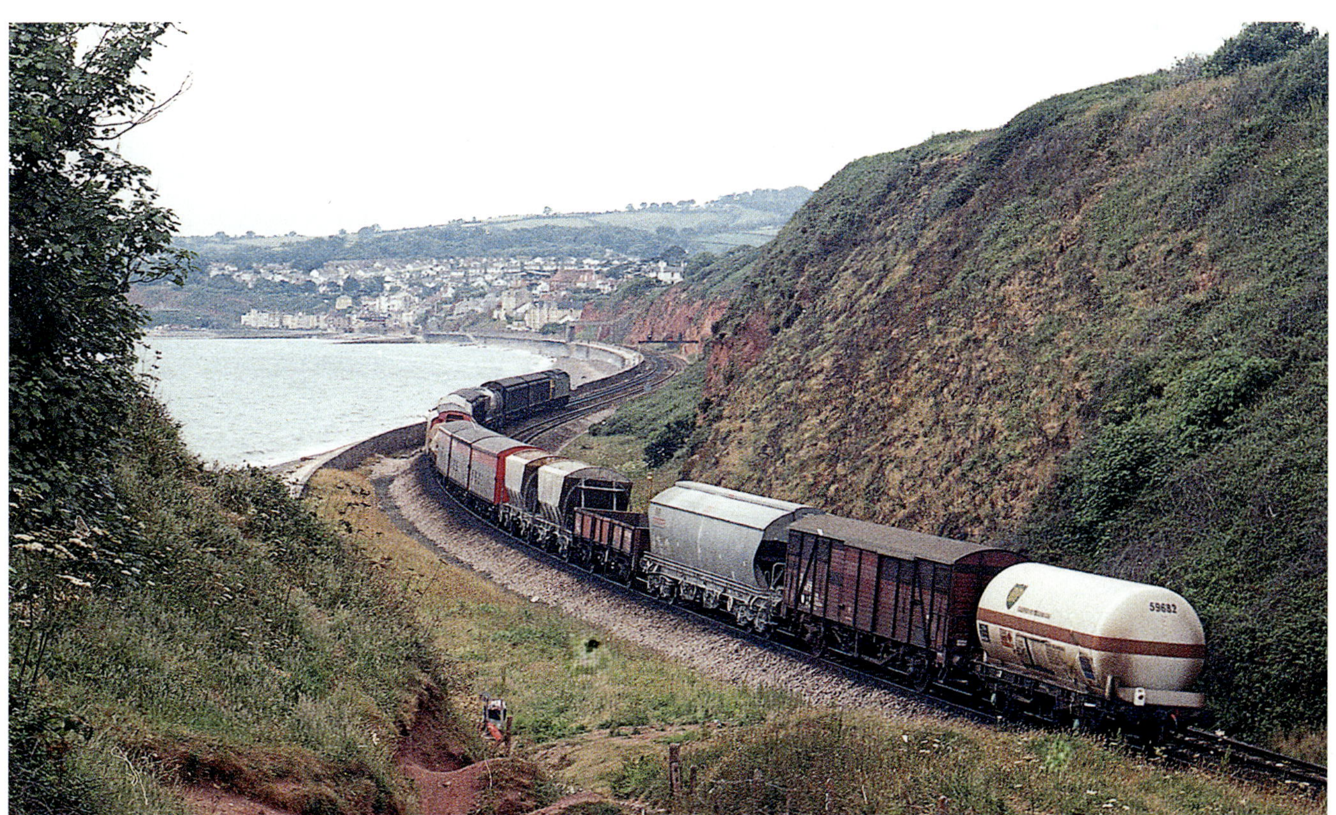

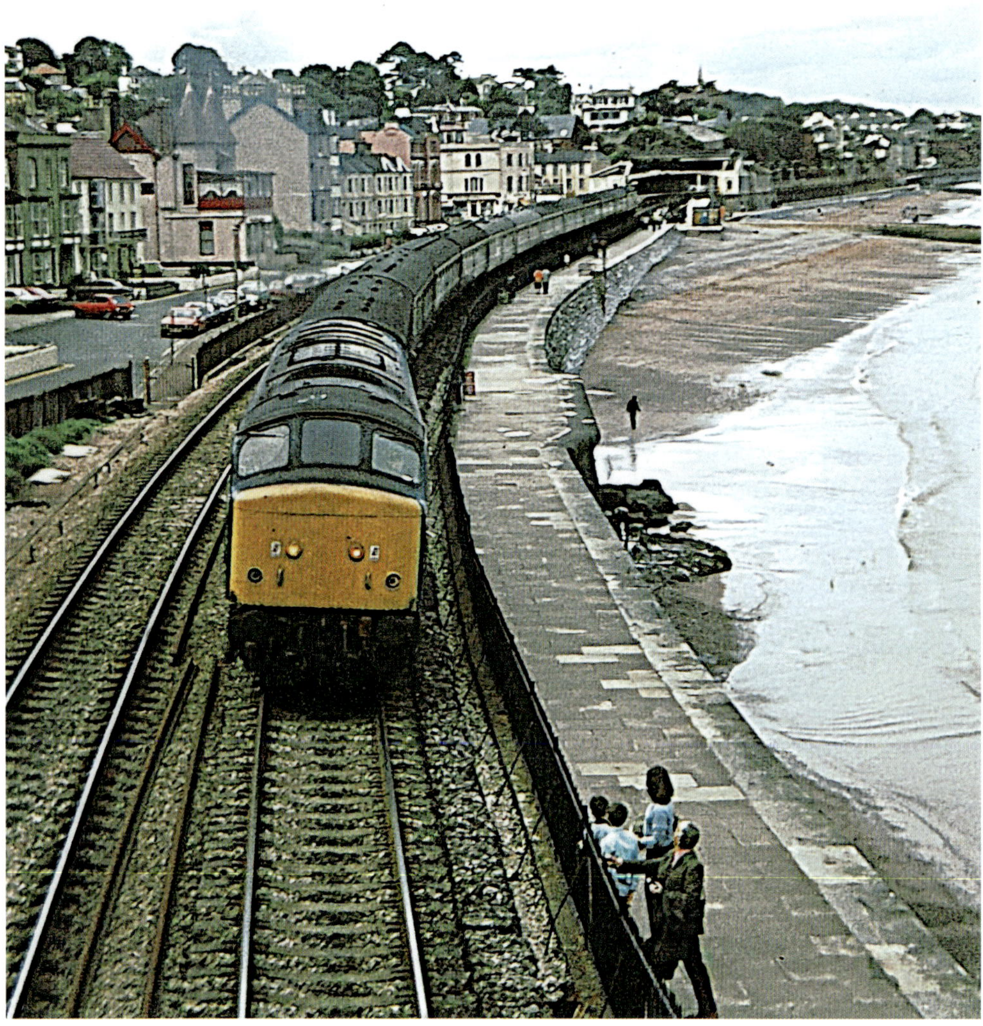

Left: Dawlish on 27th May 1981 as a Peak heads a Southbound train for either Plymouth or Paignton. John captured the family in the foreground happily watching trains pass.

Photo by John Stanford

Below: Dawlish in better weather and a class 47 wheels a passenger train to the station on a hot afternoon the same year.

Photo by Trevor Riddle

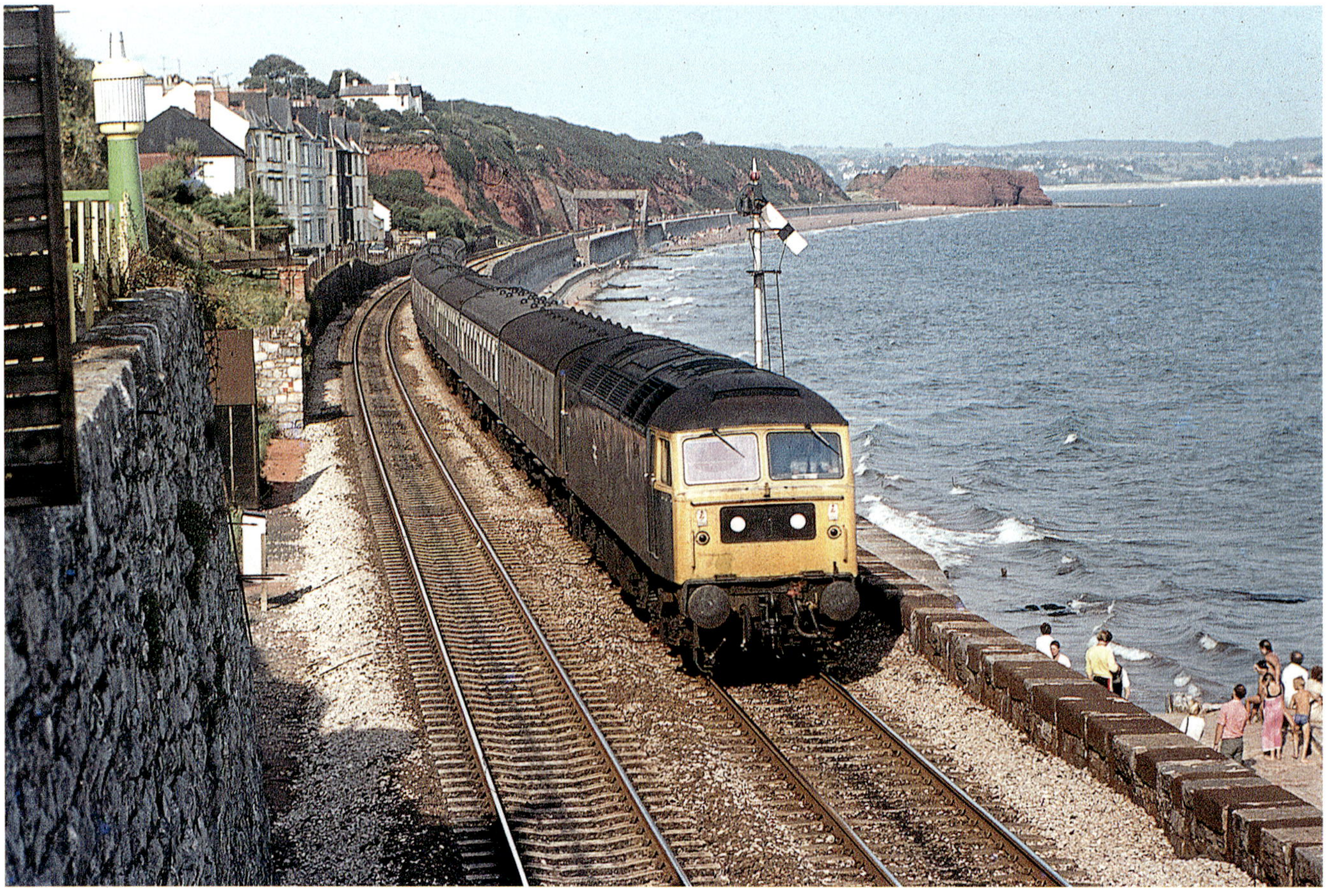

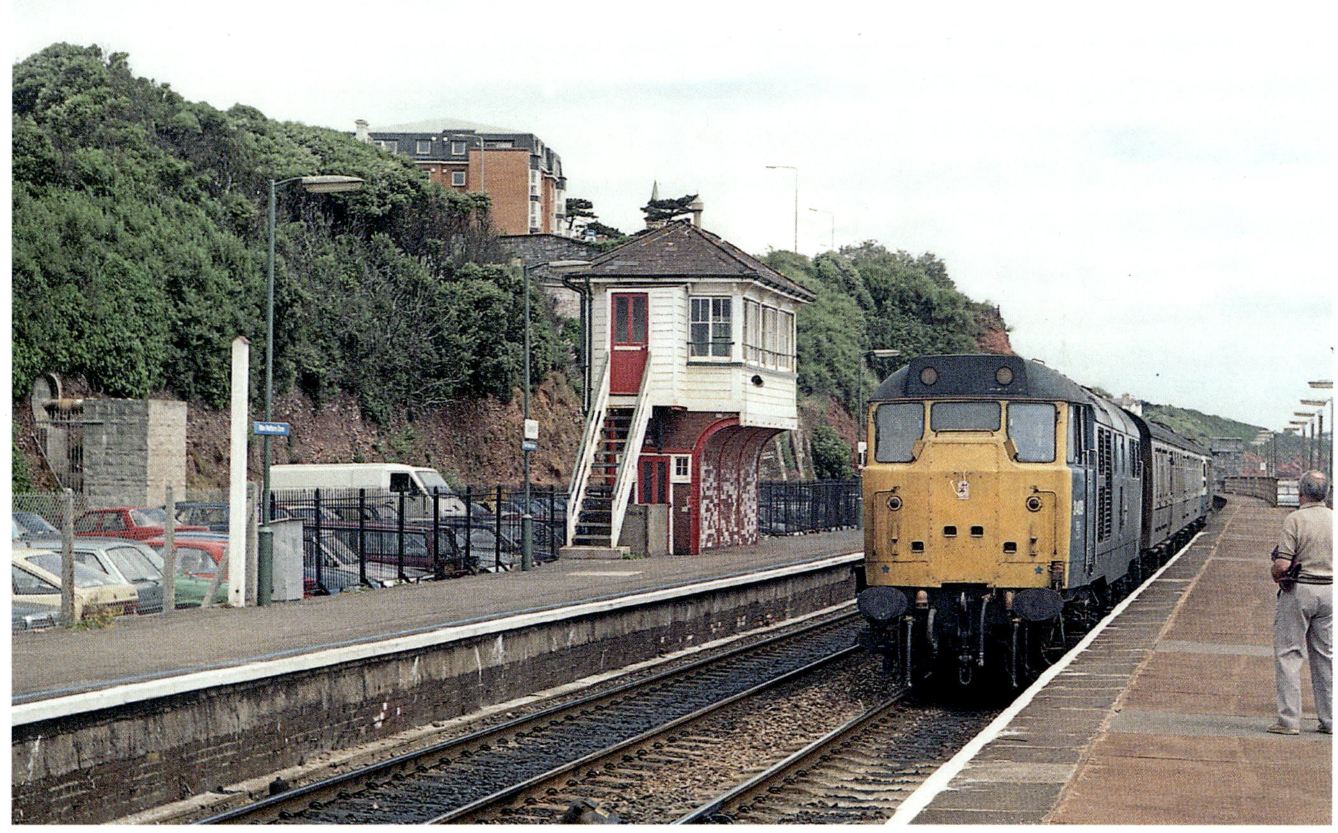

Dawlish six years later in July 1989, a year after Peak locos had disappeared and a class 31 draws in with a Paignton train. Local loco-hauled trains were in their twilight then.

Dawlish nearly 40 years later to the day from John's shot and a friendly wave from the GWR driver, with the enhanced sea wall evident. The author's team when he was a delivery director led the work to enhance the sea-wall following the February 2014 breach: with hydrology studies to determine the nature of wall enhancement and sea behaviour.

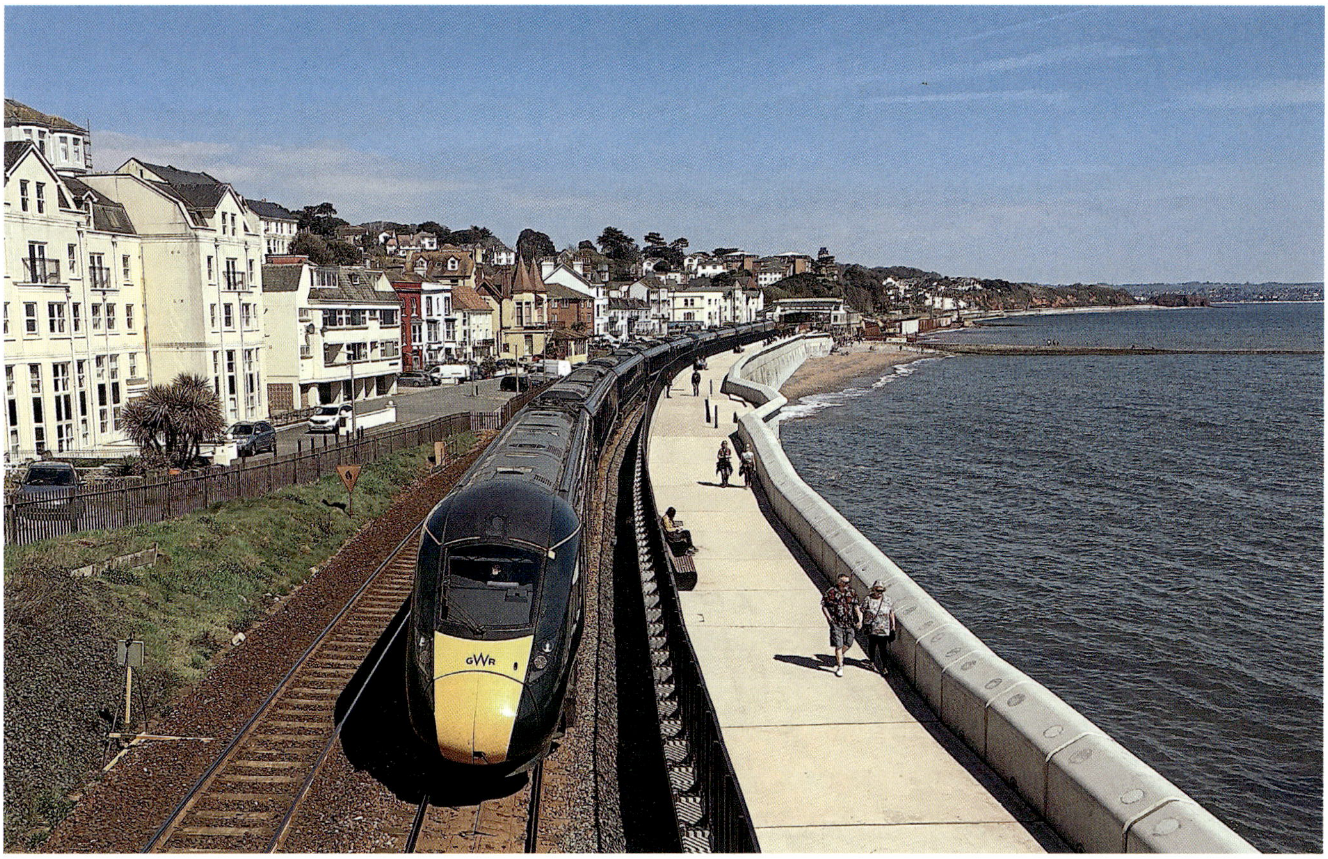

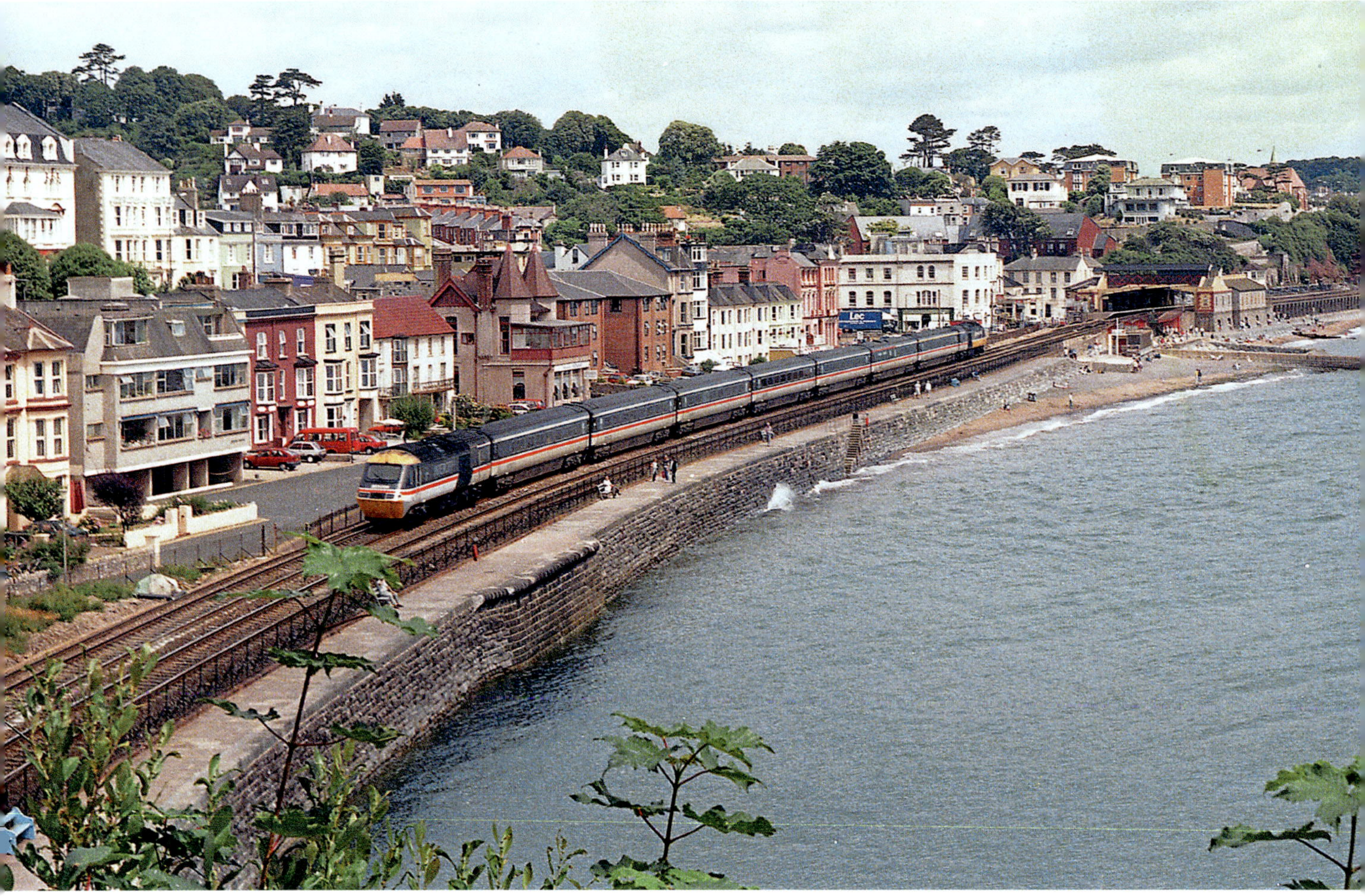

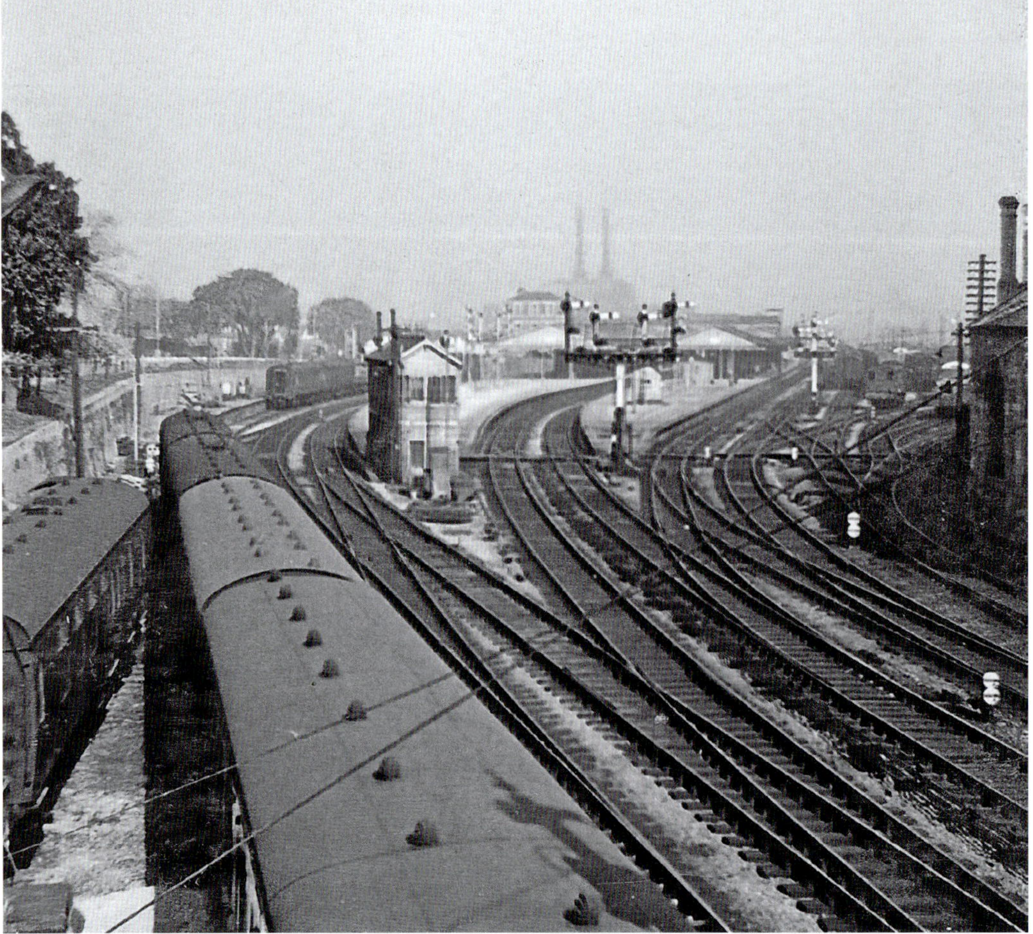

Above: Dawlish high up in summer 1990 captures an inter-city HST travelling toward Exeter. By then the consistent colours of BR's business sectors had become commonplace as BR blue with blue and grey coaches were coming to an end.

Left: Newton Abbot was still a busy hub in the 1960s, following huge expansion of the station in the 1930s to cope with West Country holiday traffic. The layout existed almost complete in this form until the May 1987 re-signalling and large-scale rationalisation, reflecting reduced holidaymaker and freight traffic. This image was taken on 4th August 1961. *Photo by John Stanford*

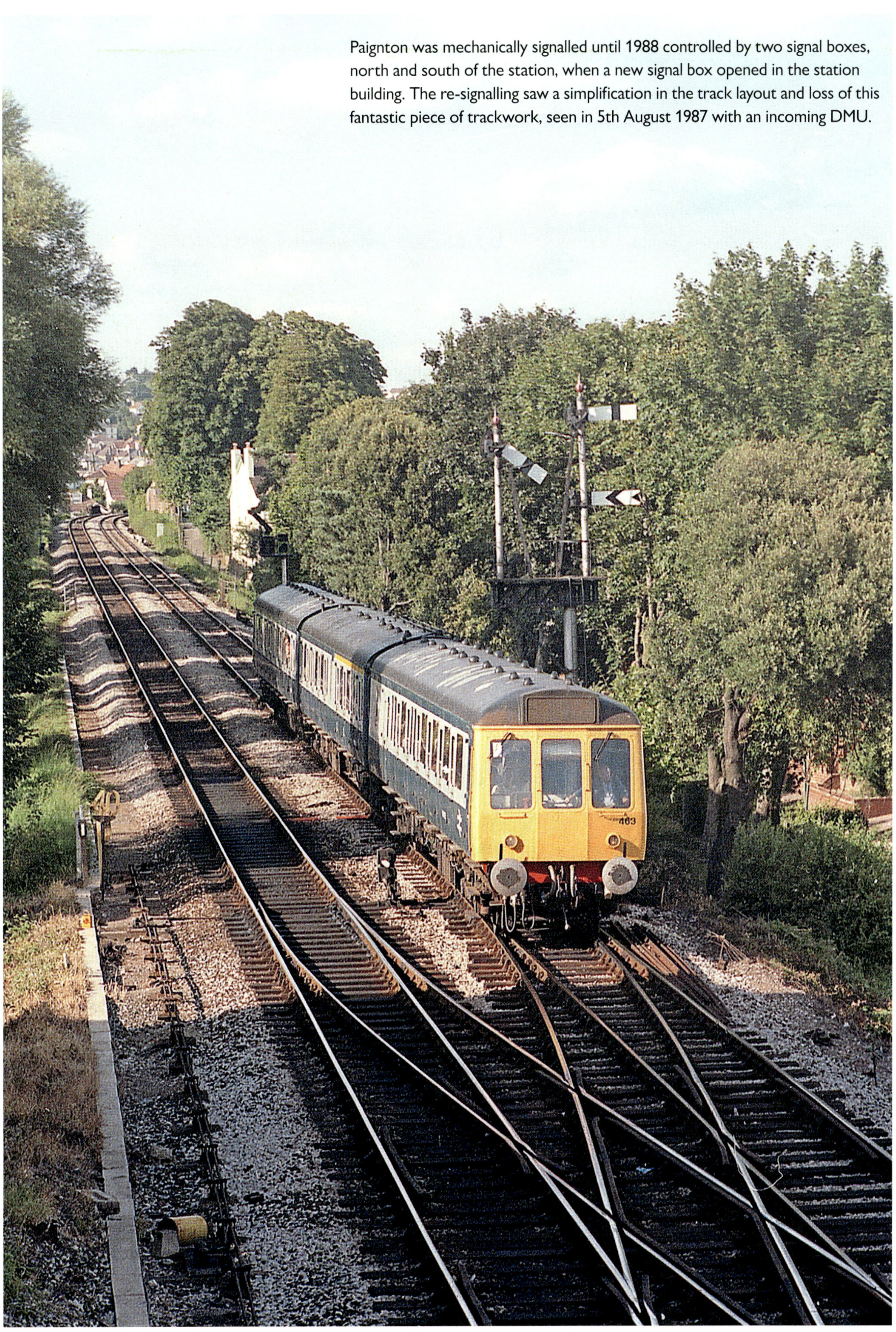

Paignton was mechanically signalled until 1988 controlled by two signal boxes, north and south of the station, when a new signal box opened in the station building. The re-signalling saw a simplification in the track layout and loss of this fantastic piece of trackwork, seen in 5th August 1987 with an incoming DMU.

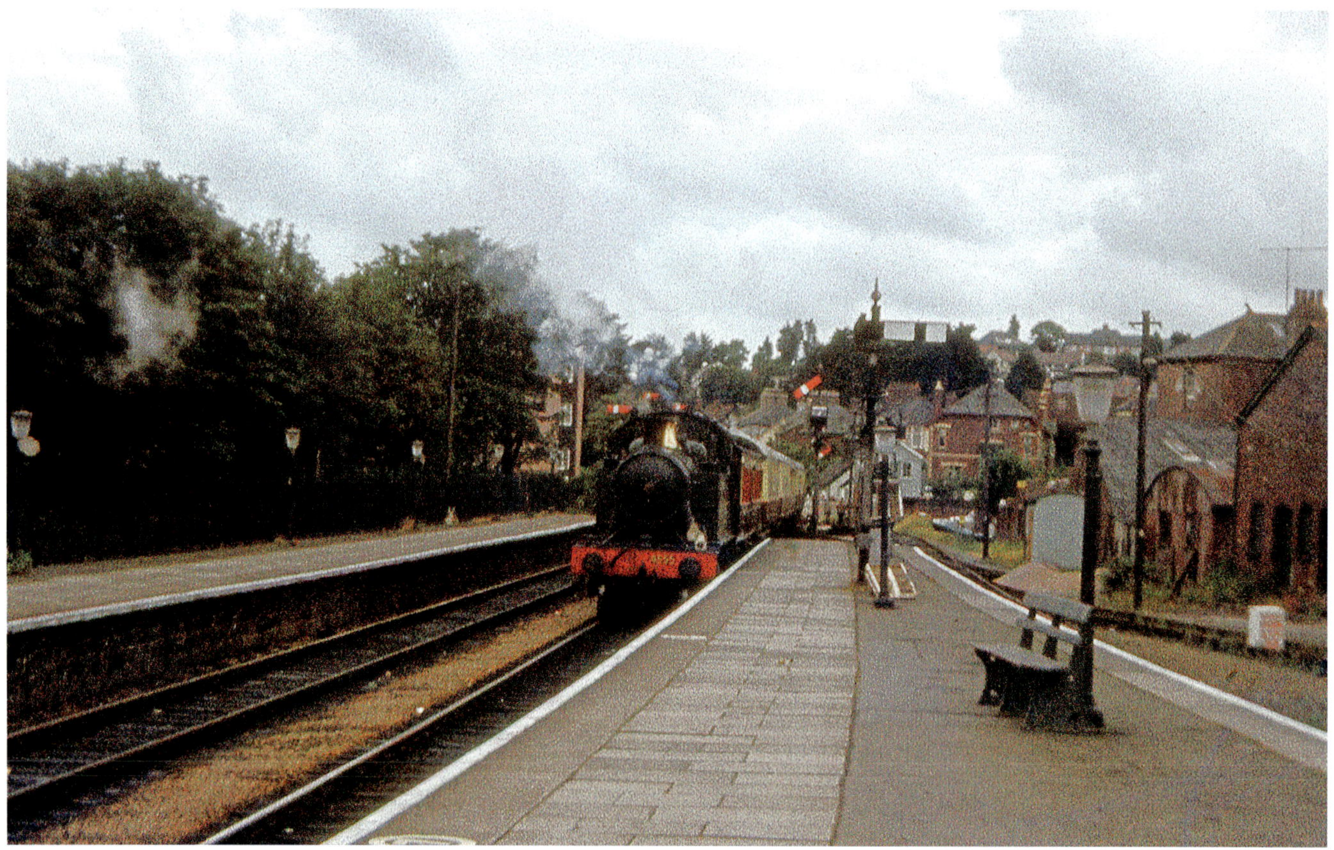

Paignton of course has established itself as the start point for the excellent Dartmouth Steam Railway – properly opened in 1973 after the line from here to Kingswear was purchased by the Dart Valley Railway Co. John purchased shares in the company and travelled a special trial steam hauled service in July 1972, seen here during shunt moves. *Photo by John Stanford*

Paignton South level crossing on 27th May 1968 and a Western class diesel hydraulic departs the station with empty stock for Goodrington Carriage Sidings. Note the superb disc signal. *Photo by John Stanford*

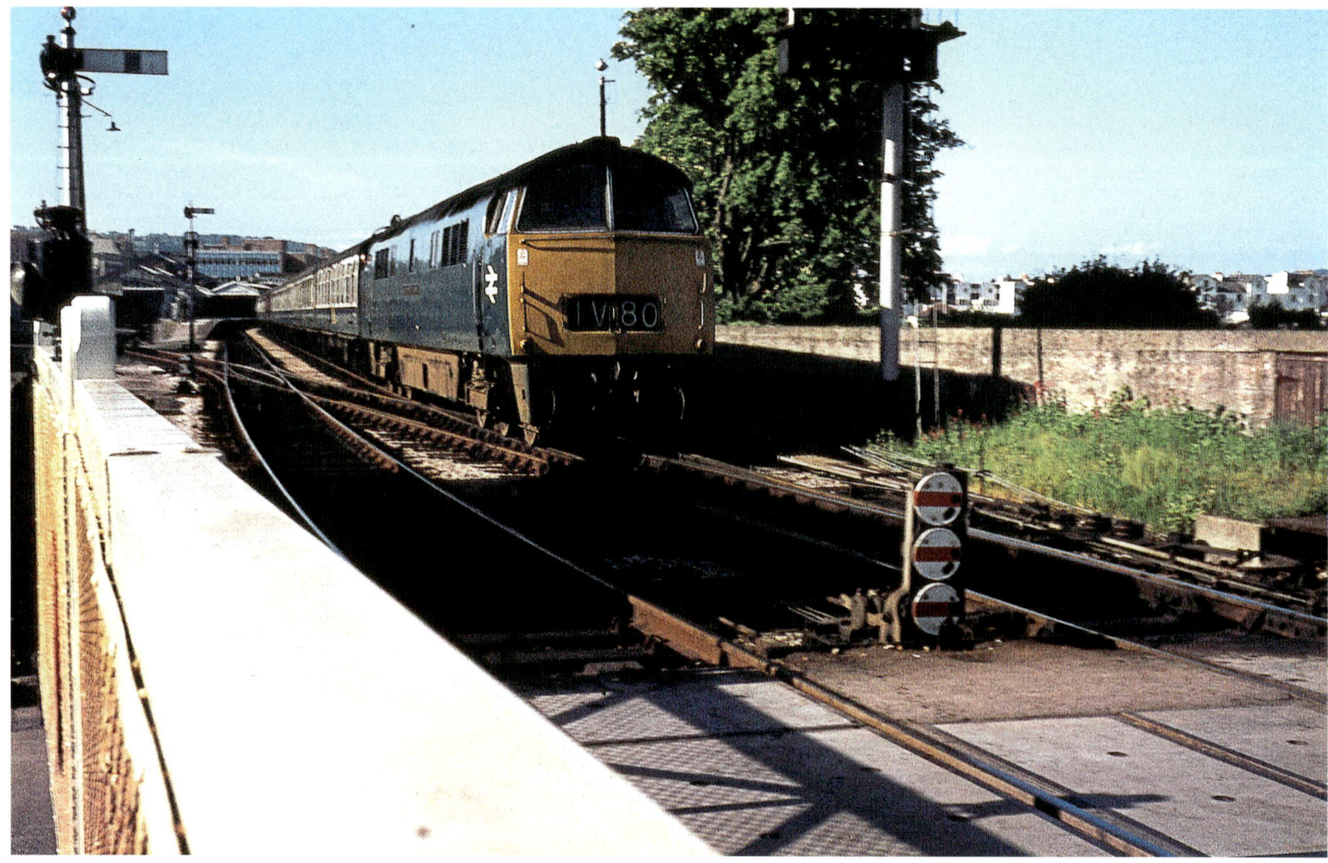

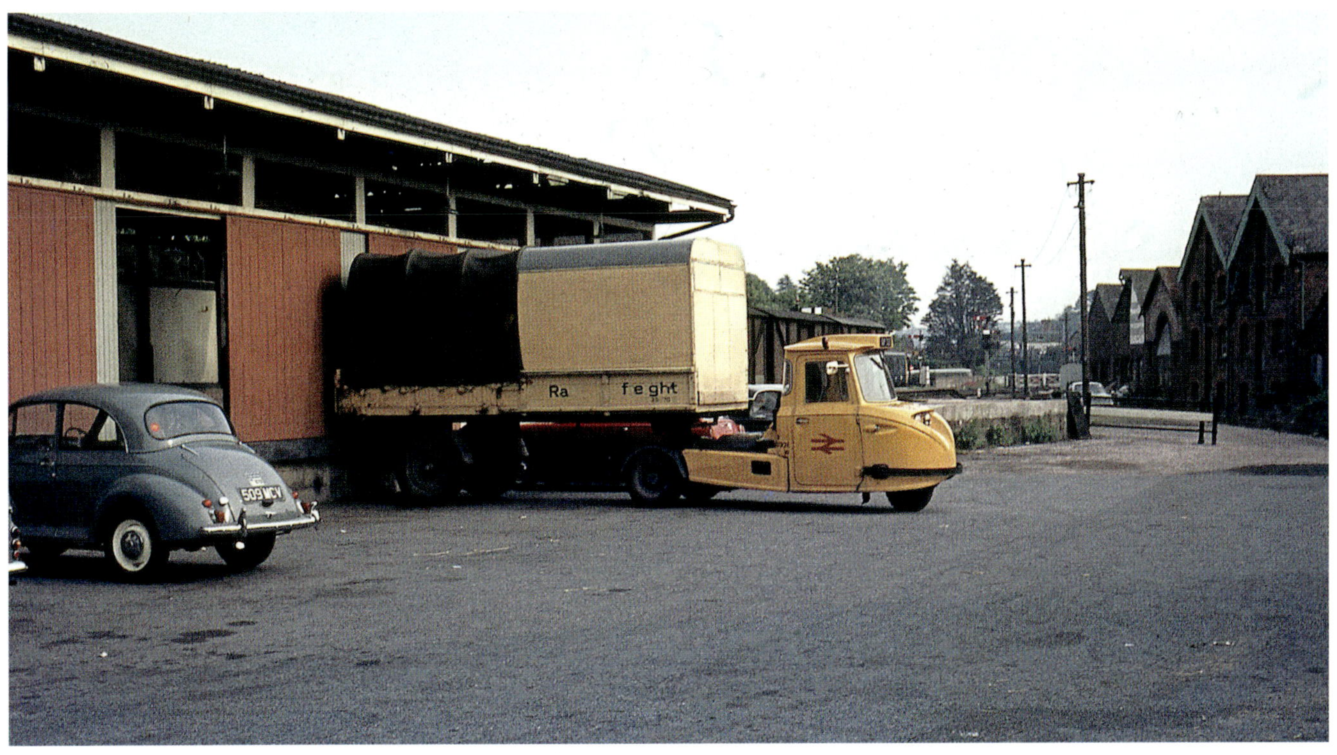

Paignton Goods Yard was still active in 1968 when John caught this three-wheeled Scammell Karrier being loaded as part of BRs collection and delivery service. The yard ceased to see rail traffic by 1972 and was then lifted. The level of weekday passenger train service at Paignton is now at its highest at 82 passenger trains a day, compared with 41 in 1987 and a slightly lower figure in the 1960s when John started his railway career. No.1 in the charts when this picture was taken was Young Girl by Gary Puckett & The Union Gap. *Photo by John Stanford*

Paignton South level crossing in July 1968 and D847 *Strongbow* hauls a teatime Goodrington to Newton Abbot freight over the crossing. The train consisted of four wheel box vans and empty coal wagons. *Photo by John Stanford*

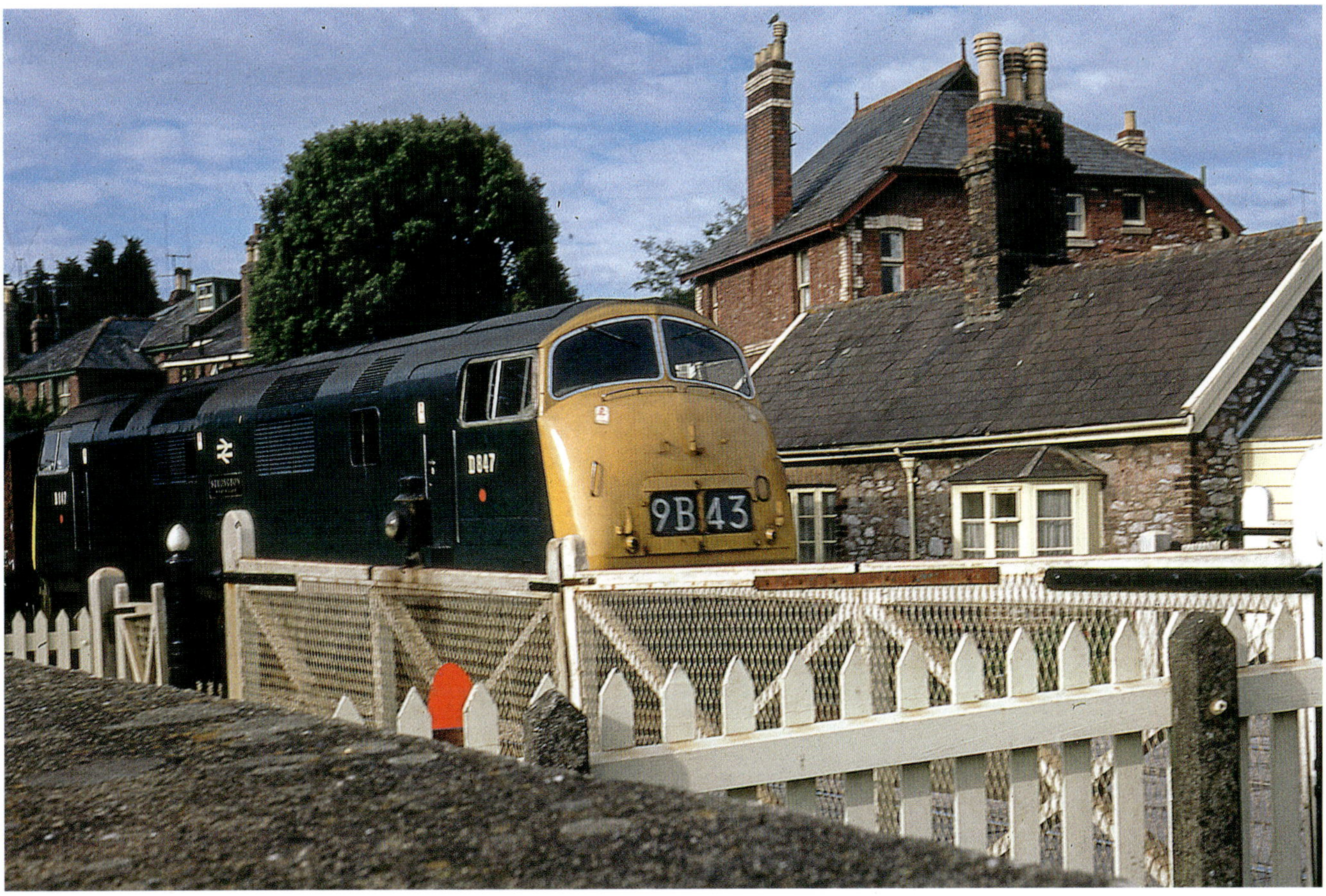

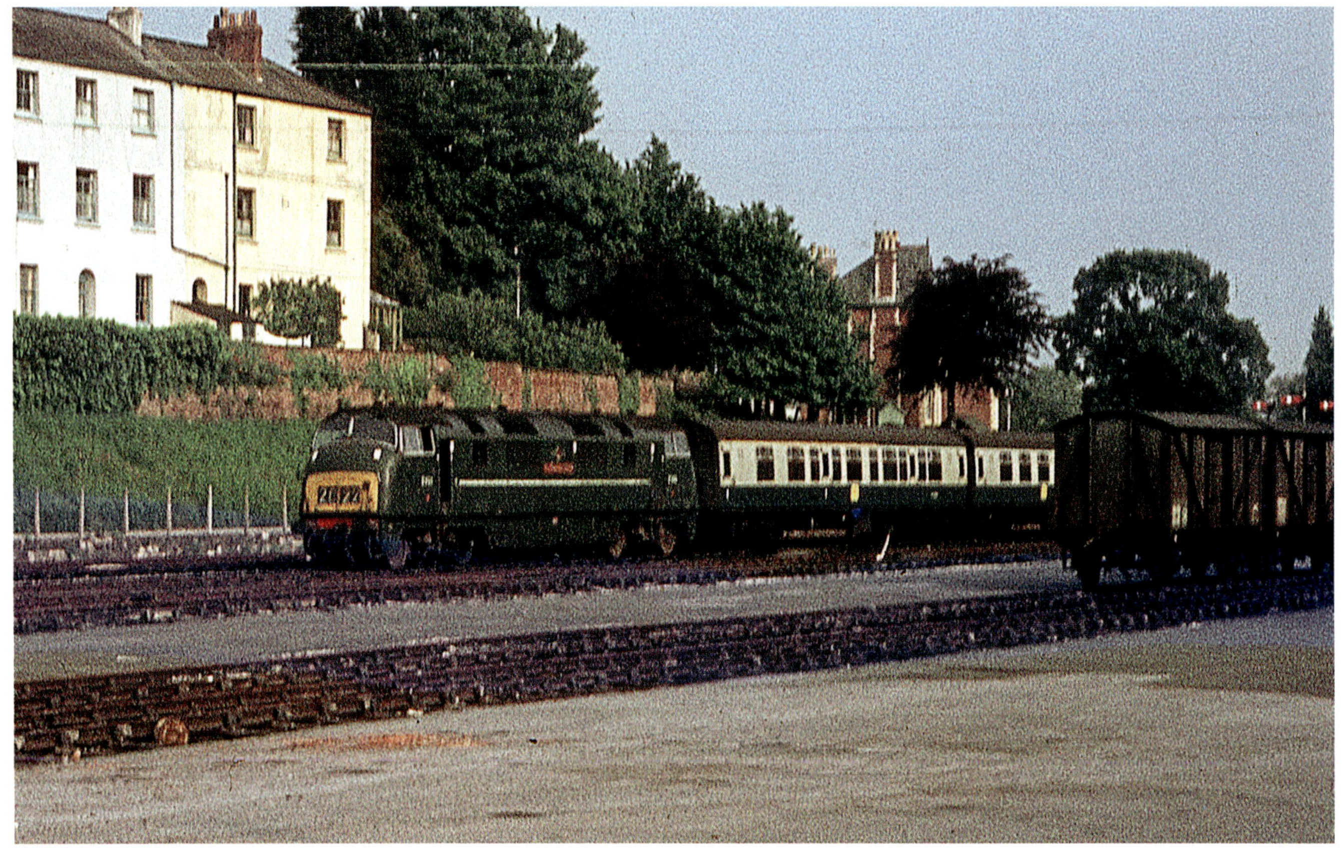

Goodrington Carriage Sidings on 28th May 1968 and green Warship class loco D800 *Sir Brian Robertson* awaits departure. In his notebook, John recorded most Warships he saw that week were blue or maroon. *Photo by John Stanford*

Goodrington Carriage Sidings earlier the same day with Warship locos D823 and D829 running round their train. Until the 1950s a level crossing existed here until the road bridge was built. *Photo by John Stanford*

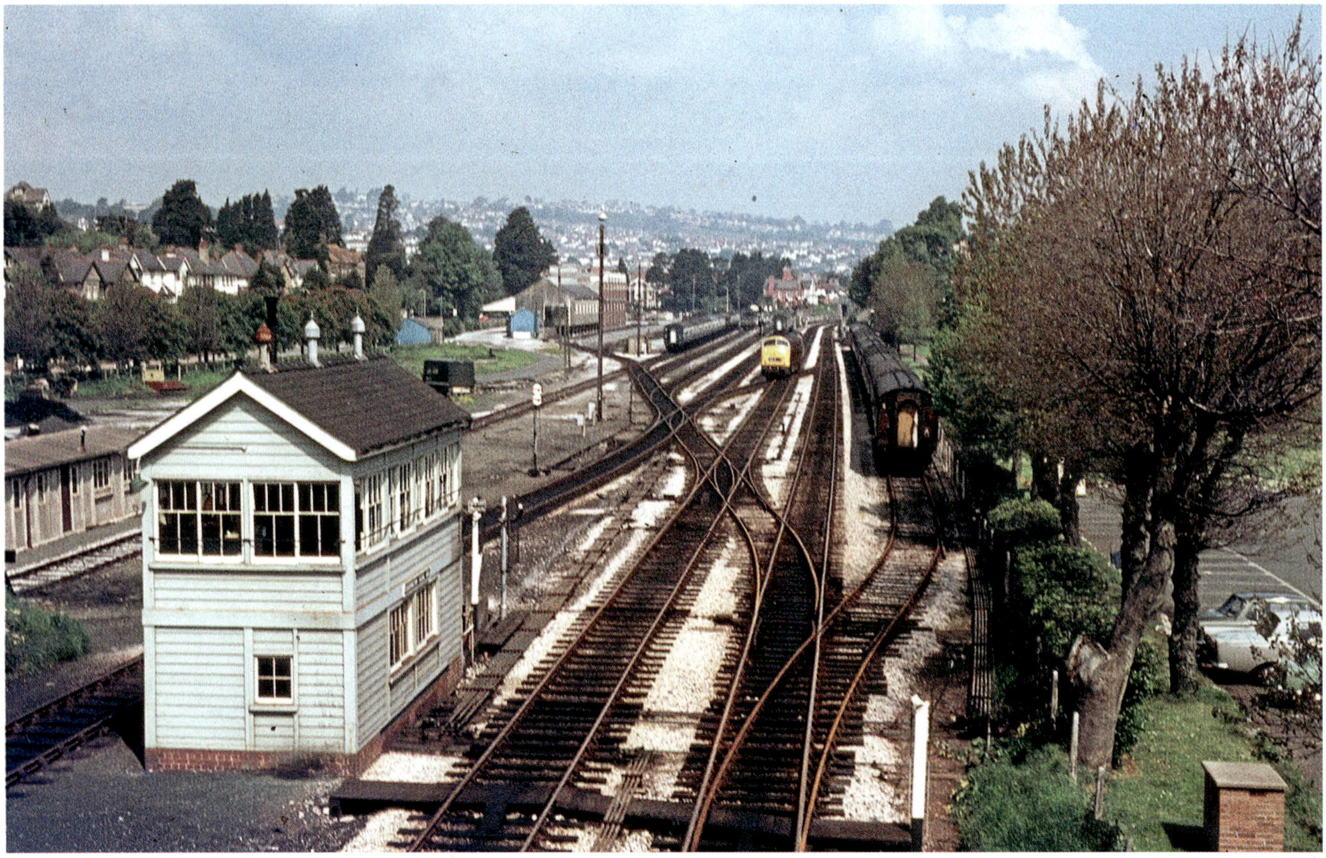

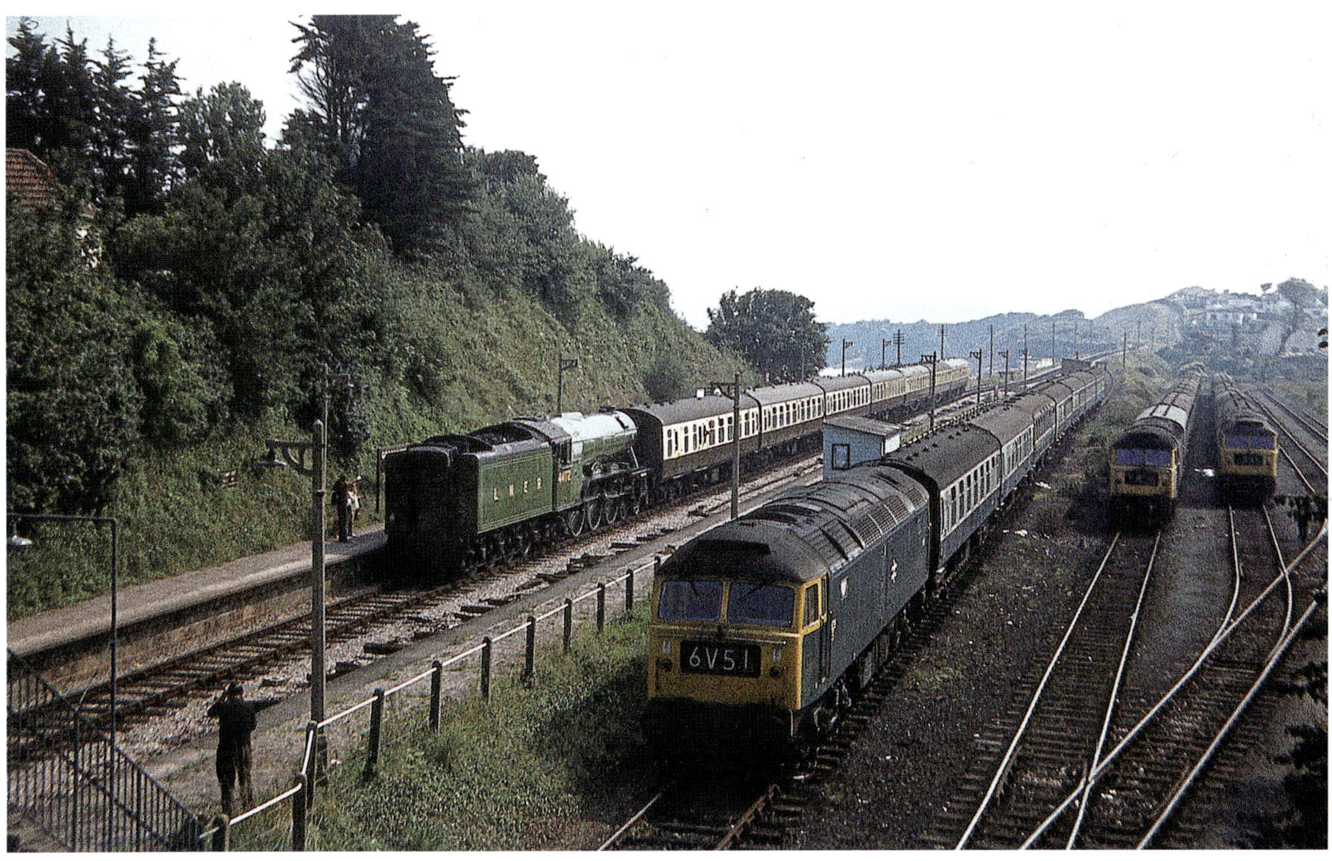

Goodrington Happy Valley Carriage Sidings in August 1973 and John captured 4472 *Flying Scotsman* arguably the most famous steam locomotive in the world, running in past multiple class 47s, one of which has a Gresley buffet car in its train. *Photo by John Stanford*

Sultan Cove and a beautiful sunny August in 1972 witnesses the passing of a Class 103 2 car 'Park Royal' DMU set (numbers 50414 & 56169). This was a regular DMU on the branch and was then preserved on the West Somerset Railway although sadly it was later scrapped due to the state of the bodywork. Its sister survives on the Helston Railway. *Photo by John Stanford*

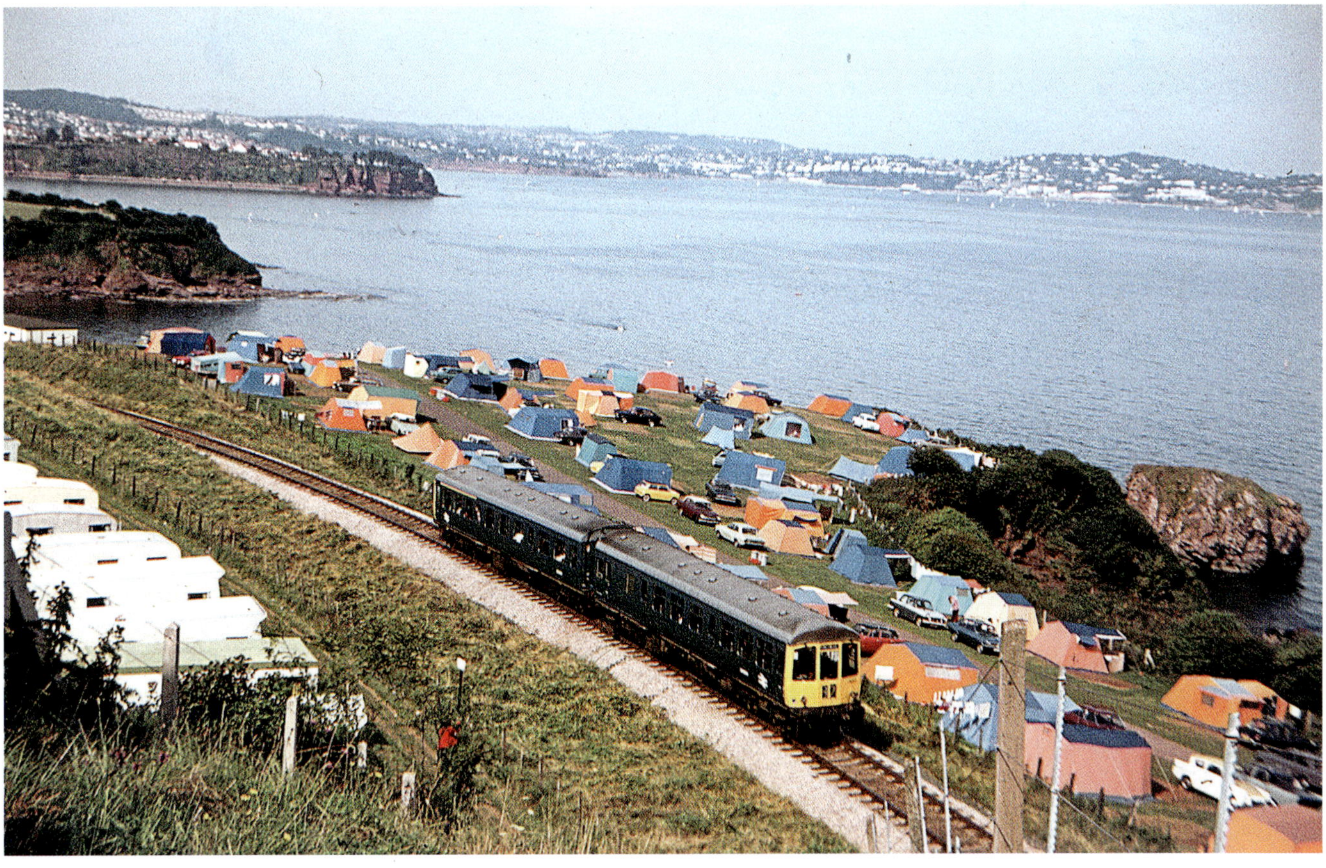

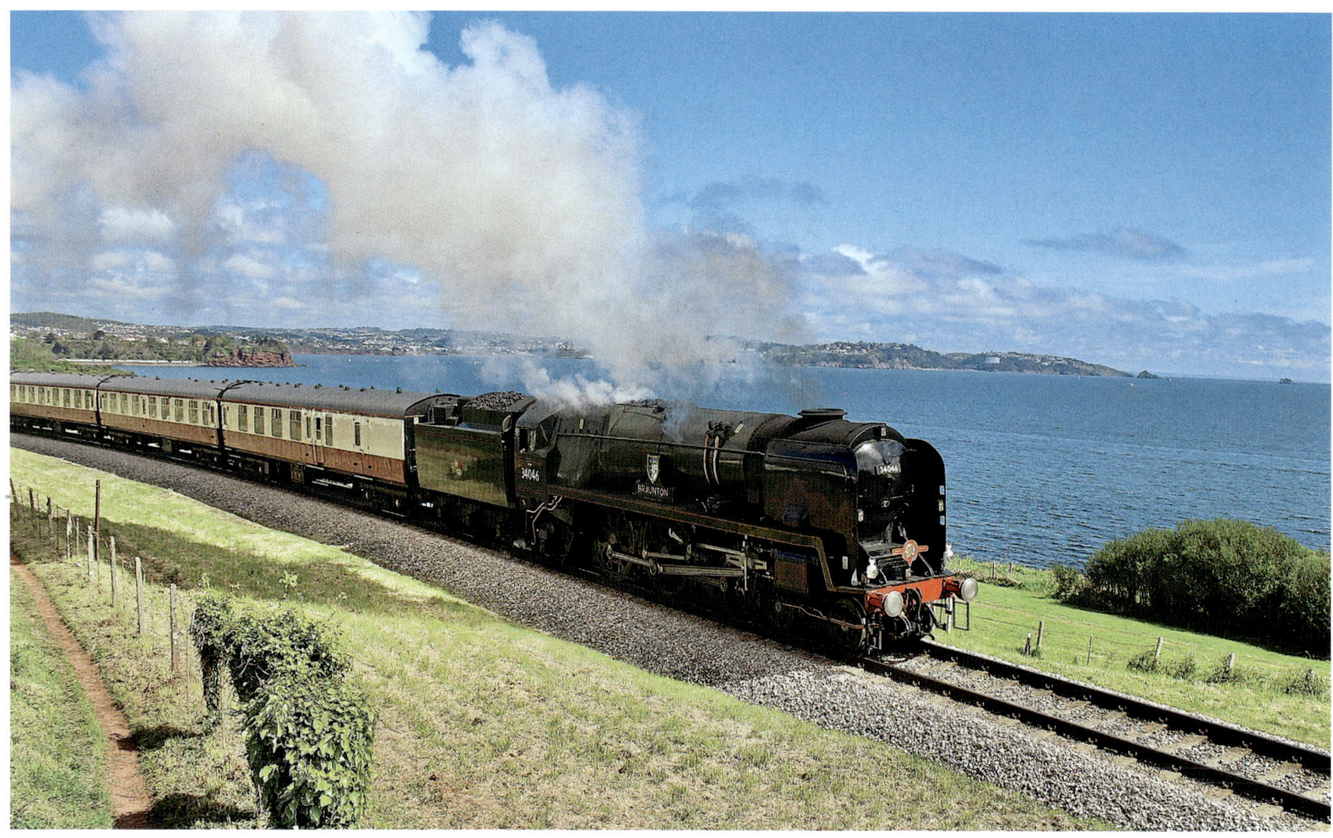

Sultan Cove again, as the family love of Torbay has endured. This scene looks superb as Southern Railway Bullied pacific *Braunton* hauls a special Locomotive Services Ltd train from Nantwich to Kinsgwear on 4th May 2024. The line frequently hosts special trains and flourishes as one of the premier heritage railways in the UK, with great scenery, and continuing passenger growth and profitability. Fiona was on board, taking her dad Bill to celebrate his 80th birthday – he even 'cabbed' the Bullied pacific loco.

Churston on 20th August 1972 and Peak loco D154 passes through on a return Mystex (BR coding for a mystery excursion); the 13.30 from Kingswear to Gloucester formed of Mark 1 coaches. Peaks were extremely rare South of Goodrington Carriage Sidings, so this was a fortuitous catch by John. *Photo by John Stanford*

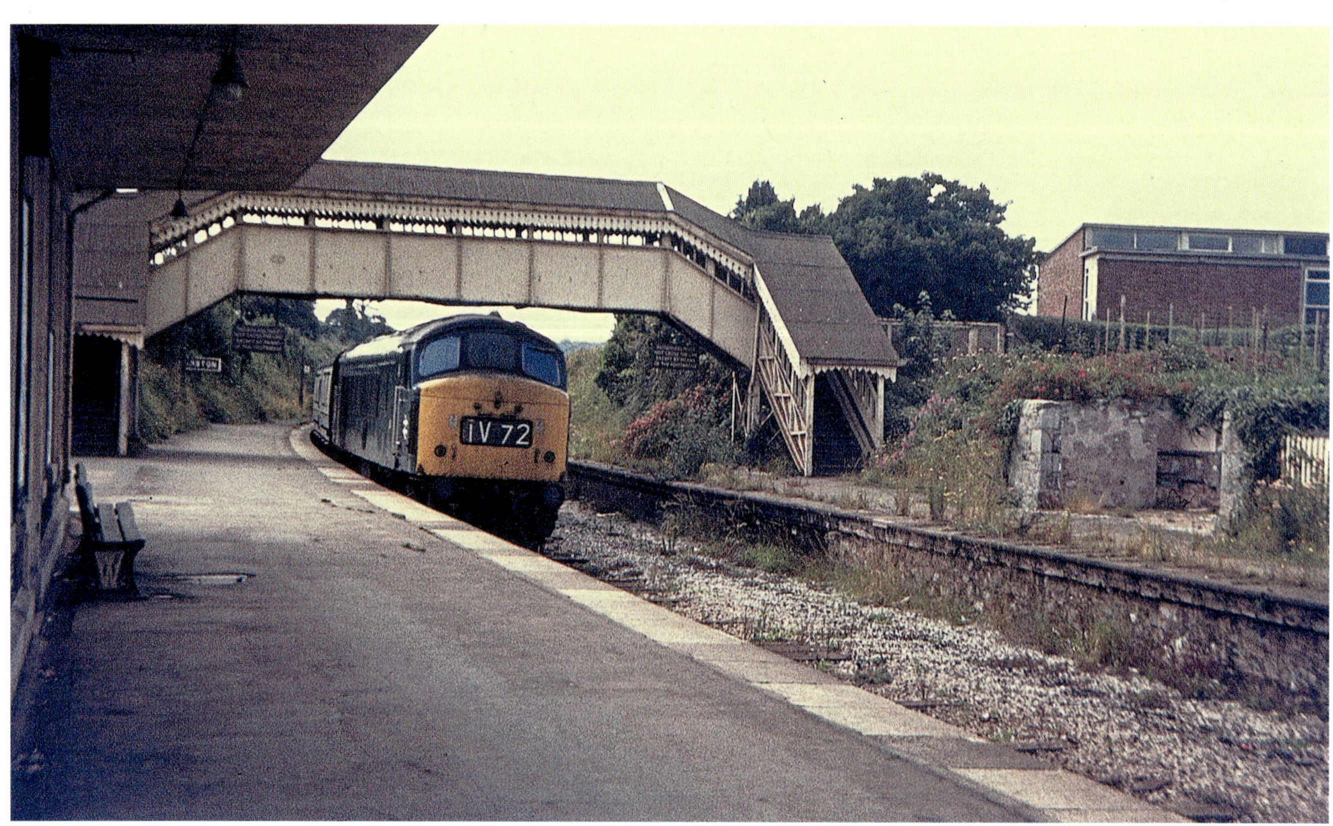

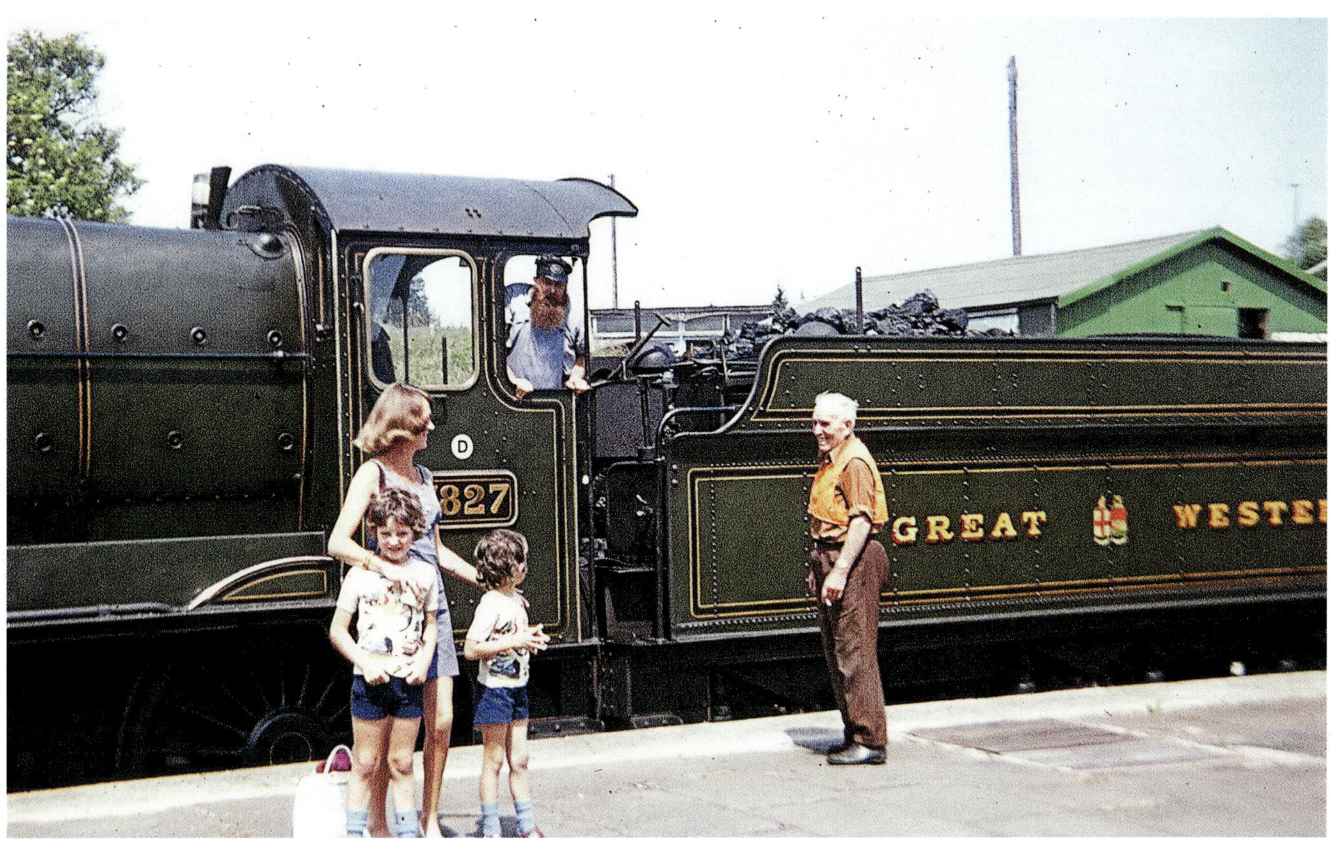

Churston on 25th June 1976 and Wendy talks to the Dart Valley Railway track ganger with Mark talking to Peter 'Jesse' Janes the fireman on 7827 *Lydham Manor*; the author's favourite GWR loco. The area was visited for the annual family holiday from 1970 to 1985, after John and Wendy honeymooned here four years earlier when they both worked for BR. The nuptial linkage in the area continued, see page 108. *Photo by John Stanford*

Kingswear in 1968 and the remnants of the freight yard still existed although not for much longer – by the following year just a run round loop remained. A BR blue DMU sits in the platform awaiting custom. *Photo by John Stanford*

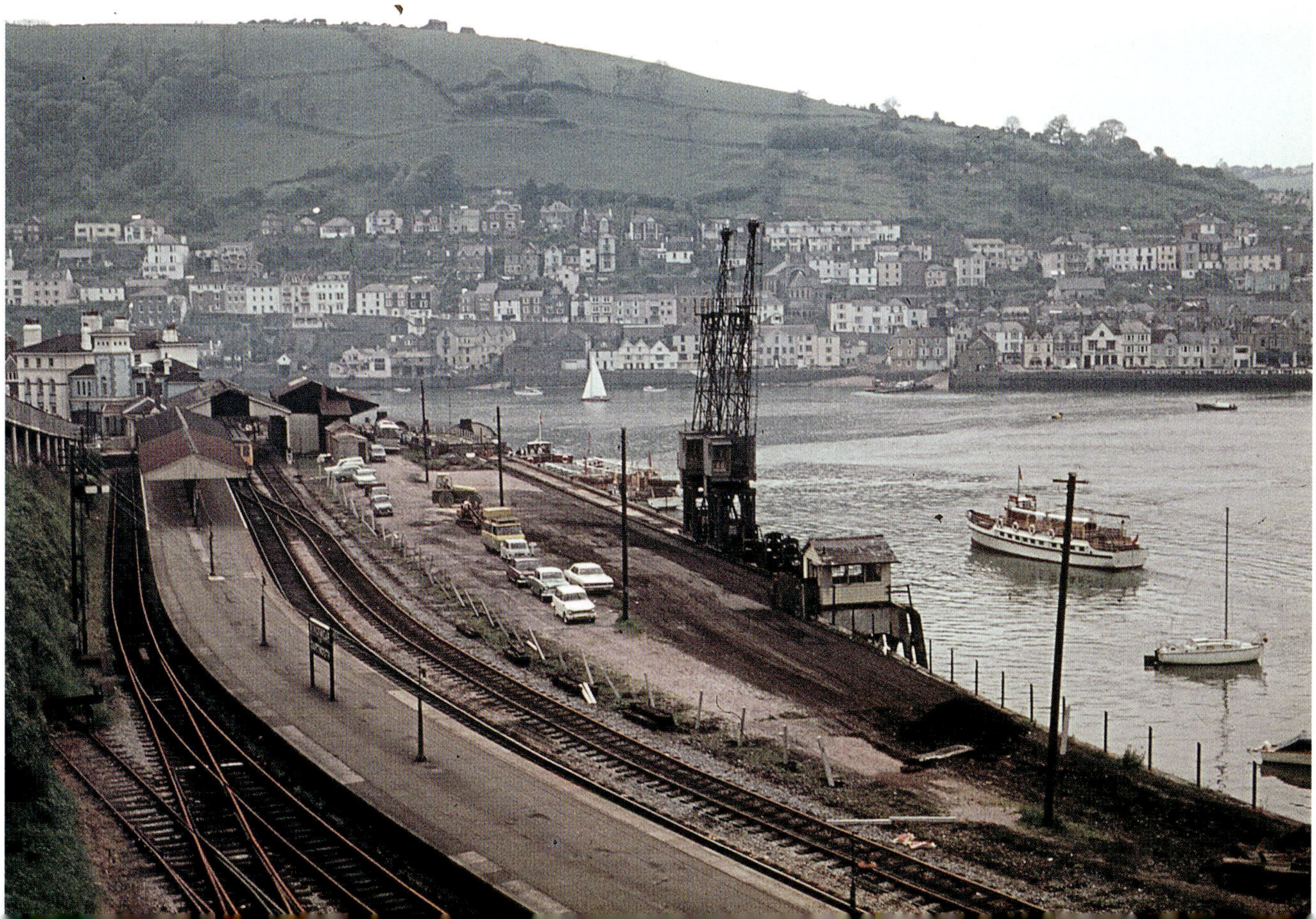

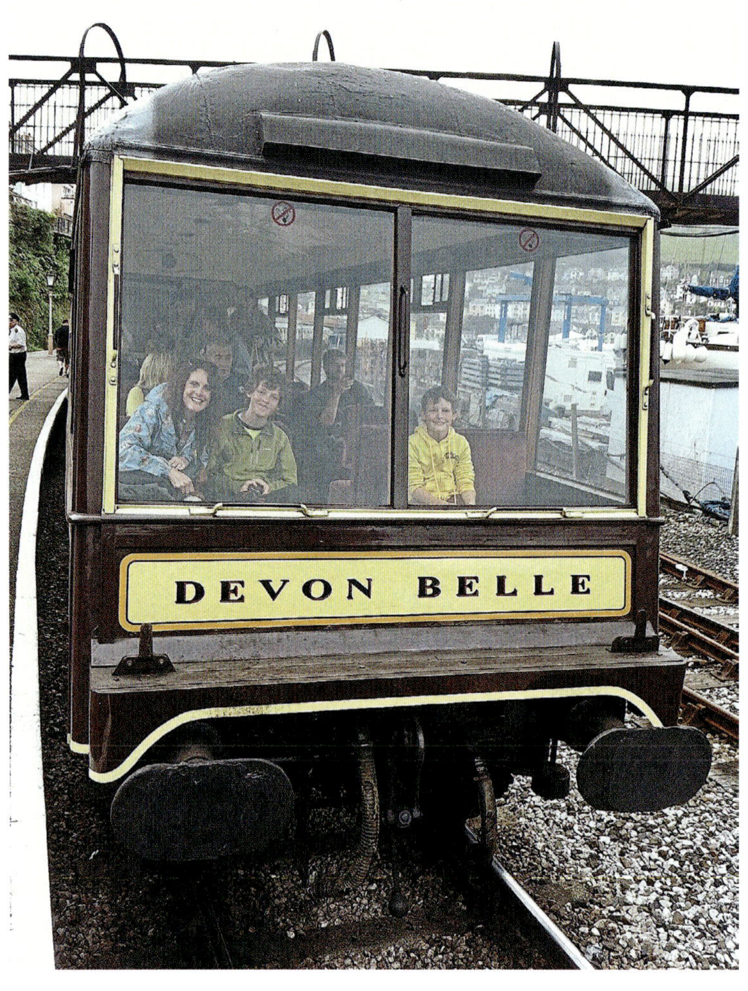

Left: Kingswear with the Devon Belle observation saloon, occupied by Fiona and sons Olly and Toby in August 2012. Paul proposed to Fiona in this vehicle hauled by *Lydham Manor* from Kingswear on 2nd October 1991, after they had met at a party hosted by his friends from BR in 1988. They married two years after engagement in 1993.

Below: Buckfastleigh in May 1967 with GWR auto-tank loco 1420 visible. The lady at left photo-bombed the shot, although now nearly 60 years later gives an insight to dress styles. John was a member of the supporting society seeking to preserve Ashburton to Totnes from the outset after involvement with the aborted scheme to preserve the Heathfield line at the start of the 1960s. *Photo by John Stanford*

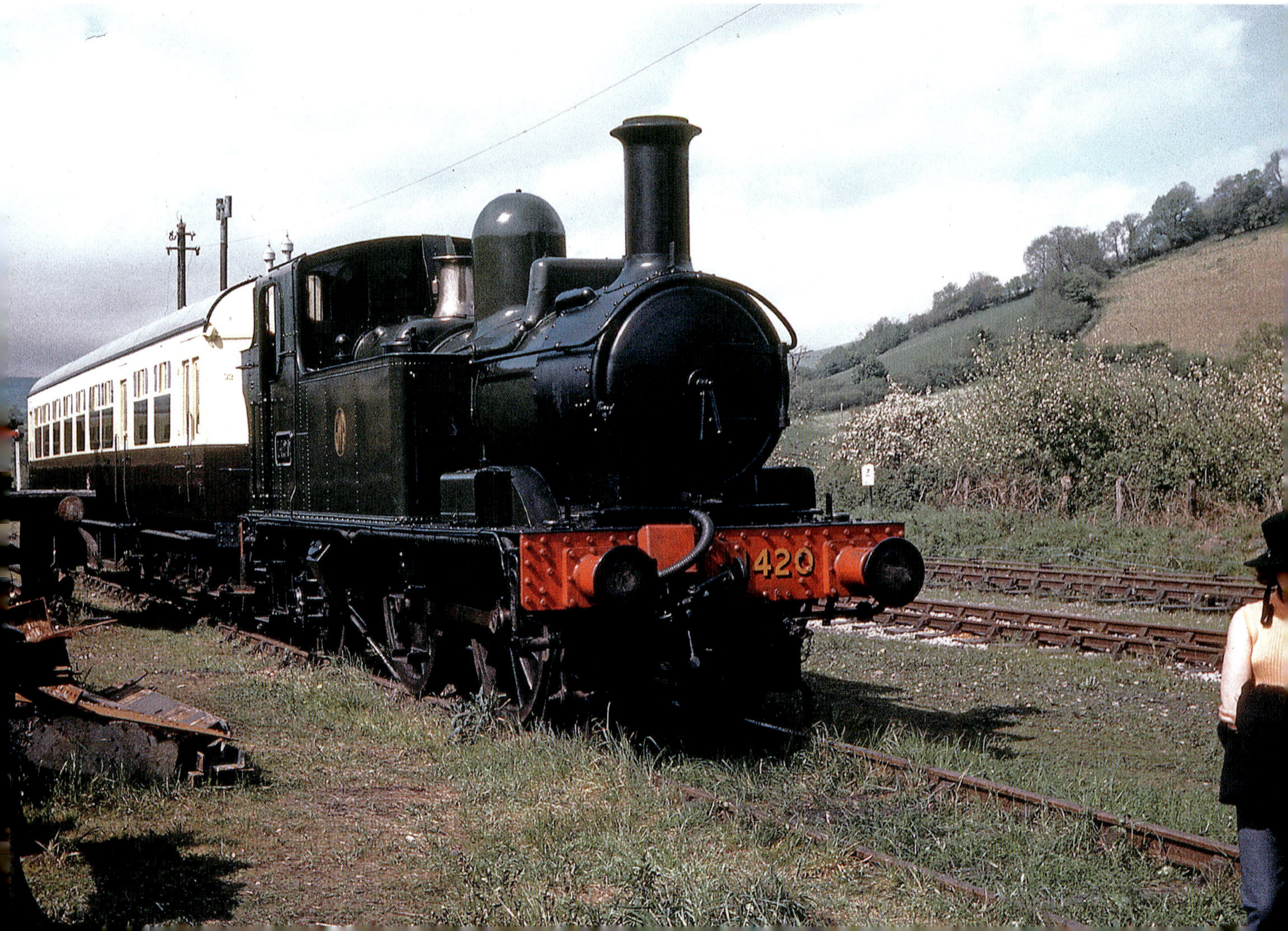

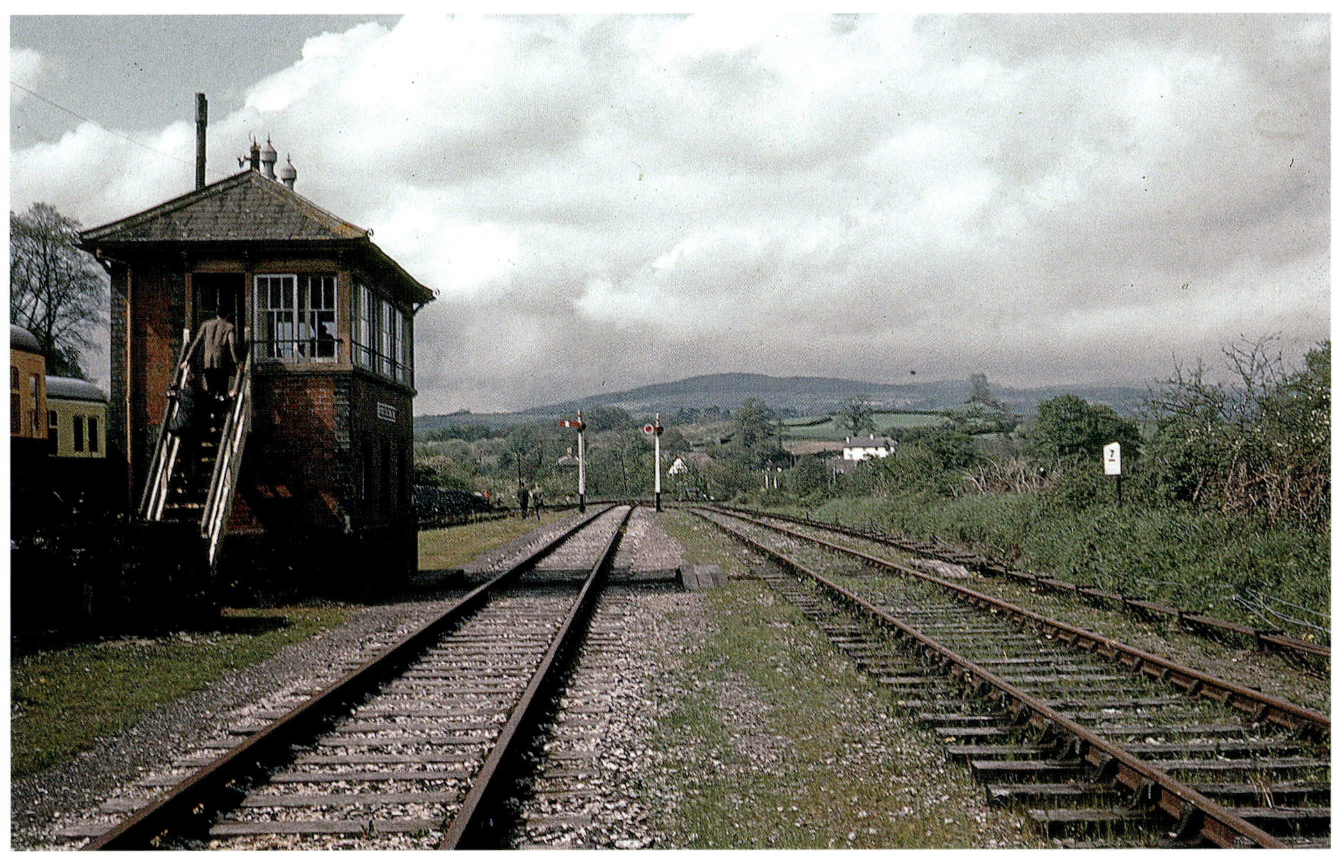

Buckfastleigh signal box on 13th May 1967 looking toward Ashburton and the section of line lost to the A38 dual carriageway, which totally changed the scenery on this area. *Photo by John Stanford*

Buckfastleigh on 28th March 1970 as GWR pannier, number 6412, gets a train underway for Totnes with author in shot, backed by a Rover P6, a Mk1 Ford Escort and what appears to be a Lada. The loco also worked the Kingswear line, until sale in 1976 – see Minehead entry. *Photo by John Stanford*

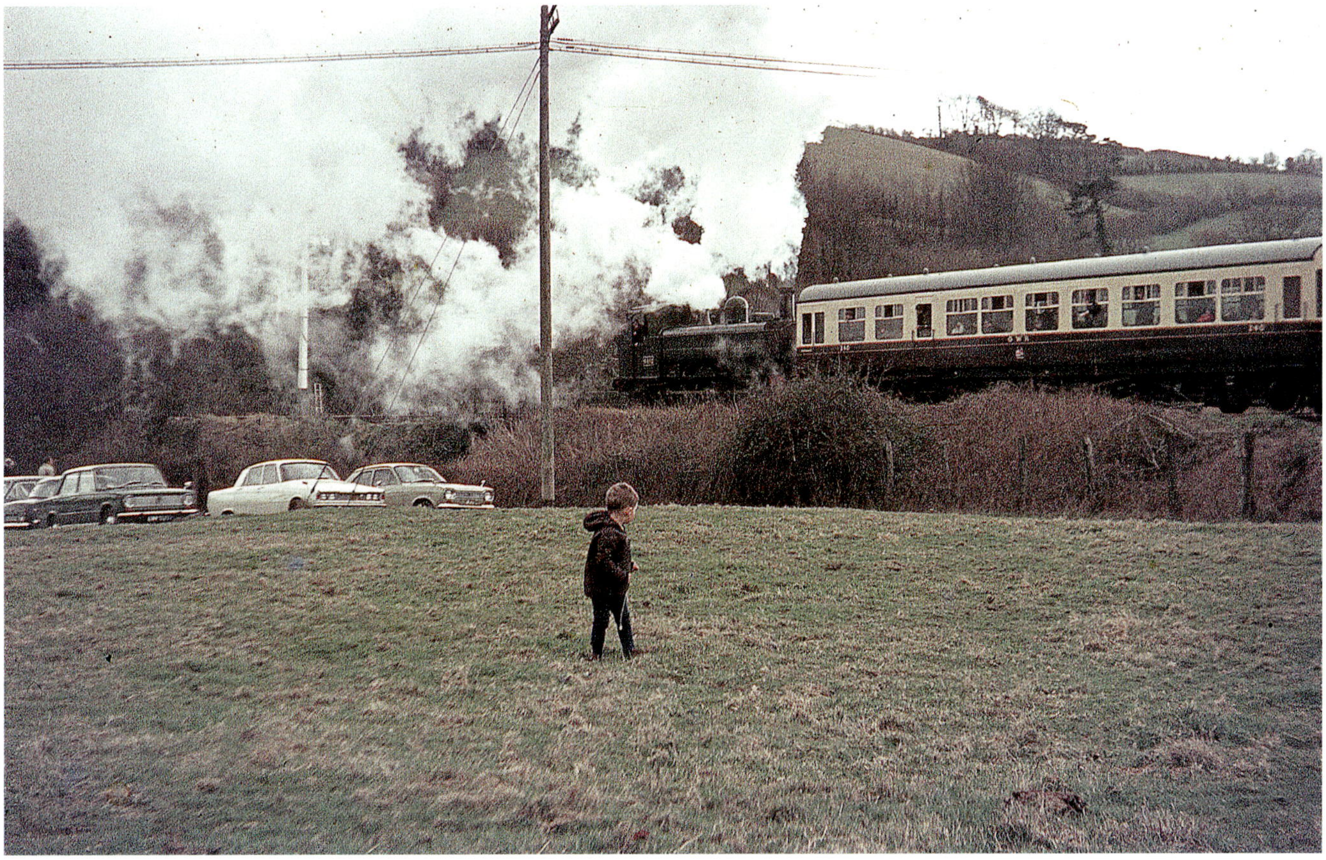

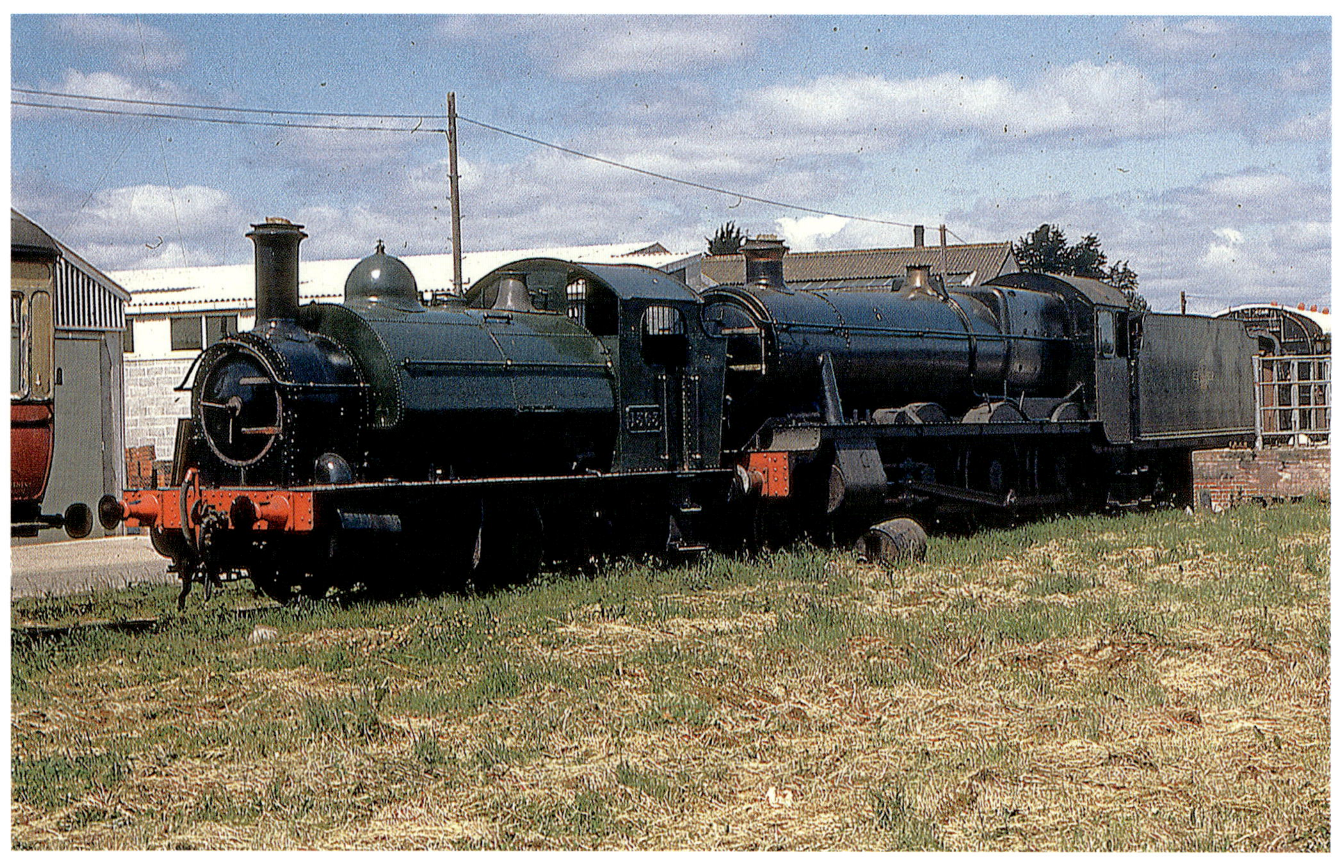

Totnes Quay Branch was home to Great Western Society stock items in the early days and 1363 and GWR Hall 6998 and some stock resided here, captured by John on 13th May 1967. He attended some open days when engines were steamed. Both locomotives now reside at Didcot GWS. *Photo by John Stanford*

Plymouth in 2001 with a Hall and Castle en route to Penzance. The author travelled on 16th April 2001 with lifelong friend Alan Taylor, successfully experiencing steam over Dainton Bank this time. John, Paul and Alan would attend meetings in the prominent office block in their railway careers – what was BR's Inter-City House. Now in 2025 it is part of Plymouth University.

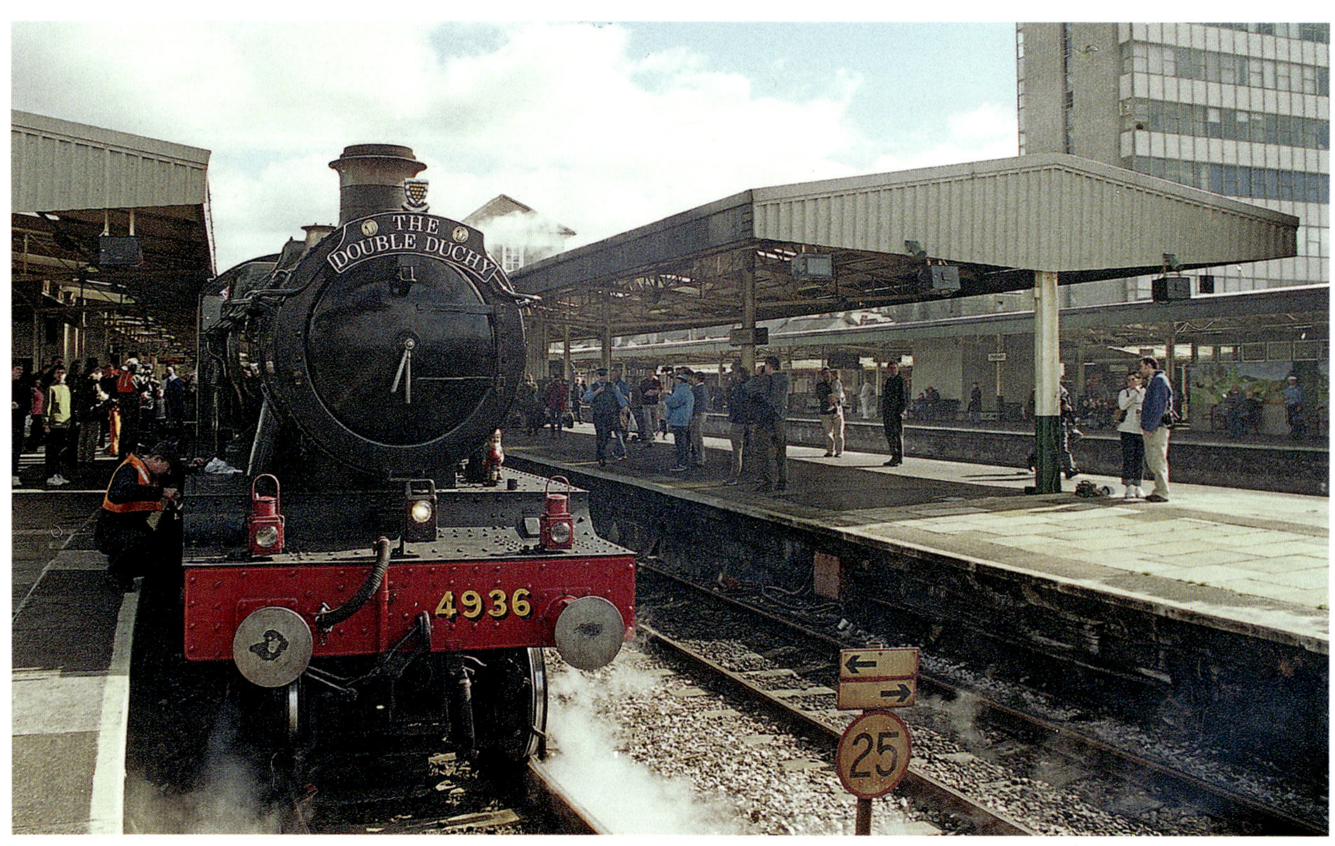

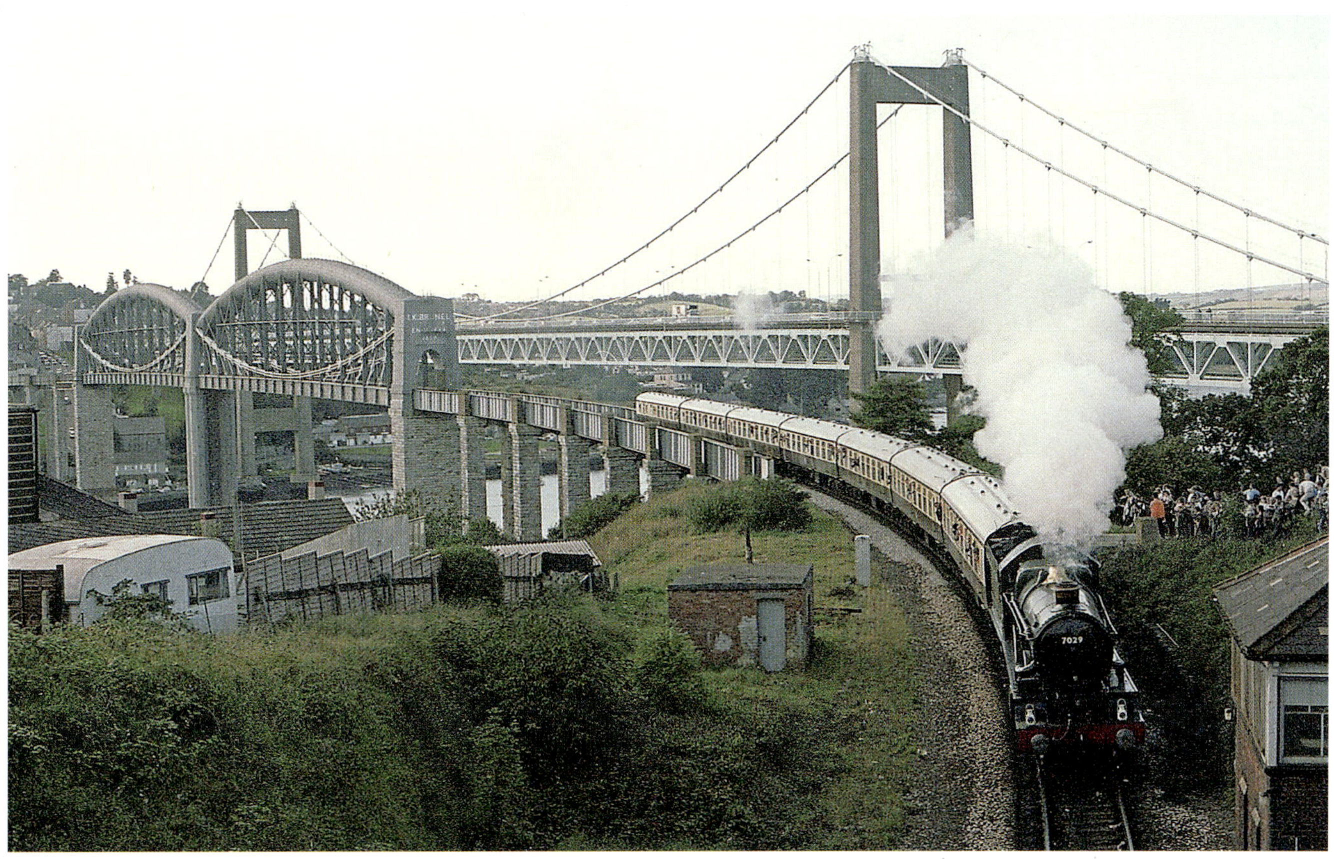

River Tamar and the Royal Albert Bridge with 7029 *Clun Castle* officiating on 6th September 1985 with crowds massed and traffic coming to a stand on the road-bridge to watch the spectacle – such was the magnetism of the first steam for over 20 years over the bridge and on the Cornish main line. And from the opposite end in September 2024 an up HST passing viewed from a drone, HSTs now in their twilight. The bridge remains a superb tribute to GWR chief engineer I.K. Brunel. *Photos by Richard Giles and the author*

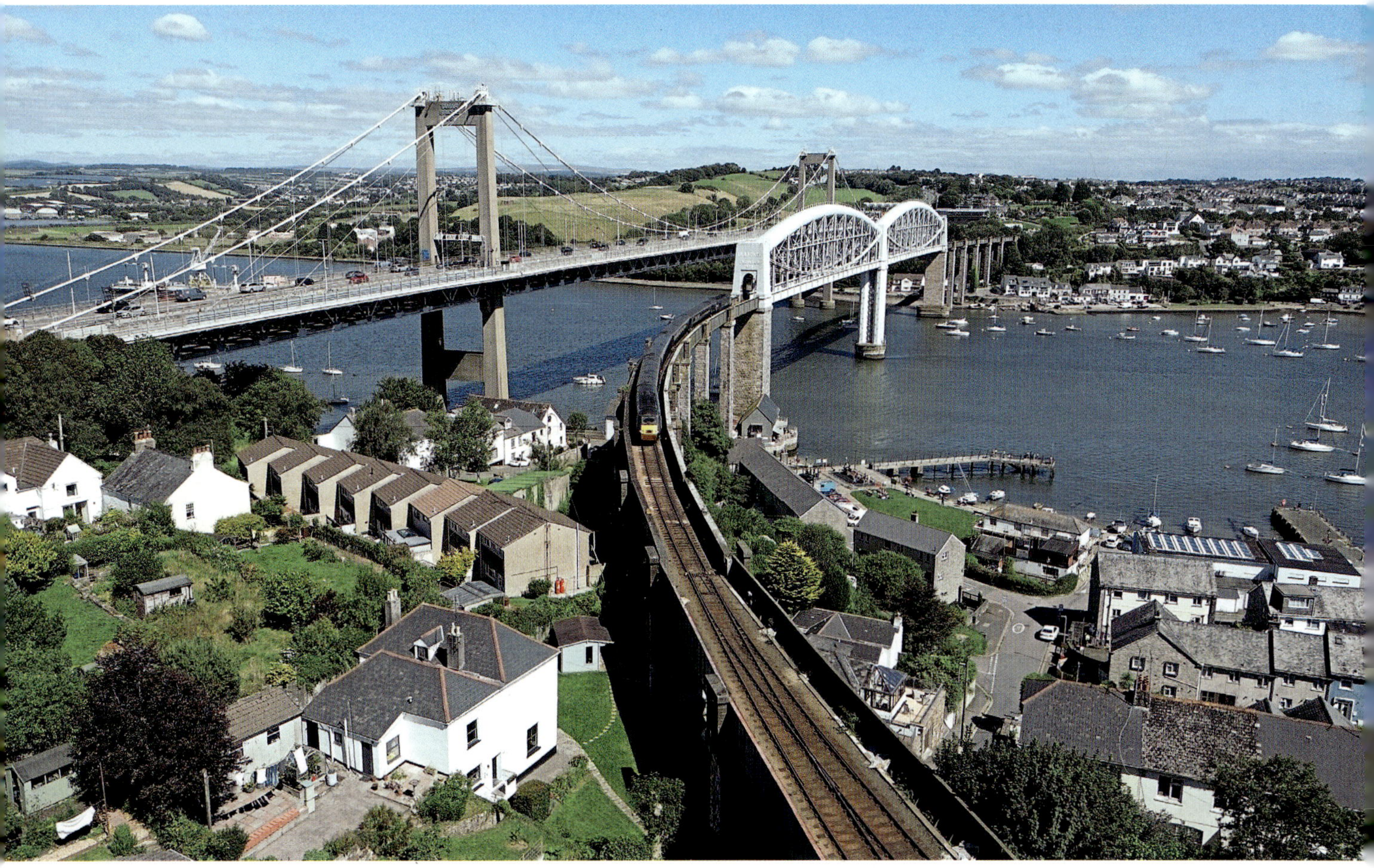

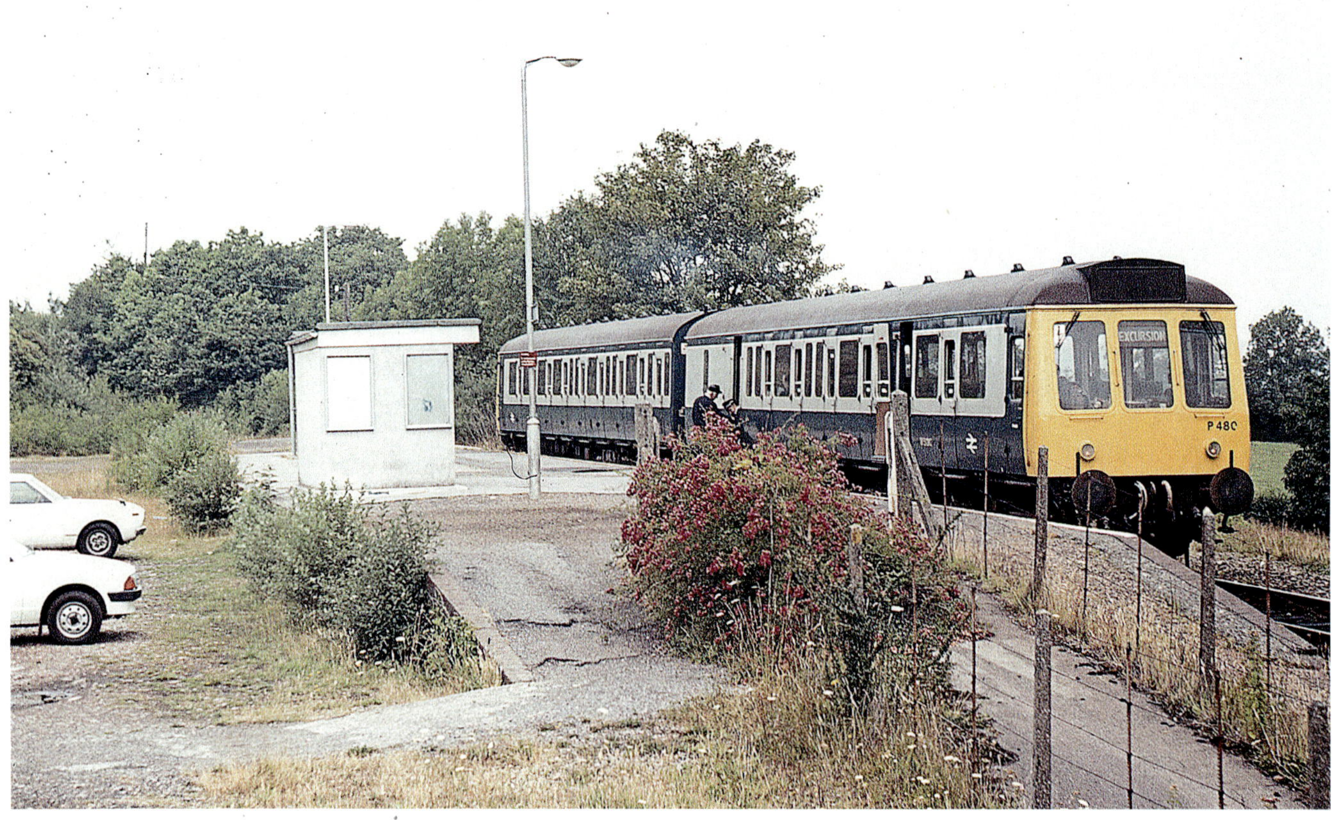

Gunnislake on 22nd July 1984. Over time from 1970 John managed to travel all West of England lines open, apart from the Wadebridge and Retew lines. This shot was just as the author had finished school, with the summer off before starting with BR on 7th September 1984. *Photo by John Stanford*

Liskeard in July 1983 as the family ticked off travelling another branch whilst on holiday. The fact that the Looe branch platform is at right angles to the main line is derived from a historical need to link the Liskeard Looe and Caradon Railway to what became the GWR main line to Cornwall. *Photo by John Stanford*

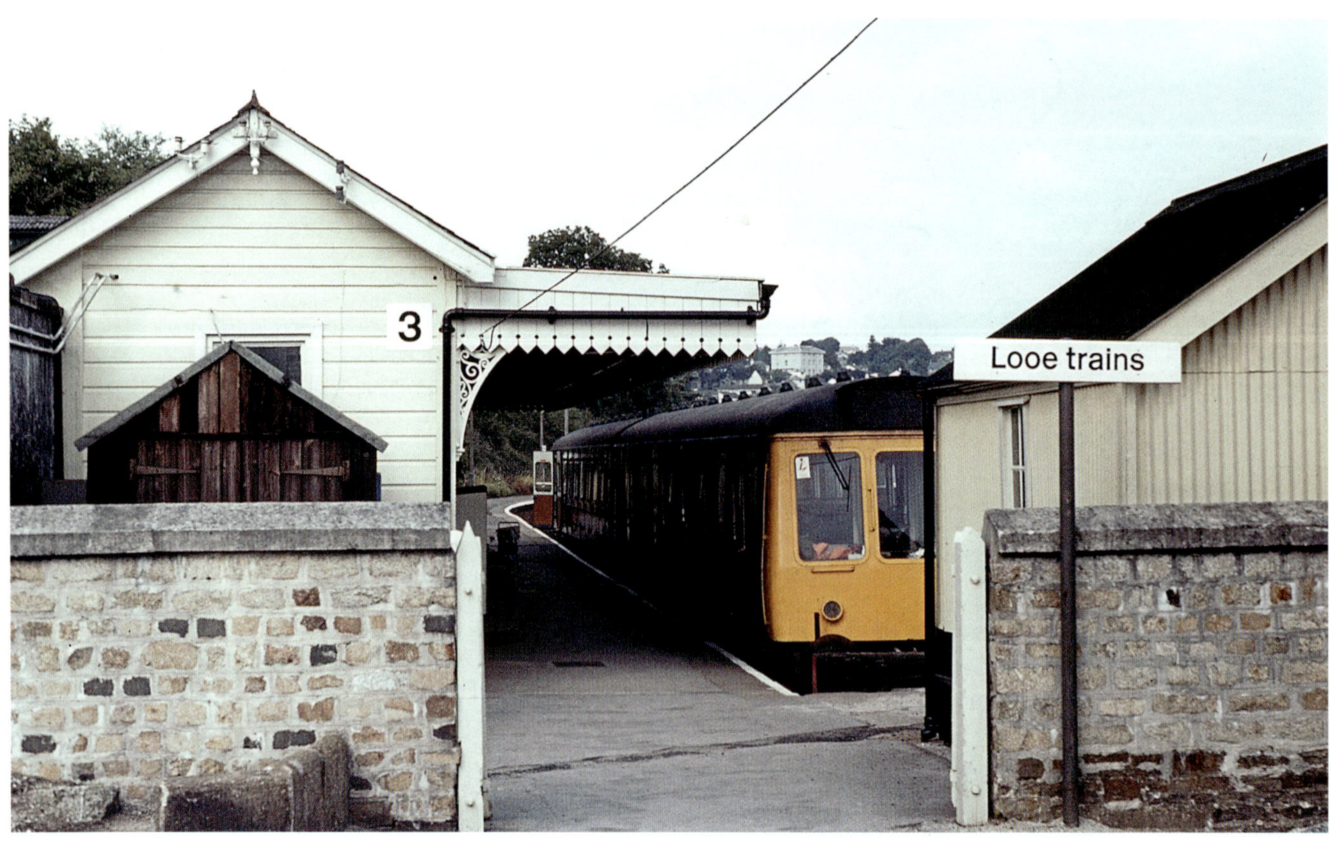

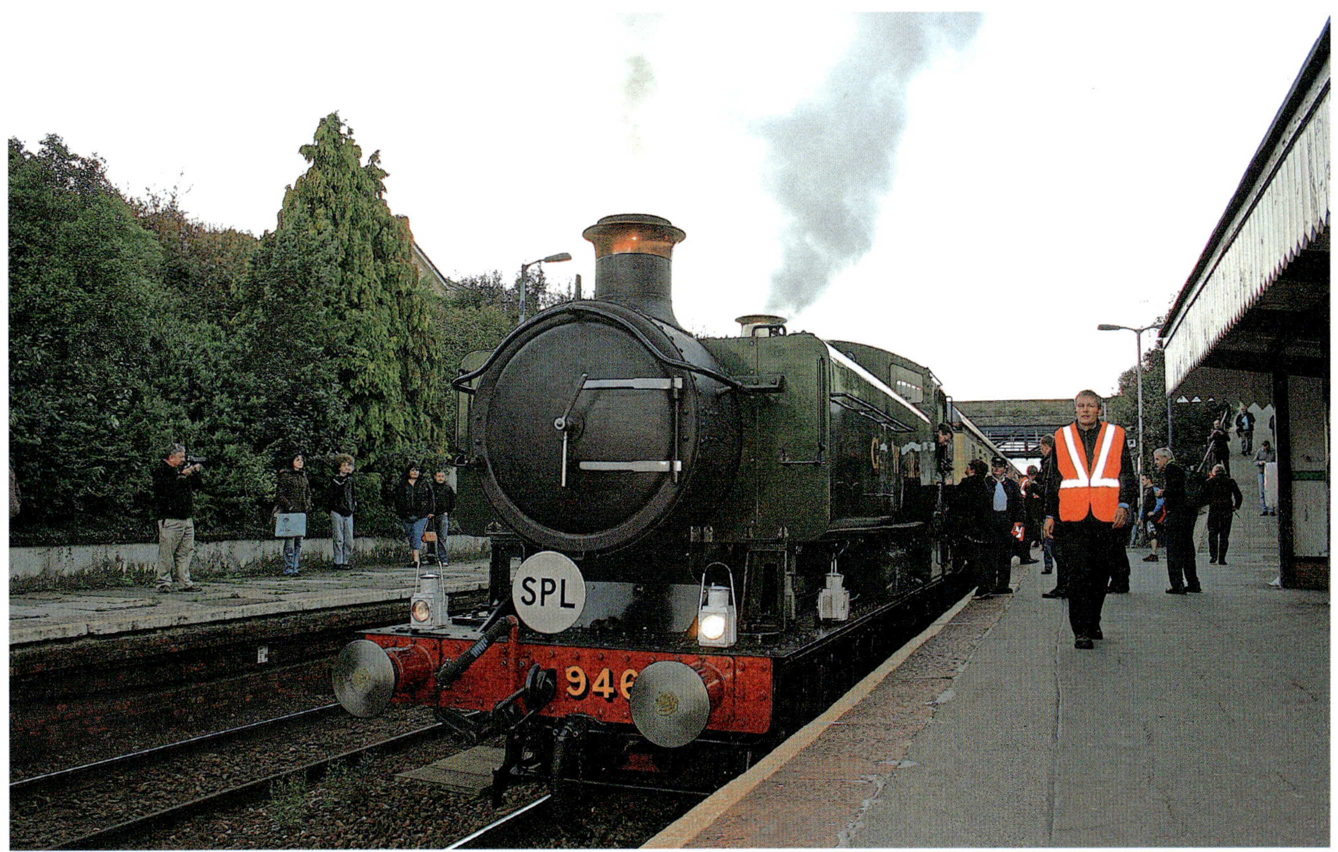

Liskeard in 26th September 2010 as 9466 awaits to head to Plymouth having come up from Looe. Walking towards the camera is Network Rail mobile operations manager Barry Trout, who was overseeing the special operations. The author first met Barry in 1989 when they worked in train and personal accident investigation roles.

Coombe Halt witnesses a freight movement to service Moorswater which was a freight location until December 2020. The railway first appeared here in 1844. After cessation of clay traffic in 1997, two years later the author secured cement traffic into here working with Blue Circle Cement and EWS; arranging for class 66 loco and cement wagon clearance, with the Permanent Way maintenance engineer assessing and upgrading the line. In the last few weeks of cement traffic 70815 is seen in a sylvan setting hauling PCA wagons for unloading.

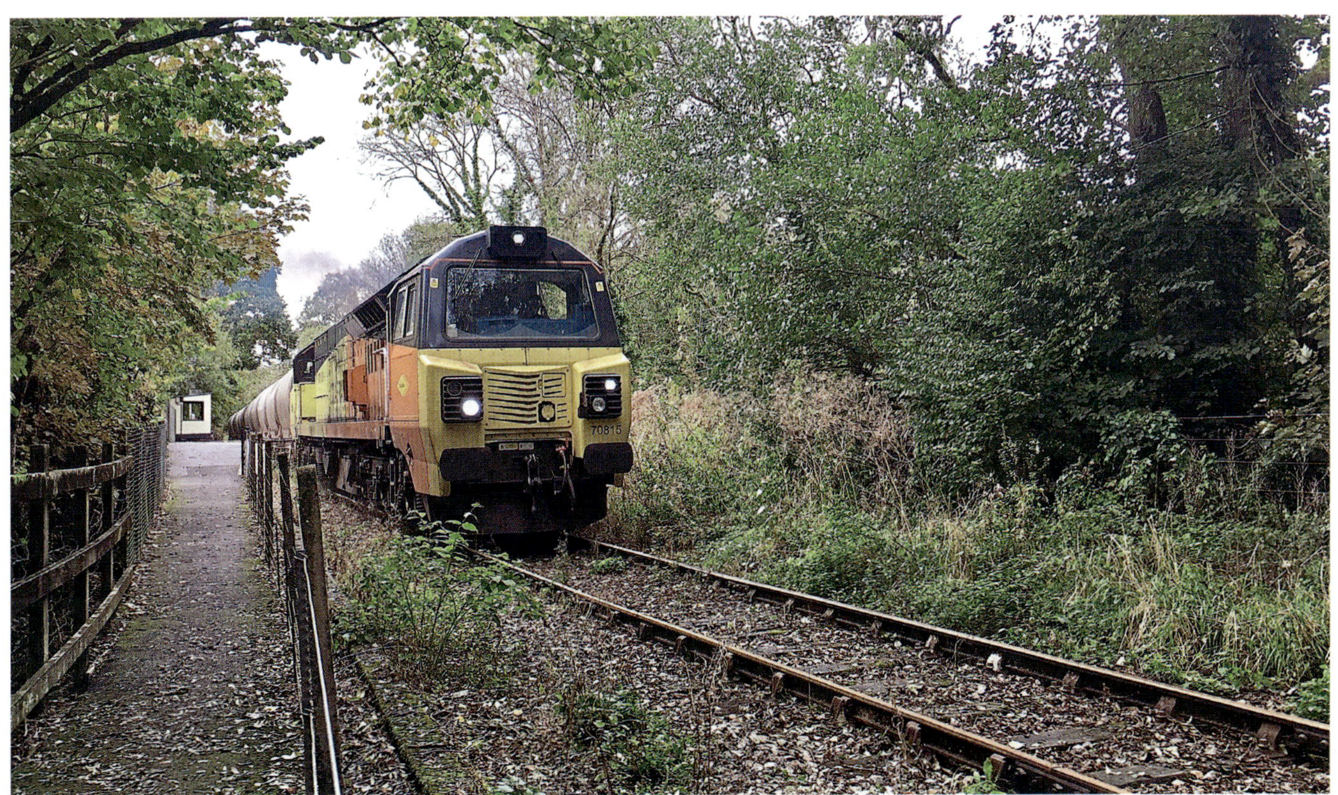

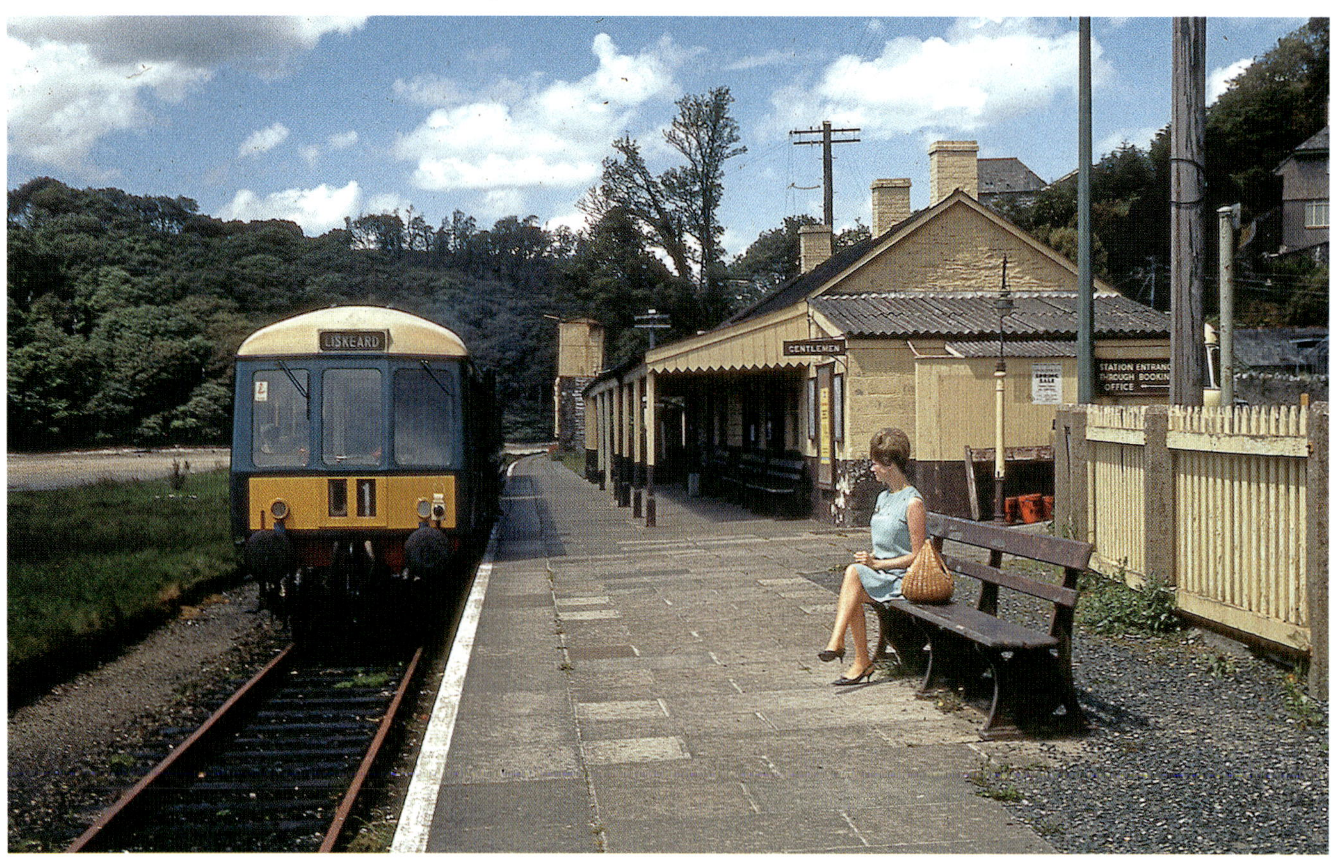

Looe in June 1967 with a DMU awaiting departure and the author's mum Wendy in shot, taking in the sunshine, a few months before the author's birth. The station was subsequently demolished and the track cut back, reflected in the next photograph.

Photo by John Stanford

Looe nearly 30 years later captured by John after working a morning shift in Yatton Booking Office. First generation BR DMUs were in their twilight and this time is reflective of the situation pertaining in the 1980s and early 1990s with a 1st generation bubble car.

Photo by John Stanford

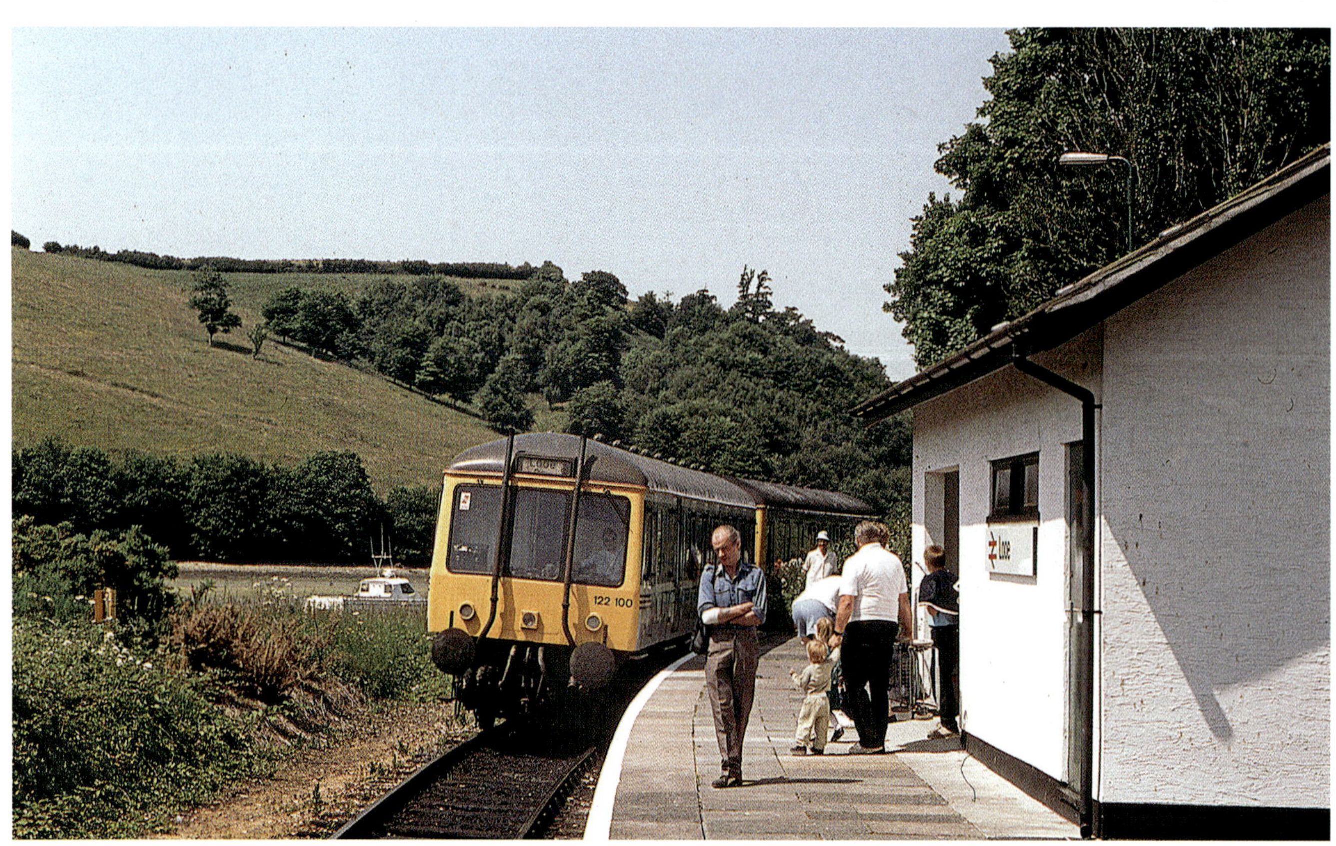

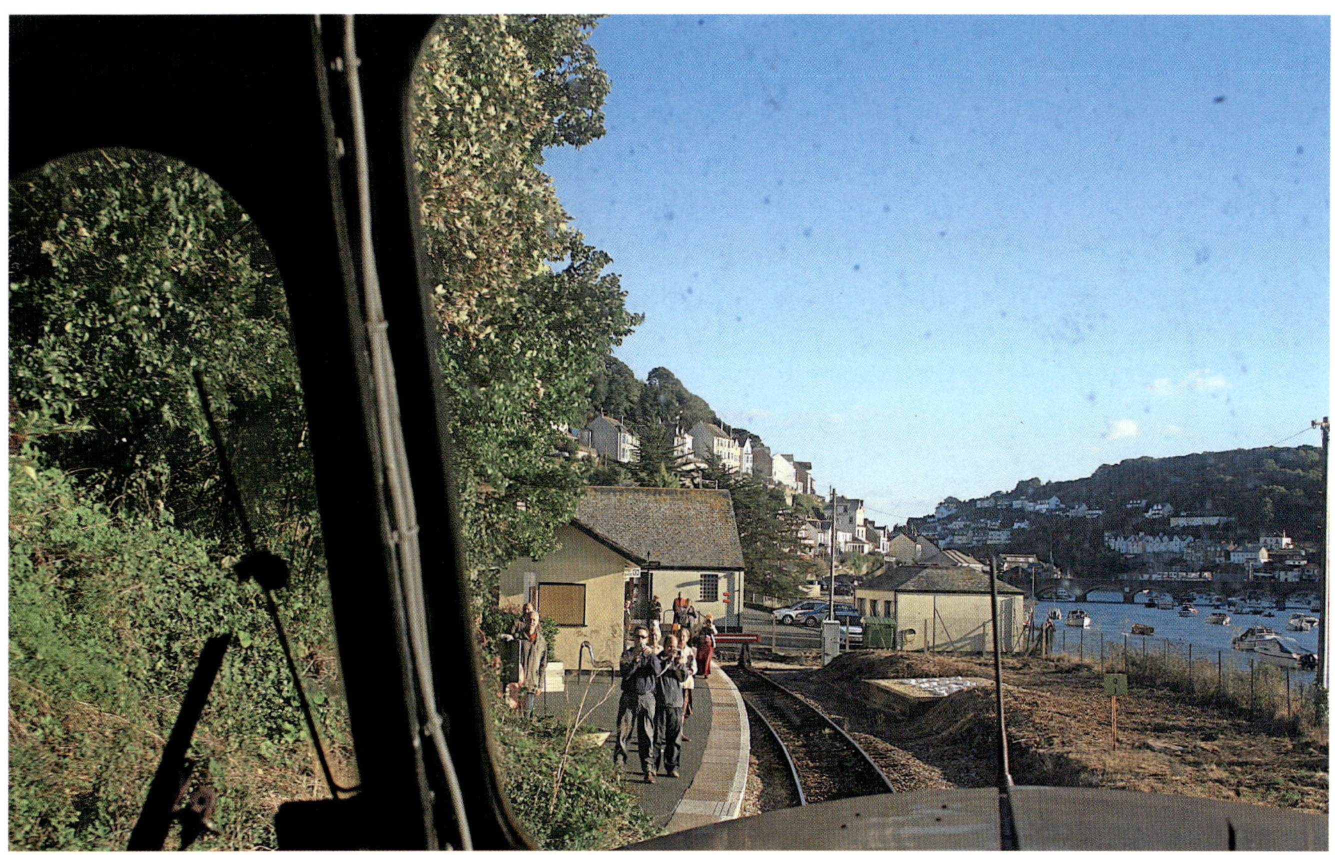

Looe Branch. In late September 2010 a series of special steam trains operated. The author was invited to travel on them by West Coast Railways and GWR, as he had secured dispensation from engineering colleagues for the GWR pannier to travel on the line, which exceeded established weight limits, here is the view from the cab of 37 685, loco 9466 was at rear for movements to Looe and hauled trains the opposite direction.

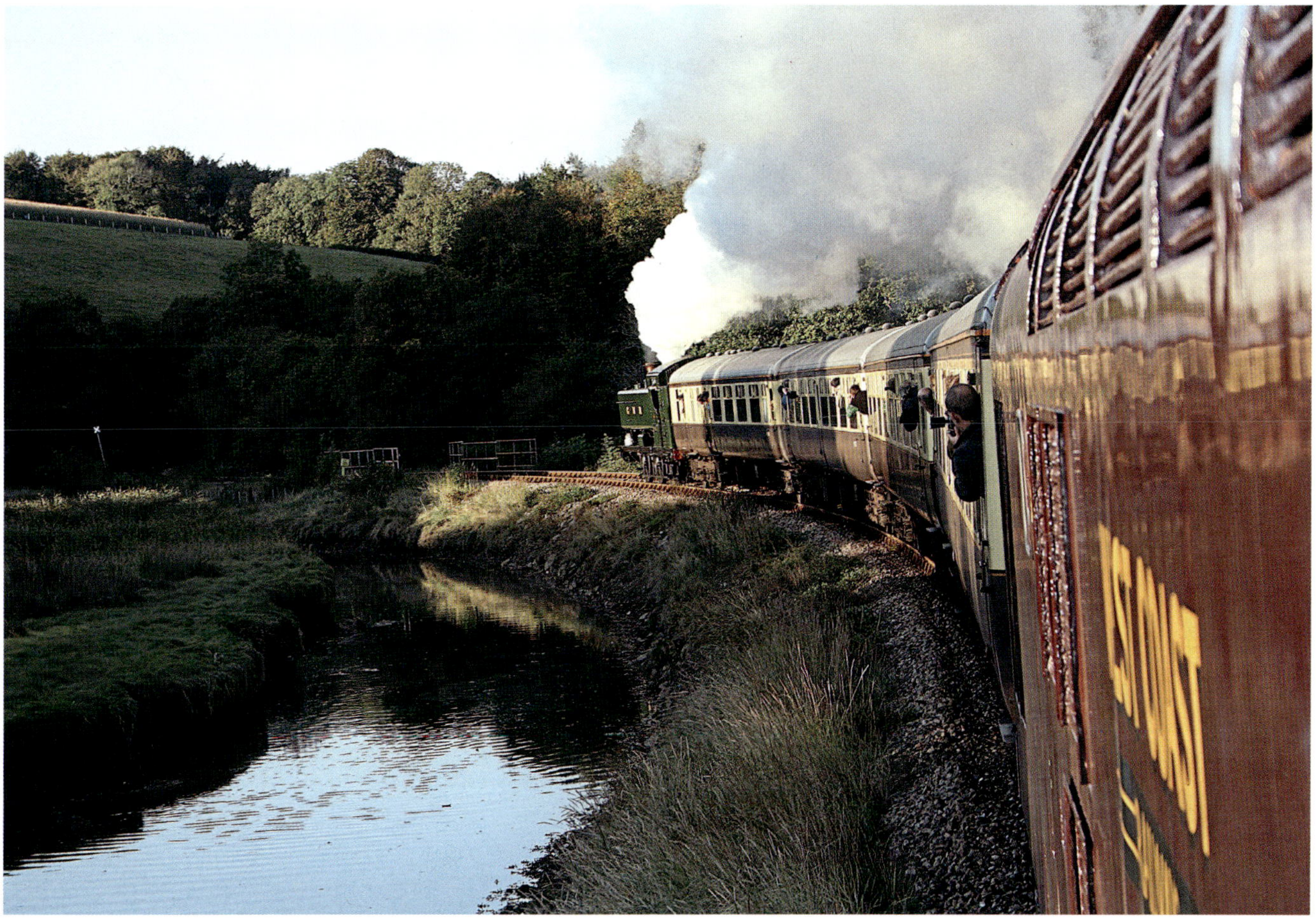

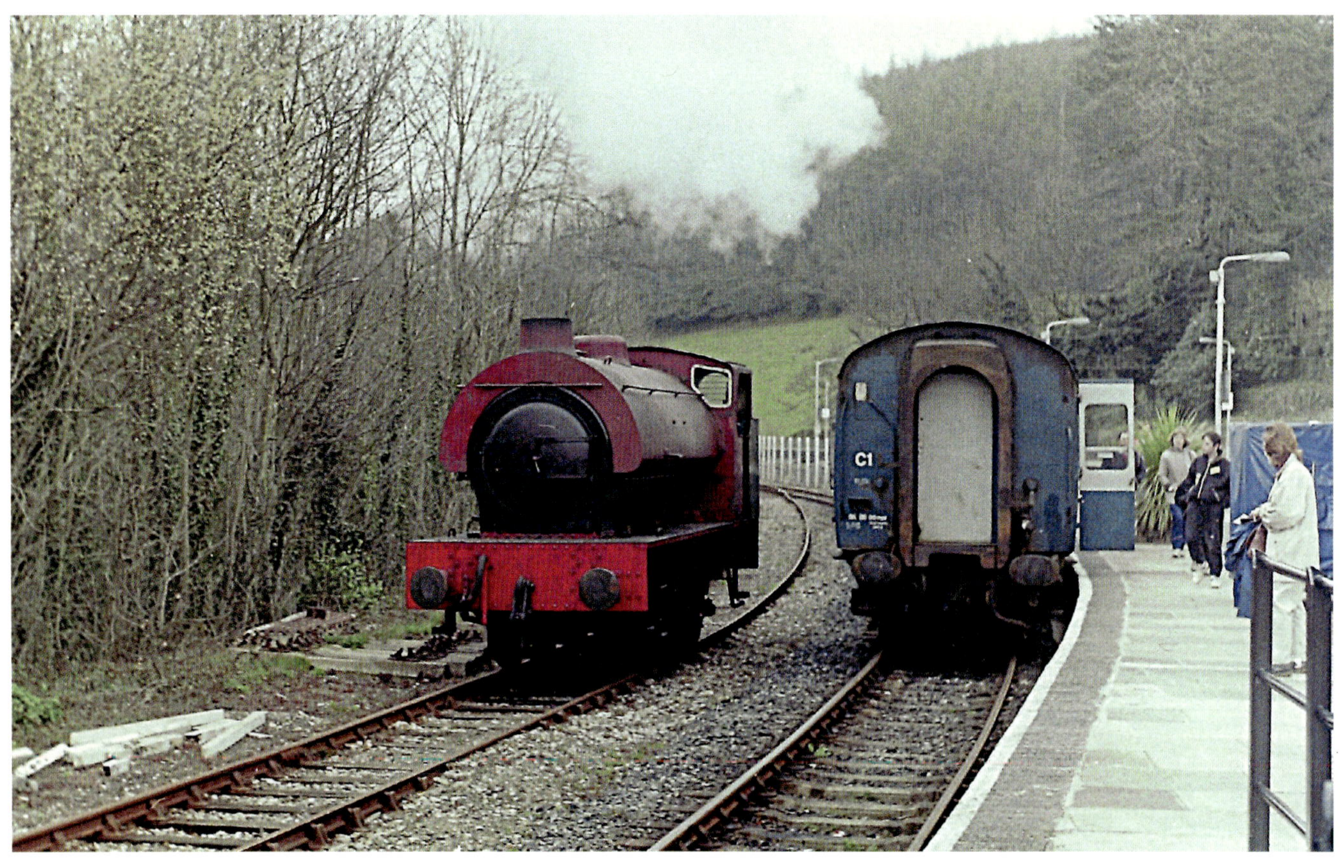

Bodmin Parkway is the point where the line to Bodmin and Wadebridge departs and Bodmin. This ceased BR freight traffic in 1983 and happily was preserved, commencing train rides from Bodmin Parkway in 1990. The author visited on Easter Saturday 1991 and was hauled by Austerity saddle tank *Swiftsure* formerly of Cadley Hill Colliery.

Boscarne Jn on 19th November 1983 with the BR-operated railtour of Cornish branch lines organised by John's BR friends. The author was in the cab of the leading loco, with John panicking as to his whereabouts. The Cornish Railways train-crew allowed him and a gaggle of other young enthusiasts to remain in the cab until Bodmin General. *Photo by Trevor Riddle*

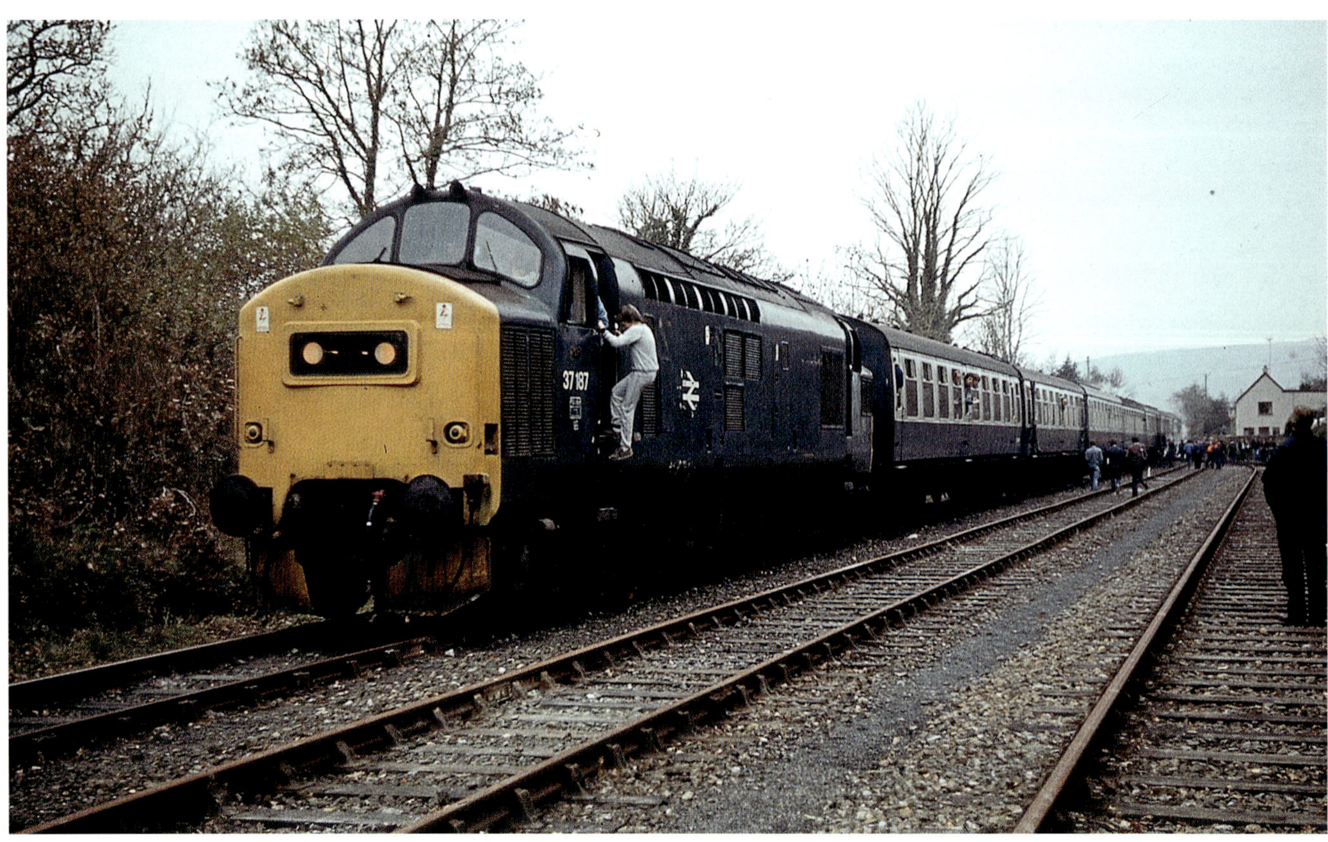

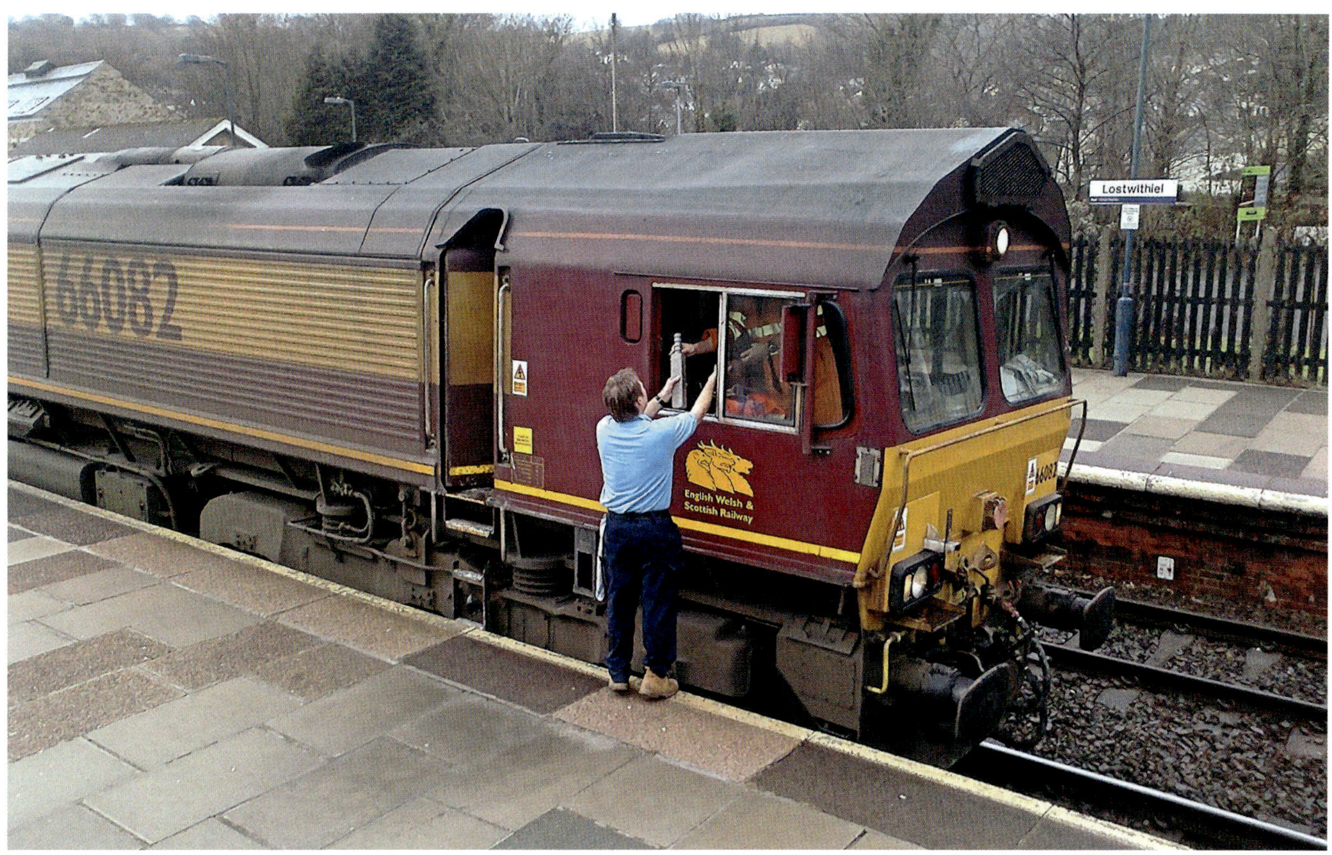

Lostwithiel was, until March 2024, the signal box that controlled access to Fowey; that is now under Exeter Signalling Centre. Here level crossing manager Rob Aston, a lifelong friend of John and Paul, captured signalman David Baker taking the single token for the Fowey Branch from the driver. *Photo by Rob Aston*

Fowey on 19th November 1983 when the author was taken by John on the railtour of Cornish freight branches. Here one of the resident class 10 shunt locos is seen. Frost does not sully the trees – it is china clay dust as a result of the loading process. *Photo by John Stanford*

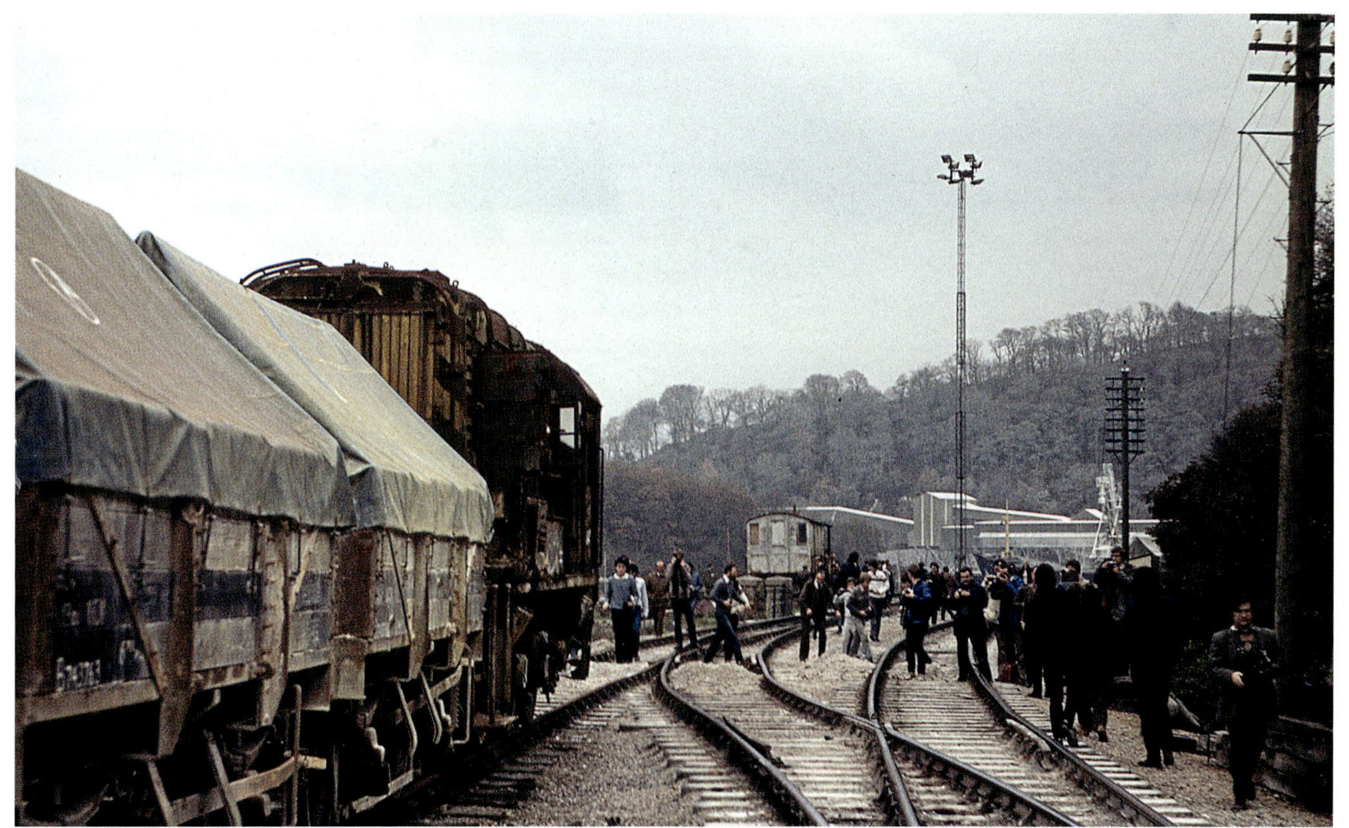

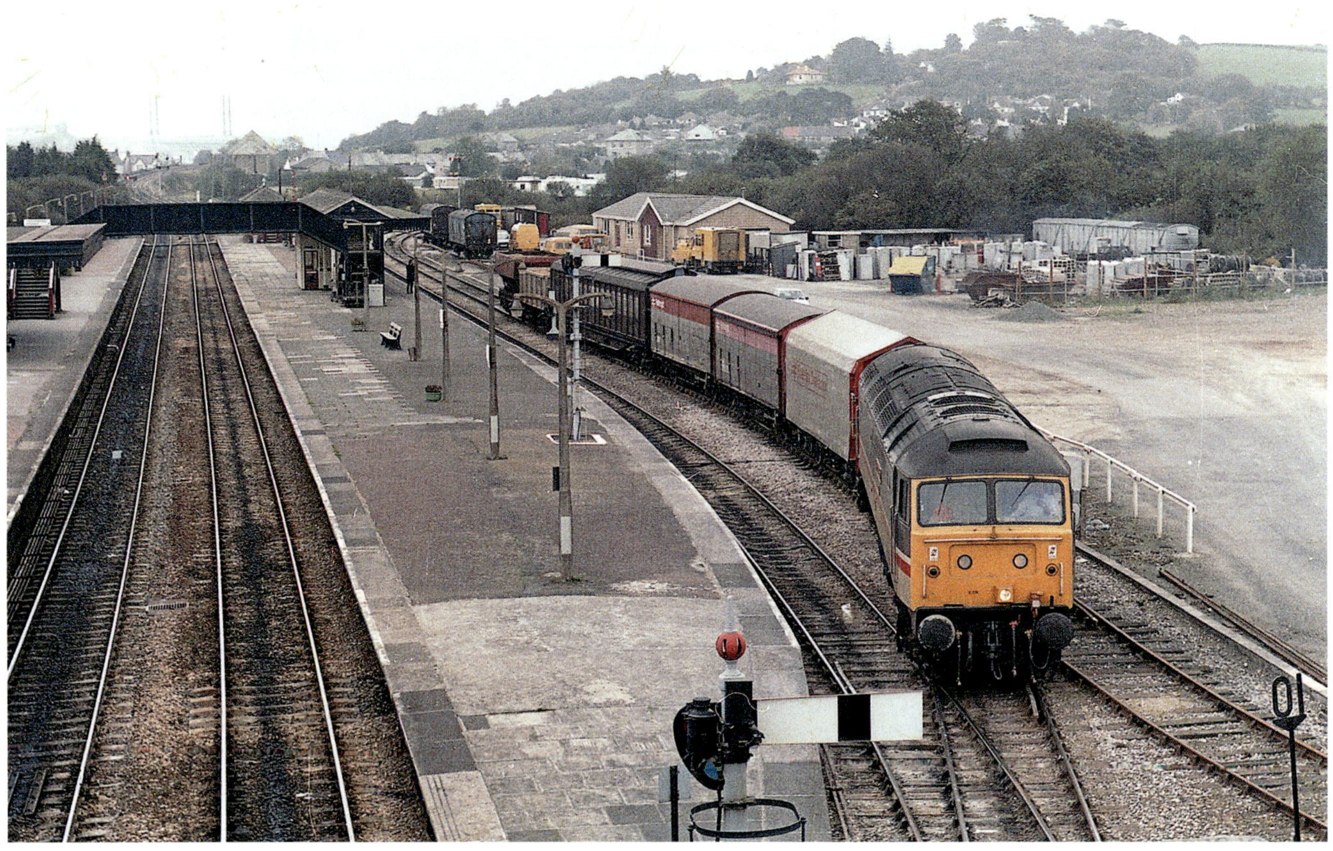

ar, 15th October 1988 and the afternoon St Blazey Speedlink train gets underway heading north toward Plymouth. The last two wagons behind 47508 convey seaweed; loaded latterly at Truro until 2001. It was used as a fertiliser.

Par in October 1988 and 37672 absolutely blasts through the station for Fowey. The author as a 21-year-old in the train planning unit could never have imagined that 10 years later he would be regional freight manager, routinely coming for meetings with EWS and English China Clays and other customers about existing and new railfreight traffic.

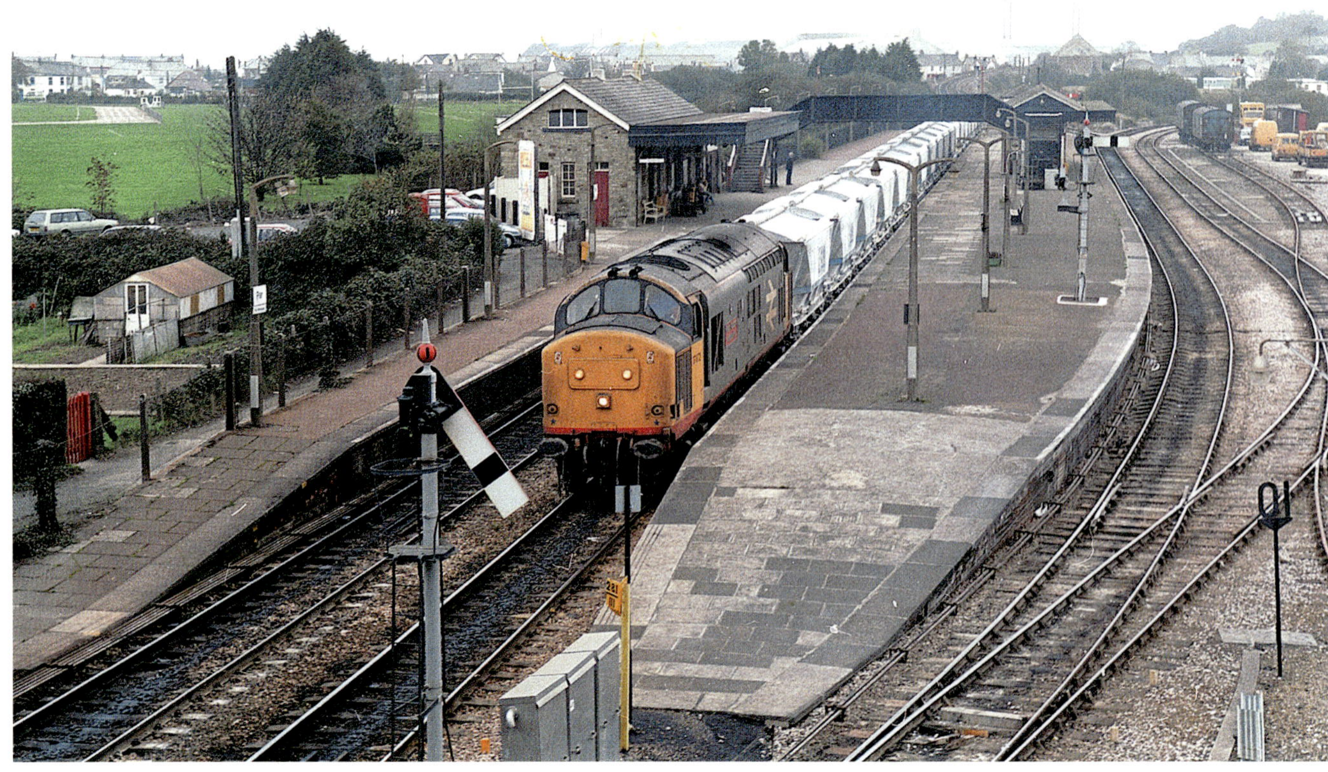

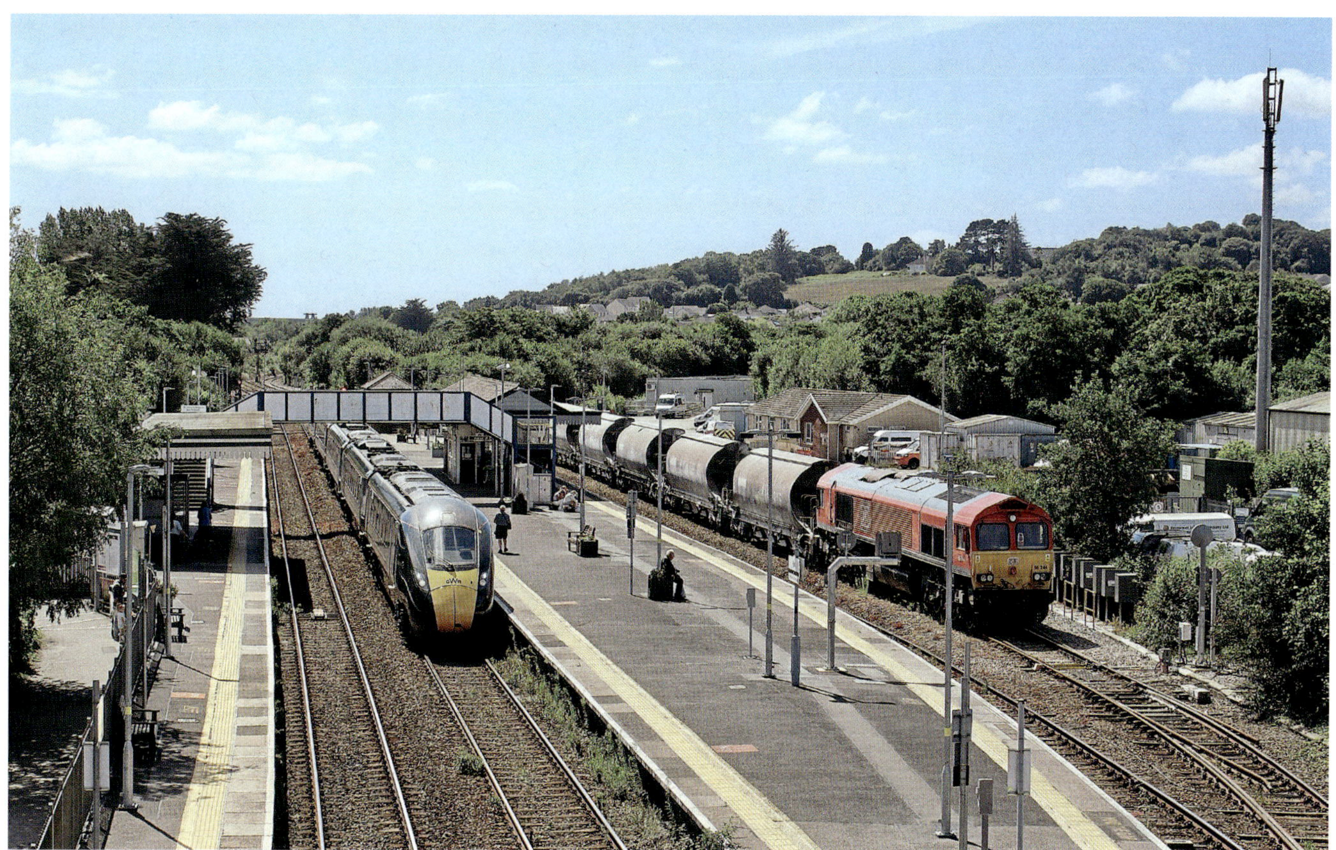

Par from a similar viewpoint on 14th August 2024 which neatly shows the layout of the station as DB Cargo 66244 stands with seven loaded JIA wagons, off the Parkandillack line, with 'white gold' for the Potteries. The wagons replaced the CDA wagons exactly year earlier.

St Blazey in 2025 it is still the hub for remaining regular rail freight with a small admin hub, for traincrew operating clay traffic. This 2024 scene highlights the facilities, from wagon stabling, covered workshops from wagon maintenance and a loco stabling point. In 1998, the author's first visit to the depot, there were circa 40 drivers, now it is just a handful. Loco 66152 is nearest the camera, named after the late Derek Holmes, a brilliant railwayman and former mentor to the author.

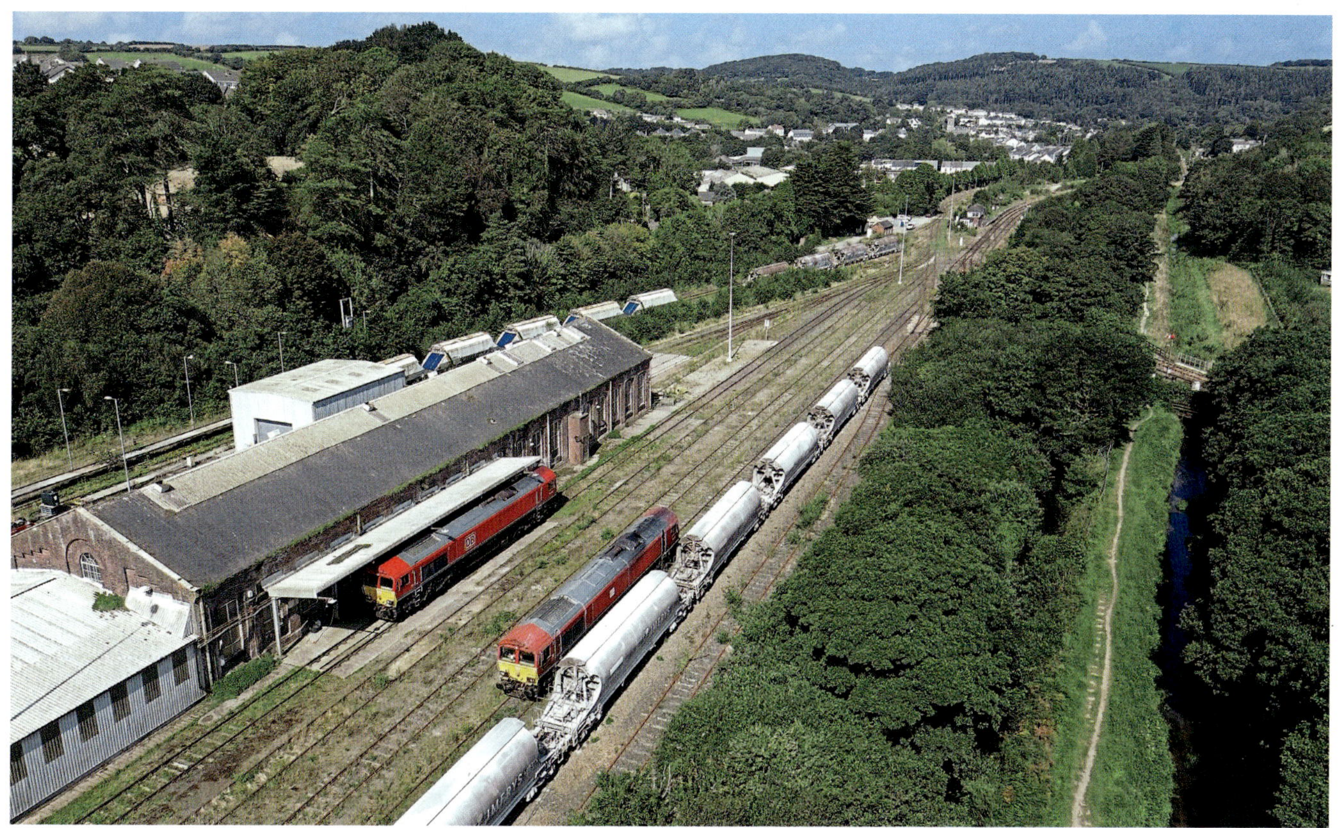

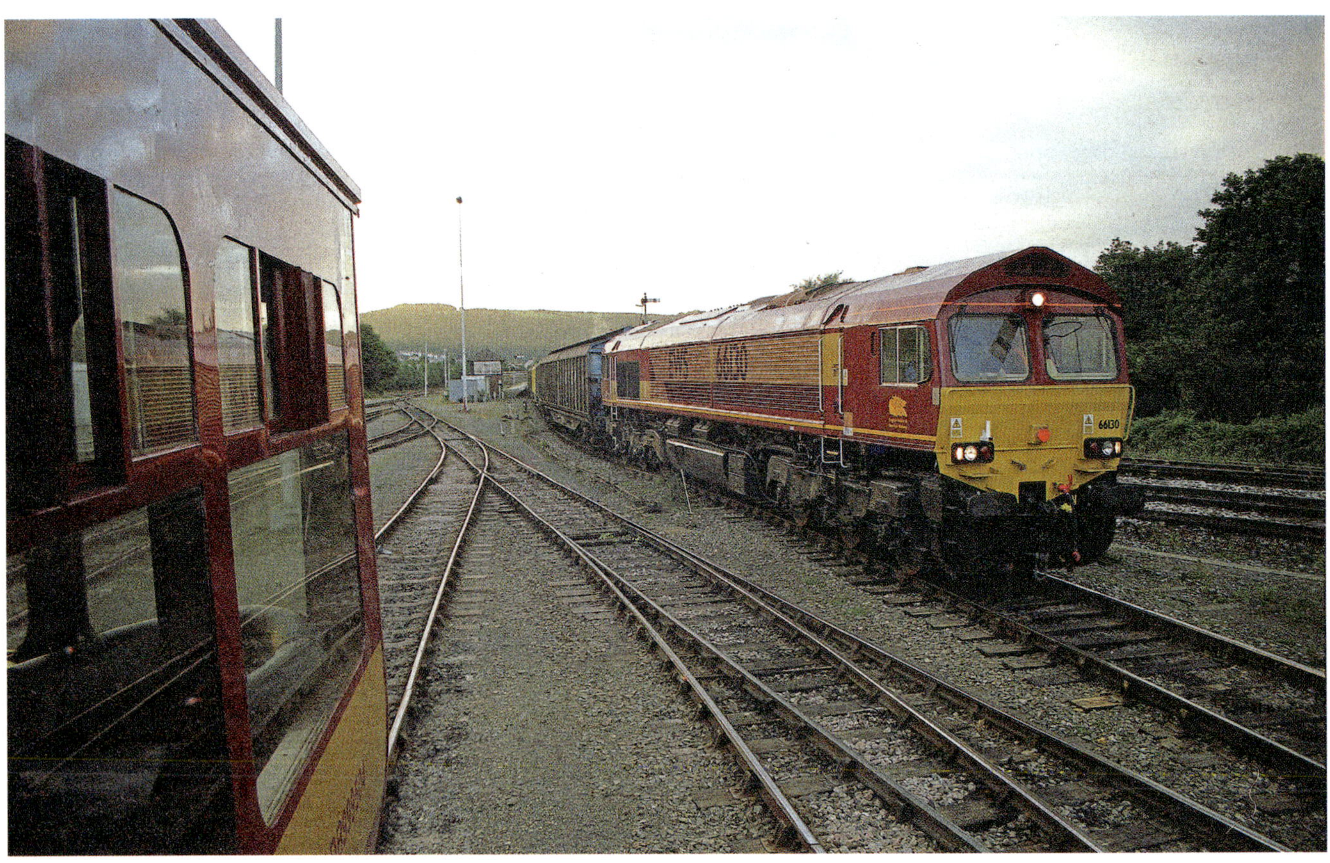

St Blazey on the evening of 10th August 1999 as new class 66 loco pushes its train of empty cement wagons from the yard, ready to return to Hope in Derbyshire. This was the author's first large rail flow he established in Cornwall working with Blue Circle Cement and EWS. He was waiting to depart with a class 37 and upon an inspection saloon to Penzance, travelling with friend and colleague EWS Rail Services manager Huw Philips. This journey enabled the author to route learn, in connection with his movements manager duties at Burngullow the following day.

Par Docks in October 1988 and bagged clay is evident in German box vans. A class 08 loco would pootle along the line a few times a week to drop off or pick up a few clay wagons. Now once a week a large train usually leaves here for Stoke on Trent for the ceramics industry.

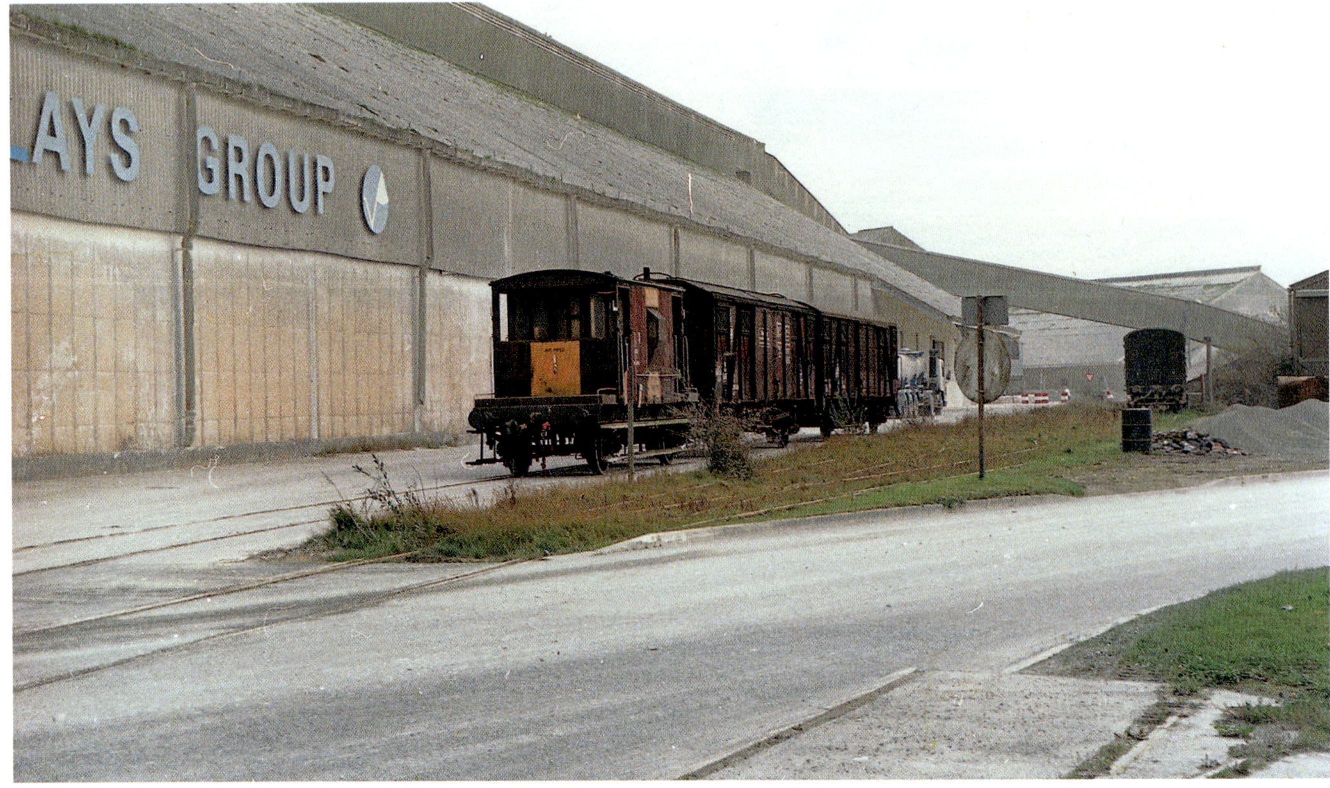

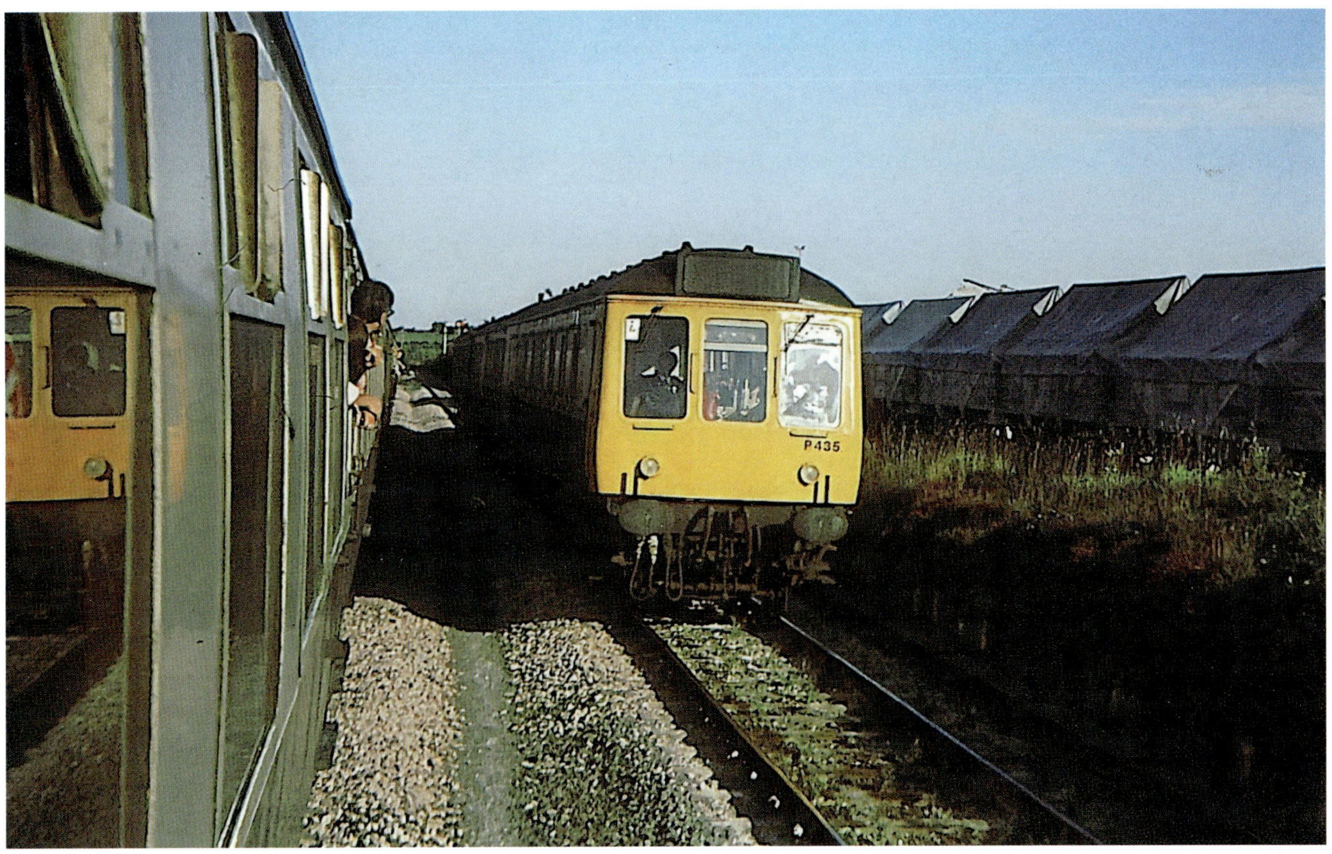

Goonbarrow, near Bugle, on 16th August 1982 and John captures a service train from the charter service. He, Wendy and their boys travelled for a day out in Newquay. At right are Clay Hoods with only another five years of working life ahead. *Photo by John Stanford*

Burngullow and on 10th August 1999, 37689 blasts away with three PBA wagons for loading on the Parkandillack branch. Minutes earlier the young St Blazey driver said to the author that he enjoyed driving 37s on the branches. The author said he felt guilty, as he got the support of his structure engineer colleagues to route clear from here to Parkandillack for new, heavier, class 66 locomotives.

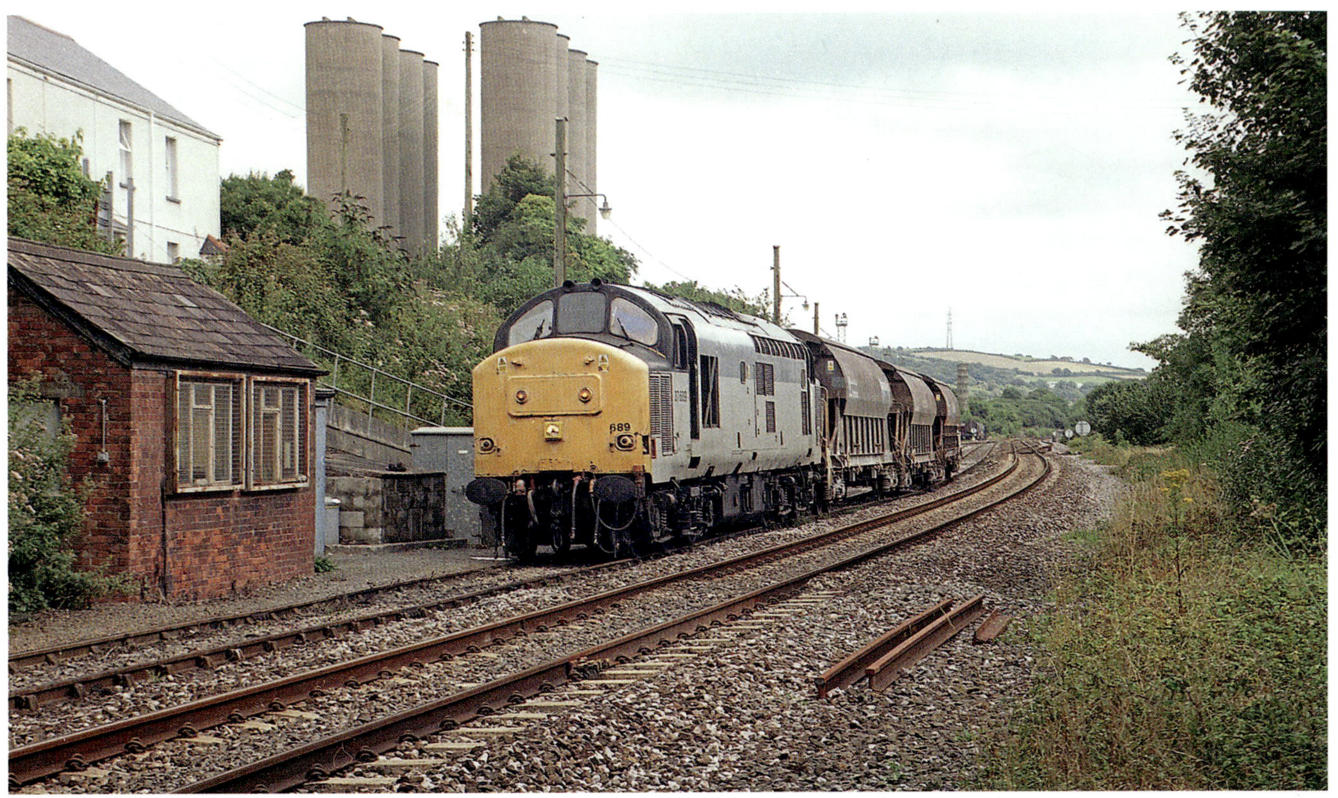

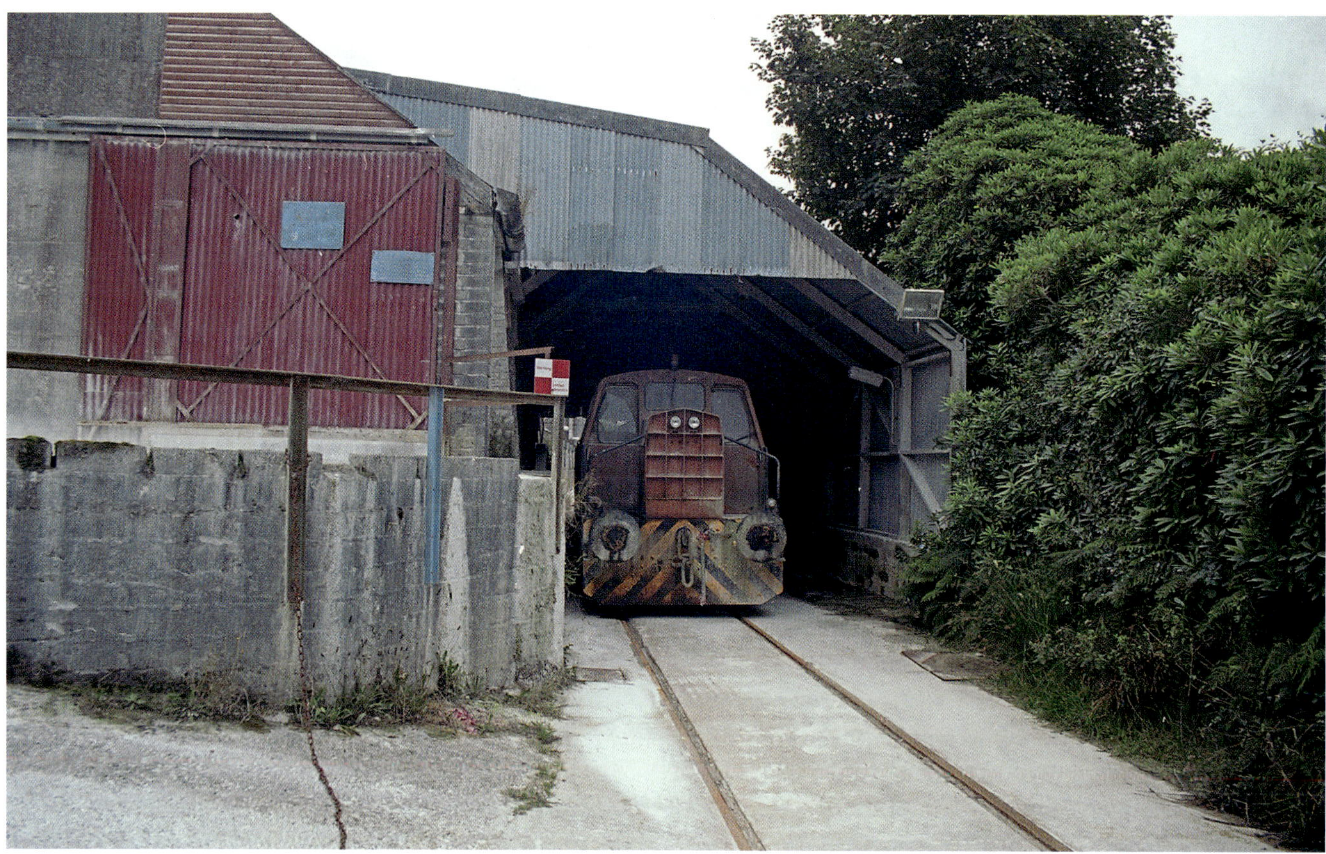

Burngullow on 11th August 1999 was bereft of freight traffic and clay works activity; as the Eclipse saw a focus on passenger trains. The author was based at Burngullow for the day and after all trains successfully reached their destinations in time for the eclipse, went for a wander round deserted clay works; which closed some eight years later as the clay industry contracted.

Parkandillack is situated on what was a through line; lifted in the 1960s. When John first visited the line in 1983 it was on a railtour. Previously he attended freight meetings at St Blazey depot, once in a boat with area manager Rusty Eplett and at John Keay House in St Austell with English China Clays.

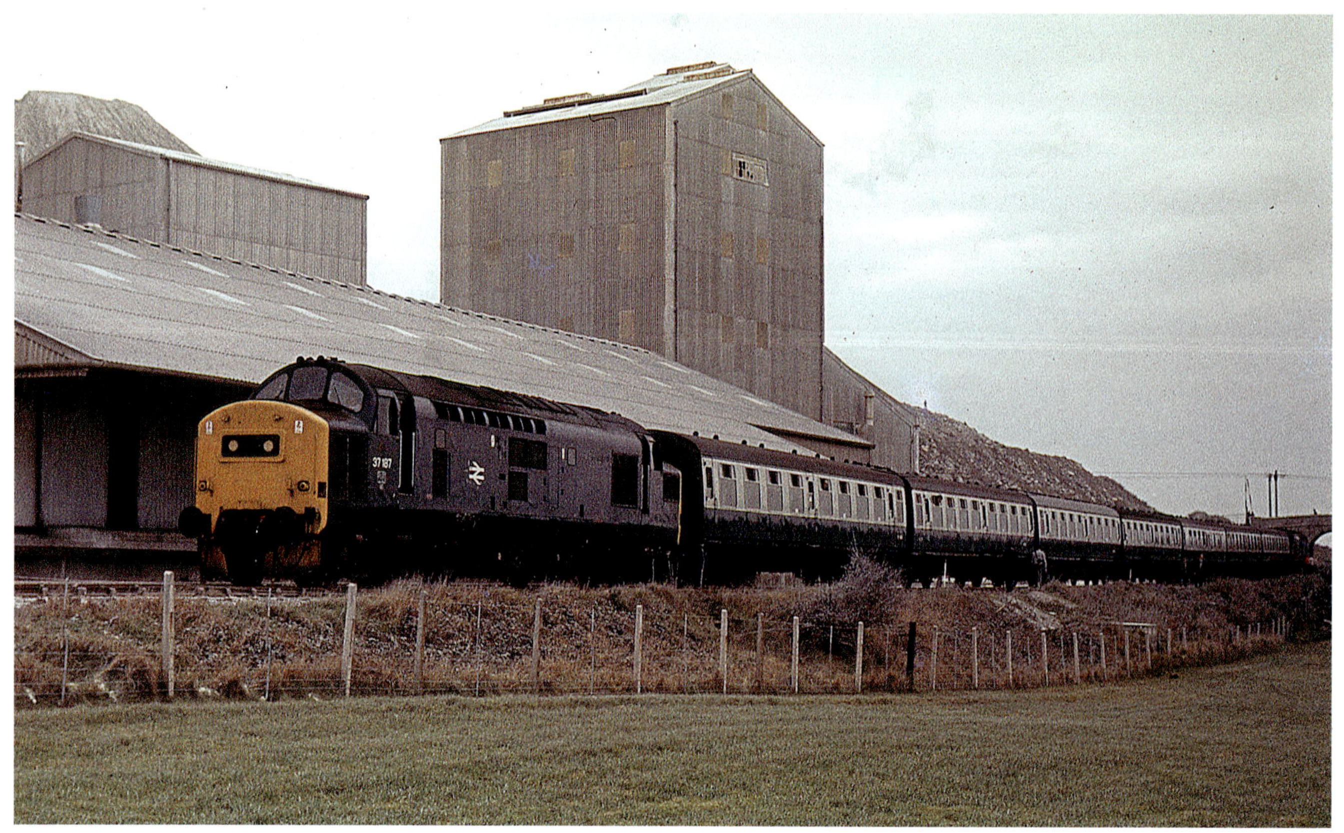

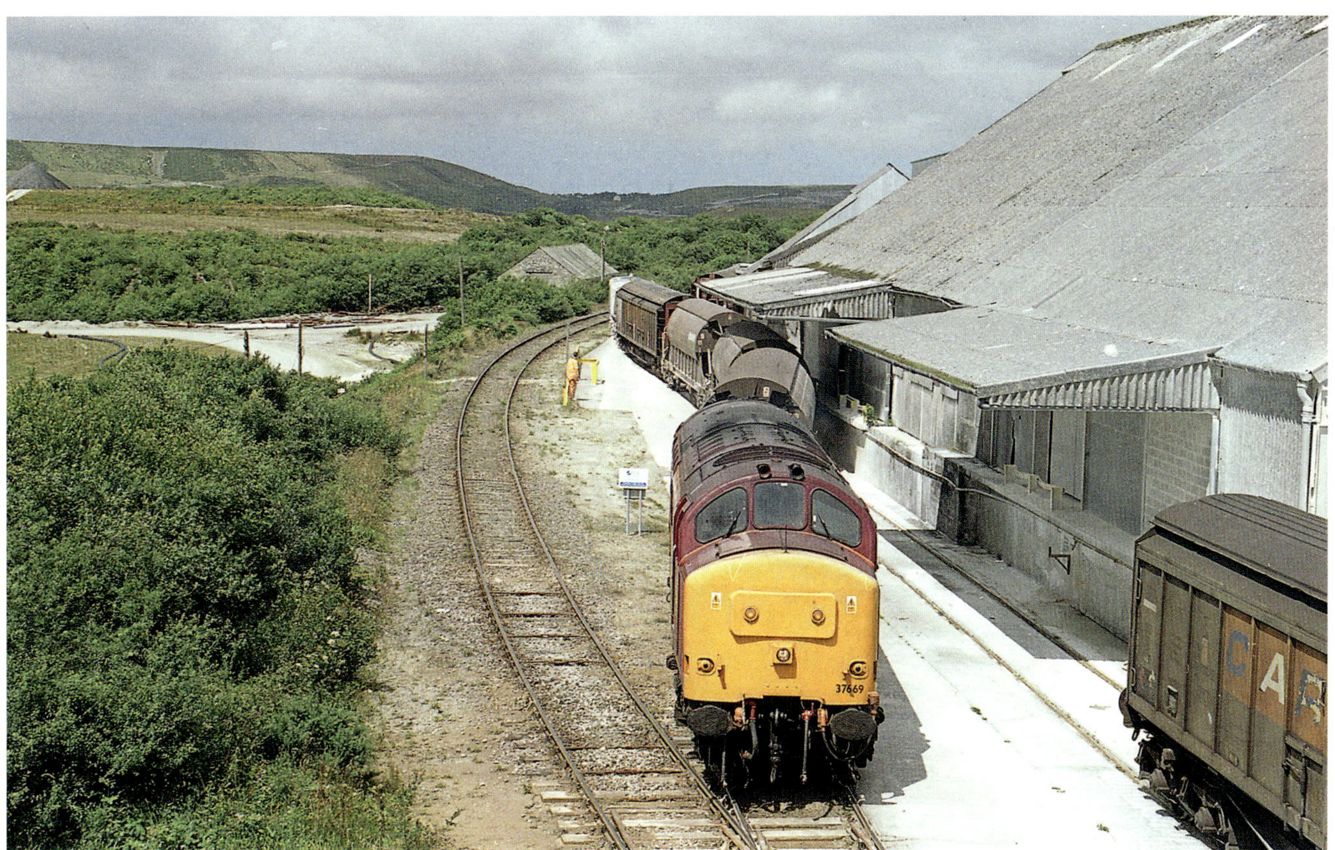

Treviscoe in July 1998 on the Parkandillack branch; when the author was polishing up his freight knowledge whilst on holiday. Later that year he took up the role of Regional Freight Manager Western Region for Railtrack. The appointment was in April but he was not released from his safety critical operations manager role until year-end. The class 37 is shunting wagons destined for Stoke.

Falmouth Docks in August 1980 still hosted a working steam loco and Sentinel diesel shunter. In view is a Hudswell Clarke saddle tank; the non working machine was on display near the entrance to the dockyard. Then, internal rail traffic operated plus fish traffic onto the national network. *Photo by John Stanford*

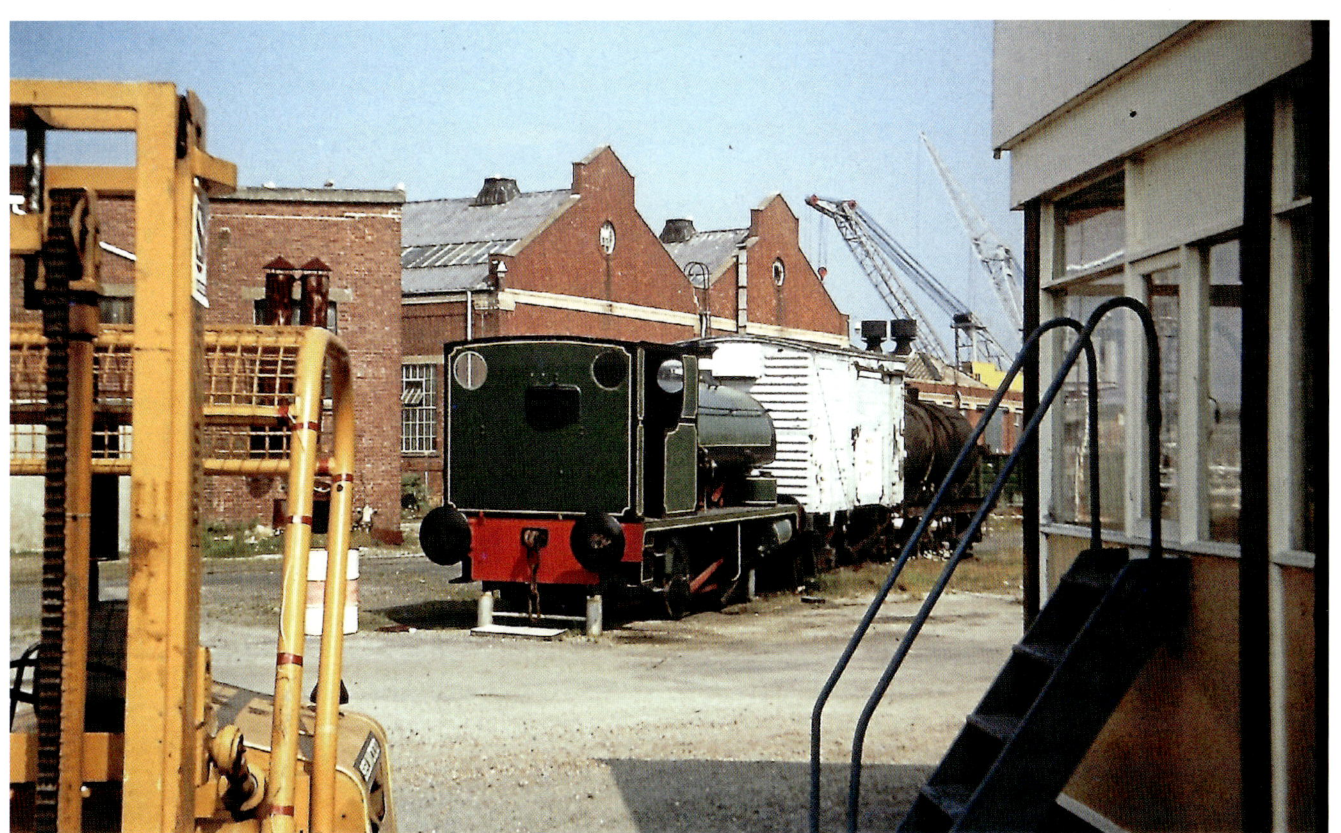

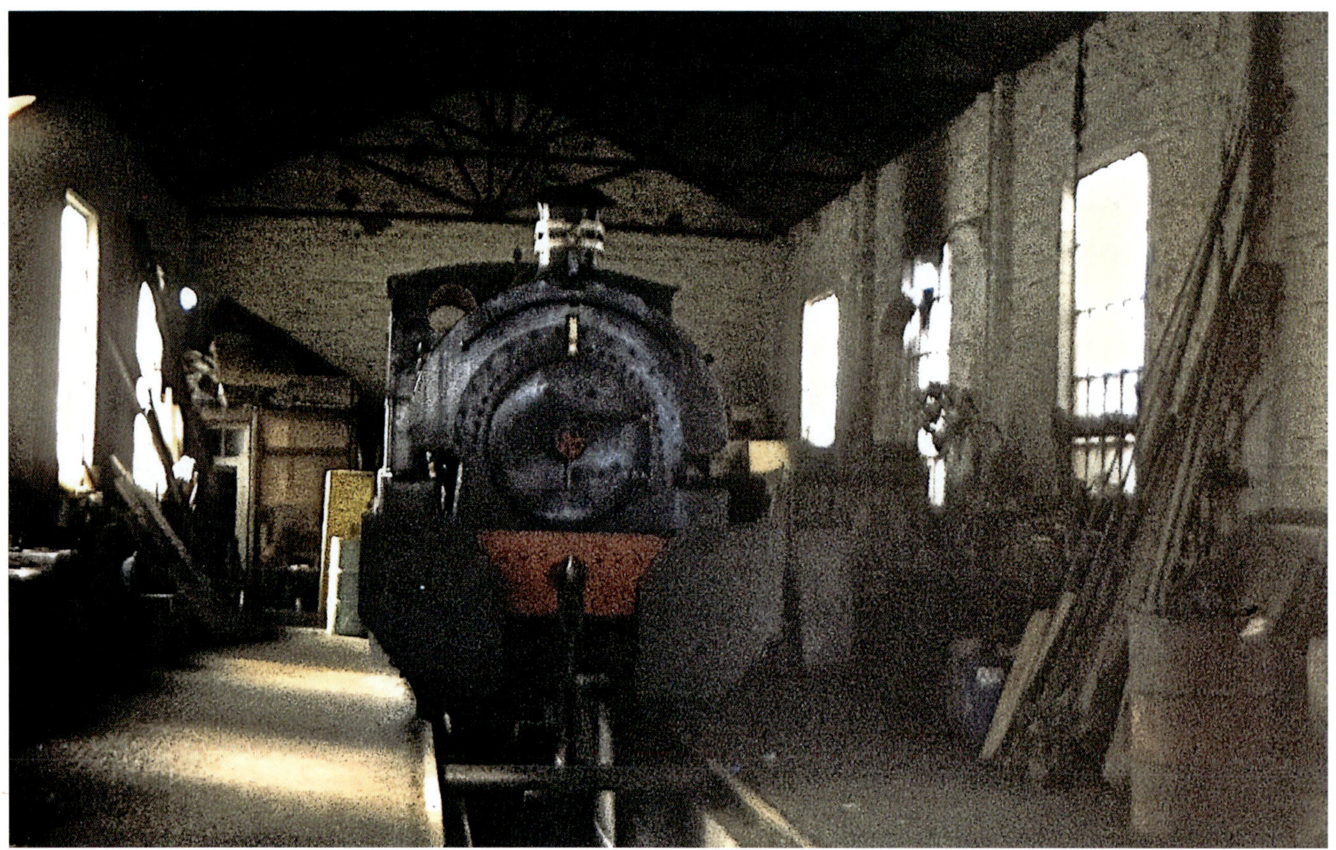

Falmouth Docks was revisited by the author early in his railway career on 5th March 1985 to see the remaining working steam engine; built by Hawthorn Leslie. Lovingly cared for by its regular driver Roy, it is seen here in the shed. The Sentinel diesel had been working the day of the visit; however, a year later the working steam loco was retired and preserved. The last rail traffic at the docks was coal in 1997 and containerised shot blast waste from ships the following year.

St Ives was first visited by John and the family in the 1980s, and many times since. Here in August 2020; the author hiking with Fiona from St Erth to Marazion caught a GWR 150 Unit, now 40 years old, heading back to St Erth.

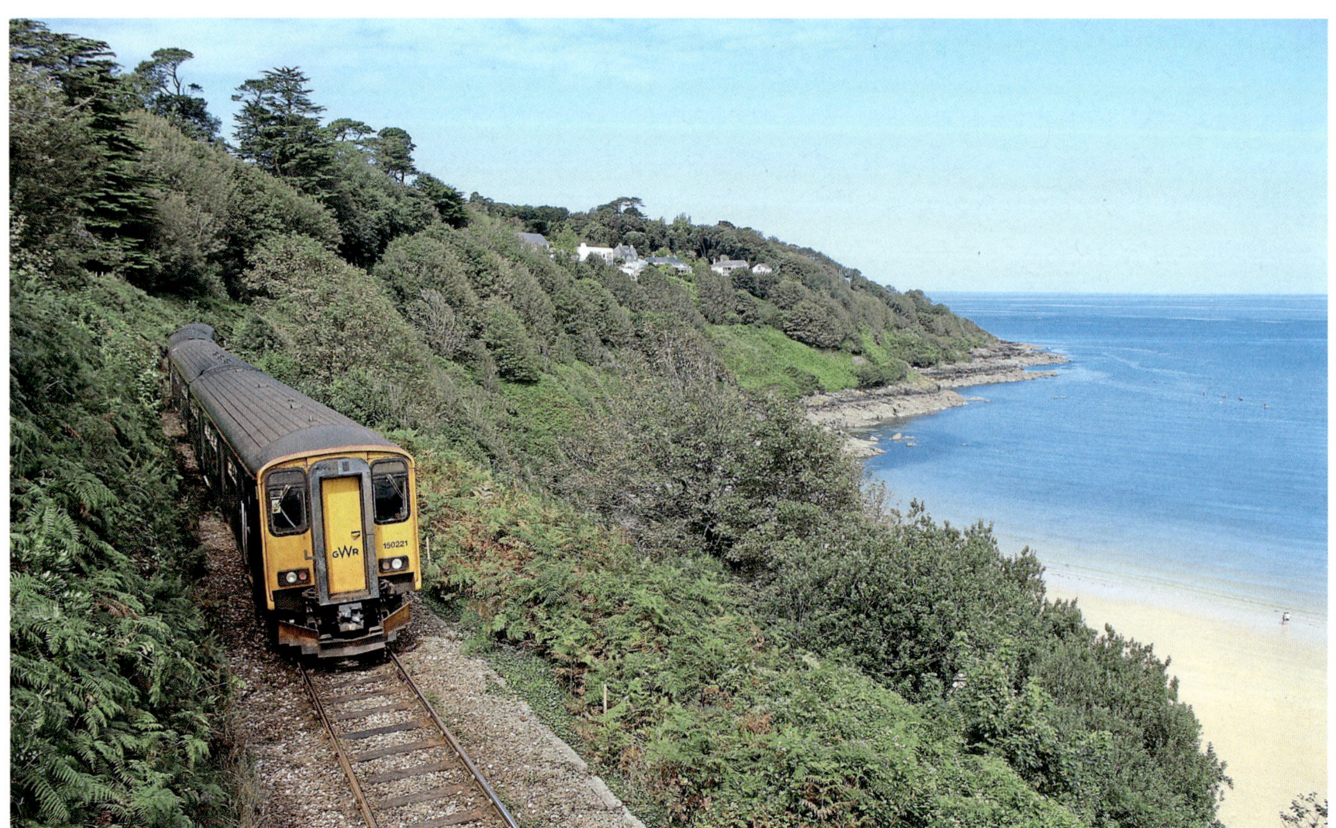

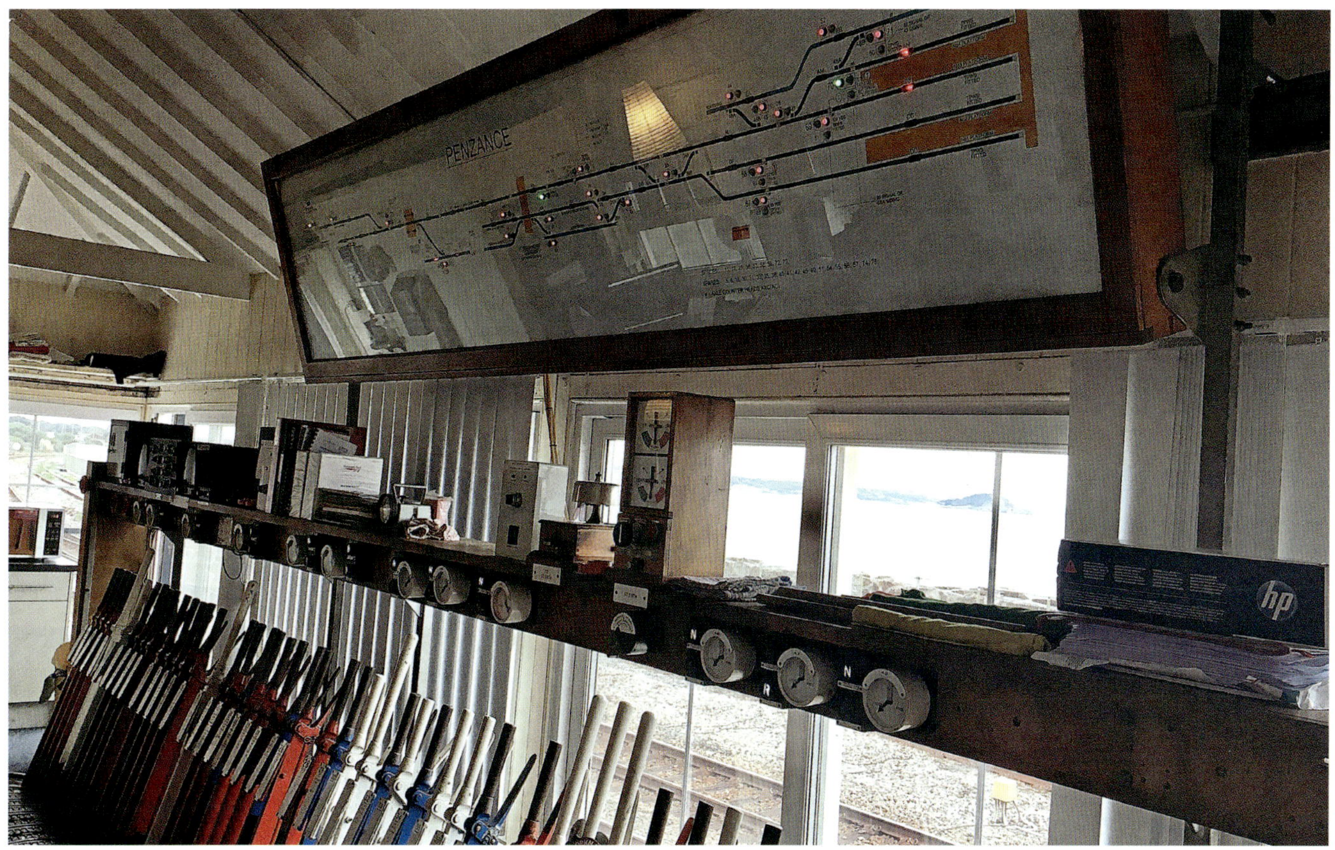

Penzance signal box; possibly the box with the best view on the network including both the sea and St Michael's Mount (visible in the photo).The author visited whilst doing a safety tour with friend and colleague Barry Milsom, then performance director, at train operator GWR on 11th September 2020.

Penzance and the end of the line, physically and metaphorically. The Night Rivera sleeper train at journey's end, on which the author travelled to do a day of safety tours at Network Rail and GWR locations. The author's final work in summer 2021 before the end of his full-time railway career was a report on the reunification of the railway to align with the Keith Williams review and better operating the network. Cornwall was used as a worked case study. He was absolutely delighted; this work was highly acclaimed by the chief executive of Network Rail. Subsequently some of the elements in the report have been adopted on the Western Region.

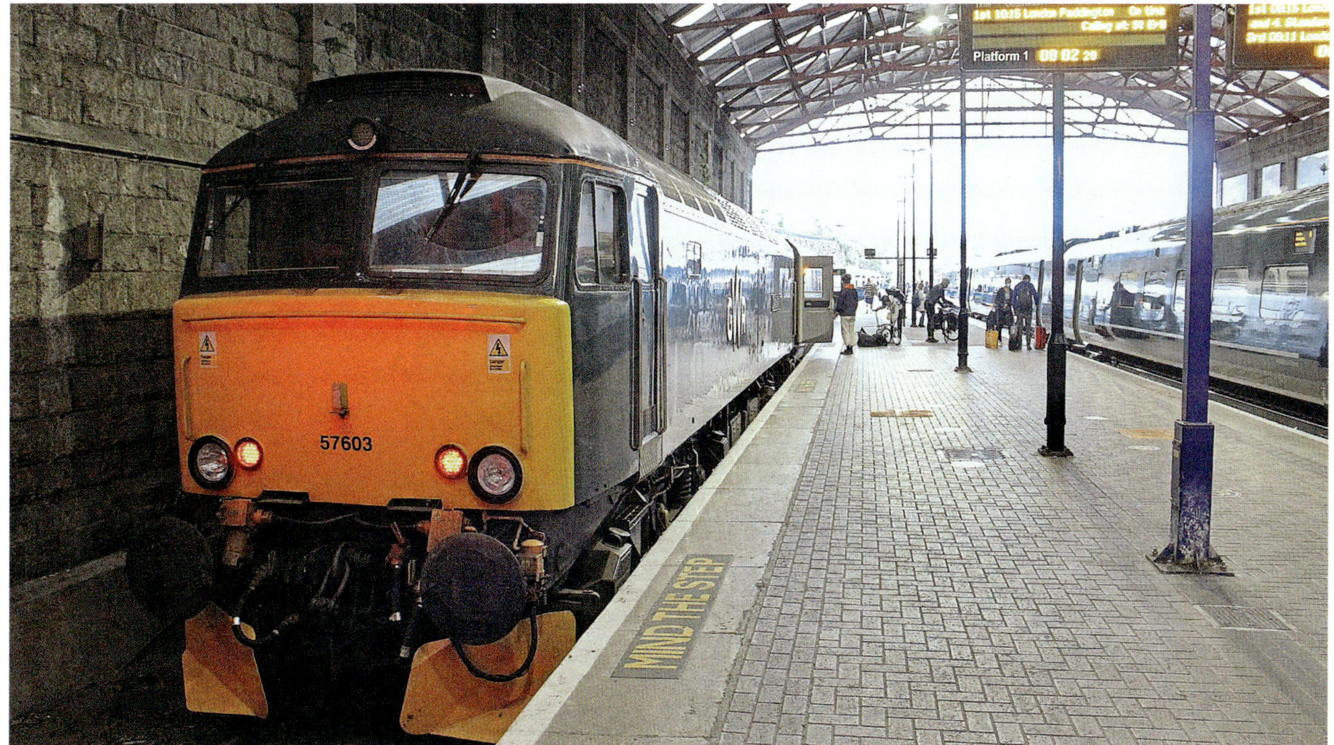

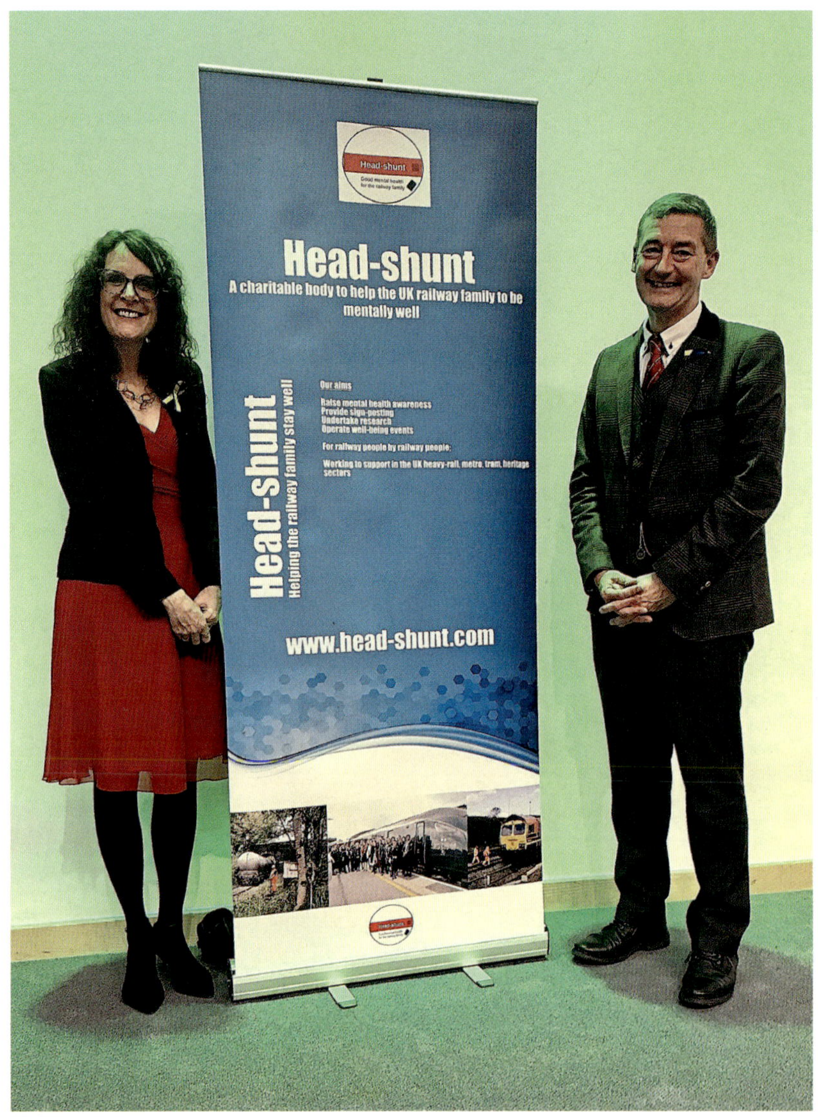

Epilogue

Fiona and I decided in 2021, in line with my taking early retirement from the railway after 37 years, to start a small rail charity to help the railway family uphold good mental health. This was part of a desire to put something back into an industry which was key to my family for 150 years. Appropriately it is called Head-shunt; the name was Fiona's idea.

At the time of writing, more than 5,000 rail staff have heard details of my mental experiences ranging from my post traumatic stress disorder (PTSD) because of my attending train accidents and rail suicides, through to coping with consequential anxiety and depression and of course learning techniques to stay well. Some great supporters have come from within the railway family to help us in this charity endeavour both practically and financially.

The charity aims to educate people and 'break the ceiling' and encourage people – not limited to the railway family – to speak up about their needs, plus of course to upskill people, often using our collective lived experience and that of our other supporters to help and inform people and companies about mental health and wellbeing.

Bibliography

PRIMARY DATA REFERENCES

British Railways; Western Region Staff Magazine 1960 to 1965
British Railways; (and successors) operational publications; including the Western Region Sectional Appendix and re-signalling notices including Bristol re-signalling 1970-72, Bristol re-signalling 2018
British Railways; Public and working timetables over period 1960 to 1987
Cadbury Ltd; Bournville Works Magazine and Bournville Reporter Newspaper 1895 to 1976
Cadbury Ltd; Minutes of directors' meetings over period 1890 to 1976
Cadbury Ltd; Bournville 1925 – Transport; Cadbury Ltd publication
Cadbury Ltd; Staff records held at Cadbury Bournville for Stanford family 1907 to 1973
Great Western Railway; Staff magazine; editions over period 1898 to 1920
Her Majesty's Stationary Office; Financing of Britain's Railways 1982 by Sir David Serpell KCB
Office of Rail and Roads; website for passenger utilisation of UK railways; https://dataportal.orr.gov.uk/statistics/usage/passenger-rail-usage/
Office for National Statistics; Census documents 1875 to 1915
Stanford family; Personal notes and diaries of John and Paul Stanford taken during their railway career 1960 to 2021

SECONDARY DATA REFERENCES

Cadbury Ltd; Cadbury Bournville – a century of progress 1831 – 1931; 1931
Industrial Railway Society; Locomotive Handbooks – multiple handbooks, for geographic areas featured; published over multiple years
Maggs, Colin; Rail Centres – Bristol; 1981
Maggs, Colin; Rail Centres – Exeter; 1985
Maggs, Colin; The Birmingham to Gloucester Line; 2013
Port of Bristol Authority; Port of Bristol – A motorway port; 1973
Six Bells Junction website; 'The Railtour Files'; www.sixbellsjunction.co.uk
Sharp, Derek; The Railways of Cadbury and Bournville; 2002
Williams, Ned; Railways of the Black Country (the byways); 1984

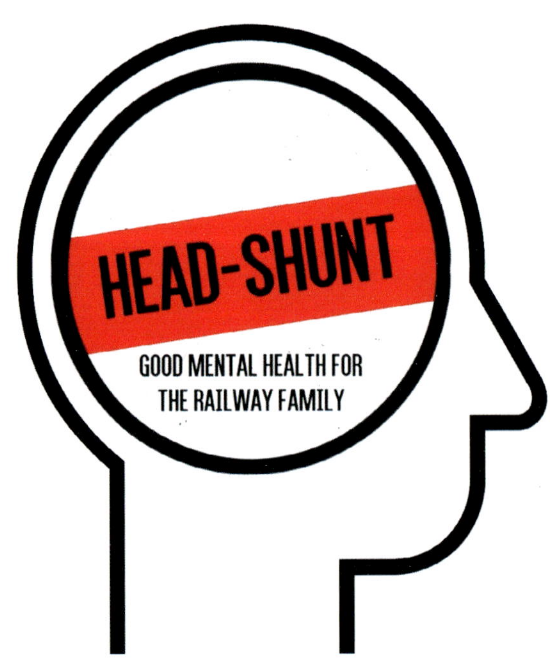

www.head-shunt.com

Author royalties from sales of this book will be used to help other members of the railway family be mentally well and resilient, to face the challenges the rest of the 21st century brings in operating Britain's railway.